T0290609

Fair Progress?
Economic Mobility across Generations around the World

Ambar Narayan, Roy Van der Weide,
Alexandru Cojocaru, Christoph Lakner,
Silvia Redaelli, Daniel Gerszon Mahler,
Rakesh Gupta N. Ramasubbaiah,
and Stefan Thewissen

WORLD BANK GROUP

CONTENTS

FIGURES

MAPS

TABLES

FOREWORD

Dick Whittington rose from humble origins to become Lord Mayor of London and a favorite bedtime story. Ragged Dick, the fictional New Yorker whose journey from shoeshine boy to pillar of the middle class, is at the heart of the American Dream.

These timeless stories are retold because of the universal desire to succeed in life and to make sure that our children do better than ourselves. Today, the question is more pertinent than ever: If you are born into a low-income family, what are the chances that you will rise higher regardless of your background?

The ability to move up the economic ladder matters for reducing poverty and inequality and can help boost economic growth. Every day, nearly 400,000 babies are born around the world. None of them get to choose their gender, race, where they are born, or the social and economic condition of their families. Life's starting point is a lottery. But the future needn't be left to chance.

Drawing on our new Global Database of Intergenerational Mobility, with its unprecedented coverage of 96 percent of the world's population over the past half century, this report paints a detailed picture of socioeconomic mobility and inequality of opportunity around the world.

Its findings give us cause for concern as well as optimism. Trends in mobility in the developing world have stalled since the 1960s, making it harder to harness human potential for generating greater, and more widely shared, prosperity. Yet, some developing regions have made impressive progress. And even in the regions with the lowest mobility, rising enrollments in the past two decades may be increasing the share of those with more education and therefore helping to increase mobility for today's young people.

Narrowing the gaps between the rungs on the mobility ladder requires public investments and policies that create more equal opportunity.

Fair Progress? makes the case for investing in people, particularly in children as early as possible. It also argues for reducing inequalities of wealth and assets through tax and spending policies and for creating more and better jobs by promoting competition in markets and by fostering economic opportunity among disadvantaged groups.

The World Bank's Human Capital Project, which aligns closely with this report, will help countries invest more, and more effectively, in their people. Let's not forget that there are at least 400,000 reasons a day to invest in better policies to promote mobility.

Kristalina Georgieva
Chief Executive Officer
The World Bank

ACKNOWLEDGMENTS

This study was written by a team led by Ambar Narayan and Roy Van der Weide with core team members Alexandru Cojocaru, Christoph Lakner, Daniel Gerszon Mahler, Rakesh Gupta N. Ramasubbaiah, Silvia Redaelli, and Stefan Thewissen. David Newhouse, Fedja Pivodic, and Patrizio Piraino contributed key inputs. The study was prepared under the supervision of Francisco Ferreira and Carolina Sanchez-Paramo and under the overall guidance of Jan Walliser. The team is also grateful for guidance and advice from Asli Demirgüç-Kunt, Shanta Devarajan, Roberta Gatti, Ana Revenga, and Carlos Silva-Jauregui.

Miles Corak and Luis-Felipe Lopez-Calva peer-reviewed the report, and Andrea Brandolini and Roberta Gatti served as additional peer reviewers at the concept stage. The team also appreciates the many helpful comments and suggestions received from colleagues in and outside the World Bank. In particular, the team would like to thank Kathleen Beegle, Maurizio Bussolo, Andrew Dabalen, Maria Davalos, Gabriela Inchauste, Vito Peragine, Martin Rama, Paul Roemer, and Albert Zeufack.

Robert Zimmermann edited the volume, and Paul McClure edited the Preview published in October 2017. The production of the full study was led by Rumit Pancholi (production editor), Michael Harrup (production editor), Patricia Katayama (acquisitions editor), and Deborah Appel-Barker (print coordinator). Maura Leary, supported by Venkat Gopalakrishnan, led the communication and messaging during the launch of the Preview. David Sharrock, Venkat Gopalakrishnan, Yanina Budkin, and Indira Chand led the communication and messaging efforts for the report's launch and dissemination. Messaging and communication support were also provided by Paul Gallagher, Phillip Jeremy Hay, Victoria Smith, Mikael Reventar, and other colleagues. Additional support was provided by Anna Regina Rillo Bonfield, Pamela Gaye Gunio, Karem Nathalia Edwards de

Izquierdo, and Estella Malayiki. Mary Donaldson Lewis provided support on graphics. All cartographic maps were produced by Bruno Bonansea.

For their advice and support in creating the Global Database on Intergenerational Mobility, the team thanks the following World Bank colleagues: Frank Adoho, Raul Andres Castaneda Aguilar, Saniya Ansar, Sam Asher, Aziz Atamanov, Joao Pedro Wagner de Azevedo, Reena Badiani-Magnusson, Kathleen Beegle, Tom Bundervoet, Jean-Pierre Chauffour, Andrew Dabalen, Carolina Diaz-Bonilla, Olivier Dupriez, Freeha Fatima, Samuel Freije-Rodriguez, Isis Gaddis, Emanuela Galasso, John Giles, Nadia Belhaj Hassine, Jake Hess, Yang Huang, Jonathan Kastelic, Leora Klapper, Aart Kraay, Ghazala Mansuri, Federica Marzo, Kris Mcdonall, Maria Ignacia Contreras Mediano, Claudio Montenegro, Jose Montes, Rose Mungai, Tu Chi Nguyen, Minh Cong Nguyen, Theresa Osborne, Gbemisola Oseni, Truman Packard, Paul Andres Corral Rodas, Prem Sangraula, Kinnon Scott, Dorothe Singer, Diane Steele, Hiroki Uematsu, Rashiel Velarde, Ayago Esmubancha Wambile, and Judy Yang. Acknowledgements are also due to the following external colleagues: Paolo Brunori, Daniele Checchi, Philippe de Vreyer, Muhammed Abdul Khalid, Sylvie Lambert, Paolo Mauro, Guido Neidhöfer, Paul Novosad, Vito Peragine, and Eleni Yitbarek.

Estimates of income mobility for many of the countries included in the global database were obtained through the Equal Chances project hosted at the University of Bari, for which the team is most grateful. The Equal Chances project also kindly agreed to make the global database available on its website, allowing public users to visualize the global trends and patterns in intergenerational mobility.

The report is a joint project of the Development Research Group in the Development Economics Vice Presidency and the Poverty and Equity Global Practice in the Equitable Growth, Finance and Institutions Vice Presidency of the World Bank.

ABBREVIATIONS

FCV	fragility, conflict, and violence
GDIM	Global Database for Intergenerational Mobility
GDP	gross domestic product
HOI	Human Opportunity Index
IEO	inequality of economic opportunity
IGM	intergenerational mobility
IGP	intergenerational persistence
IHDP	Infant Health and Development Program
IMF	International Monetary Fund
ISCED	International Standard Classification of Education
ISSP	International Social Survey Program
MLD	mean log deviation
MTO	Moving to Opportunity
NLSY	National Longitudinal Survey of Youth
ODID	Oxford Department of International Development
OECD	Organisation for Economic Co-operation and Development
OLS	ordinary least squares
PISA	Program for International Student Assessment
PSID	Panel Study of Income Dynamics
RCT	randomized controlled trial
SES	socioeconomic status
TSTSLS	two-sample two-stage least squares
WDI	World Development Indicators
WVS	World Values Survey

Overview

Introduction

Economic mobility across generations, also known as intergenerational mobility (IGM) in the economic literature, is a key element of human progress. In most countries, parents would like to see their children have a higher living standard—and with it a better life—than they have had themselves. And most individuals would like the opportunity to move up to a higher place on the economic ladder than the point on it where they happened to be born. For sustainable and inclusive growth, public policy must help give scope to such aspirations. But evidence suggests that, in too many parts of the world, mobility poses a challenge. This concern is especially acute for developing countries: in most of them, it is harder than in wealthier countries to move from the bottom to the top of the economic ladder.

This study measures the extent of IGM in economies across the world, how it has evolved over time and across generations, and the factors that might be associated with higher mobility, to draw implications for policy. By reporting findings on a global scale, it fills an important gap in the empirical evidence on IGM. For its global analysis, this study focuses primarily on mobility in education, which is important in its own right and is an essential element of economic mobility. A newly created database—the Global Database of Intergenerational Mobility (GDIM)—covering more than 95 percent of the global population—forms the basis for most of the primary data analysis. To complement the global story of educational mobility, IGM in income is measured or compiled from existing studies for a smaller set of economies to shed some light on the patterns and drivers of income mobility and its relationship with educational mobility.

Higher mobility across generations is interpreted here in two distinct but related ways. *Absolute upward IGM* is the extent to which living standards of a generation are higher than those of their parents. This type of mobility reflects a universal human aspiration of parents hoping for a better life for their children. Higher absolute upward mobility is closely associated with income growth and a rise in shared prosperity or income growth of the bottom 40 percent, when these improvements are sustained over an extended period. The focus on upward mobility is crucial because mobility can also mean downward movement, driven, for example, by uncertainty and vulnerability to uninsured risks.

Relative IGM is the extent to which an individual's position on the economic scale is independent of the position of his or her parents. Higher relative mobility across generations is associated with lower inequality of opportunity, which is the extent to which people's life achievements are affected by circumstances they are born into, such as parental education and income, race, gender, and birthplace.[1] Such circumstances remain crucial: children born every day around the world face starkly different life prospects because of the circumstances they inherit.

Both types of mobility are important for economic progress and for sustaining a social contract that addresses the aspirations of society. Without absolute mobility, living standards cannot improve, and social cohesion may be at risk as the different groups in society compete for slices of a fixed or shrinking economic pie. Meanwhile, a lack of relative mobility is not only deeply unfair and perpetuates inequality across generations, but it is also harmful to economic growth because of wasted human potential, which leads to misallocation of resources. A lack of relative mobility over time, therefore, may constrain absolute upward mobility.

This book finds both absolute and relative mobility in education to be significantly higher, on average, in high-income economies than in developing economies, for cohorts born between the 1940s and 1980s. Although absolute IGM has been converging between the two groups of economies over time, progress in the developing world has stalled since the 1960s, at a relatively low level of educational attainment compared with high-income economies. On relative IGM, high-income economies have improved more than developing economies have; today, all 15 economies that rank in the bottom 10 percent by relative IGM are developing economies.

Among developing economies, educational IGM—both absolute and relative—varies significantly for the current generation. For example, about 12 percent of adults born in the 1980s in some low-income or fragile economies of Sub-Saharan Africa (referred to as Africa hereafter) have more education than their parents, compared with more than 80 percent of the same generation in parts of the East Asia and Pacific region (referred to as East Asia hereafter). Average relative mobility for economies in South Asia and Africa is significantly lower than that for the other developing regions.

Relative IGM in income, for a subset of 75 economies, combining the book's own estimates with those compiled from existing studies, exhibits a pattern that has some similarities with that of relative IGM in education. Income IGM tends to be lower in the developing regions than in the high-income economies; 24 out of the 25 economies in the bottom third by income mobility are developing economies. In the developing world, most of the economies with low relative IGM are in the Africa, South Asia, and Latin America and Caribbean regions (referred to as Latin America hereafter). In several developing economies, mostly in Africa, the Middle East and North Africa (referred to as Middle East hereafter), and Latin America, income mobility trails behind educational mobility; labor market deficiencies may be contributing significantly to this gap.

Gender gaps in educational mobility are closing fast. In advanced economies, the gaps for tertiary education and absolute mobility, which used to favor boys, reversed for individuals born in the 1960s and have widened, with girls acquiring more education than boys, in recent decades. Girls are catching up with boys in developing economies as well. However, achieving similar improvements in income mobility among girls will also require reducing the widespread gender disparities in labor market outcomes.

Mobility from the bottom half of the education ladder to the top quartile has fallen over time in developing economies, whereas persistence at the bottom has increased. In the median developing economy for the 1980s generation, less than 15 percent born into the bottom half make it to the top quarter, while more than two-thirds stay in the bottom half. High persistence, both at the top and at the bottom, is a concern not just in developing economies but in most economies around the world.

The patterns observed in the global database suggest that economies with higher IGM in education are better placed to generate future growth, as well as reduce poverty and inequality. Stalled progress in absolute mobility, low relative mobility, and high persistence at the bottom of the education ladder in large parts of the developing world thus add up to concern about future progress. These concerns are heightened for Africa and South Asia, where the prospects of children are still tied to the socioeconomic status of their parents more closely than in any other developing region, which suggests that relative mobility in these two regions will continue to be low in the near future.

At the same time, the rise in educational mobility observed in many high-income economies and in parts of East Asia, Latin America, and the Middle East for individuals born between the 1950s and the 1980s provides cause for optimism, suggesting that changing the status quo is possible with policy action. There is some cause for optimism in Africa and South Asia as well. According to rough predictions, rising enrollments in the past two decades may have increased absolute mobility in both regions among those born in the 1990s.

Intergenerational Mobility in Education around the World

The existing empirical evidence on IGM is primarily on relative (and not absolute) mobility, and skewed toward high-income economies and toward men (from father to son). A recent review of the existing literature finds that comparable estimates of relative IGM in income can be compiled for just 42 economies, of which only 12 are low- or middle-income economies; and the most comprehensive global study to date on relative IGM in education similarly covers 42 economies.[2] In contrast, this book includes estimates of absolute and relative mobility in education for economies that are home to more than 95 percent of the world's population. Such a comprehensive coverage allows for an analysis of global trends and patterns in absolute and relative mobility in education for men and women alike. Estimates of relative IGM in income are compiled for a subset of economies, using own estimations to complement comparable estimates compiled from the existing literature.

Educational Mobility Is a Key Element of Economic Mobility across Generations

Because education is a key dimension of human progress, educational mobility is important in its own right and is an essential element of economic mobility, when economic mobility is understood in terms of well-being rather than income alone. Moreover, because education tends to be a strong predictor of lifetime earnings, mobility in education is a key factor influencing income mobility, but with two important limitations. First, education mobility is measured here without considering the quality of learning, which makes the outcome an unreliable indicator of the skills that will influence an individual's earnings as an adult. Second, the relationship between mobility in education and mobility in income depends on several factors, such as how labor markets reward skills and how parental connections affect economic opportunities—all of which can vary across economies and over time.

Economic theories predict that IGM in education and IGM in income are positively correlated, given that persistence of income across generations occurs as a result of inherited endowments and parental preferences to invest for the benefit of their children.[3] Empirically, the correlation is observed to be strong among economies for which estimates for relative mobility in both education and income are available for comparable cohorts (figure O.1).[4] However, the association is also imperfect, which means that the relative rankings of economies can change depending on which measure is used. In general, mobility in education and income will be more closely associated, the more similar economies are in terms of returns to education and the better education predicts income in both generations.

Intergenerational mobility in Education: Trends and Patterns

To assess the evolution of IGM in education across space and over time, absolute upward mobility in an economy is measured by the share of respondents in a nationally representative survey who have higher education levels than the maximum level of education among the parents of the respondent (excluding individuals whose parents have tertiary education).[5]

FIGURE O.1   Relative IGMs in education and income are correlated, but imperfectly

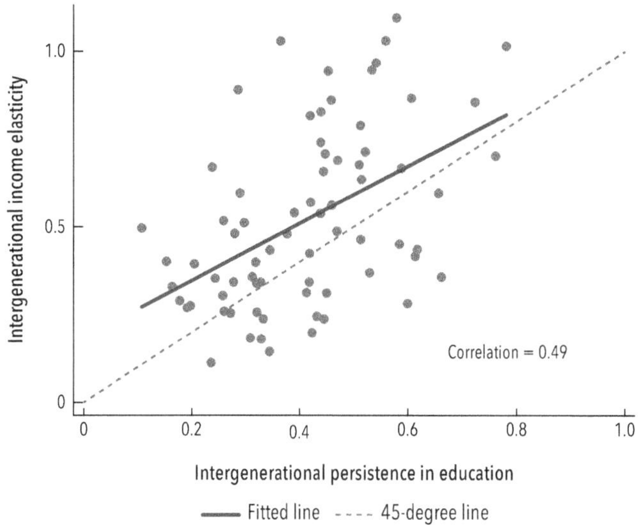

Source: Estimates based on GDIM 2018 (World Bank); Equalchances 2018; compiled from multiple studies.
Note: Higher elasticity (persistence) indicates lower IGM. Income elasticity estimates are for the 1960s or 1970s cohort approximately; education persistence estimates are for the 1980s cohort. IGM = intergenerational mobility.

Relative mobility is measured by the extent to which the educational attainment of individuals is independent of the education of their parents, using the coefficient from regressions of children's years of education on the education of their parents. Higher values of this regression coefficient indicate greater persistence, and hence lower relative mobility.[6] IGM is estimated among adults for 10-year cohorts born between 1940 and 1989. For example, a "child" of the "1980s cohort" refers to the generation born between 1980 and 1989, and "parents" refers to the parents of this generation. The 1980s cohort is the latest whose members are likely to have completed their education and therefore represents the latest generation of adults, which also implies that the IGM trends shown here do not reflect any changes in educational attainment that may have occurred in the last decade or so.

Absolute and relative IGMs in education are estimated for the 1980s cohort in 148 economies, which are home to 96 percent of the world's population. These include 111 developing economies covering 96 percent of the population in the developing world. In all regions but the Middle East, the population coverage is greater than 90 percent. For 111 of 148 economies, with 87 percent of the world's population, IGM is estimated for multiple cohorts. All mobility measures reported for groups of economies are simple averages unweighted by population. Thus, they should be interpreted as the average IGM of all economies in a group, and not as IGM of the average individual in that group.

Absolute mobility and relative mobility are lower in developing economies than in high-income economies

The rate of absolute IGM in education has historically been greater in high-income economies than in developing economies and continues to be so among the 1980s cohort (figure O.2, panel a).[7] Among the 1980s generation, the average relative IGM in developing economies is also significantly lower than the average in high-income economies (figure O.2, panel b). Seven of the 15 economies in the top decile of relative IGM among the 1980s generation are high-income economies, whereas all economies ranked in the bottom decile are developing economies.[8] The gap is consistent with the pattern of relative IGM in income being low in developing economies, using available estimates that have a much narrower global coverage.[9]

Whereas the gap in absolute mobility between high-income and developing economies has been closing, absolute mobility in developing economies has stopped rising since the 1960s

Absolute mobility has converged to some extent between high-income and developing economies (see figure O.2, panel a). The underlying trends are less positive, however; the gap is closing because absolute IGM has been falling in advanced economies since the 1950s cohort, while staying on a flat trajectory in developing economies since the 1960s cohort. Some 47 percent of the 1980s generation in an average developing economy have more education than their parents, which is almost unchanged from the 1960s generation. Among the 1980s generation in the average high-income economy, 57 percent have more education than their parents, which is lower than the rate among the 1950s generation.

Progress in absolute mobility stalled in the average developing economy at a much lower level of educational attainment compared with the average high-income economy. Convergence in absolute IGM does not imply convergence in average educational attainment between high-income and developing economies; that gap is as large today as it was 40 years ago (figure O.3). Sons and daughters are on average better educated than their parents almost everywhere. However, the developing world today is roughly where the high-income world was 40 years ago.

Developing economies have increasingly fallen behind high-income economies in relative mobility

Relative IGM improved at a more rapid rate among high-income economies than among developing economies between the 1940s cohort and the 1980s cohort. This has widened the gap between the two groups of economies over time (see figure O.2, panel b). This is particularly true of the period between the 1970s cohort and the 1980s cohort, when relative IGM in the average developing economy showed no improvement, but was rising in the average high-income economy. Relative IGM among the 1980s generation in the average developing economy is close to that of the 1940s generation in the average high-income economy.[10]

FIGURE O.2 Changes in absolute and relative mobility over time, developing and high-income economies

a. Share of adults with more education than their parents (*absolute upward mobility*)
(excluding adults whose parents have tertiary education)

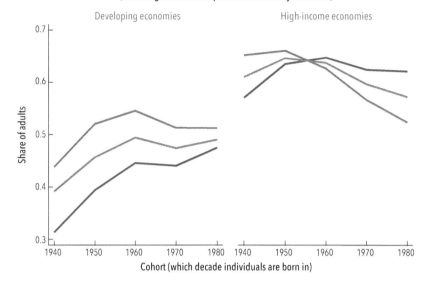

b. Intergenerational persistence in education (*relative mobility*)
(higher persistence indicates lower mobility)

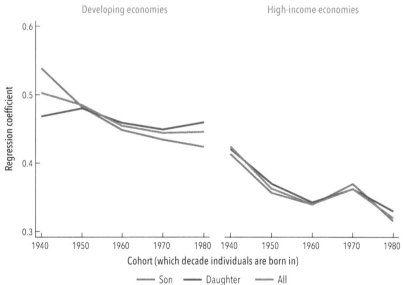

Source: Calculations based on data in GDIM 2018 (World Bank).
Note: Absolute upward mobility is the share of individuals with more education than the maximum educational attainment of their parents (excluding adults whose parents have tertiary education), where education is defined in terms of five categories based on UIS (2012). Intergenerational persistence is measured by the coefficient from a regression of children's years of schooling on the years of schooling of their parents. Higher persistence indicates lower relative mobility. The averages for developing and high-income groups are simple averages (unweighted by population) across economies in each group.

FIGURE 0.3   Share of population in different cohorts with tertiary education

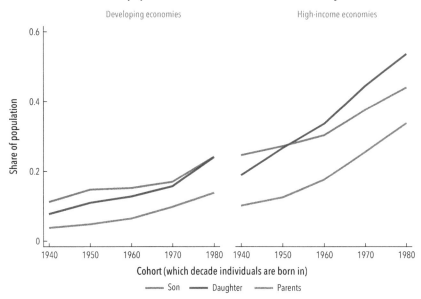

Source: Calculations using GDIM 2018 (World Bank).
Note: Averages for developing economies and high-income economies are simple (unweighted by population) averages across economies in each group.

Absolute mobility and relative mobility in education among the 1980s generation are correlated, but imperfectly

On average, economies with a higher share of adults who are more educated than their parents are also economies in which the educational attainment of individuals is less dependent on the educational attainment of their parents (figure O.4). This is consistent with the view that absolute and relative mobility complement and reinforce each other. A lack of relative mobility leads to lower and less-inclusive growth, which, in turn, limits absolute mobility over time. However, the relationship is imperfect with significant outliers, such as some economies in East Asia that have very high absolute mobility (for example, Republic of Korea and Malaysia) because of a rapid rise in education levels from a lower starting point, compared with economies that developed earlier (for example, Denmark and Japan) that have similar levels of relative mobility.

Intergenerational mobility has improved in some developing regions, but declined or stagnated in other regions

Although IGM on average has improved across the developing world since the 1950s cohort, the improvements are highly uneven. Between the 1950s cohort and the 1980s cohort, positive changes are largely concentrated in East Asia, Latin America, and the Middle East. In contrast, absolute IGM and relative IGM have declined in Eastern Europe and Central Asia and stagnated in Africa. In South Asia, there have been improvements in

FIGURE O.4 Absolute mobility and relative mobility are correlated, but with many outliers

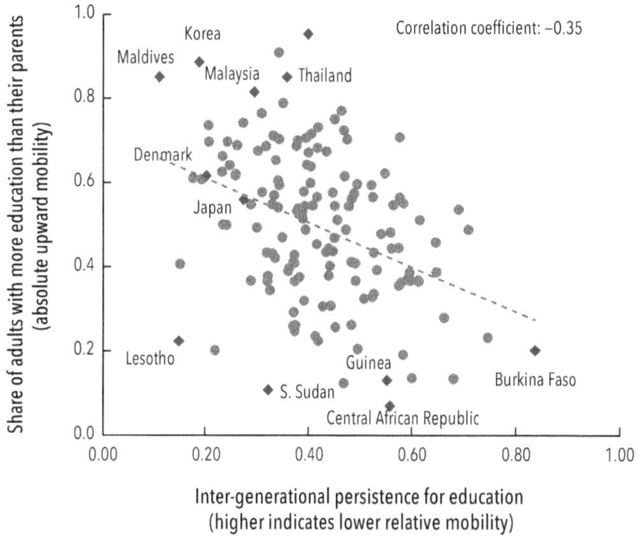

Source: Calculations based on data in GDIM 2018 (World Bank).
Note: 1980s cohort only.

absolute mobility, but not in relative mobility. The findings on Africa are broadly consistent with estimates available from earlier research for a smaller number of countries.[11]

Because of such uneven progress, IGM in education varies widely within the developing world. Average absolute mobility in East Asia, Latin America and the Middle East is at or above the high-income average (figure O.5). In relative mobility, East Asia is ahead of the other developing regions but still below the high-income average. At the other end of the spectrum is Africa, where absolute and relative mobility are well below the average in developing economies. In the average economy of Africa, 35 percent of people born in the 1980s exhibit higher educational attainment than their parents, compared with roughly 60 percent of the same generation in the average economy of East Asia, Latin America, or the Middle East.

Mobility among the current generation varies significantly among developing economies, with the lowest mobility seen in some of the poorest or most fragile economies

The gap between the well- and low-performing developing economies in terms of IGM is vast (map O.1). Looking at absolute mobility, for example, only 12 percent of the individuals born in the 1980s in the Central African Republic, Guinea, and South Sudan have achieved higher education levels than their parents have, compared with more than 80 percent of residents of Malaysia and Thailand born in the same decade. Economies affected by fragility, conflict, and violence (FCV) are found to have lower average absolute and relative mobility compared with the developing economy averages

FIGURE O.5   Absolute mobility and relative mobility, averages by region and income group

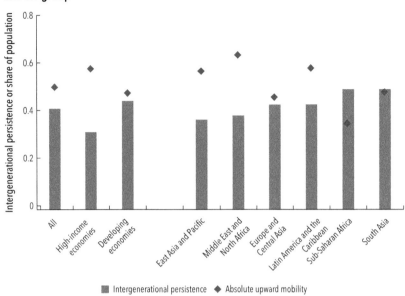

Source: Calculations based on GDIM 2018 (World Bank).
Note: Averages are not weighted by population. Higher persistence implies lower relative IGM. Regions are sorted in decreasing order of relative IGM. 1980s cohort only.

for all cohorts.[12] Of the 15 economies in the bottom decile of absolute mobility for the 1980s cohort, 12 are in Africa, and 5 of these 12 are FCV. In relative mobility, 10 of the 15 economies in the bottom decile are in Africa, including four that are FCV.

Educational Mobility from the Bottom to the Top across the World

The relative mobility measure used so far does not distinguish between upward and downward mobility, and the measure of absolute mobility does not capture the influence of parental background on one's educational attainment relative to individuals in the same generation. To complement these measures, it is useful to also look at the share of individuals who make it to the top quartile of education in their generation out of those who were born to parents with education in the bottom half of their generation.[13]

Mobility from the bottom to the top is low almost everywhere, but the lowest rates occur mostly in developing economies
In a large majority of economies across the world, one's chances of reaching the top quarter of the ladder of educational attainment depend largely on where one's parents stood on that ladder (figure O.6). This share would be 0.25 if one's ability to obtain an education did not depend on how well educated one's parents are. However, there are very few economies in which the share exceeds 0.20. Among the bottom 50 economies by this share among the 1980s generation, 46 are developing, whereas only 4 are high

MAP O.1   IGM across the world: the 1980s generation

a. Share of adults with more education than their parents: Absolute upward mobility

IBRD 43642 | APRIL 2018

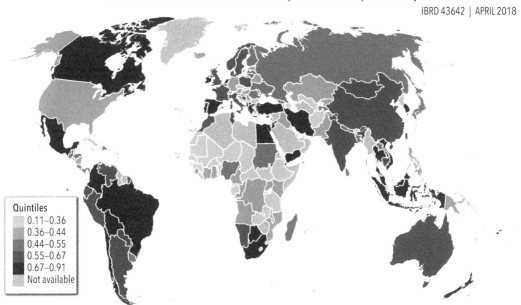

Quintiles
- 0.11–0.36
- 0.36–0.44
- 0.44–0.55
- 0.55–0.67
- 0.67–0.91
- Not available

b. Intergenerational persistence in education: Relative mobility

IBRD 43643 | APRIL 2018

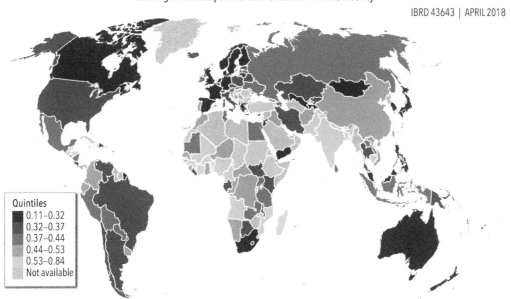

Quintiles
- 0.11–0.32
- 0.32–0.37
- 0.37–0.44
- 0.44–0.53
- 0.53–0.84
- Not available

Source: Calculations based on data in the GDIM 2018 (World Bank).
Note: Absolute upward intergenerational mobility (IGM) is the share of individuals with higher educational attainment than their parents (excluding adults whose parents have tertiary education). Intergenerational persistence is the coefficient from the regression of children's years of schooling on parents' years of schooling. Greater persistence indicates lower relative IGM. The darker shade indicates higher relative or absolute IGM.

FIGURE O.6   Share of individuals in the 1980s cohort who are born into the bottom half and who have reached the top quartile in education

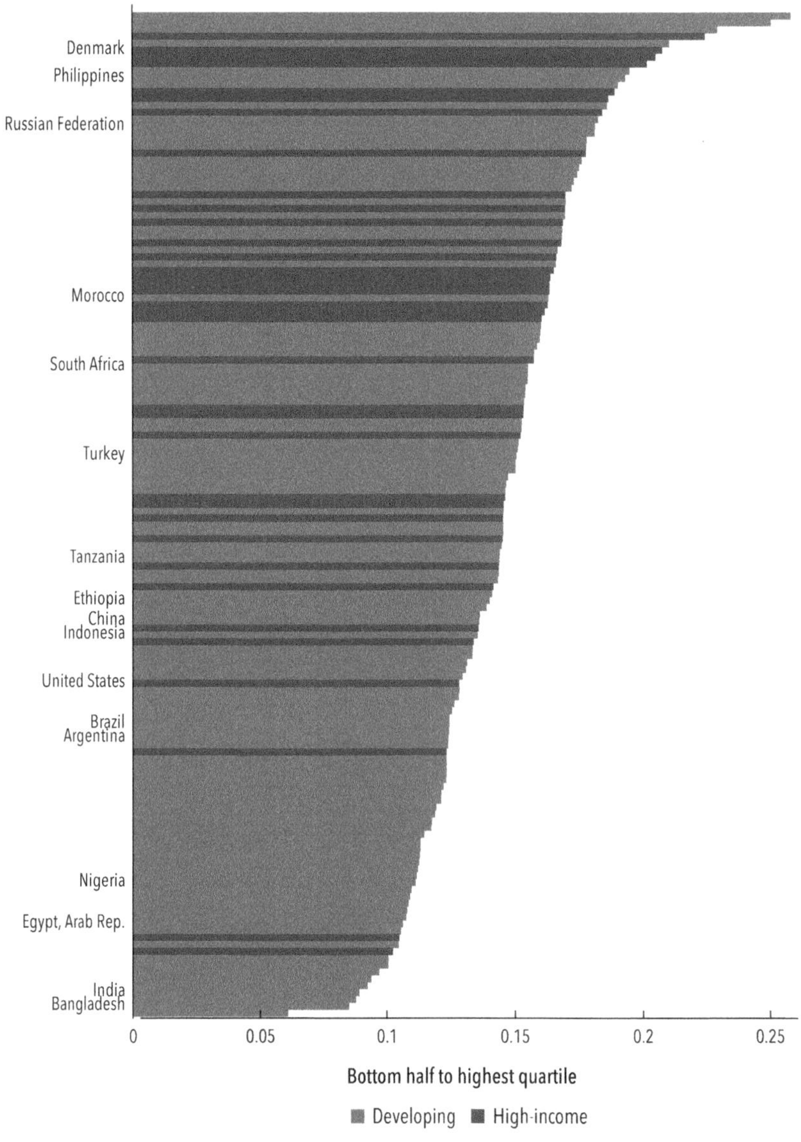

Source: Calculations based on data in the GDIM 2018 (World Bank).
Note: The figure depicts the 1980s cohort only and shows data for 146 economies: for illustrative purposes, only a few are named.

income, including the United States. In the median developing economy, less than 15 percent of individuals born in the bottom half make it to the top quarter, whereas more than two-thirds stay in the bottom half.

Upward mobility is declining in the developing world, whereas persistence at the bottom is rising

The rate of upward mobility from the bottom half to the top quartile was higher in developing economies than in high-income economies for the

1940s cohort. It has since moved in the opposite direction so that, for the 1980s cohort, the share of individuals born in the bottom half who reach the top is slightly higher in high-income economies than in developing economies. As upward mobility from the bottom has declined, persistence at the bottom has increased in developing economies to exceed the persistence rate in high-income economies for the recent cohorts. Thus, the opportunity for individuals born in poorer households to climb the ladder is narrowing in many economies in which average living standards are still low compared with high-income economies.

Girls have moved ahead of boys in absolute IGM in high-income economies and are rapidly closing the gap in developing economies
Girls in high-income economies now exhibit higher rates of tertiary education and absolute IGM than boys (see figure O.2, panel a, and figure O.3). The reversal of the gender gap occurred for the 1960s cohort, and the advantage of girls has since grown in high-income economies. Since the 1960s cohort, girls also have higher rates of mobility from the bottom to the top and lower rates of persistence at the bottom than boys.

In the developing world, the trend is in the same direction. Women have already caught up with men in tertiary education, and the gender gap is narrowing rapidly in absolute mobility (figure O.2, panel a). These trends suggest a not-too-distant future when upward mobility relative to parents will be greater among girls than among boys in the developing world. The likelihood of climbing from the bottom to the top has also been rising among girls relative to boys in the developing world.

Many of the global patterns identified above carry over to six large developing economies
Looking closely at six large developing economies, namely Brazil, China, the Arab Republic of Egypt, India, Indonesia, and Nigeria, absolute mobility rose in all of them from the 1940s cohort to the 1980s cohort. Relative mobility increased in Brazil, Egypt, India, and Indonesia, whereas it fell in China and Nigeria. In the case of India, even though relative mobility has been improving, it is still low by international standards and the lowest among the six large developing economies observed in this book. Provinces with greater absolute IGM tend to also show greater relative IGM in most of these economies, but the correlation is imperfect, and there are several outliers.

What Do Today's Enrollment Patterns Suggest about IGM in the Next Generation?

Standard estimates of IGM discussed so far are reflections of what has happened in the past, whereas current patterns of child educational outcomes and the ways these are associated with parental socioeconomic status can offer a window into future mobility. Recent school enrollment patterns show that poverty and low parental education continue to reinforce each other in creating vast inequalities in access to education for children and entrenching low IGM. In low- and low-middle-income econo-mies, the likelihood of enrollment among different age groups is signifi-cantly lower when household income and parental education are lower.[14] Moreover, given the well-documented problems in learning outcomes among children in poorer households, inequality in education is likely to be much higher than suggested by enrollment profiles once the quality of learning is considered.

Across regions, the prospects of relative mobility are the lowest among children in Africa and South Asia

To see the potential mobility of future generations, an alternative measure of educational attainment can be defined for those born after the 1980s, which is the "education shortfall" or the difference between the observed years of schooling completed and the years of schooling that should have been completed on the basis of a child's age.[15]

Figure O.7 shows the average persistence between the education short-fall and parental years of schooling among children of ages 6–11 years and 12–17 years in five developing regions.[16] Regional averages of relative IGM for the 1980s cohort are included for comparison. Average persistence among the younger cohorts appears to be the highest in Africa and South Asia, similar to the pattern in relative mobility seen for the adults belonging to the 1980s cohort. Among children of ages 6–11 years, the gaps in per-sistence between Africa and South Asia and the other regions are smaller, but still present. If these trends persist, the prospects of the next generation of adults will continue to be tied to parental educational attainment more closely in Africa and South Asia than in any other region of the world.

FIGURE O.7   Intergenerational persistence in education among children

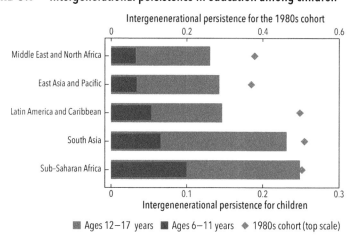

Source: Calculations based on data in the GDIM 2018 (World Bank).
Notes: Intergenerational persistence for children is the regression coefficient of a Tobit regression of children's "education shortfall" on parental years of schooling. Education Shortfall = Observed Years of Education − (Age of Child − 5).

In absolute mobility, Africa may be catching up with other developing regions among younger cohorts

In Africa, average enrollment in primary school increased from 73 to 98 percent between 1996 and 2014, which may signal an increase in absolute mobility among children born during the 1990s.[17] Rough predictions of what absolute mobility might look like for the 1990s cohort suggest that average absolute IGM in Africa may indeed be improving faster than in the previous two decades and catching up with the developing economy average. Similar predictions also suggest that absolute IGM among the 1990s cohort in South Asia may have already caught up with the developing economy average.

Pathways to Intergenerational Mobility in Education and Income

Absolute Upward Mobility Is Linked to Growth and the Distribution of Growth

Absolute upward IGM is likely to be high in a society in which rising prosperity is broadly shared and sustained. Growth in average incomes, which increases the size of the economic pie, is necessary but not sufficient for a high rate of absolute mobility, which also requires a more equitable distribution of the benefits of growth. For example, the sharp decline in absolute mobility in the United States between individuals born in the 1940s and those born in the 1980s was driven more by the unequal distribution of economic growth than the slowdown in aggregate growth since the 1940s.[18]

But even if absolute upward IGM increases with rising prosperity, relative IGM may not necessarily follow, as seen from the imperfect association between the two (see figure O.4). The average economy in South Asia, for example, experienced rising absolute mobility in education between the 1950s and the 1980s generations but had almost no improvement in relative mobility. Improving relative mobility and, in particular, upward mobility from the bottom of the ladder also requires equalizing opportunities to reduce disadvantages because of circumstances such as parental education or income, gender, or location.

What Matters for Relative IGM in Income, at Different Stages of the Life Cycle

Why incomes persist from one generation to the next

The different channels through which parental income influences income of the next generation can be identified by decomposing the coefficient of intergenerational income persistence, under certain simplifying assumptions, into shares that reflect the effects of (1) parental education on offspring's income through offspring's education; (2) parental education on the determinants of offspring's income that are independent of education; and (3) parental characteristics (other than education) on offspring's income. The first channel gets stronger as IGM in education declines, and as returns to education of the offspring's generation rise relative to the parents' generation. The second channel becomes stronger, for example, if parents who are more educated help their offspring acquire better non-cognitive skills that increase their earnings for a given level of education. The third channel is strengthened, for example, if the offspring enjoy advantages in factor markets or receive better quality of education because of the social status or wealth of their parents, which translate to higher earnings.

Decompositions for 49 economies suggest that the third channel is typically the strongest, accounting for an average of about 80 percent of the persistence of income. This is not surprising, given that this channel reflects the share of income persistence attributable to all parental characteristics, including unobservable ones, that are associated with income but independent of the quantity of parental education. Three types of effects are likely to be important contributors to the third channel. One is the effect of distorted labor markets, which reward those with parental connections, legacies, or social privilege. The second is the effect of where one lives—richer parents may cluster together in places that allow their children to have better access to information, services, jobs and networks, and positive spillover effects from peer groups and role models. The third is the effect of the offspring of richer parents getting an education of higher quality, which is not accounted for in the first or the second channels. Identifying the drivers of income persistence requires looking closely at these effects.

The relative size of the third channel increases, whereas that of the first channel declines with per capita gross domestic product (GDP). Accordingly, the association between IGM of income and IGM of education tends to be stronger among developing economies than among high-income economies. This probably occurs because, when GDP is higher, relative mobility of education tends to be higher and education tends to be a weaker predictor of income. As that happens, the third channel becomes more important for income persistence across generations.

Relative IGM of income—how does it compare with IGM in education?
The map of income IGM (map O.2) should primarily be used for comparisons with education IGM (map O.1) rather than as a definitive picture of mobility, given the strong assumptions that underlie most of the income IGM estimates, the varied sources of these estimates, and the widespread gaps in geographic coverage. Relative IGM in income tends to be lower in the developing regions than in the high-income economies, like what is seen for relative IGM in education. In the developing world, low IGM in income is seen primarily in parts of Africa, Latin America, and South Asia. The United States appears to be less income mobile than are most high-income economies.

Income and education IGMs line up well with each other in most of East Asia, Eastern Europe and Central Asia, Latin America, and South Asia, and in high-income economies (comparing maps O.1 and O.2). Income mobility in Africa tends to be low for the economies with available estimates, even compared with their low levels of relative mobility of education. Income mobility lags education mobility in other countries as well, mostly in the Middle East and Latin America. In all these cases, the previously

MAP O.2   Relative intergenerational mobility of income across the world

a. IGM for selected economies for which estimates are available

IBRD 43644 | APRIL 2018

Intergenerational
Income
Persistence

0.6
0.5
0.4
0.3
0.2
Not available

Source: Estimates using GDIM 2018 and Equalchances 2018, compiled from multiple studies.
Note: Darker colors indicate higher relative IGM of income (or lower persistence). Gray shading indicates economies for which data on IGM for income are not available. The estimates are for the 1960s or 1970s cohorts, approximately.

mentioned third channel of income persistence is important, where labor markets and location-specific factors may be playing key roles in driving a wedge between education mobility and income mobility.

Understanding the drivers of inequality of opportunity, which is the inequality attributable to predetermined circumstances, such as parental education, geographical location of residence or birth, gender, and race, can help uncover the true impediments to higher relative mobility. This is because advantages passed on from generation to generation, even if they are correlated with parental education or income, may be attributable at least in part to the other circumstances that are included in the inequality of opportunity framework. In the decompositions above, where one lives, or one's gender, ethnicity, or other markers of social status, for example, could affect the size of the third channel, through direct and indirect routes, or the first channel, through their effect on returns to education.

Inequality of opportunity emerges at various stages of the life cycle
Circumstances of an individual at birth interact with policies, markets, and institutions to shape opportunities at various stages, which, in turn, influence the individual's adult earnings and thus IGM in income. Circumstances influence the opportunities available to an individual in two ways: direct effects, at every stage of the life cycle, and indirect effects, given that opportunities at each stage of life influence outcomes in subsequent stages.

For example, parental incomes influence investments in children's human capital that will, in turn, affect their incomes later in life, which is the first channel of income persistence mentioned earlier. Because monetary investments in children and parental human capital often complement each other in influencing human capital formation among children, parents with more education, who are also likely to be richer, are likely to invest more in their children relative to less-educated parents.[19] In the presence of credit constraints, the link between parental incomes and parental investments in children becomes stronger because parental investments are constrained by the resources available to the parents.[20] Parental status can also exert a direct influence on adult incomes, through networks and connections in labor and other factor markets, as in the third channel mentioned earlier. Other circumstances, such as geographic location, gender, and race, can affect the earnings of the next generation through a similar combination of direct and indirect pathways.

Circumstances begin affecting opportunities early in a child's life. Children's endowments at birth are affected by maternal nutrition and health during gestation, as well as by nonmonetary endowments or traits inherited from parents, all of which may be associated with circumstances such as parental education, income, and geographic location.[21] Circumstances then affect the critical inputs into human capital development throughout childhood, including nutrition, access to health care, basic services such as safe water and sanitation, and access to quality education. The schooling and noncognitive skills attained by children affect incomes later in life through the returns the children obtain for their human capital in the labor market and interactions with other factor markets.

At each stage of the life cycle, a few external actors are key to mediating the process of equalizing opportunities. These include, for example, the systems of maternal and early childhood care at the first stage; the school system at the second stage; and the institutional structure of factor markets—labor, capital, and land—at the third stage. The private sector plays a key role not only in generating demand for labor, but also in the provision of services. Governments can influence these external actors in crucial ways, for example, through regulations and policies that affect markets and the provision of services, and through public investments that seek to equalize opportunities, as mentioned earlier.

Economies with greater inequality of opportunity tend to have lower relative IGM

Education mobility estimates in GDIM confirm the pattern found by earlier studies: economies with greater inequality of opportunity, measured by the inequality of economic opportunity (IEO) index, are likely to show lower relative IGM (figure O.8).[22] IEO, which measures the share of total income inequality that is attributable to circumstances, is distant enough from relative IGM in education for the correlation between the two to be meaningful rather than inevitable. The correlation is consistent with the idea that the path to a more mobile society goes through lower inequality of opportunity.

FIGURE O.8   Greater inequality of opportunity is associated with lower relative mobility in education

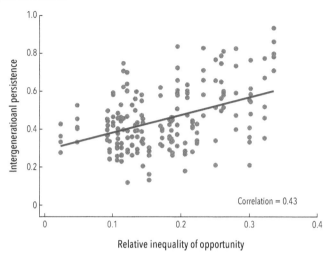

Source: Calculations using data from Brunori, Ferreira, and Peragine 2013; and GDIM 2018 (World Bank).
Note: Higher intergenerational persistence indicates lower relative intergenerational mobility in education. Relative inequality of opportunity refers to the share of total inequality attributed to circumstances.

Higher Public Spending Contributes to Greater Relative IGM in Richer Economies

Even though relative IGM in education is found to be higher in richer economies, this association should not be seen as an automatic consequence of growth. Existing theory suggests that the relationship can go either way because of opposing effects. On the one hand, as economies become richer and credit markets become more efficient, the effect of credit constraints may decline, which would tend to reduce intergenerational persistence in education.[23] On the other hand, as economies become richer and average education levels increase, parental investments in their children's education are likely to become more "efficient" in terms of producing outcomes, which raises intergenerational persistence unless inequality in parental education were to decline significantly.[24]

Given these opposing effects, relative IGM is more likely to improve with income levels if richer economies invest, on average, more public resources on equalizing opportunities, which appears to be the case. The data show that public spending on education as a share of GDP, which is an imperfect but useful proxy for investments to equalize opportunities, rises with per capita GDP and is associated with higher relative IGM (figure O.9). Regressions show that higher public spending (on education or on aggregate) is associated with higher relative IGM in education, after controlling for an economy's per capita GDP.[25] This is consistent with the theory that public spending helps equalize opportunities through investments that compensate for the gap in private investments between children of rich and poor parents.

FIGURE 0.9   Public spending on education is higher for richer economies, and associated with higher relative mobility in education

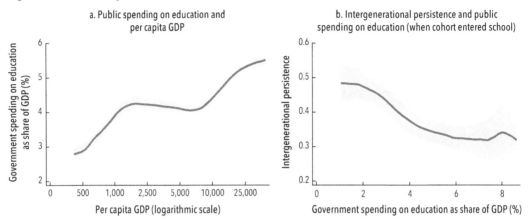

a. Public spending on education and per capita GDP

b. Intergenerational persistence and public spending on education (when cohort entered school)

Source: Calculations based on GDIM 2018, the Maddison Project, and United Nations Educational, Scientific, and Cultural Organization.
Note: Intergenerational persistence of each cohort is matched to gross domestic product (GDP) and public spending for the year when the average individual in the cohort is 5 years old (for example, intergenerational mobility of the 1980s cohort is matched to GDP and public spending in 1990). The shaded areas indicate 95 percent confidence intervals.

But just higher levels of spending are not enough. To improve relative IGM, public investments need to be effective, and "progressive," so that the relatively poor benefit more than those who are more well-off.

Why Does Intergenerational Mobility Matter?

The "Virtuous Cycle" of Greater IGM and Better Economic Outcomes

There is a strong positive association between IGM in education, both relative and absolute, and the level of economic development, across and within economies. Economic literature theorizes that, in economies with credit constraints that disproportionately affect the poor, IGM and economic growth may reinforce each other in a virtuous cycle. Greater relative mobility is also associated with a more inclusive pattern of development—low relative IGM is both a cause and a consequence of higher inequality, and has adverse consequences for social stability.

Greater IGM in education is associated with higher growth and poverty reduction in subsequent years

Greater absolute IGM and relative IGM in education among a generation are both associated with higher economic growth and less poverty when the generation reaches adulthood, according to cross-country regressions using GDIM.[26] In the case of poverty, the relationship is largely driven by a strong association between the poverty rate and upward mobility among individuals born to parents with low education levels. These results do not necessarily mean that higher IGM causes higher growth and poverty reduction, but rather that economies with higher IGM in education are also likely to have higher growth and poverty reduction subsequently. A simple calculation based on the same regressions illustrates the strength of the association: the rise of an economy from the bottom quartile of economies (sorted by relative IGM) to the top quartile is associated with an increase in GDP per capita of about 10 percent when the generation reaches adulthood.

IGM *in education tends to be greater in richer economies and in richer areas within economies*

Greater educational mobility is associated with higher levels of GDP. A similar association is also found within five of the six large developing economies mentioned earlier, where provinces with greater mobility among the 1980s generation are likely to exhibit higher GDP per capita. China is the only exception—provinces with greater relative mobility in China tend to be poorer. The relationships are nonlinear. Relative IGM increases with per capita GDP if the latter exceeds a certain level (figure O.10, panel a). Absolute mobility also increases with national income but is unchanged for per capita GDP above a certain level (1990 purchasing power parity) (figure O.10, panel b). Raising educational attainment probably becomes more difficult once an economy crosses an income level at which a certain threshold of education attainment is also reached.

Raising relative IGM can set in motion a virtuous cycle of higher mobility and higher growth

Higher relative mobility in education and income promotes economic growth because it leads to more efficient allocation of resources: individuals with higher innate abilities—rather than individuals with wealthier or more-educated parents—are more likely to obtain more education and

FIGURE O.10   Intergenerational mobility versus GDP per capita

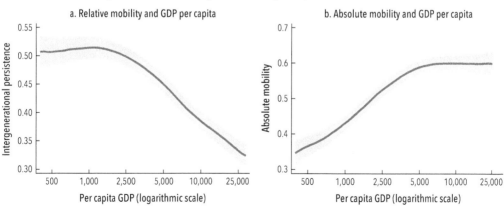

Source: Calculations based on data in the GDIM 2018 and the Maddison Project. The shaded areas indicate 95 percent confidence intervals.
Note: GDP = gross domestic product.

more productive jobs.[27] Economic growth may, in turn, help increase relative mobility, primarily by weakening the credit constraints that limit investment in education among the poor, although there can also be opposite forces that work toward reducing relative mobility as economies get richer. If the net effect of growth on relative mobility is positive, the virtuous cycle is set in motion: as countries grow, mobility rises more, which, in turn, stimulates growth further.

Policies to raise relative mobility are likely to promote long-run growth as well, by harnessing human potential more effectively and reducing the inefficiencies caused by misallocation of human and financial capital, the costs of which accumulate systematically over generations in an economy with low relative mobility. And the virtuous cycle between mobility and growth is likely to be stronger if the resources generated by higher growth are used to finance more progressive public spending that expands opportunities and helps level the playing field between the haves and the have-nots.

Empirical evidence exists to support the view that inequality of opportunity that leads to lower relative IGM is damaging to a country's long-term growth prospects. Recent research from the United States suggests that improving opportunities for upward mobility could enhance economic growth by increasing the rate of innovation in a society.[28] Inequality of opportunity may be particularly harmful for long-term growth by discouraging innovation and human capital investments. There is some evidence for the pernicious effects of inequality of opportunity on growth in Brazil and the United States,[29] but the cross-country evidence is more mixed.[30]

Greater relative mobility is associated with lower inequality

Lower relative IGM in income is associated with higher income inequality, as illustrated by the Great Gatsby curve found by various researchers and shown here with available estimates for 75 economies (figure O.11). Similar patterns are obtained for relative mobility in education. Higher education inequality during the schooling years of a cohort is associated with lower relative mobility, which is akin to a Gatsby curve in education. Lower relative mobility in education among a generation is also associated with higher income inequality during the peak earning years of that generation. Both correlations are much stronger in developing economies than in high-income economies.

These relationships are likely to be the consequence of a two-way relationship noted by other studies: higher inequality tends to limit relative mobility, which worsens inequality over time.[31] This happens because higher inequality leads to more unequal parental investments in children and affects the policies, institutions, and balance of power in society that shape opportunities. Unequal opportunities, in turn, lead to lower relative mobility and more inequality in the next generation, which is consistent with the strong association between relative mobility and inequality of opportunity shown earlier (figure O.8). Breaking the cycle of low relative mobility and

FIGURE 0.11   Higher relative IGM in income is associated with lower income inequality

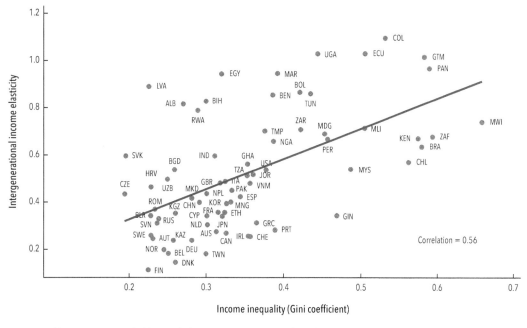

Source: Equalchances 2018, compiled from multiple studies; GDIM 2018 (World Bank); World Development Indicators for income inequality.
Note: Higher intergenerational income elasticity indicates lower relative intergenerational mobility (IGM).

high inequality will require equalizing opportunities to reduce the disadvantages faced by individuals because of circumstances outside their control.

Promoting Relative IGM Can Be Good for Social Stability

Higher absolute mobility is critical in meeting the aspirations of people. Nonetheless, in many societies, this may not be sufficient to induce the sense of fairness that is the bedrock of social cohesion and stability. The lack of relative mobility and pervasive inequality of opportunity can erode the perceptions of a population about fairness and trust in their society, which affects the social contract that supports growth and social stability. Behavioral experiments show that people are highly averse to inequality perceived as unfair.[32] Expectations of future mobility are important as well. If perceptions of higher mobility induce more tolerance for inequality, higher relative IGM could lead to greater acceptance for policies that increase growth and prosperity in the long run, but with some trade-off in inequality today.[33]

Low mobility, if perceived as such, can also lower one's aspirations, hopes, and ambitions for the future and thus reduce investments in human capital, reinforcing the cycle of low IGM and low levels of economic development. Perceptions of mobility are important building blocks of the process by which individuals form aspirations, both for themselves and for their children. When taken to the extreme, the vicious cycle of low perceived mobility and low aspirations can push individuals to opt out of socioeconomic processes, leading to marginalization and conflict.[34]

Evidence on direct links between social cohesion and perceptions of mobility, fairness, and inequality is difficult to find. However, it seems relevant that strong perceptions of downward mobility and lower tolerance for inequality were noted in at least three countries in the Middle East and North Africa region in 2012 relative to a decade earlier.[35] For social stability, it is the perceptions of the population regarding mobility—which are associated with actual mobility only imperfectly—that seem to matter. Perceptions of mobility can even diverge from actual mobility, particularly if comparisons are made across countries.[36] Some evidence from the Europe and Central Asia region also suggests that perceptions of absolute mobility are associated with actual relative mobility, but not with actual absolute mobility.

Policy Drivers to Improve Intergenerational Mobility

Evidence from the economic literature and cross-country patterns obtained using the GDIM can help identify the key drivers of long-term outcomes that are likely to improve mobility. This exercise is not intended to generate a definitive ranking of policy priorities, which must be guided by individual country contexts and societal preferences. Rather, it is an attempt to provide a broad range of candidate policies, which countries can assess to identify the package of priorities that are suitable for their own contexts. The implicit selection of policy drivers that are highlighted below is guided not only by the strength of the evidence, but also by the mobility-enhancing potential of interventions based on their underlying theories of change. Even when evidence is inadequate, it is important to consider the potential effects on IGM of policies that have been less studied, either because they are less amenable to rigorous evaluations or because they are designed with other, more proximate development objectives in mind.

The focus will be primarily on relative mobility. In the developing world, absolute IGM and relative IGM often complement each other as policy objectives—better opportunities for individuals from socially disadvantaged backgrounds would raise relative mobility and generate greater absolute mobility for the society as a whole. But even when the two objectives diverge, the case for prioritizing relative mobility is compelling, given its importance for long-term growth, inequality, and social cohesion. Relative mobility may even influence perceptions of absolute mobility, as mentioned earlier.

To promote relative mobility, the state can play a proactive role in "compensating" for differences in individual and family starting points to level the playing field in opportunities. Policies should also aim to equalize opportunities across space, given the contribution of location to inequalities in most countries. The state also has a prominent role to play in making markets work more efficiently and equitably, given that discrimination, anticompetitive behavior, and market concentration are likely to constrain IGM. Fiscal policy is the most effective public policy tool for realizing many of these objectives, by raising resources for investments in public goods and reducing inequality through redistribution.

Reducing Inequality of Opportunities Attributable to Individual Circumstances

Leveling the playing field can take several forms, depending on a country's context and stage of development. In most developing economies, where relative mobility in education tends to be low, building ladders to opportunities at the early stages of an individual's life is critical for promoting IGM. Such interventions can seek to influence behavior and decisions of households in ways that lead to improvements in children's long-term outcomes that matter for mobility.

Equalizing opportunities in utero and early childhood

Improving the early life environment is critical because gaps that emerge early in life are difficult to offset through interventions later in life. Child malnutrition, for example, can generate learning difficulties, poor health, and lower productivity and earnings over a lifetime.[37] Consistent with this, economies with lower rates of stunted growth among children at age 5 are also likely to have higher relative and absolute IGM in education (figure O.12).

Interventions to equalize opportunities must begin even before a child is born because maternal health is a key determinant of a child's health at birth, and the deprivations suffered in utero can reduce the effectiveness of postnatal investments.[38] Policy measures aimed at disadvantaged women of childbearing age can have a positive effect on infant health and longer-term outcomes of children. These include food supplementation programs that

FIGURE 0.12   Higher mobility is associated with lower rates of stunting

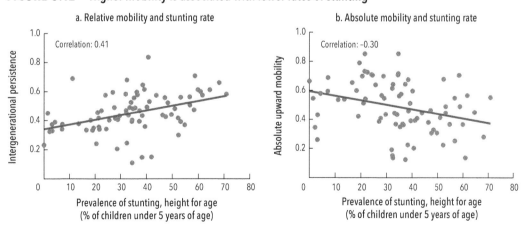

Source: GDIM 2018 (World Bank); Institute for Statistics, United Nations Educational, Scientific and Cultural Organization; World Development Indicators database, World Bank, (http://data.worldbank.org/products/wdi).
Note: The figure shows intergenerational mobility estimates for cohorts born in the 1980s. The rates of stunting, height for age (percentage of children under 5 years of age), refer to averages in 1986–95, including economies with at least one observation during this period. The period is chosen roughly to match the early childhood years of the 1980s cohorts.

might involve relatively inexpensive nutritional supplements for mothers and programs to build awareness among mothers, for example through visits by health workers.

Intervening in the postnatal period is also effective, particularly if this is accomplished early in a child's life. Programs targeting nutritional and health improvements in early childhood can yield long-term benefits in education outcomes and wages; nutritional supplements seem to have the strongest effects when they are given to children of age 2 years or younger.[39] Universal preschool programs can play an important equalizing role because skill formation is a dynamic process in which early inputs strongly affect the productivity of later inputs (Heckman 2006). Reviews of the evidence indicate that intervening during preschool years is more effective than later interventions, and only programs that start before children reach the age of 3 years seem to have long-lasting effects on cognitive abilities.[40]

Cognitive skills are not the only determinants of long-term outcomes. Intensive preschool programs such as the Perry Preschool and Abecedarian projects in the United States had large long-term effects also because they improved noncognitive skills among children, starting around age three.[41] Although most of the research on the long-term effects of early childhood programs has been conducted in high-income countries, one important example in a developing country setting finds that interventions to improve children's socioemotional skills during the first three years of life can have a positive and significant effect on labor earnings in adulthood.[42]

Although small, intensive, model programs such as Perry demonstrate the frontier of possibilities with early childhood development (ECD) programs, research on the long-term effects of the Head Start Program in the United States—one of the longest-running and largest preschool programs in the world targeting low-income children—suggests what is possible with large-scale ECD programs.[43] Despite the challenges of implementation and the inefficiencies associated with scaling up, the benefits can still be substantial.

The evidence on the long-term benefits of other programs and policies that could potentially equalize opportunities in childhood is somewhat thin. On subsidized childcare, a key policy instrument whose effects on long-term outcomes are not well documented, the experience of Norway is illuminating. In the four years after a reform in 1975 in Norway, childcare coverage almost tripled among three- to six-year-olds. The program led to an increase in life-cycle labor income and educational attainment, with the largest effects occurring among girls and the children of less-educated mothers.[44] And although school meal programs have been widely adopted by governments to improve nutrition and educational outcomes, evidence on their long-term effects is available only in two high-income countries, and these effects are quite small.[45]

Reducing opportunity gaps in education—access and quality
The GDIM database shows that economies with higher absolute and relative IGM in education among cohorts of the 1980s are likely to have

smaller shares of children who were out of school and higher average test scores in primary education during the school years of these cohorts. Within economies, the gaps in learning outcomes across children of parents at different levels of income and education tend to be even larger than the gaps in access, and these gaps are particularly wide in the developing world.[46]

Investing in public education. As shown earlier, economies with more public investments in education are also likely to have greater relative mobility in education. This relationship is found to be particularly strong for developing economies, and stronger for spending on primary education than other levels of education. That said, developing economies showing greater relative and absolute mobility seem to invest more public resources in all levels of education. The relationship between public education spending and absolute mobility is much weaker. This is consistent with public education spending having an equalizing effect, given that equality of opportunity is more closely related to relative IGM than to absolute IGM.

However, higher public spending on education is likely to promote economic mobility only if the spending translates to better access to and quality of education for disadvantaged groups. The level of public spending in education is found to be weakly correlated with average learning outcomes across countries and statistically insignificant after controlling for the country's income level;[47] however, there is evidence that more public spending is associated with lower inequality in learning achievement.[48] It seems intuitive that just spending more is not enough to improve the quality of learning and equity in access to education. What also matters is how efficient the spending is in producing the key inputs into education and how equitable the allocation of spending is across groups and across space.

According to the GDIM database, both absolute IGM and relative IGM tend to be greater in economies with a higher teacher–student ratio in primary education, which is a broad measure of one of the inputs that are crucial to the quality of education. Other key inputs that influence the quality of education, such as the quality of teachers, curricula, facilities, and so on, are likely to matter as well for whether more education spending in an economy translates to better learning outcomes among disadvantaged children.

Education reforms. Relative mobility benefits from policy changes that improve the accessibility of education among disadvantaged students. Existing research suggests that reforms that weaken the practice of tracking students by academic ability or postpone it until students are older promote equality of opportunity, as seen from examples of such reforms in three Nordic countries.[49] Other policy changes can affect the implicit or explicit costs of education. The instruments are varied, such as reducing the duration of education for tertiary degrees (as was done in Italy), and increasing the years of compulsory schooling (as in Norway).

Improving the accessibility of secondary schooling is likely to become a priority in many developing economies as primary school enrollments approach 100 percent. A recent policy experiment in rural Ghana found large effects of secondary school scholarships on the education and labor market outcomes of low-income students.[50] This highlights the potential benefits of free secondary schooling, as well as the need for developing economies to consider such policy experiments to build the evidence that informs future education reforms.

Improving the quality of learning and reducing vast inequalities in learning outcomes require education policies that address the proximate and systemic causes of the "learning crisis" described by the 2018 *World Development Report* (World Bank 2018a). The same report organizes the policy actions to address proximate causes—such as children arriving to school unprepared to learn, teachers lacking the skills or motivation to teach, inputs that are unavailable or of inferior quality, and poor management and governance of schools—and the deeper systemic causes into three broad categories. These are assessing learning through better measurement and tracking, acting on evidence to make schools work for all learners, and aligning actors to make the entire education system work for learning.

Breaking the cycle of low aspirations and low mobility

Beliefs about mobility and aspirations influence each other because the behavior of individuals depends on the belief systems impressed upon them by society, and actual mobility contributes to the formation of these belief systems.[51] Evidence suggests that mobility trajectories and long-run beliefs are determined jointly and thus depend on each other. A well-known theory refers to an aspirations window, or the set of similar (or attainable) individuals whose lives and achievements help form one's future goals, which is broadened by higher (perceived) mobility.[52] The aspirations window of an individual is shaped by multiple reference groups, whose composition is influenced by the individual's socioeconomic status, as well as social hierarchies and norms.

Aspirations are critical to mobility. For example, in Mexico, poor youth of ages 12–22 years with higher mobility aspirations have been found to stay in school longer, exhibit better health behavior, and engage less in self-destructive behavior.[53] High aspirations of 12-year-olds in Telangana and Andhra Pradesh in India are positively associated with the amount of time devoted to education and, ultimately, with educational outcomes at age 19 years.[54]

The aspiration window of children of low socioeconomic status is likely to be narrow because children in such families are likely to grow up in a social environment that contributes to the narrowing of their aspiration window. Moreover, parental aspirations, which influence the aspirations of children and their own investments in their children, may be lower among families of low socioeconomic status. Rigid social hierarchies may contribute to or compound the effects of low aspirations. For example, an experiment in India shows that providing cues to one's place in the caste order influences the ability of low caste boys to learn and the willingness of high caste boys to expend effort.[55]

Policies to influence aspirations—indirectly or directly. Exposing children and parents to information, experiences, and role models that influence the shaping of aspirations may help widen the aspiration window in some settings. For example, providing information on the returns to education to students in the Dominican Republic at the end of compulsory schooling significantly improved their perceptions of the returns to schooling relative to similar schoolchildren in a control group.[56] Interventions that help the creation of role models can also raise aspirations. For example, a random assignment of female leaders in selected village councils in a state in India led to a significant reduction in the gender aspirations gap among parents and among adolescents.[57]

Evidence is inadequate so far on whether interventions directly aimed at raising the aspirations of children or parents can improve education outcomes. Interventions to improve aspirations and attitudes among school-age children have shown some positive effects; the evidence is weaker on the effects of interventions to raise parental aspirations.[58] Thus, more evidence is needed, particularly from behavioral interventions that target aspirations, before policy conclusions can be established.

Given the dynamic ways in which aspirations are formed and sustained, interventions that aim directly at raising aspirations are not the only answer. Some studies have argued that, for many youths from disadvantaged backgrounds, the stalling of aspirations during their formative years is what is salient, rather than a shortage of high aspirations.[59] This calls for greater support to young people from socially disadvantaged backgrounds in maintaining their aspirations—including better opportunities in education and jobs, better teachers, and better career advice, mentoring, and training.

Labor market policies and institutions to promote mobility

As seen earlier, labor markets play a significant role in shaping the persistence of income inequality across generations. In the decompositions, the functioning of the labor market influences the size of the first channel through returns to education, and that of the third channel through the effect of parental circumstances other than education on an individual's earnings. Both effects can be influenced by circumstances other than parental characteristics, such as an individual's gender or race.

The labor market can limit income IGM by compounding any preexisting inequality that affects an individual before his or her entry into the labor market. Although the labor market directly affects individuals at their adult stage of life, it has a feedback effect on human capital formation as well. Because investments in human capital are "priced" in the labor market, policies and institutions affecting these prices have feedback effects on investment decisions that parents make for their children's education, and on the decisions made by the children themselves.

How the labor market affects income IGM and its relationship with education IGM. One of the indicators of a healthy labor market is the labor force participation rate (LFP). For economies with low LFP, the association between relative IGM in education and income is much weaker than for those with high LFP (figure O.13), which is also confirmed by regression analysis.[60] This suggests that, in an economy with low LFP, investments in human capital are harder to monetize, which leads to a larger "wedge" between educational and income IGMs. Once the effect of the LFP is considered, the economy's per capita GDP does not have a strong effect on the relationship between education IGM and income IGM, which suggests that for this relationship, an economy's labor market conditions matter more than its level of development.

The labor market is also more likely to be a barrier to IGM in income when the allocation of jobs and differences in earnings are influenced by an individual's circumstances that are unrelated to his or her productivity. For example, the role of parental social networks can be a key barrier to relative mobility when jobs are rationed and unemployment is high. A study of young adults in a city in South Africa finds that the father's occupational networks have a strong effect on the son's labor market outcomes.[61] In the Middle East, personal connections, or the so-called culture of *wasta*, appear to play a strong role in compounding the effects of weak job creation on IGM.[62]

FIGURE O.13   When labor force participation is higher, relative IGMs in income and education are more closely associated with one another

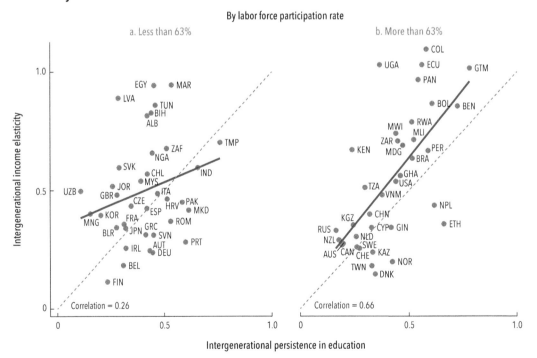

Source: GDIM 2018 (World Bank); Equalchances 2018; and ILOSTAT.
Note: Sixty-three percent is the median labor force participation rate for countries with available estimates of income and educational intergenerational mobility (IGM).

The effect of parental networks on labor market outcomes is compounded by discrimination based on characteristics unrelated to productivity, such as gender, race, caste, or religion. Discrimination can also interact with social networks in transmitting disadvantage across generations, contributing to a high degree of "inertia" that can cause discrimination to persist in labor markets long after legislative interventions are put in place.

Around the world, women are found to be less likely to actively participate in the labor market; and for those who choose to work for pay, labor market disparities persist in terms of wages, occupation, and sector of employment.[63] Because of these disparities, although gender gaps in IGM in education have closed or even reversed in much of the world, the same may not have occurred for gender gaps in income IGM. Several factors contribute to gender disparities, including differences in time use, social networks, and gender roles between women and men, and discrimination by employers. Social norms can play a role in reproducing gender disparities in the labor market from one generation to the next.

Policies to level the playing field in the labor market. In general, labor market institutions and policies can support higher IGM by limiting the extent or effect of unemployment spells, easing labor market access of vulnerable categories and youth, improving competitions among employers, and increasing protection of workers who are discriminated against. Policies and regulations that promote competition and market integration are also likely to be good for IGM. The less segmented and more competitive the labor market is, the less likely distortionary practices such as discrimination and network effects are to survive in equilibrium.

A combination of active and passive labor market policies can help reduce the negative and long run consequences of unemployment, particularly in advanced economies. Weak labor market conditions for young entrants to the job market, as seen during the 2008 financial crisis, have long-lasting effects on their productivity, incomes, and prospects for upward mobility. The income effect of job loss can be minimized by unemployment benefits or, in case of informal labor markets, by social assistance measures that may reduce the likelihood of disinvestment in children's human capital.

Facilitating the integration of youth into the labor market is essential to reduce the chances of lifetime income losses as a result of a poor start. Giving incentives to employers to hire young people, such as through wage subsidies, targeted reductions in the labor tax wedge, or tax credits at the lower end of the wage scale, are potential policy options whose effects may be small or temporary.[64] Programs such as training or subsidized employment can also be beneficial for youth, especially during a recession. In general, however, active labor market policies may be limited in what they can achieve. A recent study finds that the effect of active labor market policies in developing economies is relatively small and tends to be largely offset by their cost.[65]

Labor market and social policies such as parental leave, flexible workplace arrangements, and the provision of affordable and high-quality childcare have been found to have a positive effect on women's LFP. Moreover, reserving some part of the parental leave for fathers has been found not only to limit the gendered effect of family-related work interruptions, but also to reduce differences in time use between men and women that contribute to inequality of opportunities between genders.[66]

Mitigating the effects of capital market imperfections on mobility
Credit constraints and lack of insurance can limit upward mobility of the poor and lead to poverty traps in developing economies, where capital markets tend to be underdeveloped. These imperfections also provide an additional incentive for wealth transfers to the next generation, which increases persistence in earning differentials across generations, given that only those with access to inherited wealth can finance investments that can potentially enhance their earnings. Intergenerational persistence of earnings has been found to vary between different points of the distribution of parental income in some developing economies, which hints at the presence of credit constraints.[67] For example, relative mobility of income in Brazil is found to increase, on average, with the father's wage and is substantially lower for sons of fathers with below-median wages.[68]

Capital market imperfections strengthen the case for redistributive policies. When capital market imperfections are taken into account, the distribution of wealth among a generation has important effects on the distribution of income as well as on aggregate efficiency and output.[69] This implies that redistributive policies can promote IGM by improving both distribution and efficiency, when the dynamic effects of wealth inequality in the presence of credit constraints are considered. These arguments also strengthen the case for taxation of capital income and property.

Moreover, given the role of credit constraints, broadening access to financial services may arguably improve IGM, particularly at the lower end of the income distribution. The same argument applies to targeted transfers to lower-income families, such as conditional or unconditional cash transfers, and tax credits for the working poor. Also, in the presence of credit constraints, lack of collateral among the poor becomes a critical barrier to investments, which suggests that policies that facilitate legalization of existing assets or broader ownership of assets can be mobility enhancing. By a similar argument, ensuring that women and men have equal rights to inherit and own assets in countries where women lack such rights can improve economic mobility of women, and possibly that of their children.[70]

Reducing the barriers to economic transformation
In most developing economies, the process of economic transformation strongly influences how factor markets work.[71] Many of the usual forces of transformation—such as employment shifts toward more productive sectors, rising geographic mobility, and weakening of restrictive social norms—are likely to improve IGM. For example, in India, IGM among

scheduled castes and tribes is found to have increased and converged toward that of other groups as economic transformation has accelerated.[72] Conversely, skill-based technological change that accompanies transformation can reduce relative mobility by raising returns to education and, with that, wages at the top.

The positive effects of transformation can be muted by existing factor market distortions or rigidities. For example, land market distortions can constrain spatial mobility, and distortions in land and labor markets can interact with restrictive social norms to restrict economic transformation processes.[73] For these reasons, as transformation progresses, the trajectories of economic mobility can vary a lot within the same economy. In China, for example, one study finds that relative IGM in both education and earnings has fallen more among women and residents of economically disadvantaged regions since the beginning of the economic transition.[74]

One reason why IGM trends vary widely across groups and regions within a country may be the significant adjustment costs workers face in changing locations or industries, which can prevent them from exploiting new opportunities in a transforming economy that is trading more with the rest of the world. A recent World Bank study finds that the effects of exports on labor outcomes in South Asia are localized, most likely because of the presence of significant worker-level adjustment costs.[75] In general terms, reducing barriers to spatial mobility—so that people can freely move or connect to better jobs, services, and opportunities wherever these exist—is likely to benefit IGM.

Equalizing Opportunities across Space

For mobility and opportunity, it matters where one is born in a country, in addition to the social status of the family one is born into. Although much more research is needed, the combined evidence so far underscores the importance of focusing locally—from the level of provinces down to the level of neighborhoods—for improving IGM.

Local drivers of mobility matter

The global data on educational mobility reveal a few patterns suggesting the importance of local drivers of mobility. Globally, economies with lower levels of spatial segregation by education levels are also likely to have higher absolute and relative educational mobility (figure O.14). The same pattern is seen across provinces within the six large developing economies. In economies (or provinces) with lower levels of segregation, children from disadvantaged backgrounds plausibly get more chances to share the same public services as children from richer backgrounds and benefit from positive spillovers.

In the same six economies, in provinces with a higher concentration of "privilege" (the more educated), those at the bottom of the ladder have higher chances of making it to the top, possibly because of more economic dynamism, better services, and other positive spillovers from the highly educated.[76]

FIGURE 0.14   Economies with higher educational mobility tend to have lower levels of spatial segregation by education

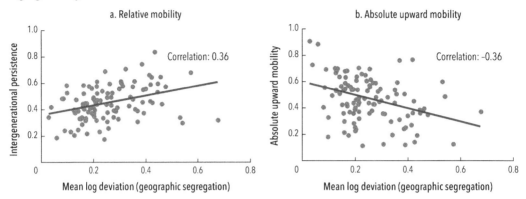

Source: Calculations using GDIM 2018 (World Bank).
Note: Intergenerational mobility estimates for cohort born in the 1980s. Mean log deviation refers to segregation measured by the share of between-primary sample unit inequality in education out of total inequality, using sample of all adults from surveys underlying GDIM 2018 (World Bank).

But these provinces also have higher inequality in upward mobility between those in the bottom half and others. To ensure that the advantages offered by these "mobility poles" are available more equitably, policies need to focus on narrowing the opportunity gaps between children born with different parental backgrounds living in these areas.

Evidence on the drivers of mobility at the neighborhood or community level is compelling, but limited mostly to high-income economies. The Moving to Opportunity project in the United States has highlighted the important effect of better neighborhoods and local environments on long-term outcomes for children, including their incomes as adults, if the change occurs at an early age.[77] Neighborhood characteristics such as income segregation and concentrated poverty, inequality, racial segregation, quality of schools, crime rates, and the share of two-parent families have been found to be important determinants of IGM. At least half of the variance in IGM across areas in the United States is attributable to the causal effect of location.[78]

Public policies to strengthen the local drivers of IGM
Although national-level policies are important, social mobility needs to be addressed also at the local level. Several characteristics that influence the key pathways for local effects on mobility can be influenced by policy, such as safety, accessibility, infrastructure, and the quality and availability of childcare, health care, educational institutions, and recreational facilities. Interventions aimed at reducing the concentration of poverty and the socioeconomic segregation of neighborhoods can be particularly beneficial for mobility.

For example, location-specific investments in housing and infrastructure may be able to reduce the economic segregation of communities and improve connectivity to markets. Local incentives and subsidies to promote the creation of jobs in distressed neighborhoods have helped in some cases to reduce concentrated poverty and improve the social environment.[79] Mentoring programs, interventions through social networks, and internships at local companies have been suggested as potential ways to motivate and help children from disadvantaged backgrounds.[80] There is also increasing recognition of the need for more comprehensive approaches to building neighborhood social capital, combining service delivery, housing, and public and private investment, and building resident governance structures.[81]

A Fiscal System to Balance Efficiency with Equity in Developing Economies

A fiscal system that raises sufficient resources to support public investments to promote IGM must balance efficiency and equity objectives for developing economies. There are compelling arguments to suggest that, with imperfect capital markets, redistributive policies can improve efficiency; but trade-offs between equity and efficiency may exist for specific policies. This calls for a comprehensive approach that considers the combined redistributive and efficiency effects of taxes and spending, and that encompasses both design and administration considerations.

Raising resources through progressive taxation
In developing economies, limited levels of taxation and the composition of revenues limit fiscal redistribution relative to advanced economies.[82] Developing economies rely heavily on indirect taxation, which has a limited redistributive effect compared with direct taxes that translates to lower effect on improving IGM. In the GDIM database, economies with lower tax revenues and share of direct taxes in total revenue tend to have lower IGM in education—relative and absolute.

Enhancing redistribution requires that developing economies raise more fiscal resources through taxation. To achieve that, a policy strategy could aim to broaden the income tax base and increase progressivity, strengthening tax compliance as a prerequisite. Other than meeting resource needs, such a strategy can also help moderate inequality of outcomes today, which will help raise relative IGM tomorrow. Property taxes can provide a relatively efficient way of improving the progressivity of taxes and raising revenues, if the necessary investments in administrative capacity are made. Inheritance taxes are another direct way to address persistence and raise resources. These taxes currently contribute little to fiscal revenues despite a rising flow of inheritances in recent years in many economies.

In-kind spending and transfers
To improve IGM, for most developing economies, there is a compelling case for prioritizing investments that equalize opportunities for children and mothers. This includes in-kind spending on systems and programs to

improve maternal and child health, education, nutrition, and ECD, and well-targeted transfer programs that benefit long-term outcomes of children. Transfer programs can mitigate the effects of credit constraints on investments in children. Although conditional and unconditional cash transfers have been widely adopted in the developing world and found to have positive short-term effects, more long-term studies are needed to find robust evidence on their long-term effects.[83] A recent review concludes that cash transfer programs have had positive effects on schooling outcomes, whereas the evidence on employment and income effects is more mixed.[84]

Research from some high-income economies demonstrates what transfer programs can potentially achieve. For example, studies have found that exposure in teenage years to the Earned Income Tax Credit in the United States—a tax benefit targeted to low-income households, which is in effect one of the largest transfer programs in the country—has a positive effect on test scores; the likelihood of completing high school, completing college, and being employed; and earnings as a young adult.[85] As mentioned earlier, a recent policy experiment also suggests that scholarships for secondary school students could be an important policy tool to improve educational mobility in developing economies. In contrast with these priorities, fiscally expensive universal price subsidy schemes, which are found to be an inefficient approach to protect the poor, have limited redistributive effect in the short or long run.[86]

Spending priorities will vary by country context, including the extent to which barriers to income mobility are different from those limiting educational mobility. For example, public spending on infrastructure can be a priority for improving income mobility in economies where barriers to connectivity prevent workers from accessing jobs, or firms from accessing markets. In economies with high unemployment, investments in active labor market programs and social protection systems for workers might help improve relative mobility and prevent downward mobility among workers.

Adopting the Right Policies Requires Evidence and Better Governance

Lack of evidence about what works, and how, may sometimes be a reason why policies that promote long-term inclusive growth are not adopted by governments. Even monitoring IGM and inequality of opportunity at the national level has proved to be difficult in some developing countries—a data gap that can be addressed at a reasonably low cost by adding a few questions to existing household surveys, which ask adult respondents about the education, occupation, and birth year of their parents. For setting policy priorities, policy makers also need to know more about the factors that influence mobility, evidence on which can be generated using a variety of possible sources. These include "big data" from administrative records and censuses that are becoming more useable with rapid technological advances, which also help address the security and privacy concerns about the use of such data. For evidence on the impacts of potential interventions, policy makers need to draw on the findings of academic research and test them in local contexts with carefully evaluated pilots. To help with this process, academic research needs to focus more on filling the gaps in evidence on the drivers of the long-term outcomes that determine IGM, particularly in developing-country settings.

But too often, governments find it hard to adopt or implement many of the policies to achieve fair progress, even when compelling evidence exists to guide these decisions. In explaining why this happens, the 2017 *World Development Report* (World Bank 2017) notes that the adoption and implementation of effective policies are influenced by who has a place at the bargaining table during the process of designing and implementing policy. That process, which can be termed *governance*, underlies how institutions in a country function to support policies that promote long-term prosperity and fairness. Persistence of outcomes across generations can often be traced to policies being influenced more by the preferences of the rich than by those of the poor and the disadvantaged. Inequality in a society often reflects power asymmetries; and persistence of outcomes across generations, in turn, reflects the transmission of power asymmetries through the status inherited by a child from his or her parents. Policies that promote the greater good, including mobility, may be difficult to introduce and implement because the groups in society who benefit from the status quo may be powerful enough to resist reforms.

History offers numerous examples in which rules, institutions, and processes have improved in societies, often incrementally, and existing institutions have been adapted to deliver effective policy solutions. World Bank (2017) argues that what matters for policy effectiveness is whether those institutional forms can perform their intended functions in a particular setting, and it identifies commitment, coordination, and cooperation as the three core functions of institutions that determine policy effectiveness.

Conclusion: A Few Principles for IGM-Enhancing Policies

For sustainable and inclusive growth, public policy must support a social contract that addresses people's aspirations. Such a contract, in most countries, is likely to be one where all parents can expect their children to have better lives than themselves (absolute upward IGM) and where an individual's position on the income scale is less tied to the status of his or her parents (relative IGM). Policies that achieve success on both these fronts can create a positive feedback loop, because citizens' perceptions of higher mobility can, in turn, lead to a social consensus that improves the environment for policies of the future.

Policies supporting the drivers of economic growth—such as promoting macroeconomic stability, a better investment climate, and greater integration with global markets—are also likely to be good for IGM, absolute and relative. Conversely, higher mobility, both relative and absolute, has a positive feedback on growth in the long run, by increasing the stock of human capital and innovation, promoting a more efficient allocation of resources, and building support for a social consensus around policies that contribute to the greater good. But higher growth, even when it is distributed such that it improves the living standards of most individuals in a society, may not be enough to ensure greater relative mobility. A society with high inequality is also likely to have greater inequality of opportunity, which leads to lower relative mobility that, in turn, leads to further inequality in outcomes and opportunities, and so on.

To break the cycle of high inequality and low mobility, a government would need to prioritize policies that raise opportunities for the least advantaged groups at various stages of life, as appropriate for a country's own context. In most developing economies, where relative mobility in education tends to be low, investments and policies aimed at the initial stages of an individual's life cycle are necessary for promoting IGM in education as well as income.

However, for most economies, promoting educational mobility may not be enough. Labor market inefficiencies and distortions can pose a strong barrier to IGM of income, over and above the factors that limit educational mobility. The capital market can also play a constraining role by affecting the ability of the poor to make optimal investment decisions, which constrains mobility in education and income alike. Barriers to mobility across space and industries can distort labor markets and lead to the benefits of transformation being locally concentrated instead of being shared widely across an economy.

Evidence from the literature and cross-country patterns provide a few insights on the broad directions for policies to raise IGM. First, the state can play a proactive role in equalizing opportunities attributable to individual circumstances, where the priorities may include (1) interventions targeted to maternal health and to early childhood, because gaps that emerge then are often irreversible; (2) reducing gaps in access to and quality of education between the haves and have-nots; (3) enhancing the effectiveness of interventions by considering the role of aspirations and social norms in influencing the decisions of households and individuals; and (4) making markets work more efficiently and equitably, and reducing barriers to mobility across space and industries.

Second, the state may need to be proactive about equalizing opportunities across space. How policies and investments are applied at the local level matters, from provinces down to individual communities. Interventions to improve neighborhoods and social environments, by reducing socioeconomic segregation, investing in services and infrastructure, and building social capital, are likely to be beneficial for IGM. In making their investment decisions, policy makers must consider not just the short-term effects of investments, but also the potential long-term benefits for the children and youth belonging to those communities, which, in turn, have a positive effect on the next generation, and so on.

Third, fiscal policy can influence IGM in education and income in multiple ways. The goal of a mobility-enhancing fiscal policy would be threefold: mobilize resources to finance public investments that promote higher IGM, boost relative IGM by moderating income inequality, and balance these objectives with the objective of promoting efficiency and growth. A policy strategy could aim to broaden the tax base for income tax, increase progressivity through tools such as property and inheritance taxes, and strengthen tax compliance, while investing in building administrative capacity. On spending to improve IGM, in addition to investments to equalize opportunities for children and mothers, well-targeted transfer programs can mitigate the effects of credit constraints on human capital investments of families. In some countries, these priorities may need to replace universal price subsidy schemes for items like fuel, which are often an inefficient way to protect the poor while consuming a large share of scarce resources.

Last, governance can play a crucial role in mitigating the power asymmetries that prevent the right policies from being adopted even when there is compelling evidence on what needs to be done. Inequities in the policy-making system prevent policies from being more responsive to the needs of the poor and the disadvantaged. This causes inequality to persist across generations, which, in turn, strengthens power asymmetries and perpetuates the cycle. World Bank (2017) suggests that positive change requires shifting the incentives of those with power, reshaping their preferences to support positive outcomes, and increasing the contestability of policy decisions by considering the interests of those who are typically excluded from the policy arena.

Such changes can catalyze reforms that unlock the human potential among the poor and the disadvantaged and set in motion a virtuous cycle. Higher intergenerational mobility can lead to greater efficiency and economic growth and lower inequality, which is likely to promote a more level playing field and reduce asymmetries in power. This, in turn, is likely to boost the mobility of future generations and place a country on a higher, more self-sustaining path of long-term development.

Notes

1. See, for example, Roemer (1998) and Van de Gaer (1993).
2. Hertz and others (2007).
3. See, for example, Solon (2004).
4. Figure O.1 combines income IGM estimates from other studies with own estimates, while ensuring some degree of comparability in methodology across estimates (see chapter 2).
5. Excluding individuals with parents who have tertiary education mitigates the "ceiling effect" in educational mobility (that education levels cannot exceed tertiary). An alternative method for mitigating this effect leads to roughly similar results (see chapter 3 of the book).

6. An alternate measure of relative IGM used in the mobility literature, the intergenerational correlation of educational attainment, is also computed to check the robustness of results reported with the regression coefficient.

7. The gap in absolute mobility among the 1980s generation between high-income and developing economies is almost equally large if the measure of absolute IGM includes individuals whose parents have tertiary educational attainment (instead of dropping them) and considers these individuals as upwardly mobile if they have at least as much education as their parents.

8. The gap between developing and high-income economies in relative mobility is also significant if the correlation coefficient between parental and offspring educational attainment, rather than the regression coefficient, is used as the measure of intergenerational persistence (not shown here).

9. See, for example, Corak (2016b) for reviews of the evidence.

10. The widening gap between high-income and developing economies is also observed if the correlation coefficient between parental and offspring educational attainment is used as the measure of intergenerational persistence.

11. Beegle and others (2016); for a more detailed comparison with that study, see chapter 3.

12. The FCV group of economies is based on the World Bank Group's Harmonized List of Fragile Situations (Fiscal Year 2018): http://www.worldbank.org/en/topic/fragilityconflictviolence/brief/harmonized-list-of-fragile-situations. Of the 36 economies in the list, IGM estimates for all cohorts can be computed for 7 economies and IGM estimates for the 1980s cohort can be estimated for 26 economies (see chapter 3 of the book).

13. This indicator, termed *poverty-to-privilege rate* in the book, is identical to the indicator referred to as *rags to riches* in Corak (2016a).

14. These findings are reported from Evans, Newhouse, and Suarez-Becerra (forthcoming).

15. The educational shortfall of a child of age T = observed years of education – (T – 5). This indicator is used in lieu of educational attainment, because those who are born after the 1980s cohort may not necessarily have completed their education by the time of the survey.

16. Average persistence is measured by the average of regression coefficients from regressions of educational shortfall on parental education for every country. Regional averages include only those economies on which the shortfall variable can be constructed.

17. World Development Indicators (2018).

18. Chetty, Hendren, and Katz (2016).

19. For example, see Becker and others (2015).

20. See Piketty (2000) for an overview of the literature.

21. Becker and Tomes (1979, 1986); Currie (2009).
22. IEO is measured as the share of total income inequality attributed to predetermined circumstances. The estimates of IEO are taken from Brunori, Ferreira, and Peragine (2013), who compiled them from multiple studies. In most cases, the circumstances include parental education, geographical location of residence or birth, and gender, and, in some cases, race, ethnicity, and religion.
23. See, for example, Maoz and Moav (1999), and Owen and Weil (1998).
24. For example, in the model by Becker and others (2015), which assumes perfect credit markets and no government intervention, an increase in average parental education and income is predicted to raise the level of intergenerational persistence unless inequality in parental education were to decline significantly.
25. Based on linear regressions of relative IGM in education on public spending on education or total public spending (as a share of GDP) and (the logarithm of) per capita GDP of an economy, pooling cohorts from the 1960s to the 1980s and including cohort fixed effects (see chapter 4).
26. This observation is supported by regressions of (logarithm of) GDP or headcount poverty rates on measures of absolute or relative mobility, at the time when the cohort was about 15 years old, controlling for lagged (log) GDP levels just before the individuals were born and economy or region-specific effects (see chapter 3).
27. See, for example, Owen and Weil (1998), Galor and Tsiddon (1997), and Hassler and Mora (2000).
28. Bell and others (2017).
29. See Marrero and Rodriguez (2013) for the United States, and Teyssier (2013) for Brazil.
30. Ferreira and others (2017).
31. See the discussion in Corak (2013), who also shows an earlier example of the Gatsby curve.
32. See, for example, Fehr and Fischbacher (2003) and Fleib (2015).
33. Benabou and Ok (2001). This seems to be supported by empirical evidence in several countries: see, for example, Alesina, Stantcheva, and Teso (2018) and Gaviria, Graham, and Braido (2007).
34. Esteban and Ray (1994).
35. Krishnan and others (2016).
36. Alesina, Stantcheva, and Teso (2018).
37. Alderman, Hoddinott, and Kinsey (2006) and Hoddinott and others (2008).
38. See, for example, Aizer and Currie (2014).
39. See, for example, Hoddinott and others (2008, 2013) and Bharadwaj, Løken, and Neilson (2013).
40. Heckman, Pinto, and Savelyev (2013).
41. Heckman and Kautz (2014).
42. Gertler and others (2014).
43. Deming (2009).

44. Havnes and Mogstad (2011).
45. Butikofer, Mølland, and Salvanes (2016); and Alex-Petersen, Lundborg, and Rooth (2017).
46. For example, socioeconomically disadvantaged students across OECD countries are almost three times more likely than advantaged students not to attain the baseline level of proficiency in science (OECD 2016).
47. World Bank (2018b).
48. Balcazar, Narayan, and Tiwari (2015).
49. Tracking refers to the common practice of separating pupils by academic ability and having them follow different curricula within a school or placing them in different schools. For evidence on the effect of tracking, see Brunello and Checchi (2007); Pekkarinen, Uusitalo, and Kerr (2009); Aakvik, Salvanes, and Vaage (2010); and Meghir and Palme (2005).
50. Duflo, Dupas, and Kremer (2017).
51. As argued in *World Development Report 2006* (World Bank 2005).
52. See Ray (2006).
53. Ritterman Weintraub and others (2015).
54. Ross (2016).
55. Hoff and Pandey (2014).
56. Jensen (2010).
57. Beaman and others (2011).
58. See, for example, Goodman and Gregg (2010), and Gorard, See, and Davies (2012).
59. Cummings and others (2012); Kintrea, Clair, and Houston (2011).
60. "High" and "low" LFPs refer to those in the upper half and lower half of the distribution of LFPs, respectively, for the 75 countries for which income and education IGM estimates are available. Regression analysis confirms that the relationship between education IGM and income IGM is significantly stronger when LFP is higher.
61. Magruder (2010) finds that intergenerational networks can explain "nearly all employment inequality between son of present, employed fathers and other young adults."
62. Krishnan and others (2016).
63. World Bank (2011).
64. Chen and others (2018). See, for example, Katz (1998), Groh and others (2016), and Betcherman, Daysal, and Pages (2010) for the effects of wage subsidies in different economies and settings.
65. McKenzie (2017).
66. Patnaik (2016).
67. See, for example, Solon (1992), Mulligan (1997) and Corak and Heisz (1999).
68. Ferreira and Veloso (2006).
69. See, for example, Galor and Zeira (1993).
70. World Bank (2015).
71. See, for example, Beegle and others (2016) for evidence from Africa.
72. Hnatkovska, Lahiri, and Paul (2012).

73. For example, in India, labor mobility across generations may be constrained by limited land markets and a cultural obligation that makes abandoning land costly (Fernando 2016).
74. Fan, Yi, and Zhang (2015).
75. World Bank (2018a).
76. This is similar to the patterns for Canada and the United States found by Corak (2017).
77. Chetty, Hendren, and Katz (2016).
78. Chetty and Hendren (2018a, 2018b).
79. See, for example, Kline and Moretti (2014) for evidence from the United States.
80. Bell and others (2017).
81. Brown and Richman (1997).
82. Clements and others (2015) and Lustig (2017).
83. Fiszbein and others (2009).
84. Molina-Millan and others (2016).
85. Dahl and Lochner (2012); Chetty, Friedman, and Rockoff (2011); and Bastian and Michelmore (2017).
86. del Granado, Coady, and Gillingham (2012).

References

Aakvik, Arild, Kjell G. Salvanes, and Kjell Vaage. 2010. "Measuring Heterogeneity in the Returns to Education Using an Education Reform." *European Economic Review* 54 (4): 483–500.

Aizer, Anna, and Janet Currie. 2014. "The Intergenerational Transmission of Inequality: Maternal Disadvantage and Health at Birth." *Science* 344 (6186): 856–61.

Alderman, Harold, John Hoddinott, and Bill Kinsey. 2006. "Long-Term Consequences of Early Childhood Malnutrition." *Oxford Economic Papers* 58 (3): 450–74.

Alesina, Alberto, Stefanie Stantcheva, and Edoardo Teso. 2018. "Intergenerational Mobility and Preferences for Redistribution." *American Economic Review* 108 (2): 521–54.

Alex-Petersen, Jesper, Petter Lundborg, and Dan-Olof Rooth. 2017. "Long-Term Effects of Childhood Nutrition: Evidence from a School Lunch Reform." IZA DP No. 11234, Discussion Paper Series, Institute for the Study of Labor, Bonn, Germany.

Balcazar, Carlos Felipe, Ambar Narayan, and Sailesh Tiwari. 2015. "Born with a Silver Spoon: Inequality in Educational Achievement across the World." Policy Research Working Paper 7152, World Bank, Washington, DC.

Bastian, Jacob, and Katherine Michelmore. 2017. "The Long-Term Impact of the Earned Income Tax Credit on Children's Education and Employment Outcomes." *Journal of Labor Economics*. doi: 10.1086/697477.

Beaman, Lori, Esther Duflo, Rohini Pande, and Petia Topalova. 2011. "Female Leadership Raises Aspirations and Educational Attainment for Girls: A Policy Experiment in India." *Science* 335 (6068): 582–86.

Becker, Gary S., and Nigel Tomes. 1979. "An Equilibrium Theory of the Distribution of Income and Intergenerational Mobility." *Journal of Political Economy* 87 (6): 1153–89.

———. 1986. "Human Capital and the Rise and Fall of Families." *Journal of Labor Economics* 4 (3): S1–S39.

Becker, Gary S., Scott Duke Kominers, Kevin M. Murphy, and Jörg L. Spenkuch. 2015. "A Theory of Intergenerational Mobility." Working Paper, Harvard Business School, Harvard University, Cambridge, MA.

Beegle, Kathleen, Luc Christiaensen, Andrew Dabalen, and Isis Gaddis. 2016. *Poverty in a Rising Africa.* Washington, DC: World Bank.

Bell, Alexander M., Raj Chetty, Xavier Jaravel, Neviana Petkova, and John Van Reenen. 2017. "Who Becomes an Inventor in America? The Importance of Exposure to Innovation." NBER Working Paper 24062, National Bureau of Economic Research, Cambridge, MA.

Benabou, Roland, and Efe A. Ok. 2001. "Social Mobility and the Demand for Redistribution: The POUM Hypothesis." *Quarterly Journal of Economics* 116 (2): 447–87.

Betcherman, Gordon, N. Meltem Daysal, and Carmen Pages. 2010. "Do Employment Subsidies Work? Evidence from Regionally Targeted Subsidies in Turkey." *Labour Economics* 17 (4): 710–22.

Bharadwaj, Prashant, Katrine Vellesen Løken, and Christopher Neilson. 2013. "Early Life Health Interventions and Academic Achievement." *American Economic Review* 103 (5): 1862–91.

Brown, Prudence, and Harold A. Richman. 1997. "Neighborhood Effects and State and Local Policy." *Neighborhood Poverty* 2: 164–81.

Brunello, Giorgio, and Daniele Checchi. 2007. "Does School Tracking Affect Equality of Opportunity? New International Evidence." *Economic Policy* 22 (2): 782–861.

Brunori, Paolo, Francisco H. G. Ferreira, and Vito Peragine. 2013. "Inequality of Opportunity, Income Inequality, and Economic Mobility: Some International Comparisons." In *Getting Development Right: Structural Transformation, Inclusion, and Sustainability in the Post-Crisis Era*, edited by Eva Paus, 85–115. New York: Palgrave Macmillan.

Butikofer, Aline, Eirin Mølland, and Kjell G. Salvanes. 2016. "Childhood Nutrition and Labor Market Outcomes: Evidence from a School Breakfast Program." Norwegian School of Economics, Department of Economics Discussion Paper No. 15/2016, Norwegian School of Economics, Bergen, Norway.

Chen, Tingyun, Jean-Jacques Hallaert, Alexander Pitt, Haonan Qu, Maximilien Queyranne, Alaina Rhee, Anna Shabunina, Jérôme Vandenbussche, and Irene Yackovlev. 2018. "Inequality and Poverty across Generations in the European Union." IMF Staff Discussion Note 18/01, International Monetary Fund, Washington, DC.

Chetty, Raj, and Nathaniel Hendren. 2018a. "The Impacts of Neighborhoods on Intergenerational Mobility I: Childhood Exposure Effects." *Quarterly Journal of Economics*. https://doi.org/10.1093/qje/qjy007.

———. 2018b. "The Impacts of Neighborhoods on Intergenerational Mobility II: County-Level Estimates." *Quarterly Journal of Economics*. https://doi.org/10.1093/qje/qjy006.

Chetty, Raj, John N. Friedman, and Jonah E. Rockoff. 2011. "New Evidence on the Long-Term Impacts of Tax Credits." IRS Statistics of Income White Paper, Internal Revenue Service, Washington, DC.

Chetty, Raj, Nathaniel Hendren, and Lawrence F. Katz. 2016. "The Effects of Exposure to Better Neighborhoods on Children: New Evidence from the Moving to Opportunity Experiment." *American Economic Review* 106 (4): 855–902.

Clements, Benedict J., Ruud A. de Mooij, Sanjeev Gupta, and Michael Keen. 2015. *Inequality and Fiscal Policy*. Washington, DC: International Monetary Fund.

Corak, Miles. 2013. "Income Inequality, Equality of Opportunity, and Intergenerational Mobility." *Journal of Economic Perspectives* 27 (3): 79–102.

———. 2016a. "How Much Social Mobility? More, but Not Without Other Things." In *The US Labor Market: Questions and Challenges for Public Policy*, edited by M. Strain, 2–13. Washington, DC: American Enterprise Institute.

———. 2016b. "Inequality from Generation to Generation: The United States in Comparison." IZA Discussion Report No. 9929, Institute for the Study of Labor, Bonn.

———. 2017. "Divided Landscapes of Economic Opportunity: The Canadian Geography of Intergenerational Income Mobility." Working Paper 2017-043, Human Capital and Economic Opportunity Working Group, Chicago, IL.

Corak, Miles, and Andrew Heisz. 1999. "The Intergenerational Earnings and Income Mobility of Canadian Men: Evidence from Longitudinal Income Tax Data." *Journal of Human Resources* 34 (3): 504–533.

Cummings, Colleen, Karen Laing, James Law, Janice McLaughlin, Ivy Papps, Liz Todd, and Pam Woolner. 2012. "Can Changing Aspirations and Attitudes Impact on Educational Attainment?" Joseph Rowntree Foundation, York, United Kingdom.

Currie, Janet. 2009. "Healthy, Wealthy, and Wise: Socioeconomic Status, Poor Health in Childhood, and Human Capital Development." *Journal of Economic Literature* 47 (1): 87–122.

Dahl, Gordon B., and Lance Lochner. 2012. "The Impact of Family Income on Child Achievement: Evidence from the Earned Income Tax Credit." *American Economic Review* 102 (5): 1927–56.

del Granado, Francisco Javier Arze, David Coady, and Robert Gillingham. 2012. "The Unequal Benefits of Fuel Subsidies: A Review of Evidence for Developing Countries." *World Development* 40 (11): 2234–48.

Deming, David. 2009. "Early Childhood Intervention and Life-Cycle Skill Development: Evidence from Head Start." *American Economic Journal: Applied Economics* 1 (3): 111–34.

Duflo, Esther, Pascaline Dupas, and Michael Kremer. 2017. "The Impact of Free Secondary Education: Experimental Evidence from Ghana." MIT Working Paper, Massachusetts Institute of Technology, Cambridge, MA.

Equalchances. 2018. "International Database on Inequality of Opportunity and Social Mobility." University of Bari, Italy.

Evans, Martin, David Newhouse, and Pablo Suarez-Becerra. Forthcoming. "Poverty, Schooling, and the Intergenerational Transmission of Educational Disadvantage." Policy Research Working Paper, World Bank, Washington, DC.

Esteban, Joan-Maria, and Debraj Ray. 1994. "On the Measurement of Polarization." *Econometrica: Journal of the Econometric Society* 62 (4): 819–51.

Fan, Yi, Junjian Yi, and Junsen Zhang. 2015. "The Great Gatsby Curve in China: Cross-Sectional Inequality and Intergenerational Mobility." Working Paper, Chinese University of Hong Kong.

Fehr, Ernst, and Urs Fischbacher. 2003. "The Nature of Human Altruism." *Nature* 425 (6960): 785.

Fernando, A. Nilesh. 2016. "Shackled to the Soil: The Long-Term Effects of Inheriting Agricultural Land in India." Working paper, World Bank, Washington, DC.

Ferreira, Sergio Guimaraes, and Fernando A. Veloso. 2006. "Intergenerational Mobility of Wages in Brazil." *Brazilian Review of Econometrics* 26 (2): 181–211.

Ferreira, Francisco H. G., Christoph Lakner, Maria Ana Lugo, and Berk Ozler. 2017. "Inequality of Opportunity and Economic Growth: How Much Can Cross-Country Regressions Really Tell Us?" *Review of Income and Wealth*. doi: 10.1111/roiw.12311.

Fiszbein, Ariel, Norbert Schady, Francisco H. G. Ferreira, Margaret Grosh, Niall Keleher, Pedro Olinto, and Emmanuel Skoufias. 2009. "Conditional

Cash Transfers: Reducing Present and Future Poverty." Policy Research Report, World Bank, Washington, DC.

Fleib, Jurgen. 2015. "Merit Norms in the Ultimatum Game: An Experimental Study of the Effect of Merit on Individual Behavior and Aggregate Outcomes." *Central European Journal of Operations Research* 23 (2): 389–406.

Galor, Oded, and Daniel Tsiddon. 1997. "Technological Progress, Mobility, and Economic Growth." *American Economic Review* 87 (3): 363–382.

Galor, Oded, and Joseph Zeira. 1993. "Income Distribution and Macroeconomics." *Review of Economic Studies* 60 (1): 35–52.

Gaviria, Alejandro, Carol Graham, and Luis H. B. Braido. 2007. "Social Mobility and Preferences for Redistribution in Latin America." *Economía* 8 (1): 55–96.

GDIM. 2018. *Global Database on Intergenerational Mobility.* Development Research Group. Washington, DC: World Bank.

Gertler, Paul, James Heckman, Rodrigo Pinto, Arianna Zanolini, Christel Vermeersch, Susan Walker, Susan M. Chang, and Sally Grantham-McGregor. 2014. "Labor Market Returns to an Early Childhood Stimulation Intervention in Jamaica." *Science* 344 (6187): 998–1001.

Goodman, Alissa, and Paul Gregg, eds. 2010. *Poorer Children's Educational Attainment: How Important Are Attitudes and Behaviour?* York, UK: Joseph Rowntree Foundation.

Gorard, Stephen, Beng Huat See, and Peter Davies. 2012. *The Impact of Attitudes and Aspirations on Educational Attainment and Participation.* April. York, UK: Joseph Rowntree Foundation.

Groh, Matthew, Nandini Krishnan, David McKenzie, and Tara Vishwanath. 2016. "Do Wage Subsidies Provide a Stepping Stone to Employment for Recent College Graduates? Evidence from a Randomized Experiment in Jordan." *Review of Economics and Statistics* 98 (3): 488–502.

Hassler, John, and José V. Rodríguez Mora. 2000. "Intelligence, Social Mobility, and Growth." *American Economic Review* 90 (4): 888–908.

Havnes, Tarjei, and Magne Mogstad. 2011. "No Child Left Behind: Subsidized Child Care and Children's Long-Run Outcomes." *American Economic Journal: Economic Policy* 3 (2): 97–129.

Heckman, James J. 2006. "Skill Formation and the Economics of Investing in Disadvantaged Children." *Science* 312 (5782): 1900–02.

———, Rodrigo Pinto, and Peter Savelyev. 2013. "Understanding the Mechanisms through Which an Influential Early Childhood Program Boosted Adult Outcomes." *American Economic Review* 103 (6): 2052–86.

Heckman, James J., and Tim Kautz. 2014. "Fostering and Measuring Skills: Interventions That Improve Character and Cognition." In *The Myth of*

Achievement Tests: The GED and the Role of Character in American Life, edited by J. Heckman, J. E. Humphries, and T. Kautz, 341–430. Chicago, IL: University of Chicago Press.

Hertz, Tom, Tamara Jayasundera, Patrizio Piraino, Sibel Selcuk, Nicole Smith, and Alina Verashchagina. 2007. "The Inheritance of Educational Inequality: Intergenerational Comparisons and Fifty-Year Trends." *B.E. Journal of Economic Analysis and Policy* 7 (2): 1–48.

Hnatkovska, Viktoria, Amartya Lahiri, and Sourabh Paul. 2012. "Castes and Labor Mobility." *American Economic Journal: Applied Economics* 4 (2): 274–307.

Hoddinott, John, John A. Maluccio, Jere R. Behrman, Rafael Flores, and Reynaldo Martorell. 2008. "Effect of a Nutrition Intervention during Early Childhood on Economic Productivity in Guatemalan Adults." *Lancet* 371 (9610): 411–16.

Hoddinott, John, Harold Alderman, Jere R. Behrman, Lawrence Haddad, and Susan Horton. 2013. "The Economic Rationale for Investing in Stunting Reduction." *Maternal and Child Nutrition* 9 (S2): 69–82.

Hoff, Karla, and Priyanka Pandey. 2014. "Making Up People: The Effect of Identity on Performance in a Modernizing Society." *Journal of Development Economics* 106: 118–31.

Jensen, Robert. 2010. "The (Perceived) Returns to Education and the Demand for Schooling." *Quarterly Journal of Economics* 125 (2): 515–48.

Katz, Lawrence F. 1998. "Wage Subsidies for the Disadvantaged." In *Generating Jobs: How to Create Demand for Low-Skilled Workers*, edited by R. Freeman and P. Gottschalk, 21–53. New York: Russell Sage Foundation.

Kintrea, Keith, Ralf St. Clair, and Muir Houston. 2011. *The Influence of Parents, Places and Poverty on Educational Attitudes and Aspirations*. York, United Kingdom: Joseph Rowntree Foundation.

Kline, Patrick, and Enrico Moretti. 2014. "People, Places, and Public Policy: Some Simple Welfare Economics of Local Economic Development Programs." *Annual Review of Economics* 6: 629–62.

Krishnan, Nandini, Gabriel Lara Ibarra, Ambar Narayan, Sailesh Tiwari, and Tara Vishwanath. 2016. *Uneven Odds, Unequal Outcomes: Inequality of Opportunity in the Middle East and North Africa*. Washington, DC: World Bank.

Lustig, Nora. 2017. "Fiscal Policy, Income Redistribution and Poverty Reduction in Low- and Middle-Income Countries." Center for Global Development Working Paper No. 448, Center for Global Development, Washington, DC.

Maddison Historical Statistics (database), Groningen Growth and Development Centre, Faculty of Economics and Business, University of Groningen, Groningen, The Netherlands, https://www.rug.nl/ggdc/historicaldevelopment/maddison/.

Magruder, Jeremy R. 2010. "Intergenerational Networks, Unemployment, and Persistent Inequality in South Africa." *American Economic Journal: Applied Economics* 2 (1): 62–85.

Maoz, Yishay D., and Omer Moav. 1999. "Intergenerational Mobility and the Process of Development." *Economic Journal* 109 (458): 677–97.

Marrero, Gustavo A., and Juan G. Rodríguez. 2013. "Inequality of Opportunity and Growth." *Journal of Development Economics* 104: 107–22.

McKenzie, David. 2017. "Identifying and Spurring High-Growth Entrepreneurship: Experimental Evidence from a Business Plan Competition." *American Economic Review* 107 (8): 2278–307.

Meghir, Costas, and Marten Palme. 2005. "Educational Reform, Ability, and Family Background." *American Economic Review* 95 (1): 414–24.

Molina-Millan, Teresa, Tania Barham, Karen Macours, John A. Maluccio, and Marco Stampini. 2016. "Long-Term Impacts of Conditional Cash Transfers in Latin America: Review of the Evidence." IDB Working Paper Series No. IDB-WP-732, Inter-American Development Bank, Washington, DC.

Mulligan, Casey B. 1997. *Parental Priorities and Economic Inequality.* University of Chicago Press.

OECD (Organisation for Economic Co-operation and Development). 2016. *PISA 2015 Results (Volume I): Excellence and Equity in Education.* Paris: OECD Publishing. doi: 10.1787/9789264266490-en.

Owen, Ann L., and David N. Weil. 1998. "Intergenerational Earnings Mobility, Inequality and Growth." *Journal of Monetary Economics* 41 (1): 71–104.

Patnaik, Ankita. 2016. "Reserving Time for Daddy: The Short- and Long-Run Consequences of Fathers' Quotas." Working Paper, Cornell University, Ithaca, New York.

Pekkarinen, Tuomas, Roope Uusitalo, and Sari Kerr. 2009. "School Tracking and Intergenerational Income Mobility: Evidence from the Finnish Comprehensive School Reform." *Journal of Public Economics* 93 (7–8): 965–73.

Piketty, Thomas. 2000. "Theories of Persistent Inequality and Intergenerational Mobility." *Handbook of Income Distribution*, edited by Anthony Atkinson and François Bourguignon, 429–76. Amsterdam: Elsevier.

Ray, Debraj. 2006. "Aspirations, Poverty, and Economic Change." In *Understanding Poverty*, edited by Abhijit Vinayak Banerjee, Roland Bénabou, and Dilip Mookherjee. Oxford, UK: Oxford University Press.

Ritterman Weintraub, Miranda Lucia, Lia C. H. Fernald, Nancy Adler, Stefano Bertozzi, and S. Leonard Syme. 2015. "Perceptions of Social Mobility: Development of a New Psychosocial Indicator Associated with Adolescent Risk Behaviors." *Frontiers in Public Health* 3: 62.

Roemer, John E. 1998. *Equality of Opportunity*. New York: Harvard University Press.

Ross, Phillip H. 2016. "Aspirations and Human Capital Investment: Evidence from Indian Adolescents." Working paper.

Solon, Gary. 1992. "Intergenerational Income Mobility in the United States." *American Economic Review* 82 (3): 393–408.

———. 2004. "A Model of Intergenerational Mobility Variation over Time and Place." In *Generational Income Mobility in North America and Europe*, edited by Miles Corak, 38–47. Cambridge, UK: Cambridge University Press.

Teyssier, Geoffrey. 2013. "Inequality of Opportunity and Growth: An Empirical Investigation in Brazil." Unpublished manuscript, Université Paris I Panthéon-Sorbonne.

UIS (Institute for Statistics, United Nations Educational, Scientific, and Cultural Organization). 2012. "International Standard Classification of Education: ISCED 2011." UIS, Montreal. http://uis.unesco.org/sites/default/files/documents/international-standard-classification-of-education-isced-2011-en.pdf.

Van de Gaer, Dirk. 1993. *Equality of Opportunity and Investment in Human Capital*. PhD Dissertation, Catholic University of Leuven, Leuven, Belgium.

World Bank. 2005. *World Development Report 2006: Equity and Development*. Washington, DC: World Bank.

———. 2011. *World Development Report 2012: Gender Equality and Development*. Washington, D.C: World Bank.

———. 2015. *Women, Business, and the Law 2016: Getting to Equal*. Washington, DC: World Bank.

———. 2016. *Taking on Inequality: Poverty and Shared Prosperity 2016*. Washington, DC: World Bank.

———. 2017. *World Development Report 2017: Governance and the Law*. Washington, DC: World Bank.

———. 2018a. *Entangled: Localized Effects of Exports on Earnings and Employment in South Asia*. Washington, DC: World Bank.

———. 2018b. *World Development Report 2018: Learning to Realize Education's Promise*. Washington, DC: World Bank.

CHAPTER 1
Economic Mobility across Generations: Why It Matters

Economic mobility across generations, also known as intergenerational mobility (IGM) in the economic literature, is a key element of human progress. Higher mobility can be interpreted in two ways: absolute upward mobility (the extent to which living standards are better among individuals now than among their parents) and relative mobility (the extent to which the relative position of individuals on a socioeconomic scale is independent of the relative position of their parents on the scale). The first interpretation centers on a universal human aspiration among parents for a better life for their children. The second interpretation reflects an aspiration for fairness whereby everyone, regardless of their parental connections or social status, has the opportunity to climb to a rung on the economic ladder that is higher than the rung on the ladder on which they happened to be born. Promoting both types of IGM is essential for a sustainable long-term reduction in poverty and an increase in shared prosperity.

To achieve sustainable and inclusive growth, public policy must help give scope to such aspirations. However, evidence suggests that, in too many parts of the world, mobility poses a challenge. This concern is especially acute in developing economies: climbing from the bottom to the top of the economic ladder is more difficult in most of these economies than in wealthier ones. If people enjoy less potential for upward movement, economies are less able to generate future growth, reduce poverty, and narrow inequality.

This report measures the extent of IGM in economies across the world, how it has evolved across generations and over time, and the factors that may be associated with higher mobility. By reporting findings on a global scale, the study fills an important gap in the empirical evidence on IGM, which to date has been largely limited to relative mobility in high-income economies. To provide a global picture of mobility, the report primarily relies on a newly developed global database on IGM in educational attainment.

Education is a key component of an individual's well-being in its own right, which makes mobility in education an essential element of economic mobility. Since education is a critical human asset that influences the lifetime earnings of an individual, measuring mobility in education also provides important insights into income mobility, which is another key dimension of economic mobility. By compiling estimates of income IGM for economies where data are available, the report examines the relationship between educational mobility and income mobility. It concludes by deriving broad implications for policies to improve mobility in education and income, drawing on existing literature on the drivers of IGM in different contexts and cross-country patterns in the global database on mobility.

What Is Meant by Intergenerational Mobility?

Economic mobility within and across generations is interpreted in several ways in the economic literature, which is consistent with the existence of different measures (see chapter 2). This report focuses on the longer-term concept of mobility across generations, interpreting higher mobility in two distinct but related ways (box 1.1). Absolute upward IGM is the extent to which living standards are better among individuals of a generation than among their parents. The spotlight on upward mobility is crucial because mobility may also mean downward movement, driven, for example, by uncertainty and vulnerability to uninsured risks. Higher absolute upward IGM is closely associated with income growth and an expansion in shared prosperity, that is, income growth among the bottom 40 percent of the income distribution across a population (the bottom 40), if these improvements are sustained over a long period. However, the extent of absolute

BOX 1.1   Two concepts of intergenerational mobility

Socioeconomic mobility has been interpreted in several ways in the economic and sociological literature, including as mobility within and between generations and as mobility in incomes, educational attainment, and occupation. This report focuses on mobility between generations. To illustrate the two concepts of IGM used here, it is helpful to imagine two generations of adults standing on different rungs of the same economic ladder, where the rungs indicate one's economic success relative to everyone else based on, for example, lifetime income (see the figure B1.1.1). Absolute upward IGM measures the extent to which the current generation has managed to climb up the ladder relative to the previous generation or the extent to which the rungs occupied by the current generation are higher than the rungs occupied by the previous generation, that is, the parents of the current generation. Relative IGM is the extent to which every individual's position on the economic ladder is independent of the position of the individual's parents. If an individual reaches a rung of the ladder among peers that is different from what the individual's parents occupied among parents of the peers, then there has been relative mobility.

box continues next page

BOX 1.1   Two concepts of intergenerational mobility (continued)

FIGURE B1.1.1   Intergenerational Mobility

Parents   Offspring

Absolute upward
intergenerational mobility
Offspring are
better off than their parents

Relative intergenerational
mobility
Offspring of parents
who are relatively poor can
become middle class or upper
class among their generation

Although the two concepts are related, one may exist without the other. If all individuals in a generation climb two rungs relative to their parents without passing or being passed by anyone else in that generation, then there is absolute IGM, but no relative IGM. Conversely, a society may exhibit high relative IGM, but not necessarily absolute IGM, if all individuals in the current generation are on rungs that are different from the rungs occupied by their parents, while the current generation as a whole occupies the same rungs of the ladder as the previous generation. In this case, the standard of living of the society overall has not improved.

Relative IGM is consistent with the interpretation of mobility as origin independence applied in an intergenerational context. In a society with high relative IGM, the lifetime incomes of individuals are influenced less by the origin of the individuals, that is, their parents. Origin independence is closely related to the concept of equality of opportunity (Roemer 1998).

upward IGM depends not only on whether growth has occurred on average, but also on the extent to which growth has led to improvements in living standards among families from one generation to the next.

Relative IGM is the extent to which an individual's position on the economic scale is independent of the position of the individual's parents. Higher relative mobility across generations is associated with lower inequality of opportunity, that is, the extent to which an individual's life achievements are affected by the circumstances of the individual's birth, such as race, gender, birthplace, or parental educational attainment or income.[1] The lack of relative mobility across generations is driven by the stubborn fact that children born every day around the world face starkly different life prospects. Some, who have wealthier, more educated parents, will grow up in a healthier environment, receive a better education, and can expect to earn more in better jobs, compared with many others who do not inherit these advantages.

Both types of mobility are important for economic progress and for sustaining a social contract that addresses the aspirations of society. Without absolute mobility, living standards cannot improve, and social cohesion may be at risk as the different groups in society compete for slices of a fixed or shrinking economic pie. Meanwhile, a lack of relative mobility not only is deeply unfair and perpetuates inequality but also leads to wasted human potential and inefficient allocation of resources, which are harmful for growth. A lack of relative mobility over time, in other words, may constrain absolute upward mobility.

Why Is Mobility across Generations Important?

Absolute Mobility Is about Long-Term Improvement in Living Standards for All

The concept of absolute IGM revolves around the long-term improvement in living standards among families and individuals. By adding a new dimension to aggregate indicators such as growth rates in gross domestic product (GDP), it furthers the understanding of progress. An indicator of absolute IGM may be used to measure the extent of progress across generations of each family, for all families in a society, rather than the average amount of progress or the progress achieved by an average family. It would seek to capture the extent to which a universal human aspiration—of parents hoping for better lives for their children—is being met by society.

"One of the defining features of the 'American Dream' is the ideal that children have a higher standard of living than their parents," write Chetty et al. (2017, 1) citing Samuel (2012). It is fair to conclude that the same ideal guides the aspirations of most people all over the world, irrespective of their location.

Absolute upward IGM tends to be high in a society in which rising prosperity is broadly shared and sustained. Growth in average incomes, which increases the size of the economic pie, is necessary for high absolute mobility. In Vietnam, for example, GDP per capita grew more than 20-fold between 1990 and 2014. The average living standards of the current generation of Vietnamese and of people in many other rapidly growing developing economies are thus much better than the living standards of their parents, which also translates into high rates of upward mobility among families across generations (see chapter 3). Upward mobility, however, is likely to be much lower in economies that have not been able to sustain long spells of growth, including many that are characterized by low income, fragility, or conflict. Moreover, growth in average income does not guarantee a high rate of absolute mobility. In Vietnam, absolute mobility is high because growth is also broadly shared, as suggested by the almost 75 percent decline in the poverty rate between 1990 and 2014.[2]

Research conducted recently in the United States starkly illustrates the importance of not just growth, but also the distribution of growth for absolute IGM.[3] The share of individuals earning more than their parents in the United States, a reasonable measure of absolute IGM, fell from 90 percent among individuals born in the 1940s to 50 percent among people born in the 1980s, who are the latest generation of adults of earning age. The decline was driven more by the unequal distribution of economic growth than the slowdown in aggregate growth since the 1940s. In a simulated U.S. economy in which GDP is maintained at the current level, but distributed across income groups as it was distributed among individuals born in the 1940s, absolute mobility among people born in the 1980s would have been 80 percent, which is 60 percent higher than what is observed.[4]

The concept of absolute mobility thus combines notions of growth and how growth is distributed, and the measure reflects changes in the well-being of families. Higher absolute mobility is, therefore, an indication not only of a growing economy, but also of an economy in which a larger proportion of the population can share in the progress. Arguably, this measure of human progress should be at least as important for economies as growth rates in aggregate or average income because it plumbs the core of what is important if a society is to meet the aspirations of its people.

The Case for Relative Intergenerational Mobility

Although, intuitively, there is a compelling case for considering absolute upward mobility as a measure of progress, it may not be as obvious why economies, including developing economies, should also be concerned about relative IGM. If absolute living standards are improving among most families from one generation to the next, why should the fact that different generations of the same family remain on the same rung of the economic ladder relative to other people in the same generation be a cause of concern?

High absolute IGM does not necessarily translate into high relative IGM. If a man in Vietnam earns double the amount another man earns, the first man's son may be expected to make, as an adult, nearly 50 percent more than the son of the lower-income man. This is a high degree of persistence in income across generations. Persistence is greater in countries such as Peru and South Africa, where the son of the man who earns more in the example above would make almost 70 percent more than the son of the lower-income man, and even greater in some other countries where he would expect to earn more than double that of the other son.

Low relative mobility also implies that privilege and poverty alike are highly persistent across generations in many societies. For example, in the United States, a quarter of the sons born to fathers in the top 10 percent of earnings are also among the top 10 percenters as adults, and most sons born to top 10 percent fathers are at least in the top 30 percent. By contrast, 22 percent of sons born to fathers in the bottom 10 percent remain in the bottom decile as adults, and half remain in the bottom 30 percent.[5]

To understand why governments should also care about relative IGM, one must examine the channels through which higher relative IGM may translate into better development outcomes. The weight of evidence seems to suggest that relative IGM is desirable because it promotes economic growth and a more inclusive growth process in the medium to long term (figure 1.1). It is also desirable from the perspective of fairness, perceptions of which contribute to social cohesion and stability.

Low relative mobility is associated with high inequality

An important reason to care about relative IGM is the mutually rein-forcing relationship between the phenomenon and income inequality. Lower relative IGM is associated with greater income inequality, as depicted by the so-called Great Gatsby curve—a relationship that has been noted by numerous studies.[6] This is most likely because of a two-way relationship: more inequality tends to limit relative mobility,

FIGURE 1.1   Low relative IGM is both a cause and consequence of inequality

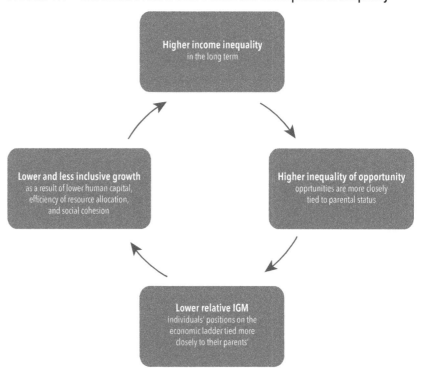

Source: World Bank.
Note: The figure should be considered a highly stylized representation of complex relationships. IGM = intergenerational mobility.

which tends to aggravate inequality over time. If endowments, such as monetary bequests and nonmonetary traits, can be inherited from parents and if parents attach a value to investing in their children, the result may be the persistence of income levels across generations and thus greater inequality in incomes (box 1.2).[7] Models that incorporate these features show that persistence and income inequality are both likely to be greater if the heritability of endowments and traits is stronger, the returns to investments in the human capital of children are higher, and public investment in children's human capital is more progressive. However, relative IGM and cross-sectional inequality are not perfectly correlated, in part because economies differ in the diversity of inherited endowments and traits.

BOX 1.2   A theory of intergenerational mobility and the relationship with inequality

Extending the seminal work of Becker and Tomes (1979), Solon (2004) provides an intuitive theoretical model of IGM. According to this model, earnings levels can persist across generations because of heritable monetary and nonmonetary endowments and parental preferences for investment for the benefit of their children. The model assumes that parents derive utility from their own consumption and from the incomes of their children later in life and thus make decisions on investment in the human capital of their children based on the nature of their preferences and the returns available to human capital investment. A child's human capital is a function of parental and government investments, as well as an inherited human capital endowment, which represents the combined effect of many attributes of children influenced by nature, nurture, or both.

"Children are assumed to receive endowments of capital that are determined by the reputation and 'connections' of their families, the genetic constitutions of their families, and the learning, skills, goals, and other 'family commodities' acquired through belonging to a particular family culture," according to Becker and Tomes (1979, 1,158). The model predicts that, in steady state, a country would have lower relative IGM (higher intergenerational elasticity) and more inequality (the cross-sectional variance of log earnings) if it has more extensive heritability of endowments, higher returns to human capital investment, or less progressive public investment in the human capital of children. However, IGM and cross-sectional inequality do not fully determine each other: two societies with similar intergenerational elasticity might differ in cross-sectional inequality because they differ in the heterogeneity of endowments, which might be monetary or traits related to ability.

Source: Solon 2002, 2004.

Capital market failure is another important reason why lower relative mobility is associated with greater inequality. If credit is constrained, as is the case in most developing economies, high income inequality can lead to large differences in parental investments in their children, which generate differences in the earnings levels that persist across generations and cause inequality to increase more.[8] Piketty (2014) finds similar underlying processes that lead to greater persistence and higher income inequality in a credit-constrained society. An increase in the capital–income ratio because the returns to capital exceed the pace of income growth leads to a greater divide among incomes given that capital income tends to be more concentrated at the top of the distribution. Although labor incomes can be correlated across generations, this is much more the case among capital incomes because capital can be more easily inherited and passed down through generations.[9] In the presence of credit constraints, larger wealth transfers will increase the persistence of earning levels across generations.

More generally, inequality affects the policies, institutions, and balance of power that shape the opportunities in a society. Unequal opportunities, in turn, lead to lower relative mobility and more inequality in the next generation.[10] Breaking the cycle of low mobility and high inequality will require equalizing opportunities to reduce the disadvantages faced by individuals because of circumstances of birth, such as parents of low social or economic status or residence in a poor neighborhood, village, or region. Empirical evidence also shows that economies characterized by lower relative mobility tend to exhibit greater inequality of opportunity, which is the share of inequality attributable to circumstances at birth.[11]

Equalizing opportunities should be a priority for economies seeking to reduce income inequality in the long term, an emerging aim among governments across the world. Narrowing income inequality is necessary to ensure that growth translates into shared prosperity, namely, sufficient increases in the incomes of the bottom 40. Moreover, achieving the global goal of a 3 percent extreme poverty rate in 2030 also requires economies to increase the shared prosperity premium, that is, the difference in the income growth rate of the bottom 40 and the average income growth rate, which is akin to reducing inequality (World Bank 2016).

Higher relative mobility and higher economic growth can reinforce each other
Long-term growth is another important reason policy makers should focus on raising IGM by equalizing opportunities. Economic literature theorizes that, in economies with credit constraints that disproportionately affect the poor, relative IGM and economic growth may reinforce each other in a virtuous cycle (box 1.3).

Intuitively, higher relative mobility is good for growth in an economy because it leads to more efficient allocation of resources: individuals with higher innate abilities—rather than individuals with wealthier or more educated parents—are more likely to obtain more education and more

BOX 1.3   Higher relative mobility and economic growth can reinforce each other in a virtuous cycle

Several dynamic growth models in the economic literature suggest that relative IGM and economic growth may reinforce each other, so that IGM increases along the growth path. These models propose different channels through which higher relative IGM has a positive effect on long-term growth. Individuals' outcomes are assumed in these models to be a function of innate ability and the social circumstances the individuals grow up in. In a more mobile society, the correlation between human capital accumulation and ability will be stronger because individuals with higher abilities—rather than those with the wealthiest parents—will tend to obtain more education. This may lead to a more efficient allocation of educational resources, resulting in higher economic growth (Owen and Weil 1998). Higher relative IGM can also imply more efficient "sorting" in the labor market, which has a positive feedback on growth. For example, the highly educated and high-ability individuals may be more likely to end up in the technologically advanced sectors, which increases the likelihood of developing and adopting modern technologies (Galor and Tsiddon 1997). Also, when the sorting of individuals into entrepreneurship is based more on innate ability than on social background, there are efficiency gains that induce higher economic growth (Hassler and Mora 2000). Although these arguments apply primarily to relative IGM, it is easy to see that absolute IGM is also likely to benefit long-term growth, by increasing the aggregate stock of human capital and the likelihood of adopting modern technologies.

These dynamic models also propose a few different channels through which economic growth can increase IGM. For example, growth can weaken credit constraints to investments in education (Maoz and Moav 1999), which promotes both relative and absolute IGM. This can occur, for example, when skilled and unskilled workers are complements in production in a fast-growing society. As the share of the employed who are highly skilled increases with growth, the relative wage of low-skilled workers rises, which weakens their credit constraints and reduces the incentives for high-income families to invest in higher education, raising relative IGM (Owen and Weil 1998). Also, high-growth societies may undergo faster technological change, which would make any informational advantage individuals receive from their parents less valuable and innate ability more valuable, thus fostering relative IGM (Hassler and Mora 2000). At the same time, there are other channels through which growth may affect relative mobility in the opposite direction (see chapter 4, box 4.4). The net effect of growth on relative IGM would depend on which of the channels dominate, as well as the extent to which public spending, which tends to be higher for richer economies, plays a role in promoting social mobility (chapter 4).

box continues next page

BOX 1.3   Higher relative mobility and economic growth can reinforce each other in a virtuous cycle (continued)

Economic theories suggest that policies to promote IGM are also likely to benefit economic growth when capital markets are imperfect. When relative IGM is low, inequalities in income and wealth are perpetuated across generations. An unequal distribution of wealth can lead to misallocation of resources and lower output when capital markets are imperfect, whose costs accumulate over generations. For example, with credit market imperfections, the initial distribution of wealth can affect aggregate investment and output in both the short and long runs (Galor and Zeira 1993). And by influencing the occupational choice of individuals, the initial wealth distribution can affect the output and the overall development path of an economy (Banerjee and Newman 1993). In such a scenario, policies to raise IGM—such as public funding of quality education for the less well-off and fiscal policies to reduce inequality in the distribution of wealth—are likely to also increase aggregate output (see, for example, Piketty 2000).

productive jobs. Resources to develop human capital are matched more optimally with ability in a high-mobility society, which results in greater realization of human potential. In contrast, in an economy with low mobility, human and financial capital are misallocated systematically at different stages of the life cycle of individuals. This can happen, for example, because the poor are unable to invest optimally to develop the human potential of their children as a result of credit constraints, or because labor and capital markets reward those born with privileges inherited from parents or discriminate on the basis of race, gender, or other social markers. Thus, policies to raise relative mobility are likely to promote long-run growth as well, by reducing the inefficiencies due to misallocation of human and financial capital, the costs of which accumulate systematically over generations in an economy with low relative mobility (see box 1.3).

Conversely, economic growth may increase relative mobility, primarily by weakening the credit constraints that limit investment in education among the poor. But there can also be countervailing forces that work toward reducing relative mobility as economies get richer (see chapter 4). The net effect of growth on IGM is more likely to be positive if higher economic growth generates greater resources to finance higher public spending of the kind that has a moderating effect on inequality of opportunities. If the net effect of growth on relative mobility is positive, the virtuous cycle is formed: as economies grow, mobility rises, which in turn stimulates growth further. The empirical patterns seen in this report (chapter 3) appear to be consistent with this prediction.

Empirical evidence exists to suggest that inequality of opportunity that leads to lower relative IGM is damaging to an economy's long-term growth prospects. Bell et al. (2017) provide a telling example from the United States on the effect of lost human potential due to low social mobility.[12] They find that the probability a child will become an inventor is many times greater among children in rich families than among children in lower-income families and that a large share of this innovation gap can be attributed to differences in childhood environment. Thus, improving opportunities for social mobility could benefit not only the disadvantaged children, but also the overall society by increasing the rate of innovation and economic growth. More generally, realizing the wasted human potential would generate a rise in the overall stock of human capital in an economy, which could have a strong impact on long-term growth.[13]

Emerging evidence also suggests that inequality of opportunity may be particularly harmful to long-term growth because it discourages innovation and human capital investment. In contrast, inequality produced by differences in effort unrelated to circumstances at birth may even be good for long-term growth up to a point because it could incentivize innovation and effort. Recent research has found evidence for the contrasting effects of circumstances at birth and effort—the two components of inequality—on growth in Brazil and the United States.[14] However, the cross-country evidence is more mixed, suggesting that this relationship may not be universally true.[15]

A related strand in the literature finds evidence that inequality in human development among children in different socioeconomic groups, which is a proxy for certain dimensions of inequality of opportunity, leads to lower economic growth. One study finds a significant negative effect on economic growth associated with inequality in child health measured by the differences in mortality among children born to mothers with different educational attainment. By a conservative estimate, a 5 percent reduction in the under-five mortality rate among children born to mothers with low educational attainment would lead to an almost 8 percent increase in GDP per capita after a decade.[16] On the basis of a historical dataset of nearly 100 countries, another study finds that, among children, inequality in educational attainment attributable to circumstances at birth has a negative impact on per capita GDP.[17]

Higher mobility—absolute and relative—promotes social cohesion and higher aspirations

Higher absolute mobility is critical in meeting the aspirations of people (see above). Nonetheless, in many societies, this may not be sufficient to induce the sense of fairness that is a bedrock of social cohesion and stability. Economic mobility in terms of changes in relative rank and position by income is often said to mitigate static inequality and contribute to long-term fairness.

> Consider two societies that have the same distribution of annual income. In one, there is great mobility and change so that the position of particular families in the income hierarchy varies widely from year to year. In the other,

there is great rigidity so that each family stays in the same position year after year. Clearly, in any meaningful sense, the second would be the more unequal society. (Friedman 2002, 171)

This intuition would apply even more strongly to mobility across generations. If it is undesirable for a society to exhibit great rigidity in the position of families in the income hierarchy from year to year, such rigidity that persists across generations would be an even greater cause for concern.

Lack of relative mobility and high inequality of opportunity can erode the perceptions of a population about fairness and trust in their society. This affects the social contract that supports growth and social stability. Evidence suggests that, as a cause of negative perceptions about fairness, inequality of opportunity, which is closely related to relative mobility, may matter more than overall inequality.[18] This is consistent with behavioral experiments showing that people are highly averse to inequality perceived as unfair.[19] People may even be willing to accept greater inequality of outcomes if it is perceived to be associated with merit.[20] Expectations of future mobility are important as well. Hirschman and Rothschild (1973, 552) refer to a tunnel effect in arguing that people will be more inclined to accept the status quo if they expect their well-being to improve, whereas the immobile "experience the turnaround from hopefulness to disenchantment" (box 1.4).

If perceptions of higher mobility induce more tolerance for inequality, higher relative IGM could lead to greater acceptance for policies that increase growth and prosperity in the long run, but with some trade-off in inequality today. This seems to be supported by empirical evidence in several countries (see box 1.4). Some inequality in earnings is an unavoidable consequence of the incentives needed to spur the effort, innovation, and risk taking that lead to higher economic efficiency and prosperity. Individuals may be more inclined to tolerate such inequality if they believe that the society they live in will provide them or their children with a fair chance to climb the economic ladder.

Low mobility, if perceived as such, can also lower one's aspirations, hopes, and ambitions for the future and thus reduce investments in human capital and reinforce the cycle of low IGM and high inequality (see chapter 5). Perceptions of mobility are important building blocks of the process by which individuals form aspirations, both for themselves and for their children. The poor and the disadvantaged who live in societies with low mobility may come to think of their places in the social order as unchangeable.[21] When taken to the extreme, the vicious cycle of low perceived mobility and low aspirations can push individuals to opt out of socioeconomic processes, leading to youth disenfranchisement, marginalization, and conflict.[22]

Evidence on direct links between social cohesion and perceptions of mobility, fairness, and inequality is difficult to find, given the complexity of forces that cause social instability. However, it seems relevant that

BOX 1.4   The policy preferences of individuals can be shaped by perceptions of IGM

Hirschman and Rothschild (1973) use the analogy of a two-lane tunnel that is so long the end is not visible. All the traffic is heading in the same direction and at a standstill. If a driver suddenly notices cars beginning to accelerate in the next lane, he will initially take it as a sign that his lane might also start to move sometime soon. This is the tunnel effect, an acceptance of the status quo. However, if, after a while, the driver's own lane does not begin to move, the tunnel effect wears off, and he will become frustrated, no longer accept the status quo, and switch lanes even if that violates traffic rules. Benabou and Ok (2001) extend this intuition to argue that the prospect of upward mobility among individuals who are poorer than average can lead them to oppose lasting redistribution under certain conditions. These individuals are not especially strong advocates of redistributive policies because of the belief that they or their children are likely to climb the income ladder and, one day, become well off. Support for this theory has been encouraged by a few empirical studies, including Cojocaru (2014), who finds that the expectation of upward mobility reduces the preference for redistribution among relatively poor individuals if their degree of risk aversion is not too high. Other studies find that perceptions of mobility are correlated with redistribution preferences, and this correlation is stronger in the case of policies that promote equality of opportunity rather than equality in outcomes (Alesina, Michalopoulos, and Papaioannou 2016; Gaviria, Graham, and Braido 2007).

heightened perceptions of inequality and unfairness have been associated with the onset of the Arab Spring, although income inequality was low and even declining in some of the affected countries.[23] Strong perceptions of downward mobility were noted in at least three countries, where a much smaller share of the population identified with the upper classes in 2012 relative to a decade earlier.[24] In all three countries, the tolerance for inequality declined. Although the simultaneous rise in perceptions of downward mobility and preferences for less inequality in these countries by no means explain the Arab Spring, it seems reasonable to argue that they indicate shifts in public opinion that contributed to the upheaval in the region that started in 2010.

It is the expectation or perception of mobility that seems to matter for social cohesion and policy preferences. Actual mobility matters in shaping these perceptions to some extent (see chapter 5). Evidence suggests that those who have experienced mobility are likely to be more optimistic about it.[25] Parents in societies with higher educational mobility seem to be more optimistic about their children's future, as expressed in terms of the opportunity of the children to learn and grow. However, perceptions of mobility can also diverge from actual mobility, particularly if comparisons are made across countries. For example, perceived mobility is higher among Americans compared with Europeans, despite mounting empirical evidence that relative IGM is lower in the United States than in several European countries.[26]

Thus, governments concerned about social stability should pay attention not only to the extent of mobility in society, but also to the perceptions of the population about mobility. The two are far from synonymous: although the actual extent of mobility shapes perceptions to some extent, other factors are also likely to matter, and this may be difficult to analyze. Arguably, these factors include the visibility of the pathways available for mobility, the fairness of processes, and the institutions and policies that shape these processes.

Measuring Economic Mobility Globally with Education

How do economies around the world, including developing economies, fare in terms of absolute and relative IGM? How has IGM changed across generations, and how is it related to other indicators of development? This report seeks to address these questions, focusing primarily on educational mobility. Because education is a key dimension of human progress, educational mobility is important in its own right and an essential element of economic mobility, when economic mobility is understood as mobility in well-being rather than as mobility in income alone. Applying this broad concept of economic mobility, this report examines trends and patterns in IGM across the world through the lens of educational mobility. Most of the original analysis is based on a global dataset compiled for this report (the Global Database on Intergenerational Mobility or GDIM) that measures mobility, both absolute and relative, in terms of educational attainment, using comparable data sources and estimation methods across economies. The report complements the analysis of educational mobility by providing a snapshot of income mobility and its relationship with educational mobility for a large subset of economies where estimates of income IGM are available.

The report fills an important gap in the global evidence base on IGM. The existing empirical evidence on IGM is primarily on relative (and not absolute) mobility, and skewed toward high-income economies and toward men (from father to son). A recent review of the existing literature finds that comparable estimates of relative IGM in income can be compiled for just 42 economies, of which only 12 are low-income or middle-income economies; and the most comprehensive global study to date on relative IGM in education similarly covers 42 economies.[27] In contrast, this report includes estimates of absolute and relative IGM in education among the cohort of individuals born in the 1980s—the most recent generation of adults—for economies that are home to 96 percent of the world's population. For 87 percent of the world's population, IGM can also be estimated for older cohorts to show trends in educational mobility over time—from those born in the 1940s to those born in the 1980s. Such a comprehensive coverage allows for an analysis of global trends and patterns in absolute and relative mobility in education for men and women alike.

Because education is a critical human asset that affects the earning potential of an individual, mobility in education also has important implications for income mobility, which is another key dimension of economic mobility. Standard theoretical models predict that IGM of education and IGM of income should be positively correlated, since persistence of income across generations occurs because of inherited monetary and nonmonetary endowments and parental preferences to invest for the benefit of their children (see box 1.2).[28] Empirical evidence supports this prediction among economies for which estimates for relative IGM in both education and income are available for roughly comparable cohorts. Economies with higher persistence in education across generations (or lower relative IGM) are likely to also have higher persistence in incomes, and vice versa (figure 1.2).[29] Because of data limitations, estimates of relative IGM in income—combining existing studies with own estimates—are available for only 75 economies, and that too with no information on changes over time and with methodological differences across studies that make comparisons difficult (see chapter 2).

Although IGMs in education and income are associated with each other, there are two key reasons why the association is imperfect. First, education mobility is measured here without considering the quality of learning,

FIGURE 1.2 Relative IGM in education and income are correlated, but imperfectly

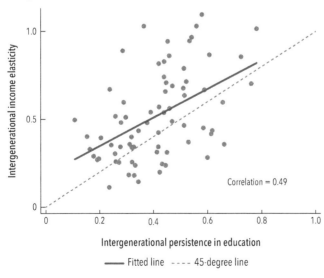

Source: GDIM 2018; Equalchances 2018.
Note: Higher elasticity/persistence indicates lower IGM. IGM = intergenerational mobility.

which makes the analysis an unreliable indicator of the skills that will influence an individual's earnings as an adult. Second, the relationship between mobility in education and mobility in income depends on several factors, including how the labor market rewards skills and the extent of income redistribution, which can vary across economies and over time (see chapter 4). Other factors matter as well, such as the effect of parental education on an individual's noncognitive skills and the effect of parental networks and connections on an individual's access to jobs and credit. In general, IGM in education and income are more closely associated when economies are more similar in terms of returns to education and the extent to which education predicts income (see chapter 4).

A Road Map of the Report

Chapter 2 discusses in some detail the measures of IGM that are used in the report and the data they are based on, explains the rationale for the selected measures, and situates them in the broader context of concepts and measures of mobility in general. Chapter 3 reports historical trends and geographical patterns in IGM in education using the global dataset developed for this study. Although this fills an important gap in evidence, most readers would also be interested in knowing what the drivers of IGM are and what they imply in terms of policies to promote greater mobility. These are highly complex and context-specific issues, and evidence derived from program evaluations also tends to be thin because of the length of time it takes for intergenerational impacts to be revealed and studied. Chapters 4 to 6 take small steps toward addressing these questions by reviewing the insights available in the literature and the data on the key drivers of IGM in education and income and related policies.

Chapter 4 provides a framework that is used to organize the discussion of drivers of mobility in chapters 5 and 6. The chapter starts by presenting relative IGM of income for a subset of economies around the world, using own estimations to complement comparable estimates compiled from existing literature, and then examining the relationship between relative IGMs in education and income. This is done by analytically partitioning the channels through which an individual's income is influenced by parental income, and distinguishing between the contribution of parental *education* and the contribution of all other circumstances to income persistence.

A life-cycle framework is then used to link income persistence across generations to the concept of inequality of opportunity. The framework reflects the ways in which a broad range of circumstances shape opportunities in interconnected ways at successive stages of life to drive income persistence across generations, as well as the role of markets, policies, and institutions in mediating how circumstances matter at every stage. Although the framework is an intuitive way to organize chapters 5 and 6, it has its limitations, because the drivers of mobility at the different stages of life affect (and interact with) each other. For example, fiscal and social policy tools that act directly on the earnings and assets of adults can affect the incentives and ability of parents to invest in the education of their children, which in turn affects the next generation's mobility of education and income.

Using the life-cycle framework, chapter 5 focuses on the drivers that act upon individuals in childhood, prior to the typical age of entering the labor market, to influence IGM in education. This entails identifying the factors, including policies, that determine the extent to which children born into different circumstances face a level playing field in their effort to realize their human capital potential, which is a key driver of economic status in adulthood. Given that educational mobility does not necessarily translate into income mobility (see above), chapter 6 looks at the available evidence on the drivers of IGM of income that act upon individuals during their income-earning years. The chapter focuses on the role of factor markets—labor and capital—and broader forces of economic transformation in determining economic mobility, and derives a few implications for fiscal and social policy tools that can be deployed to improve economic mobility. The chapter also discusses briefly the political economy factors underlying the reasons why policies that are likely to enhance mobility are not adopted or implemented effectively as often as they should be.

Notes

1. See, for example, Roemer (1998); Van de gaer (1993).
2. Doan and Nguyen (2016).
3. Chetty et al. (2017).
4. In contrast, if GDP growth since the 1980s were restored to the level of GDP in the 1940s and 1950s, but distributed across income groups as GDP is distributed today, 62 percent of the 1980s generation would have been earning more than their parents (Chetty et al. 2017).
5. Corak (2016).
6. See, for example, Corak (2016).
7. Becker and Tomes (1979) developed the earliest version of this theoretical model, which has since been extended and refined by numerous researchers. In particular, see Becker and Tomes (1986), Piketty (2000), and Solon (2002, 2004) for an overview.
8. For an overview, see Loury (1981); Piketty (2000).
9. This would also imply that as the share of capital and, thus, inheritances rises, the persistence (the intergenerational elasticity) of labor earnings could favor an underestimation of the extent to which advantages are passed down from one generation to the next.
10. See, for example, Corak (2013).
11. See Brunori, Ferreira, and Peragine 2013.
12. World Bank (2005) also suggests that inequality of opportunity imposes a cost on economic growth because of the wasted human potential it implies.

13. See, for example, Barro (2001) on the effects of the quantity and quality of schools and Grimm (2011) for an overview of the effects of the health of children on long-term growth.
14. See Marrero and Rodriíguez (2013) on the United States and Teyssier (2013) on Brazil. Higher inequality of opportunity has also been associated with lower growth in the future incomes of the poor in the United States between 1960 and 2010 (Marrero, Rodríguez, and Van Der Weide et al. 2016).
15. Ferreira, Filmer, and Schady 2017.
16. See Grimm (2011), who uses a cross-national panel dataset of 62 low- and middle-income countries between 1985 and 2007.
17. Molina, Narayan, and Saavedra-Chanduvi 2013.
18. In the Europe and Central Asia region, perceptions of fairness and life satisfaction seem to be associated more strongly with the component of inequality attributable to between-group differences than with overall measures of inequality (Abras et al. 2013).
19. See, for example, Fehr and Fischbacher (2003). Also see Cappelen et al. (2013).
20. Fleib (2015).
21. Hoff (2012).
22. Esteban and Ray (1994).
23. See Ianchovichina, Mottaghi, and Devarajan 2015 (2015); Krishnan et al. (2016).
24. Krishnan et al. (2016), using World Values Surveys for the Arab Republic of Egypt, Morocco, and Jordan. See WVS (World Values Survey) (database), King's College, Old Aberdeen, UK, http://www .worldvaluessurvey.org/wvs.jsp.
25. Alesina, Michalopoulos, and Papaioannou 2016.
26. Alesina, Michalopoulos, and Papaioannou (2016); Causa and Johansson (2010).
27. Hertz et al. (2007).
28. See, for example, Solon (2004).
29. Figure 1.2 includes 74 economies for which comparable estimates of relative IGM of income are available—of which estimates for 42 economies are compiled from existing studies (Equalchances 2018) and the rest are calculated for this report—while ensuring some degree of comparability in methodology across estimates (see chapter 2).

References

Abras, Ana, Alejandro Hoyos, Ambar Narayan, and Sailesh Tiwari. 2013. "Inequality of Opportunities in the Labor Market: Evidence from Life in Transition Surveys in Europe and Central Asia." *IZA Journal of Labor & Development* 2 (1): 7.

Alesina, Alberto, Stelios Michalopoulos, and Elias Papaioannou. 2016. "Ethnic Inequality." *Journal of Political Economy* 124 (2): 428–88.

Banerjee, Abhijit V., and Andrew F. Newman. 1993. "Occupational Choice and the Process of Development." *Journal of Political Economy* 101 (2): 274–98.

Barro, Robert J. 2001. "Human Capital and Growth." *American Economic Review* 91 (2): 12–17.

Becker, Gary S., and Nigel Tomes. 1979. "An Equilibrium Theory of the Distribution of Income and Intergenerational Mobility." *Journal of Political Economy* 87 (6): 1153–89.

———. 1986. "Human Capital and the Rise and Fall of Families." *Journal of Labor Economics* 4 (3, Part 2): S1–39.

Bell, Alexander M., Raj Chetty, Xavier Jaravel, Neviana Petkova, and John Van Reenen. 2017. "Who Becomes an Inventor in America? The Importance of Exposure to Innovation." NBER Working Paper 24062, National Bureau of Economic Research, Cambridge, MA.

Benabou, Roland, and Efe A. Ok. 2001. "Social Mobility and the Demand for Redistribution: The POUM Hypothesis." *The Quarterly Journal of Economics* 116 (2): 447–87.

Brunori, Paolo, Francisco H.G. Ferreira, and Vito Peragine. 2013. "Inequality of Opportunity, Income Inequality, and Economic Mobility: Some International Comparisons." In *Getting Development Right*, edited by Eva Paus, 85–115. New York: Palgrave Macmillan.

Cappelen, Alexander W., James Konow, Erik Ø. Sørensen, and Bertil Tungodden. 2013. "Just Luck: An Experimental Study of Risk-Taking and Fairness." *American Economic Review* 103 (4): 1398–413.

Chetty, Raj, David Grusky, Maximilian Hell, Nathaniel Hendren, Robert Manduca, and Jimmy Narang. 2017. "The Fading American Dream: Trends in Absolute Income Mobility Since 1940." *Science* 356 (6336): 398–406.

Cojocaru, Alexandru. 2014. "Prospects of Upward Mobility and Preferences for Redistribution: Evidence from the Life in Transition Survey." *European Journal of Political Economy* 34: 300–314.

Corak, Miles. 2013. "Income Inequality, Equality of Opportunity, and Intergenerational Mobility." *Journal of Economic Perspectives* 27 (3): 79–102.

———. 2016. "Economic Theory and Practical Lessons for Measuring Equality of Opportunities." OECD Statistics Working Papers No. 2016/02, OECD Publishing, Paris.

Doan, Quang Hung, and Ngoc Anh Nguyen. 2016. "Intergenerational Income Mobility in Vietnam." MPRA Paper 70603, Munich Personal RePEc Archive, Munich, Germany.

Equalchances. 2018. *International Database on Inequality of Opportunity and Social Mobility*. Bari, Italy: University of Bari.

Esteban, Joan-Maria, and Debraj Ray. 1994. "On the Measurement of Polarization." *Econometrica: Journal of the Econometric Society* 62 (4): 819–51.

Fehr, Ernst, and Urs Fischbacher. 2003. "The Nature of Human Altruism." *Nature* 425 (6960): 785.

Ferreira, Francisco H.G., Deon Filmer, and Norbert Schady. 2017. "Own and Sibling Effects of Conditional Cash Transfer Programs: Theory and Evidence from Cambodia." In *Research on Economic Inequality: Poverty, Inequality and Welfare*, edited by S. Bandyopadhyay, 259–98. Bingley, U.K.: Emerald.

Fleib, Jurgen. 2015. "Merit Norms in the Ultimatum Game: An Experimental Study of the Effect of Merit on Individual Behavior and Aggregate Outcomes." *Central European Journal of Operations Research* 23 (2): 389–406.

Friedman, Milton. 2002. *Capitalism and Freedom*. With the assistance of Rose D. Friedman. 40th Anniversary Edition. Chicago, IL: University of Chicago Press.

Galor, Oded, and Daniel Tsiddon. 1997. "Technological Progress, Mobility, and Economic Growth." *American Economic Review* 87 (3): 363–82.

Galor, Oded, and Joseph Zeira. 1993. "Income Distribution and Macroeconomics." *Review of Economic Studies* 60 (1): 35–52.

Gaviria, Alejandro, Carol Graham, and Luis H. B. Braido. 2007. "Social Mobility and Preferences for Redistribution in Latin America." *Economía* 8 (1): 55–96.

GDIM (Global Database on Intergenerational Mobility). 2018. *Global Database on Intergenerational Mobility*. Development Research Group. Washington, DC: World Bank.

Grimm, Michael. 2011. "Does Inequality in Health Impede Economic Growth?" *Oxford Economic Papers* 63 (3): 448–74.

Hassler, John, and José V. Rodríguez Mora. 2000. "Intelligence, Social Mobility, and Growth." *American Economic Review* 90 (4): 888–908.

Hertz, Tom, Tamara Jayasundera, Patrizio Piraino, Sibel Selcuk, Nicole Smith, and Alina Verashchagina. 2007. "The Inheritance of Educational Inequality: Intergenerational Comparisons and Fifty-Year Trends." *B.E. Journal of Economic Analysis and Policy* 7 (2): 1–48.

Hirschman, Albert O., and Michael Rothschild. 1973. "The Changing Tolerance for Income Inequality in the Course of Economic Development: With a Mathematical Appendix." *Quarterly Journal of Economics* 87 (4): 544–66.

Hoff, Karla. 2012. "The Effect of Inequality on Aspirations." Background paper for *Addressing Inequality in South Asia*, edited by Martin Rama, Tara Béteille, Yue Li, Pradeep K. Mitra, and John Lincoln Newman. Washington, DC: World Bank.

Ianchovichina, Elena, Lili Mottaghi, and Shantayanan Devarajan. 2015. *Inequality, Uprisings, and Conflict in the Arab World*. Middle East and North Africa (MENA) Economic Monitor. Washington, DC: World Bank.

Krishnan, Nandini, Gabriel Lara Ibarra, Ambar Narayan, Sailesh Tiwari, and Tara Vishwanath. 2016. *Uneven Odds, Unequal Outcomes: Inequality of Opportunity in the Middle East and North Africa*. Directions in Development. Washington, DC: World Bank.

Loury, Glenn C. 1981. "Intergenerational Transfers and the Distribution of Earnings." *Econometrica: Journal of the Econometric Society* 49 (4): 843–67.

Maoz, Yishay D., and Moav, O. 1999. "Intergenerational Mobility and the Process of Development." *Economic Journal* 109 (458): 677–97.

Marrero, Gustavo Alberto, and Juan Gabriel Rodríguez. 2013. "Inequality of Opportunity and Growth." *Journal of Development Economics* 104 (C): 107–22.

Marrero, Gustavo Alberto, Juan Gabriel Rodríguez, and Roy Van Der Weide. 2016. "Unequal Opportunity, Unequal Growth." Policy Research Working Paper 7853, World Bank, Washington, DC.

Molina, Ezequiel, Ambar Narayan, and Jaime Saavedra-Chanduvi. 2013. "Outcomes, Opportunity and Development: Why Unequal Opportunities and Not Outcomes Hinder Economic Development." Policy Research Working Paper 6735, World Bank, Washington, DC.

Causa, Orsetta, and Asa Johansson. 2010. "Intergenerational Social Mobility in OECD Countries." *OECD Journal: Economic Studies* 2010 (1): 1–44.

Owen, Ann L., and David N. Weil. 1998. "Intergenerational Earnings Mobility, Inequality and Growth." *Journal of Monetary Economics* 41 (1): 71–104.

Piketty, Thomas. 2000. "Theories of Persistent Inequality and Intergenerational Mobility." *Handbook of Income Distribution* 1: 429–76.

———. 2014. *Capital in the 21st Century*. Cambridge, MA: Harvard University Press.

Roemer, John E. 1998. *Equality of Opportunity*. Cambridge, MA: Harvard University Press.

Samuel, Lawrence R. 2012. *The American Dream: A Cultural History*. Syracuse, NY: Syracuse University Press.

Solon, Gary. 2002. "Cross-Country Differences in Intergenerational Earnings Mobility." *Journal of Economic Perspectives* 16 (3): 59–66.

———. 2004. "A Model of Intergenerational Mobility Variation over Time and Place." In *Generational Income Mobility in North America and Europe*, edited by Miles Corak, 38–47. Cambridge, UK: Cambridge University Press.

Teyssier, Geoffrey. 2013. "Inequality of Opportunity and Growth: An Empirical Investigation in Brazil." Unpublished paper, Université Paris I Pantheón-Sorbonne, Paris.

Van de Gaer, Dirk. 1993. "Equality of Opportunity and Investment in Human Capital." PhD dissertation, Catholic University of Leuven, Leuven, Belgium.

World Bank. 2005. *World Development Report 2006: Equity and Development.* Washington, DC: World Bank and Oxford University Press.

———. 2016. *Poverty and Shared Prosperity 2016: Taking on Inequality.* Washington, DC: World Bank.

CHAPTER 2
Concepts of Intergenerational Mobility, Data, and Methodology

As discussed in chapter 1, this report focuses on two distinct yet related concepts of intergenerational mobility (IGM), absolute and relative IGM. Absolute IGM is the extent to which the living standards of the members of one generation are higher than the living standards of their parents. Relative IGM is the extent to which the positions of individuals on the economic scale are independent of the positions of their parents.

Building a global database on IGM, including data on most of the developing world, is possible only if one were to measure IGM in education (chapter 1). This is because calculating income IGM for economies requires individual data on earnings (as adults) for parents and their offspring, which ideally requires long-term, nationally representative panel surveys. These surveys are rare in developing economies. In the absence of long-term panels, econometric methods are applied to estimate parental income earnings for a subset of economies for which the cross-sectional surveys used include data on labor income earnings for the respondents in addition to the retrospective data on education and age of the respondent's parents. The predicted parental earnings are then combined with observed respondent earnings to obtain estimates of IGM in earnings.

Because of the use of predicted rather than observed parental earnings data (among other data limitations), estimates of IGM in earnings will be subject to a greater degree of error compared to estimates of IGM in education. Although this approach expands the number of economies for which IGM in earnings can be estimated (beyond those economies for which parental earnings are observed by means of long panels) to about 70, this is still less than half the number of economies for which IGM in education is estimated. Furthermore, IGM in earnings can be estimated only for a snapshot in time, whereas IGM in education can be tracked over multiple cohorts spanning almost half a century.

Measures of Intergenerational Mobility in Education

Educational attainment is measured in this report by years of schooling completed and highest educational program completed. Years of schooling may be considered a continuous variable analogous to individual earnings, which is often the way they are viewed in the literature.[1]

The literature proposes several different measures of IGM.[2] In addition to distinguishing between absolute and relative mobility, mobility measures can be divided into measures that treat the outcome variable, that is, educational attainment, as continuous or as categorical. In the latter instance, common choices among categories are quintiles or quartiles, whereby individuals are sorted by educational outcome and assigned to the relevant quintile or quartile of their generation.[3] The corresponding transition probabilities—for example, the probability that an individual with parents in a low educational quintile or quartile achieves a high educational quintile or quartile (relative to others in the individual's generation)—represent natural measures of relative mobility. The matrix that organizes all possible transition probabilities is referred to as the transition matrix. For a broader taxonomy of mobility measures, see for example chapter 2 in Ferreira et al. (2013), and the references therein.

Measures Used in this Report

Absolute upward mobility in each economy is measured according to the share of survey respondents who reached higher educational attainment than their parents. (See below for details on how parental educational attainment is evaluated.) This is similar in spirit to the measure of absolute income mobility used by Chetty et al. (2017), but applied to educational outcomes instead of income.[4] In the case of relative mobility, a selection of measures is used, all gauging the extent to which the educational attainment of individuals in one generation is independent of the educational attainment of their parents. The primary measure uses the coefficient from the regression of children's years of education on the education of their parents. This is referred to as the regression coefficient or intergenerational persistence (IGP). Higher values of the regression coefficient indicate greater intergenerational persistence and, hence, lower relative mobility.

To complement this measure of relative IGM, the report also evaluates selected transition probabilities: (1) the share of individuals who reach the top quartile of education in their generation among all individuals who are born to parents with educational attainment in the bottom half of their respective generation, which is akin to moving out of relative poverty and thus referred to as the poverty-to-privilege rate; (2) the share of individuals who end up in the bottom half in educational attainment in their generation among all individuals born to parents in the bottom half of educational attainment in their respective generation, referred to as the intergenerational poverty rate; and (3) the share of individuals who reach the top quartile in educational attainment of their generation among all individuals born to parents who are in the top quartile of educational attainment in their respective generation, referred to as the intergenerational privilege rate.

IGM is estimated among adults for 10-year cohorts born between 1940 and 1989, to show how it has changed over time. For example, an individual in the 1980s cohort refers to the generation born between 1980 and 1989, and parents refers specifically to the parents of this cohort. The 1980s cohort is the most recent cohort that is likely to have already reached its maximum educational attainment and therefore represents the current generation of individuals.

In the results, average IGM measures are reported for groups of economies (developing or high-income economies or developing regions) as simple averages unweighted by population. These averages should be interpreted as the average IGM of all economies in a group for a certain generation or cohort, and not as the IGM of the average individual in the group. Simple averages are used so that each economy counts equally and so that the trends of a group are not dominated by a few large economies.

Alternative Measures of Mobility

The measures of IGM presented in this report are a small subset of a vast universe of mobility measures. The argument for limiting the choice of measures to this small but commonly used subset revolves around the need for clarity of exposition. The flip side is that some of the nuance and intricacy may go unnoticed. A natural alternative (or complement) to the measure of absolute mobility used here is a measure that evaluates growth in levels of educational attainment. In the case of relative mobility, a natural alternative to the regression coefficient would be the correlation coefficient (see below).

The transition matrix is fertile ground for a wide range of alternative measures of relative IGM. In addition to inspecting individual transition probabilities, measures of relative mobility can be derived as matrix functions that consider the entire matrix. Popular examples include the measure put forward by Bartholomew (1982), which may be interpreted as the average number of states in educational attainment (such as quartiles) crossed by individuals relative to their parents or, alternatively, the geometric means of the eigenvalues of the transition matrix.[5] In the latter case, perfect mobility is obtained if each row in the transition matrix coincides with the unconditional probabilities, which is to say if the likelihood of ending up on the lower, middle, or top rungs of the education ladder is independent of the position of one's parents on the ladder. Although this denotes an intuitive choice of perfect mobility, other choices of perfect mobility matrixes could be accommodated by adopting matrix distance functions that evaluate the distance between the empirically observed transition matrix and some benchmark matrix.[6]

Other categories of mobility measures considered in the literature distinguish among mobility as movement, mobility as origin independence, and mobility as an equalizer of long-term outcomes. Each of these offers a different lens on mobility and has been described extensively in the literature.[7]

Data for Estimating Intergenerational Mobility in Education Worldwide

The Global Database on IGM developed for this report includes estimates of absolute and relative IGM for individuals born in the 1980s in 148 economies, comprising 96 percent of the world's population. For 111 of these economies, covering 87 percent of the world's population, IGM is estimated for multiple cohorts—from individuals born in the 1940s to individuals born in the 1980s—to show trends in educational mobility over time.[8]

Identification of Relevant Surveys

Surveys collecting information on educational attainment among the parents of adults

To construct the global database, a comprehensive review was conducted of surveys that have retrospective data on parental educational attainment (for example, surveys that collect information from adult respondents on the educational attainment of their parents). In most cases, only surveys since 2006 have been considered. This is to ensure that the majority of respondents born in the 1980s have reached an age by which one may assume they have completed their education so that mobility estimates on the 1980s cohort could be accurately calculated.[9] If multiple relevant surveys were found for an economy, one was selected on the basis of sample size and the quality of the information on parental educational attainment.[10]

For most developing economies outside the Eastern Europe and Central Asia region and the Latin America and Caribbean region, cross-sectional household income or expenditure surveys are used. Social surveys such as the European Social Survey, the Latinobarómetro Survey, and the Life in Transition Survey are used for most economies in the Eastern Europe and Central Asia region and in the Latin America and Caribbean region. The social surveys tend to have small sample sizes, so, if multiple waves of the same survey contain relevant information on educational attainment, these waves are pooled.[11] For a select number of high-income economies, annual panel surveys, such as the Panel Study of Income Dynamics on the United States and the Labor and Income Panel Study on the Republic of Korea, are used (see GDIM 2018 for a complete list of surveys used for each economy).[12] In four economies (Kenya, the Lao People's Democratic Republic, Sri Lanka, and Vietnam), Skills Towards Employability and Productivity (STEP) Skills Measurement Program surveys are used. These surveys collect parental educational attainment only for a subset of respondents within households.[13]

Surveys collecting information on parental education only for co-resident adults

For many economies for which surveys with retrospective data on parental educational attainment are not available, high-quality household surveys without retrospective data are used instead. In such surveys, information on parental educational attainment can be obtained only on respondents who reside in households together with their parents as co-residents. Because co-residing adults may not be representative of the general adult population in the economy, estimates derived from this type of data may be subject to co-residency bias.[14] The magnitude of this bias depends on the share of adults who co-reside with their parents and the extent to which co-residing adults differ from adults who live away from their parents with respect to attributes that influence the association in educational attainment between adults and their parents.

To reduce the likelihood of co-residency bias, the samples are restricted to co-residents aged 21–25 at the time of the survey, and these respondents are assigned to the 1980s cohort. Thus, in these economies, IGM estimates are available only on the 1980s cohort. Furthermore, surveys from which retrospective data on parental educational attainment are available (and that reveal whether respondents co-reside with their parents) are used to estimate mobility with and without assuming co-residency to assess the magnitude of the co-residency bias. This exercise, performed by using all economies on which retrospective information on the educational attainment of the parents of adults is available, indicates that the co-residency bias is small (box 2.1). Although this does not guarantee that the bias is as small in the economies on which only co-resident data are available (where no such sensitivity check can be conducted), it does provide a reasonable degree of confidence in the IGM estimates on the 1980s cohort using co-resident data where parental information on all adults is not available.

For a handful of economies, recent surveys with co-resident data and older surveys with retrospective questions were combined: co-resident data are used for the 1980s cohort, and the older surveys are used for older cohorts. This is

---

BOX 2.1   Checking for co-residency bias

Co-residency bias appears to be small in surveys that allow a comparison between the general population of adults and co-residents. A comparison of estimates obtained on co-residents aged 21–25 against estimates for all respondents aged 21–25 by using all economies on which retrospective information on the educational attainment of the parents of adults is available is illustrated in figure B2.1.1. The mean years of schooling of co-residents and the parents of co-residents are slightly higher than the mean years of schooling of all respondents and the parents of all respondents. The estimates are almost perfectly correlated with a correlation coefficient of 0.99. A comparison of estimates of relative IGM measured by intergenerational persistence also suggests that the bias is modest. In absolute IGM, co-residents have a slightly greater chance of exhibiting higher educational attainment than their parents. The correspondence is still sufficiently high to suggest that the size of the bias is not large.

box continues next page

BOX 2.1   Checking for co-residency bias (continued)

FIGURE B2.1.1   Comparing co-residents with all respondents between ages 21 and 25 years

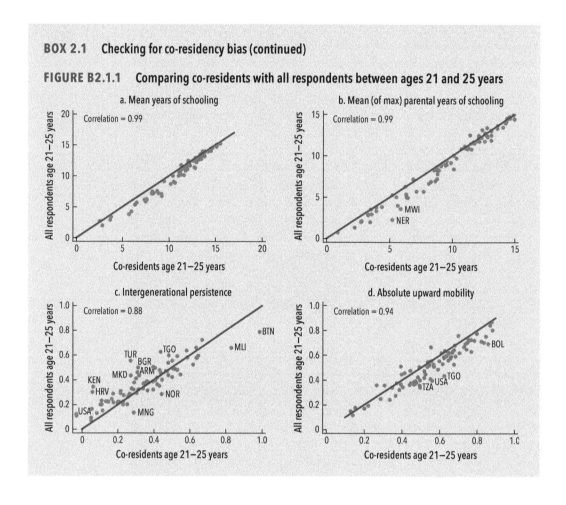

the approach on Pakistan (1991), Mauritania (1995), the Philippines (1999), Rwanda (2000), and Guinea (2002). For two economies, co-resident surveys and retrospective surveys since 2006 were not found. To maximize the coverage of economies, older surveys relying on retrospective questions are used in these cases; this is the case for New Zealand (2000) and Bhutan (2003).[15]

Coverage of the Data

The database covers 148 economies, of which the data on 111 are based on retrospective questions (table 2.1). This amounts to 96 percent of the world's population (87 percent with retrospective questions). Except for the Middle East and North Africa, the population coverage in all regions is more than 90 percent. In the case of the Middle East and North Africa, 81 percent of the population is covered (49 percent with retrospective questions). Most of the analysis that follows, with the exception of the analysis on trends in IGM, refers to the information on the 1980s cohort that is available for the full sample. If time trends are analyzed, only economies on which retrospective data are available are used, so the population coverage is somewhat lower.

TABLE 2.1 Coverage of the Global Database on Intergenerational Mobility

Income group, region	Number of economies covered		% of population covered	
	With retrospective data	Total	With retrospective data	Total
High-income economies	37	37	94	94
Developing economies	74	111	86	96
East Asia and the Pacific	8	16	92	96
Eastern Europe and Central Asia	20	20	99	99
Latin America and the Caribbean	16	16	96	96
Middle East and North Africa	5	10	49	81
South Asia	5	8	89	100
Sub-Saharan Africa	20	41	72	95
Total	111	148	87	96

Harmonizing Education Variables Worldwide

Global common denominator of five categories

To facilitate the comparability of estimates across the various surveys, a globally harmonized categorical measure of educational attainment has been constructed. To this end, the lowest common denominator across the various surveys has been adopted. This has invariably reduced the amount of detail exploited in some economies. With minor exceptions (see below), all surveys contain the following five categories, which are based on the International Standard Classification of Education (ISCED): less than primary (ISCED 0), primary (ISCED 1), lower secondary (ISCED 2), upper secondary or postsecondary nontertiary (ISCED 3–4), and tertiary (ISCED 5–8).[16] The categories refer to the highest educational level completed by the respondent. The cases where not all five categories exist are mostly high-income economies, where no category below primary is present.[17] Because these economies have instituted mandatory primary schooling, it is assumed that all individuals have completed at least primary school in these cases. Respondents who are younger than age 18 or who are still enrolled in school are excluded from the IGM estimates. The only exception involves respondents who are enrolled in school, have completed upper secondary, and are ages 20 or older. These individuals are assumed to have completed the lowest tertiary degree (ISCED 5).[18]

Mapping categories of education to years of schooling

The parental education variable always refers to the educational attainment of an individual's father or mother, whichever is greater in terms of years of schooling in the case of continuous data and in terms of the highest category of education completed in the case of categorical data. Categorical data, harmonized across economies, are used to compute absolute IGM as the share of individuals whose completed educational level (in terms of the categories described above) is higher than that of their most educated parent.

The measures of relative IGM require a continuous schooling variable. However, years of schooling do not account for differences in the quality of education. A year of schooling in Singapore may translate into a greater amount of learning than a year of schooling in other places in the world. Because of the lack of global data on educational quality, the estimates rely on years of schooling only, ignoring quality differences across and within economies. Although this is not ideal, the implication for IGM may arguably be modest. To the extent that the quality of schooling tends to be relatively stable and is likely to vary much less over time within an economy than between economies, comparisons of the educational attainment of individuals relative to their parents may be less affected by school quality. For surveys in which years of schooling are not available, other sources are relied upon to construct a measure of years of schooling (box 2.2).

BOX 2.2   Converting categories of education to years of schooling and vice versa

Many of the surveys contain direct questions eliciting information on completed years of schooling. For the surveys where no such variable is available, economy- and year-specific mapping on the duration of educational programs is relied upon to construct a measure of years of schooling.[a] The length of schooling involved in the various International Standard Classification of Education (ISCED) categories varies across economies and even within economies over time. Individuals are assigned to an educational regime on the basis of their birth year and the official age of school entry. If education reforms are known to have occurred, they are assumed to affect only those individuals who had not yet entered the target level of education at the time of the reform. For example, a reform extending lower-secondary education from three to four years is assumed not to affect children who were already enrolled in lower-secondary school at that time. The information used to carry out the mapping exercise is not available before 1970. For individuals who completed school before 1970, the duration for each educational category from 1970 is therefore applied. If information is missing in the sources for the mapping exercise, additional economy-specific information is used or the following rules of thumb for converting ISCED categories to completed years of schooling are applied: ISCED 1: 6 years; ISCED 2: 9 years; ISCED 3: 12 years; ISCED 4: 13 years; ISCED 5: 15 years; ISCED 6: 16 years; ISCED 7: 18 years; and ISCED 8: 21 years. In the few cases where information on years of schooling is available, but no information on the categories of education, the conversion is performed in reverse, using the economy- and year-specific mapping information. For example, an individual who has completed 8 years of schooling is assumed, according to the relevant rule of thumb, to have completed primary school but not lower-secondary school.

a. Two sources of information are used. The first source ("ISCED Mappings") is not available for all economies and generally only reflects the ISCED categories in the ISCED revisions of 1997 and 2011. This source is supplemented by information on the UIS. Stat database, which covers the ISCED categories annually since 1970. For the first source, see "ISCED Mappings," Institute for Statistics, United Nations Educational, Scientific, and Cultural Organization, Montreal, http://uis.unesco.org/en/isced-mappings. For the database, see UIS.Stat (database), Institute for Statistics, United Nations Educational, Scientific, and Cultural Organization, Montreal, http://data.uis.unesco.org/.

Data on Correlates of Intergenerational Mobility

To explore potential correlates of IGM, data in the Global Database on IGM are merged with a wide range of economy-level information, such as information on public spending, gross domestic product (GDP), inequality, and poverty. This information draws on numerous sources, including the Ethnic Power Relations Dataset; the Fraser Institute; Freedom House; Gallup; the Heritage Foundation; the International Center for Tax and Development; the Maddison Project; the Organisation for Economic Co-operation and Development; Transparency International; the United Nations Educational, Scientific, and Cultural Organization; the United Nations; the World Bank's World Development Indicators and PovcalNet; and the World Values Survey.[19] Economy-level estimates of returns to schooling, inequality of opportunity, IGM in income, and subnational information on GDP per capita are also incorporated from various sources.[20] A few relevant variables are constructed from the surveys in the database, such as geographical segregation and marital sorting.

Methodological Choices

The estimation of IGM between parents and children requires the specification of the parents and children to whom one is referring. This naturally has a bearing on the results: the probability of surpassing one's parents depends on whether one is referring to sons, daughters, mothers, or fathers. Unless otherwise indicated, all children have been considered in the estimates here. Whenever parental education is discussed, the reference is to the maximum level of education attained by the parents. If the schooling of either parent is unknown, the observation is dropped from the analysis. In three economies, information is available on the years of schooling of fathers, but not of mothers (Benin, Chad, and the Democratic Republic of Congo). In these cases, it is assumed that the maximum value of parental years of schooling is equivalent to the years of schooling of the fathers.

Mobility estimates based on less than 50 observations are always dropped from the analysis. If time trends are analyzed, economies in which estimates exist only on the 1980s cohort—the economies on which only co-residents are used for the estimates—are dropped to ensure that the same economies are being compared over time (unless estimates do not meet the observational cutoff). On several occasions, the required minimal number of observations is raised to 100 or 200 in analyses that do not cover time trends, averages across regions, or averages across income groups, but that examine correlations and patterns at the national or subnational level. The purpose is to guarantee that the patterns here revealed have not been distorted by sampling errors caused by small sample sizes. A variety of other methodological choices, including an assessment of their potential impacts on results, is presented in annex 2A.

Measuring Intergenerational Mobility for Developing Economies–A Pragmatic Approach

Monitoring IGM and inequality of opportunity, which are increasingly being recognized as important drivers of economic development, should be one of the priorities for data collection efforts in developing economies. Collecting information on income IGM in the "first-best" way requires long-term panels with accurate and individualized income information, which make significant demands on a developing economy's capacity and resources. But accurate estimates of IGM in education can be relatively easily obtained from retrospective data on parental education in standard household surveys.

However, national household surveys in developing economies often do not collect such retrospective data from respondents who no longer reside with their parents, even though respondents are likely to recall their parents' education with accuracy and including such information is unlikely to impose a significant cost or time burden on a survey. Among the 148 economies studied in this report, only 42 have a recent national household income or expenditure survey that includes data on parental education. For the remaining economies, a "second-best" method is adopted to estimate educational IGM. This in some cases involves using a social survey, which often provides smaller samples, does not cover all members of the household, and does not include data on household income or expenditure. Or it involves using a household income or expenditure survey without data on parental education and estimating IGM on adults co-residing with their parents, which carries the possibility of bias in the estimates and allows IGM to be estimated for only the latest cohort (see the earlier section titled "Data for Measuring International Mobility in Education Worldwide").

The less accurate methods for estimating educational IGM can be avoided if all household survey questionnaires were to include retrospective questions about the education attained by both parents of all adults living in the household. And, if a little more retrospective information on parents were available, even income IGM can be estimated with some degree of accuracy, following standard methods used in the literature. Information on parental age (year of birth) and occupation, in addition to parental education, can be used to estimate parental income because retrospective data on parental income is unlikely to be accurate.

Thus, collecting information on education, occupation, and the approximate year of birth of parents of all adults in a household, in national household surveys that are conducted at regular intervals, would allow both education and income IGM to be measured consistently over time and across regions in an economy. The same type of retrospective information would also allow standard measures of inequality of opportunity to be estimated.[21] Both types of indicators should be valuable for policy makers to monitor, given the importance of IGM and inequality of opportunity for all the reasons described in this report.

Annex 2A

The Ceiling Effect in Measuring Absolute Mobility

The fact that there is a maximum level of education any given individual can attain introduces a "ceiling effect." This upper bound—few individuals reach more than 21 years of schooling—is particularly important in measures of absolute mobility. As economies develop and the average years of schooling increase, it becomes more difficult for individuals to outperform their parents. If both parents in households in an economy frequently attain tertiary education as do all the children in these households, one may not wish to conclude that the children have failed to be mobile. If one were to reach this conclusion, a mechanical decline might become unavoidable in the share of individuals who outperform their parents in an economy at advanced stages of development. The preferred measure of absolute mobility used for this report deals with this issue by considering only individuals whose parents have completed upper secondary or less. Alternatively, one might categorize individuals as mobile if they have strictly attained more education than their parents or at least as much education as their parents if the parents have tertiary degrees.

Figure 2A.1 illustrates the extent to which the use of this alternative measure (labeled weakly) produces different results than the preferred measure for this report (labeled baseline). The use of the weaker measure gives a slightly more optimistic picture of absolute mobility in developing and high-income economies since the 1960s, which is expected because this measure adopts a more inclusive definition of mobility than the baseline measure. However, the overall trends are broadly similar to the results shown by the two measures. Absolute mobility is still lower in the average developing economy than the average high-income economy, and, since the 1960s, absolute mobility has fallen in the average high-income economy. The "weakly" measure yields a slightly more optimistic scenario for developing economies, showing a small gain between the 1960s cohort and the 1980s cohort, although the rate of increase is still much lower than in previous decades and limited to the period between the 1970s and the 1980s.

Accounting for the Extent of Growth in Absolute Mobility

Neither of the above binary measures of absolute mobility accounts for the magnitude of the extent to which children outperform their parents. Respondents who have one more year of schooling than their parents are considered as mobile as respondents who have 10 more years of schooling than their parents. This means that two economies with the same share of a generation outperforming their parents in education are deemed to have the same absolute IGM, even though the average gap in education between the offspring and their parents may be quite different in the two economies. To see how this might influence the results reported in chapter 3, an alternative measure of absolute mobility is computed: the average difference in years of schooling between parents and children (labeled mean difference in

FIGURE 2A.1   Trends in absolute mobility based on different measures

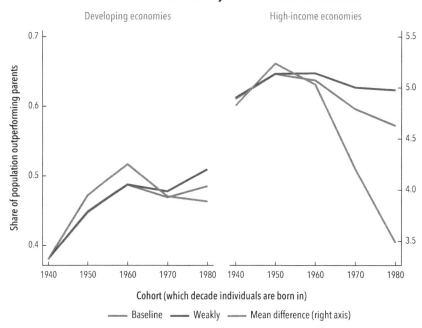

Source: Calculations based on data from the Global Database on Intergenerational Mobility (World Bank).
Note: Averages for developing and high-income groups are simple averages (unweighted by population) across economies in each group. *Baseline* shows the baseline measure of absolute mobility used in this report: the share of respondents attaining strictly more education than their parents, conditional on the parents not having tertiary education. *Weakly* shows the share attaining at least as much education as their parents. *Mean difference* shows the average difference in years of schooling between respondents and their parents, conditional on parents being in the bottom 50 percent of the national distribution.

figure 2A.1). To account for ceiling effects in this measure, only respondents whose parents are in the bottom 50 percent of the national distribution are used. Absolute mobility measured in this way shows a steeper decline over time compared with the results using the preferred measure, particularly in high-income economies.

This measure, however, provides no indication of the size or share of the population in a generation that is upwardly mobile relative to the parents. This drawback and the fact that the average difference appears to be more susceptible to the ceiling effect are the main reasons why the measure is not the preferred measure of absolute mobility in this report. Figure 2A.1 is an important reminder that absolute mobility may represent a different concept to different people. The results presented in this report are in line with an interpretation of absolute IGM as the share of a generation that outperforms their parents. This concept of absolute IGM has the advantage that it is simple and intuitive, which is also the reason why recent literature, including Chetty et al. (2017), have adopted similar measures.

Regression Coefficient versus Correlation Coefficient in Measuring Relative Intergenerational Mobility

The ceiling effect is also important in measures of relative mobility. To see why note that the coefficient of the regression of the years of schooling of respondents on the years of schooling of parents can be expressed as follows:

$$\beta = cor(educchild, educparent) * \frac{st.dev(educchild)}{st.dev(educparent)} \qquad (2A.1)$$

Because the schooling variable is bounded from above and below, the standard deviation in years of schooling tends toward zero if the average years of schooling approach either zero or the maximum. This predicts that the standard deviation follows an inverse U-shape as a function of the mean years of schooling. An implication is that, if the average years of schooling rise, then the ratio of the standard deviations of child and parent years of schooling, which enters directly into the equation for β, tends to decline over time. Consequently, for a constant correlation between the years of schooling of parents and children, one may expect β to decline as the economy accumulates more human capital.

To investigate the extent to which the choice of measure of relative mobility is important, figure 2A.2 compares time trends in the regression coefficient and the correlation coefficient. The trends are a bit less optimistic if the correlation is used as a measure of relative mobility, but most of the main findings remain unchanged, such as the higher average relative

FIGURE 2A.2   Comparing relative mobility measures

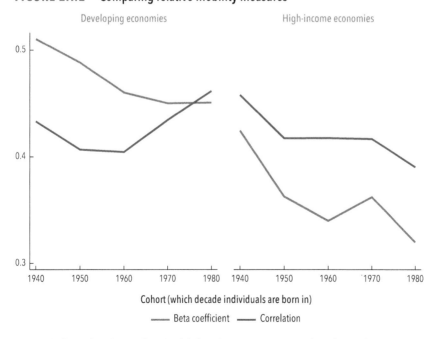

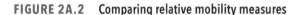

Source: Calculations based on data from the Global Database on Intergenerational Mobility (World Bank).
Note: Intergenerational persistence is measured by the coefficient from the regression of the years of schooling of children on the years of schooling of parents. The averages for developing and high-income groups are simple (unweighted by population) across economies in each group.

IGM among the 1980s cohort in the average high-income economy than in the average developing economy and the widening gap in relative IGM between high-income and developing economies since the 1960s (see chapter 3).

As a measure of relative IGM, both coefficients appear equally valid, and they are used widely in the literature. The decision to focus mainly on one in this report—the regression coefficient—is more a matter of taste than rigorous reasoning and a desire to avoid the complications that inevitably arise from using multiple measures. The interpretation of the regression coefficient appears to be (slightly) more intuitive, because it measures the extent to which a marginal (1-year) difference in the educational attainment of parents makes a difference, on average, in the expected years of schooling of their offspring.

Dealing with the Lack of Granularity in the Education Variable

Another potential issue emerges because of the lack of granularity in the education variable. In several surveys, large parts of the samples have completed the same number of years of schooling. This may be problematic, particularly in the case of transition matrix–based measures. The measures of intergenerational privilege, intergenerational poverty, and the poverty-to-privilege rate all require that each individual and each parent be placed in a quartile of the national distribution. If more than a quarter of individuals have completed the same number of years of schooling, a method to break any ties is needed to allocate individuals into quartiles. This is especially relevant among older cohorts because, in certain economies, more than half the parents in these cohorts have completed zero years of schooling. In this report, if ties become prevalent, individuals are allocated to quartiles by random assignment. To ensure that the estimates are not driven by fortunate or unfortunate random draws, each estimate is obtained 50 times using 50 different random draws. The final estimate represents the average over these 50 results.

Asher, Novosad, and Rafkin (2017) propose an alternative to breaking ties that assumes an underlying continuous distribution of human capital. Relying on modest assumptions, their method generates analytic bounds on rank-based mobility measures. If large shares of parents have no schooling, a comparison of the results of the tie-breaking method adopted in this report with the results of their method reveals substantial differences in developing economies but not in high-income economies (figure 2A.3). This is important for trends in developing economies. Whereas the method applied in this report finds that intergenerational privilege has worsened in developing economies (more children born in the top quartile are ending up in the top quartile), estimates obtained using the method of Asher, Novosad, and Rafkin (2017) suggest a more stable pattern. The measures produced by the two methods converge, however, and the gaps have been narrow since the 1970s cohort.

FIGURE 2A.3   Comparing methods to break ties

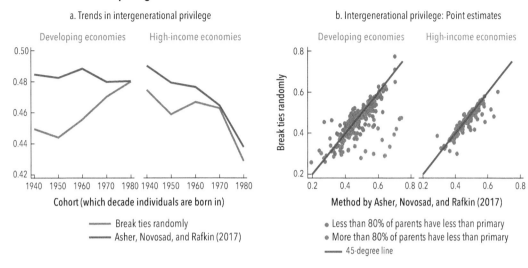

a. Trends in intergenerational privilege

b. Intergenerational privilege: Point estimates

Neither of these methods is inherently superior, and the one that is more appropriate depends on the reason behind the lack of granularity in the education variable. If more than half of parents have zero years of schooling, the random allocation method would show equal mobility among children born in the bottom quartile and the second-lowest quartile (of parental education) because the two groups will be almost identical in terms of parental education. This would be fine if half the parents truly have zero years of schooling, in which case there is no reason to believe that children born in the second-lowest quartile should perform better than children born in the bottom quartile. However, if some parents have more than zero years of schooling, but are coded to have zero years of schooling because of limited information, then the children born in the true second-lowest quartile can be expected to do better on average than children born in the true bottom quartile.

The random allocation method chosen for this report has the advantage of simplicity and transparency. It also appears to be reasonable because the lack of education is known to be widespread in developing economies among the parents of older cohorts, whose school years would correspond to the first half of the 20th century when universal education was not common in developing economies. The two methods produce similar results on the intergenerational privilege of the 1980s cohort, which is the cohort used most frequently for the analysis in chapters 3–6.

Notes

1. See Hertz et al. (2007).

2. See, for example, Fields and Ok (1999) and their references.

3. Strictly speaking, quartiles refer to the 25th, 50th, and 75th percentiles of the distribution. This report will slightly abuse this terminology by referring to the corresponding four "bins" as quartiles, for example, the first quartile will refer to those between 0 and the 25th percentile, etc.

4. Chetty et al. (2017) use this measure and find that the share of individuals earning more than their parents has declined in the United States.

5. See, for example, Dardanoni (1993); Shorrocks (1978); Sommers and Conlisk (1979).

6. See, for instance, Long and Ferrie (2007).

7. For a detailed discussion of these various concepts, see Ferreira et al. (2013), Van de Gaer, Schokkaert, and Martinez (2001), and their references.

8. Estimates of IGM for older cohorts are arguably less precise when compared to estimates for younger cohorts. Respondents born in the 1940s and 1950s who are interviewed in 2010, for example, may not provide representative samples, especially if survival rates vary with an individual's level of education. To the extent that more highly educated individuals have a higher life expectancy, estimates of educational attainment and of absolute IGM for older cohorts may be subject to a positive bias.

9. To identify relevant surveys, the literature on IGM in education was examined. This includes Azomahou and Yitbarek (2016); Hertz et al. (2008); Neidhofer, Serrano, and Gasparini (2017). The International Household Survey Network Gender Data Navigator was also explored. See Gender Data Navigator (database), International Household Survey Network, World Bank and PARIS21 Consortium, Paris, http://datanavigator.ihsn.org/. In addition, consultations were conducted with economy experts at the World Bank.

10. Similar to Neidhofer, Serrano, and Gasparini (2017), Latinobarómetro is used instead of LAPOP, which is another social survey covering the Americas. LAPOP seeks information only on the education of mothers. Meanwhile, Latinobarómetro records the highest educational attainment of fathers and mothers, which is the variable used in this report. See LAPOP (Latin American Public Opinion Project) (database), Vanderbilt University, Nashville, TN, http://www.vanderbilt.edu/lapop/; Latinobarómetro Database, Corporación Latinobarómetro, Santiago, Chile, http://www.latinobarometro.org/lat.jsp.

11. This includes three waves of the European Social Survey (from 2010 to 2014), six waves of the Latinobarómetro (from 2008 to 2015), and two waves of the Life in Transition Survey (2006 and 2011). Household (individual) weights are applied if household income or expenditure (social) surveys are used. If multiple waves of social surveys are combined, the weights are adjusted so that the sum of

weights across the waves is identical. See ESS (European Social Survey) (database), European Research Infrastructure Consortium, London; Norwegian Centre for Research Data, Bergen, Norway, http://www .europeansocialsurvey.org/; Latinobarómetro Database, Corporación Latinobarómetro, Santiago, Chile, http://www.latinobarometro.org /lat.jsp; LITS (Life in Transition Survey) (database), European Bank for Reconstruction and Development, London, http://www.ebrd.com /what-we-do/economic-research-and-data/data/lits.html.

12. See KLIPS (Korean Labor and Income Panel Study) (database), Korea Labor Institute, Sejong, Republic of Korea, https://www.kli.re.kr/klips _eng/index.do; PSID (Panel Study of Income Dynamics) (database), Survey Research Center, Institute for Social Research, University of Michigan, Ann Arbor, MI, https://psidonline.isr.umich.edu/.

13. For the STEP surveys, the household weights are adjusted to allocate the weights of household members whose information is missing to household members whose information is available. See Step Skills Measurement Program (database), World Bank, Washington, DC, http://microdata.worldbank.org/index.php/catalog/step.

14. For example, see Emran, Greene, and Shilpi (2017).

15. Tabulations show that, in Bhutan, most respondents born in the 1980s had completed their education by the time of the survey. For New Zealand, it is assumed that the estimates for the 1980s cohort are equivalent to the estimates derived for the 1970s cohort.

16. See ISCED (International Standard Classification of Education) (database), Institute for Statistics, United Nations Educational, Scientific, and Cultural Organization, Montreal, http://uis.unesco .org/en/topic/international-standard-classification-education-isced.

17. This occurs in economies where the European Social Survey or the Life in Transition Survey is used, as well as Australia; Canada; Japan; Korea; Taiwan, China; and the United States. In a few other economies, a challenge arises in assigning respondents who have completed Koranic or other religious schools. In general, it is assumed that these respondents have completed education corresponding to the primary level.

18. This assumption may affect the estimates. If most individuals who are enrolled in tertiary education and who are aged 20 or older end up completing a master's degree (ISCED 7), the assumption would assign them too little educational attainment. If these individuals also tend to have highly educated parents, the assumption would cause IGM to be underestimated. If these individuals were simply dropped from the analysis, the representativeness of the results would likely decrease. There is thus no ideal way of dealing with this group of individuals.

19. See, respectively, EPR3 (Ethnic Power Relations 3.0) (dataset), Andreas Wimmer and Philippe Duhart, University of California, Los Angeles, http://www.epr.ucla.edu/; Fraser Institute, Vancouver, https://www .fraserinstitute.org/; Freedom House, Washington, DC, https://

freedomhouse.org/; Gallup, Washington, DC, http://www.gallup.com /home.aspx; Heritage Foundation, Washington, DC, https://www .heritage.org/; International Center for Tax and Development, Institute of Development Studies, Brighton, United Kingdom, http://www.ictd .ac/; Maddison Historical Statistics (database), Groningen Growth and Development Centre, Faculty of Economics and Business, University of Groningen, Groningen, The Netherlands, https://www.rug.nl/ggdc /historicaldevelopment/maddison/; OECD.Stat (database), Organisation for Economic Co-operation and Development, Paris, https://stats.oecd .org/; Transparency International, Berlin, https://www.transparency .org/; UIS.Stat (database), Institute for Statistics, United Nations Educational, Scientific, and Cultural Organization, Montreal, http:// data.uis.unesco.org/; United Nations Statistics Division, New York, https://unstats.un.org/home/; WDI (World Development Indicators) (database), World Bank, Washington, DC, http://data.worldbank.org /products/wdi; PovcalNet (online analysis tool), World Bank, Washington, DC, http://iresearch.worldbank.org/PovcalNet/; WVS (World Values Survey) (database), King's College, Old Aberdeen, United Kingdom, http://www.worldvaluessurvey.org/wvs.jsp.

20. Data on returns to schooling have been obtained from Montenegro and Patrinos (2014), inequality of opportunity from Brunori, Ferreira, and Peragine (2013), and IGM in income from Equalchances (2018). Subnational estimates of GDP per capita have been obtained from Gennaioli et al. (2014).

21. For example, the inequality of economic opportunity or IEO measure (see chapter 4).

References

Asher, Sam, Paul Novosad, and Charlie Rafkin. 2017. "Estimating Intergenerational Mobility with Coarse Data: A Nonparametric Approach." Working Paper, World Bank, Washington, DC.

Azomahou, Theophile T., and Eleni Abraham Yitbarek. 2016. "Intergenerational Education Mobility in Africa: Has Progress Been Inclusive?" Policy Research Working Paper 7843, World Bank, Washington, DC.

Bartholomew, David J. 1982. *Stochastic Models for Social Processes*. 3rd ed. New York: Wiley.

Brunori, Paolo, Francisco H. G. Ferreira, and Vito Peragine. 2013. "Inequality of Opportunity, Income Inequality, and Economic Mobility: Some International Comparisons." In *Getting Development Right*, edited by Eva Paus, 85–115. New York: Palgrave Macmillan.

Chetty, Raj, David Grusky, Maximilian Hell, Nathaniel Hendren, Robert Manduca, and Jimmy Narang. 2017. "The Fading American Dream: Trends in Absolute Income Mobility since 1940." *Science* 356 (6336): 398–406.

Dardanoni, Valentino. 1993. "Measuring Social Mobility." *Journal of Economic Theory* 61 (2): 372–94.

Emran, M. Shahe, William Greene, and Forhad Shilpi. 2017. "When Measure Matters: Coresidency, Truncation Bias, and Intergenerational Mobility in Developing Countries." *Journal of Human Resources*: 0216–7737R1.

Equalchances. 2018. "International Database on Inequality of Opportunity and Social Mobility." University of Bari, Bari, Italy.

Ferreira, Francisco H. G., Julian Messina, Jamele Rigolini, Luis-Felipe López-Calva, Maria Ana Lugo, Renos Vakis. 2013. *Economic Mobility and the Rise of the Latin American Middle Class*. Latin America and Caribbean Studies. Washington, DC: World Bank.

Fields, Gary S., and Efe A. Ok. 1999. "Measuring Movement of Incomes." *Economica* 66 (264): 455–71.

Gennaioli, Nicola, Rafael La Porta, Florencio Lopez De Silanes, and Andrei Shleifer. 2014. "Growth in Regions." *Journal of Economic Growth* 19 (3): 259–309.

Hertz, Tom, Tamara Jayasundera, Patrizio Piraino, Sibel Selcuk, Nicole Smith, and Alina Verashchagina. 2007. "The Inheritance of Educational Inequality: Intergenerational Comparisons and Fifty-Year Trends." *The B.E. Journal of Economic Analysis & Policy* 7 (2): 1–48.

———. 2008. "The Transmission of Educational Inequality across Generations: A Global View." http://www.voxeu.org/index.php.

Long, Jason, and Joseph Ferrie. 2007. "The Path to Convergence: Intergenerational Occupational Mobility in Britain and the US in Three Eras." *The Economic Journal* 117 (519): C61–C71.

Montenegro, Claudio E., and Harry Anthony Patrinos. 2014. "Comparable Estimates of Returns to Schooling around the World." Policy Research Working Paper 7020, World Bank, Washington, DC.

Neidhofer, Guido, Joaquín Serrano, and Leonardo Gasparini. 2017. "Educational Inequality and Intergenerational Mobility in Latin America: A New Database." Discussion Paper 2017/20, Free University Berlin, School of Business & Economics. Berlin, Germany.

Shorrocks, Anthony F. 1978. "The Measurement of Mobility." *Econometrica: Journal of the Econometric Society* 46 (5): 1013–24.

Sommers, Paul M., and John Conlisk. 1979. "Eigenvalue Immobility Measures for Markov Chains." *Journal of Mathematical Sociology* 6 (2): 253–76.

Van de Gaer, Dirk, Erik Schokkaert, and Michel Martinez. 2001. "Three Meanings of Intergenerational Mobility." *Economica* 68 (272): 519–38.

CHAPTER 3

Intergenerational Mobility in Education around the World

This chapter shows how intergenerational mobility (IGM) in education has evolved around the world and across generations. It provides a snapshot of mobility among the latest generation of adults for whom data are available by presenting IGM estimates for individuals born in the 1980s in 148 economies, which are home to 96 percent of the world's population. For 111 of these economies, covering 87 percent of the world's population, IGM is also estimated for multiple cohorts—from those born in the 1940s to those born in the 1980s—to illustrate trends in mobility during the second half of the 20th century.

As described in detail in chapter 2, absolute upward mobility in each economy is measured by the share of survey respondents who have achieved higher educational attainment than their parents. Parental education is represented by the maximum educational attainment among the father and mother of the respondent. Relative mobility is the extent to which the educational attainment of a generation is independent of the educational attainment of the parents of that generation measured using the coefficient from regressions of the children's number of years of education on the number of years of education of the parents. Higher values of this regression coefficient indicate greater intergenerational persistence and, hence, less mobility. These measures are complemented by specific measures of upward and downward mobility: the likelihood that individuals born to parents with education in the bottom half of the parental generation reach the top half or stay in the bottom half of their generation. All IGM measures reported on groups of economies (developing or high-income) are simple averages unweighted by population. Thus, they should be interpreted as the average IGM of all economies in a group and not as the IGM of the average individual in that group.

There is clear value in knowing how IGM varies across economies and changes over time. The currently available empirical evidence is skewed toward high-income economies; much less is known about IGM in the developing world (see chapter 1). This chapter considerably expands the evidence base on the developing world, focusing on educational mobility, which is important for its own sake as a key element of economic mobility, and because it correlates with income mobility. The existing evidence on IGM is also skewed toward men or the intergenerational transmission from fathers to sons. This chapter studies the outcomes among both men and women, thereby filling another important gap. The exercise conducted here is similar in nature to a research project in the mid-2000s that provided comparable trends of educational mobility in 42 economies around the world.[1] The current exercise covers a much larger number of economies and provides up-to-date estimates using surveys that have become available since the earlier project was completed.

The findings highlighted in this chapter are sobering. The gains in absolute IGM in the average developing economy have stalled since the 1960s, while the average level of education of the current generation in developing economies is roughly the same as in high-income economies 30 years ago. Relative IGM is much lower in the developing world than in the high-income group for the latest generation of adults, namely those born in the 1980s. The gap between the high-income and the developing economies has been widening because relative mobility has not improved in the average developing economy since the generation born in the 1970s.

Moreover, current enrollment patterns suggest that the prospects are limited for upward mobility today among the children of poor, less educated parents in low- and low-middle-income economies. In Africa and South Asia, which are the regions with the lowest relative mobility among the latest generation of adults, the educational prospects of children remain more closely tied to the education of their parents than in other parts of the world. However, there is some cause for optimism on absolute mobility in Africa and South Asia. Rough predictions suggest that absolute mobility may have increased in both regions among those born in the 1990s, which would narrow the substantial gap between Africa and other developing regions seen for the earlier generations and bring the South Asian average up to the same level as the developing economy average.

The lack of mobility in some of the poorest parts of the world poses a substantial obstacle to the prospects for global economic progress and poverty reduction. The relationship between IGM and economic development flows in both directions: greater mobility is good for greater, more inclusive growth and vice versa, in a mutually reinforcing cycle. The near absence of this virtuous cycle in many economies, some of which are among the poorest of the world, should be a cause for global concern.

Fair Progress? Trends and Patterns in Educational Mobility

Average Educational Attainment Has Increased across Generations, but the Gap between Advanced and Developing Economies Has Persisted

Sons and daughters are on average better educated than their parents almost everywhere, including in both developing and high-income economies (figure 3.1). But, despite the rise in educational attainment across the world, the gap between developing and high-income economies is as wide today as it was 40 years ago. The developing world today is roughly where the high-income world was 40 years ago. The trends in average educational attainment do not, however, shed light on whether the progress has been fair and inclusive or the extent to which it has favored individuals with more advantaged backgrounds. Addressing these questions requires looking at both absolute and relative mobility across generations.

Absolute and Relative Intergenerational Mobility across the World and over Time

Absolute mobility and relative mobility are lower, on the average, in developing economies than in high-income economies
The rate of absolute IGM in education—the share of adults who have achieved higher educational attainment relative to their parents—has historically been greater in high-income economies than in developing economies and continues to be so among the 1980s cohort, which is the latest

FIGURE 3.1   Share of population with different educational attainment

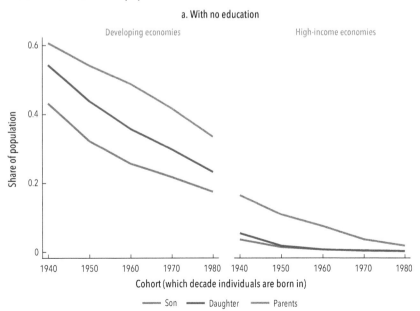

figure continues next page

FIGURE 3.1   **Share of population with different educational attainment (continued)**

b. With tertiary education

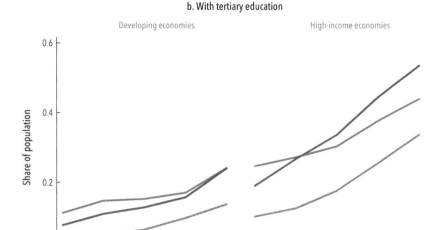

Source: Calculations based on data in the GDIM 2018.
Note: Averages for developing economies and high-income economies are simple (unweighted by population) averages across economies in each group.

generation of adults (figure 3.2, panel a).[2] Among the 1980s generation, the average relative IGM in developing economies is also significantly lower than the average in high-income economies (figure 3.2, panel b). Seven of the 15 economies in the top decile of relative IGM among the 1980s generation are high-income economies, whereas all economies ranked in the bottom decile are developing economies. The gap between developing and high-income economies in relative mobility is also significant if the correlation coefficient between parental and offspring educational attainment, rather than the regression coefficient, is used as the measure of inter-generational persistence (see box 3.1 and annex 2A). The pattern of relative income mobility is also low in developing economies examined in other studies that have much narrower coverage of the developing world (chapter 1).[3]

Although the gap in absolute mobility between high-income and developing economies has been closing, absolute mobility in developing economies has been stagnant since the 1960s

Absolute mobility has converged to some extent between the high-income and developing economies (see figure 3.2, panel a). This is consistent with the finding of a recent study that education inequality has

FIGURE 3.2   Changes in absolute and relative intergenerational mobility over time, developing and high-income economies

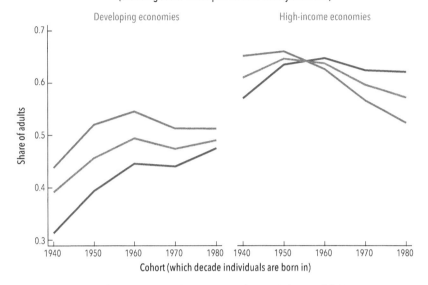

a. Share of adults with more education than their parents (*absolute upward mobility*)
(excluding adults whose parents have tertiary education)

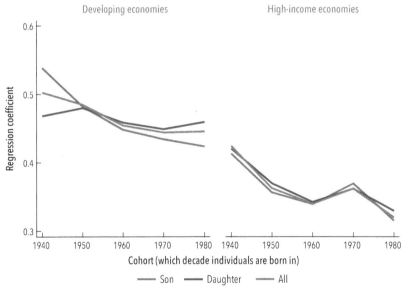

b. Intergenerational persistence in education (*relative mobility*)
(higher persistence indicates lower mobility)

Source: Calculations based on data in the GDIM 2018.
Note: Absolute upward mobility is measured by the share of individuals with more education than the maximum educational attainment of their parents, where education is defined in terms of five categories based on UIS (2012). Intergenerational persistence is measured by the coefficient from a regression of children's years of schooling on the years of schooling of their parents. The averages for developing and high-income groups are simple averages (unweighted by population) across economies in each group.

BOX 3.1   Key findings on relative mobility are unchanged if correlation is used to measure persistence

The key results on relative mobility highlighted in this chapter are robust to the choice of the correlation coefficient, instead of the regression coefficient, as a measure of intergenerational persistence. Regardless of which measure is used, relative intergenerational mobility (IGM) improved in high-income economies between the 1940s and the 1980s; the gap in relative IGM between high-income and developing economies has increased over time; and relative IGM among the 1980s generation is significantly greater in the average high-income economy than in the average developing economy. There are some differences, however, if the two different measures are used. Relative IGM in developing economies fell slightly between the 1940s and the 1980s if the correlation coefficient is used, but improved if the regression coefficient is used. Also, prior to the 1970s, the correlation coefficient shows relative IGM to be greater in the average developing economy than in the average high-income economy, whereas the former always lags the latter if the regression coefficient is used (figure B3.1.1).

The differences in the results using the two measures can be reconciled using the insights provided in annex 2A—the difference between the two measures depends on the ratio of the standard deviation of schooling in the generation of the offspring to the generation of the parents, a ratio that tends to decline as the average years of schooling increase. This ratio would also tend to be lower in high-income economies than in developing economies because the average years of schooling were much higher in the former, which explains why the average

FIGURE B3.1.1   Comparing relative mobility measures

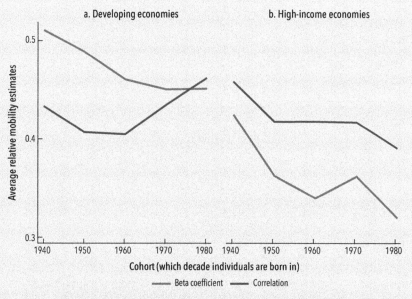

Source: Calculations based on data from the GDIM 2018.
Note: Intergenerational persistence is measured by the coefficient from the regression of the years of schooling of children on the years of schooling of parents. The averages for developing and high-income groups are simple (unweighted by population) across economies in each group.

box continues next page

BOX 3.1   Key findings on relative mobility are unchanged if correlation is used to measure persistence (continued)

developing economy prior to the 1970s exhibited a lower correlation coefficient than the average high-income economy despite the higher regression coefficient. Over time, as both the correlation coefficient and the ratio fell in high-income economies, the regression coefficient declined more than the correlation coefficient. In developing economies, the correlation coefficient actually increased, but the ratio of standard deviations fell enough to nudge the regression coefficient downward until the 1970s, after which it stagnated. Thus, the trend in relative mobility in the average high-income economy is robust to the choice of the measure of relative IGM, whereas the trend in the average developing economy is not. Both these coefficients are equally valid and widely used measures of relative IGM. The decision to focus on one of them (the regression coefficient) in this report is intended to help avoid the confusion that a multiplicity of measures can generate, and the choice is a matter of taste on account of the (slightly) more intuitive interpretation of the regression coefficient relative to the correlation coefficient.

fallen worldwide since the 1960s.[4] The underlying trends are less encouraging, however; the gap is closing because absolute IGM has been falling in advanced economies since the 1950 while staying on a flat trajectory in developing economies since the 1960s.[5] Some 47 percent of the 1980s generation in an average developing economy have more education than their parents, which is almost unchanged from the 1960s generation. Among the 1980s generation in the average high-income economy, 57 percent have more education than their parents, which is lower than the rate among the 1950s generation.

Progress in absolute mobility stalled in the average developing economy at a much lower level of educational attainment compared with the average high-income economy (see figure 3.1). Convergence in absolute IGM does not imply convergence in average educational attainment between high-income and developing economies; that gap is as large today as it was 40 years ago.

The estimates of absolute mobility may be affected by a "ceiling effect," which is a consequence of the fact that there is a maximum level of education any individual can attain. As economies develop and more individuals approach this ceiling, it becomes more difficult for offspring to outperform their parents, which may lead to a mechanical decline in absolute mobility. The absolute mobility measure used for this report deals with this ceiling effect by considering only individuals whose parents do not have a tertiary education. Using an alternate approach to deal with this ceiling effect, the main findings are found to be largely unchanged (box 3.2).

Developing economies have increasingly fallen behind high-income economies in relative mobility
Relative IGM, measured by intergenerational persistence in educational attainment, improved at a more rapid rate among high-income economies than among developing economies between the 1940s and the 1980s;

BOX 3.2   Trends in absolute mobility using alternate measures

An absolute mobility measure that fails to internalize the fact that a child whose parents have tertiary education cannot exceed that level can produce an apparent "decline" in absolute mobility as economies get richer and more educated. The preferred measure of absolute mobility used for this report deals with this issue by considering only individuals whose parents have completed upper secondary or less. To see how this assumption affects the findings, an alternate method of dealing with the "ceiling effect" is considered, whereby individuals whose parents have a tertiary education are considered upwardly mobile if they *match* their parents' level of education (see annex 2A for more details). Figure B3.2.1 compares the time-trends of this alternative measure (labeled "weakly") to the preferred measure for this report (labeled "baseline"). The "weakly" measure yields a slightly more optimistic picture of absolute mobility in developing and high-income economies since the 1960s. The overall trends, however, are broadly similar with the two alternative measures. Absolute mobility is still lower in the average developing economy than the average high-income economy; and, since the 1960s, absolute mobility has declined in the average high-income economy and improved slowly (as opposed to remaining unchanged with the baseline measure) for developing economies.

Because neither of the above measures captures the *extent* to which children outperform their parents, a third measure of absolute mobility is considered in annex 2A, as the average difference in years of schooling between parents and children. The results are, as expected, quite different, showing much more negative trends in absolute mobility since the 1960s, and particularly so for high-income economies. This measure, however, is likely to suffer from a severe ceiling effect, and provides no indication of the size or share of the population in a generation that has done better than their parents. The concept of absolute IGM as the share of a generation that outperforms their parents, used by this report, has the advantage of being simple and intuitive, which is also the reason why it has been widely adopted in recent literature, including Chetty et al. (2017).

FIGURE B3.2.1   Trends in absolute mobility based on different measures

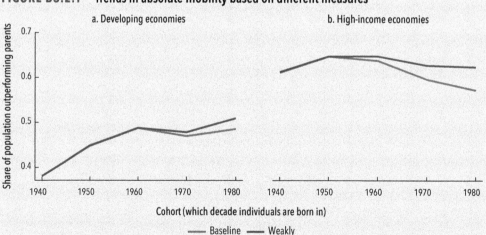

Source: Calculations based on data from GDIM 2018.
Note: Averages for developing and high-income groups are simple averages (unweighted by population) across economies in each group. *Baseline* shows the baseline measure of absolute mobility used in this report; the share of respondents attaining strictly more education than their parents, conditional on the parents not having tertiary education. *Weakly* shows the share attaining at least as much education as their parents.

this has widened the gap between the two groups of economies over time (figure 3.2, panel b). This is particularly true of the period between the 1970s and the 1980s, when relative IGM in the average developing economy showed no improvement while it was rising significantly in the average high-income economy. Relative IGM among the 1980s generation in the average developing economy is close to that of the 1940s generation in the average high-income economy. This shows the extent to which developing economies are lagging in relative mobility. The widening gap in relative IGM between high-income and developing economies is also seen if the correlation coefficient between parental and offspring educational attainment is used as the measure of intergenerational persistence (see box 3.1).

Mobility has improved in some developing regions, but declined or stagnated in two regions

Although IGM on average has improved across developing economies since the 1950s, the improvements are highly uneven and not evident everywhere. A regional breakdown of trends in the IGM between the 1950s cohort (figure 3.3, dots) and the 1980s cohort (figure 3.3, arrows) shows that positive changes are largely concentrated in East Asia and the Pacific, Latin America and the Caribbean, and the Middle East and North Africa. In contrast, absolute IGM and relative IGM have declined in Eastern Europe and Central Asia and stagnated in Sub-Saharan Africa (Africa hereafter). In South Asia, there have been improvements in absolute mobility but not in relative mobility. The findings on Africa are broadly consistent with estimates available from earlier research for a smaller number of economies.[6]

FIGURE 3.3 Changes in intergenerational mobility, by region

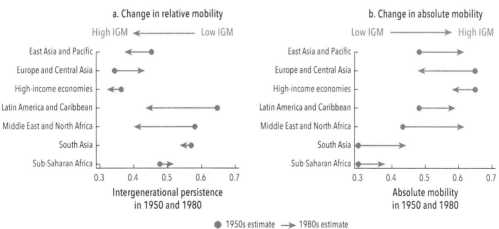

Source: Calculations based on data in the GDIM 2018.
Note: Averages are not weighted by population. Regional averages exclude high-income economies (if any). The figure does not include economies for which estimates are available only for the 1980s cohort. IGM = intergenerational mobility.

Because the mobility trends end with the 1980s cohort—the last cohort who would have completed their education at the time of survey—they do not reflect any progress made in the last decade or so. Significant increases in enrollments, particularly in regions where enrollments (and mobility) were relatively lower to start with such as in Africa, may signal an increase in mobility for individuals born in the 1990s or later. Estimates presented toward the end of this chapter suggest that regional patterns in relative mobility largely carry over to younger cohorts who have not yet reached the age at which they are expected to complete their education. On the other hand, rough predictions of absolute mobility among younger cohorts suggest that the gap between Africa and other developing regions in absolute IGM may have narrowed between the 1980s cohort and the 1990s cohort.

Comparing the trends in absolute IGM and in relative IGM, the two measures have moved in the same direction in all developing regions, but in opposite directions in high-income economies. This may have occurred because, in many high-income economies, educational attainment in the 1950s was sufficient to make more improvement in absolute mobility difficult, whereas relative mobility has continued to improve as access to education has become more equal because of public investments (see the discussion in chapter 4). In contrast, in all developing regions, improvements in educational attainment from a much lower base in the 1950s has led to a rise in absolute mobility, whereas relative mobility has improved or stagnated.

Mobility among the current generation varies significantly among developing and high-income economies alike, with the lowest mobility seen in some of the poorest parts of the world

Among developing economies, there is large variation, including geographic disparities, in absolute and relative IGM among the current (1980s) generation. Figure 3.4 shows that average absolute mobility in East Asia and the Pacific and in the Middle East and North Africa is at or above the high-income average. East Asia and the Pacific is also well ahead of the other developing regions in relative mobility. At the other end of the spectrum is Africa, where absolute and relative mobility are well below the average in developing economies.

The gap between the well- and nonperforming economies is vast (map 3.1). Only 12 percent of the people born in the 1980s in the Central African Republic, Guinea, and South Sudan have achieved higher education levels than their parents, compared with 89 percent of residents of the Republic of Korea and 85 percent of Thais born in the same decade.

Some of the lowest IGM rates are in Africa, which includes some of the poorest and most fragile parts of the world (map 3.1). Of the 15 economies in the bottom decile of absolute mobility, 12 are in Africa, and 5 of these 12 are in fragile situations. In the average economy of Africa, 35 percent of people born in the 1980s exhibit higher educational attainment than their parents, compared with 57 percent of the same generation in the average economy of East Asia and the Pacific. In relative mobility, 10 of the 15 economies in the bottom decile are in Africa, including four in fragile

FIGURE 3.4   Absolute upward mobility and relative mobility among the 1980s cohort, averages by region and income group

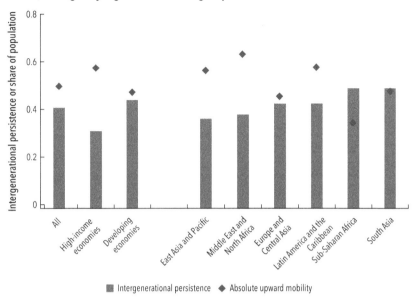

Source: Calculations based on data in the GDIM 2018.
Note: Averages are not weighted by population. Higher intergenerational persistence implies lower relative mobility. Regions are sorted in decreasing order of relative mobility.

MAP 3.1   Intergenerational mobility across the world: The 1980s generation

a. Share of adults with more education than their parents: Absolute upward mobility

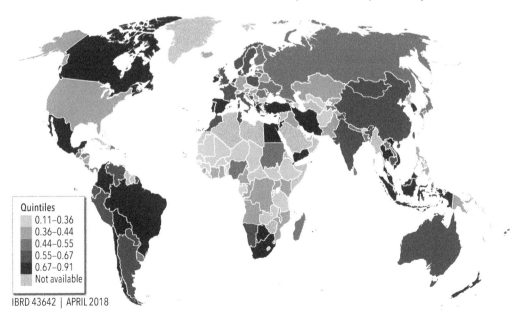

map continues next page

MAP 3.1   Intergenerational mobility across the world: the 1980s generation (continued)

b. Intergenerational persistence in education: Relative mobility

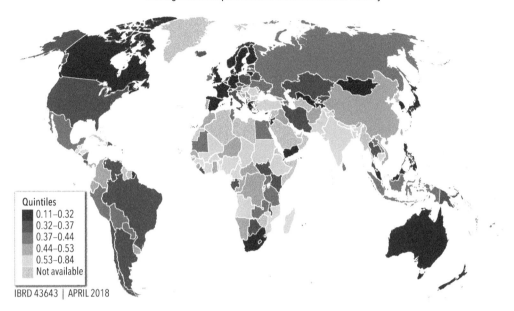

Quintiles
0.11–0.32
0.32–0.37
0.37–0.44
0.44–0.53
0.53–0.84
Not available

IBRD 43643 | APRIL 2018

Source: Calculations based on data in GDIM 2018.
Note: Absolute mobility is the share of individuals with higher educational attainment than their parents. Intergenerational persistence is the coefficient from the regression of children's years of schooling on parents' years of schooling. Greater persistence indicates lower relative mobility. The darker shade indicates higher relative or absolute mobility.

situations. The average relative IGM in economies in Africa and South Asia is almost 25 percent lower than the average in East Asia and the Pacific.

Economies affected by fragility, conflict, and violence (FCV) are an important source of concern because they appear to have consistently lower IGMs on average compared to the developing economy averages (box 3.3).[7] These findings underscore the severe challenges faced by FCV economies, both in terms of absolute improvements in welfare and fairness. The lack of improvements in either type of mobility in recent years also hints at one of the many factors that may be contributing to social instability in these economies, some of which are also among the poorest of the world.

Absolute mobility and relative mobility in education among the 1980s generation are correlated, but imperfectly

On average, economies with a higher share of adults who are more educated than their parents are also economies in which the educational attainment of individuals is less dependent on the educational attainment of their parents (figure 3.5). This is consistent with the view that absolute and relative mobility complement and reinforce each other. Extreme outliers in this association may be grouped into two main categories. One comprises high- or upper-middle-income economies that exhibit substantial absolute mobility because of a rapid rise in education levels from a lower starting point than economies that developed earlier. For example, while the Republic of

BOX 3.3   Average mobility in fragility, conflict, and violence–affected economies is lower than the developing economy average

The seven fragility, conflict, and violence (FCV) affected economies for which intergenerational mobility (IGM) can be estimated for all cohorts have lower average IGM, absolute and relative, compared to the developing economy average, for the entire period (figure B.3.3.1). The trend in average absolute IGM in these FCV economies closely follows the trend for the developing economy average, but with lower levels of absolute mobility. In relative IGM, the average for the seven FCV economies shows a decline from the 1970s cohort to the 1980s cohort, compared to almost no change during this period in the developing economy average. The historically low rates of IGM in these economies are also consistent with the view that low mobility across generations may be one of the factors that contribute to social instability over time (see chapter 1). These trends may not be representative of the FCV group because they include just 7 out of 36 FCV economies. However, IGMs for the 1980s cohort, which can be estimated for as many as 26 FCV economies, confirm that the average IGMs for this group are lower than the developing economy averages, even though they are higher than the averages for the FCV economies included in figure B3.3.1.

FIGURE B3.3.1   Mobility is consistently lower in seven fragility, conflict, and violence–affected economies than the developing-economy average

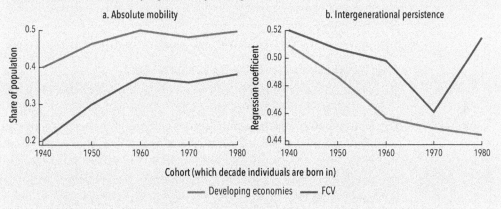

Source: Calculations based on data in the GDIM 2018.
Note: Absolute mobility is measured by the share of individuals with more education than the maximum educational attainment of their parents. Intergenerational persistence is measured by the coefficient from a regression of children's years of schooling on the years of schooling of their parents. Higher persistence indicates lower relative mobility. The averages for FCV and developing economies are simple averages (unweighted by population) for each group. The FCV group in this figure includes 7 economies (out of the 36 listed in the World Bank Group's Harmonized List of Fragile Situations for 2018): the Comoros, the Democratic Republic of Congo, Iraq, Kosovo, Liberia, Mali, and Togo. FCV = fragility, conflict, and violence.

Korea and Malaysia show high relative mobility (comparable with Denmark and Japan, respectively), they have much greater absolute mobility, indeed among the greatest in the world. The other category of outliers includes some low-income or fragile economies in which low intergenerational persistence coexists with low absolute mobility. This phenomenon demonstrates the need from an economy's development perspective to focus on both types of mobility rather than exclusively on relative mobility.

FIGURE 3.5   Absolute mobility and relative mobility are correlated, but with many outliers

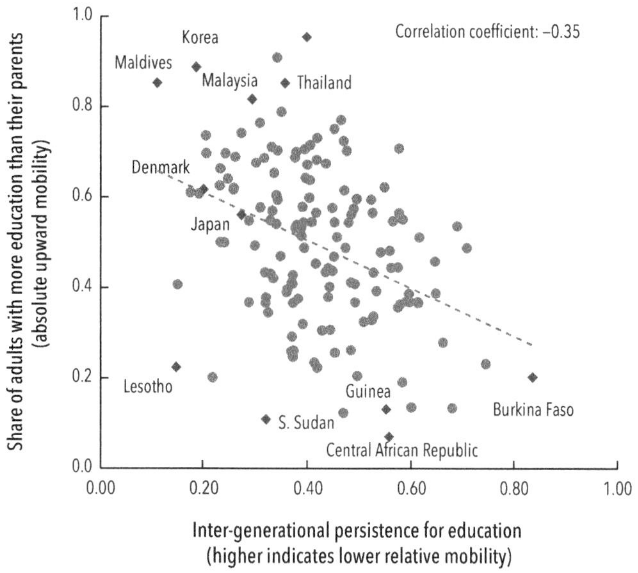

Source: Calculations based on GDIM 2018.
Note: 1980s cohort only.

Mobility from the Bottom to the Top across the World

Relative IGM obtained from a regression of the education of individuals on the education of their parents does not distinguish between upward and downward mobility. Although the measure of absolute mobility—the share of individuals with higher educational attainment than their parents—does capture a form of upward mobility, it does not capture the influence of parental background on one's educational success relative to individuals in the same generation. For example, it is conceivable that most of the individuals born to uneducated parents surpass their parents in educational attainment, even if none of the former obtains an education that places them near the top of the educational attainment among their generation. This serves as motivation to examine the so-called poverty-to-privilege rate, which refers to the share of individuals who make it to the top quartile of education in their generation out of those who were born with parents with education in the bottom half of their generation.[8]

Mobility from the bottom to the top is low almost everywhere, but the lowest rates occur mostly in developing economies

In a large majority of economies across the world, one's chances of reaching the top quarter of the ladder of educational attainment depend largely on where one's parents stood on that ladder (figure 3.6). This share would be 0.25 if one's ability to obtain an education did not depend on how well-educated one's parents are. However, there are few economies in which the share exceeds 0.20. The developing world dominates on the list of economies with the lowest share among the 1980s generation. Among the bottom 50 economies, 46 are developing, whereas only 4 are high income, including the United States. In the median developing economy, less than

FIGURE 3.6   Share of individuals in the 1980s cohort who are born into the bottom half and who have reached the top quartile

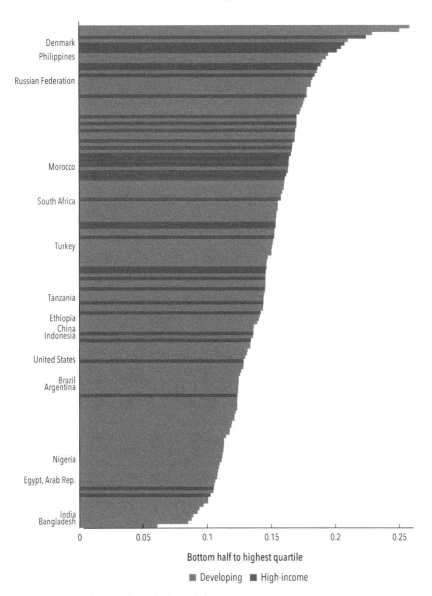

Source: Calculations based on data in the GDIM 2018.
Note: 1980s cohort only. 146 economies: for illustrative purposes, only a few are named.

FIGURE 3.7   Movement from the bottom to the top

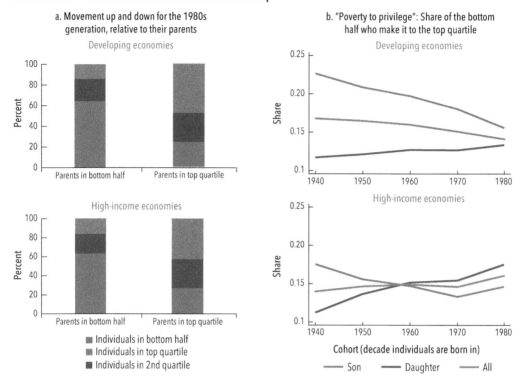

Source: Calculations based on data in the GDIM (World Bank).
Note: Panel a shows the share of individuals in each of three categories out of all individuals with parents in each of two categories.

15 percent of individuals born in the bottom half make it to the top quarter, while more than two-thirds stay in the bottom half.

The persistence at the top or the bottom is substantial around the globe and is far more common than the movement from poverty to privilege. In the average developing economy, 48 percent of individuals in the 1980s generation who had parents in the top quartile in educational attainment remained at the top, compared with 14 percent who had parents in the bottom half but who reached the top quartile (figure 3.7, panel a). The corresponding shares in high-income economies (43 percent and 16 percent, respectively) are sufficiently close to suggest that persistence at the top should be a concern across the world rather than only in developing economies. Education is not the only factor influencing earning ability, but it is sufficiently critical to suggest that a lack of income mobility at the bottom and the persistence of privilege are common almost everywhere.

Upward mobility is declining in the developing world,
whereas persistence at the bottom is rising

The poverty-to-privilege rate was higher in developing economies than in high-income economies in the 1940s. It has since moved in the opposite direction so that the share of individuals born in the bottom half who now reach the top is slightly higher in high-income economies than in developing economies (figure 3.7, panel b).

As upward mobility from the bottom has declined, results not reported here show that persistence at the bottom has increased in developing economies. This rate was lower in developing economies than in high-income economies in the 1940s, but has since risen in the former to exceed the rate in high-income economies. In developing economies, a rising trend in the intergenerational transmission of low educational attainment is a sobering development. It suggests that, among individuals born in poorer households, the opportunity to climb the income scale is narrowing in many economies in which average living standards are still low compared with high-income economies.

Trends in the Gender Gap in Mobility

Girls have moved ahead of boys in absolute mobility in high-income economies and are rapidly closing the gap in developing economies

Girls in high-income economies now exhibit higher rates of tertiary education and absolute IGM than boys (see figure 3.1, panel b and figure 3.2, panel a). While girls had a disadvantage until the 1950s, the gender gap reversed in the 1960s, and the advantage of girls has grown in high-income economies. In high-income economies since the 1960s, girls also have higher rates of mobility from the bottom to the top (figure 3.7, panel b) and lower rates of persistence at the bottom than boys (figure 3.8).

The trend in the same direction is strong in the developing world. Women have already caught up with men in tertiary education in developing economies, and the gender gap is narrowing rapidly in absolute mobility (see figure 3.2, panel a). These trends suggest a not-too-distant future when upward mobility relative to parents will be greater among girls than among boys in the developing world.

Trends in relative mobility among girls, compared with boys, present a mixed picture. Results not shown suggest that the rate of intergenerational privilege among girls is higher, that is, daughters with highly educated parents are more likely than sons to be in the top quartile in educational attainment. At the same time, in the developing world, the likelihood of climbing from the bottom to the top has been rising among girls relative to boys (figure 3.7, panel b), whereas the likelihood of staying at the bottom has been falling (figure 3.8). This was not always the case. Sons used to be less constrained than daughters by the circumstances into which they are born, particularly in the developing world. But, over the last 40 years, this gender gap has largely been closed in the average developing economy (see figure 3.7, panel b; figure 3.12). This may not be true of all economies. India and Nigeria are two prominent examples of economies in which the gender gap persists.

FIGURE 3.8   Intergenerational poverty: Probability that a child with parents in the bottom half stays there

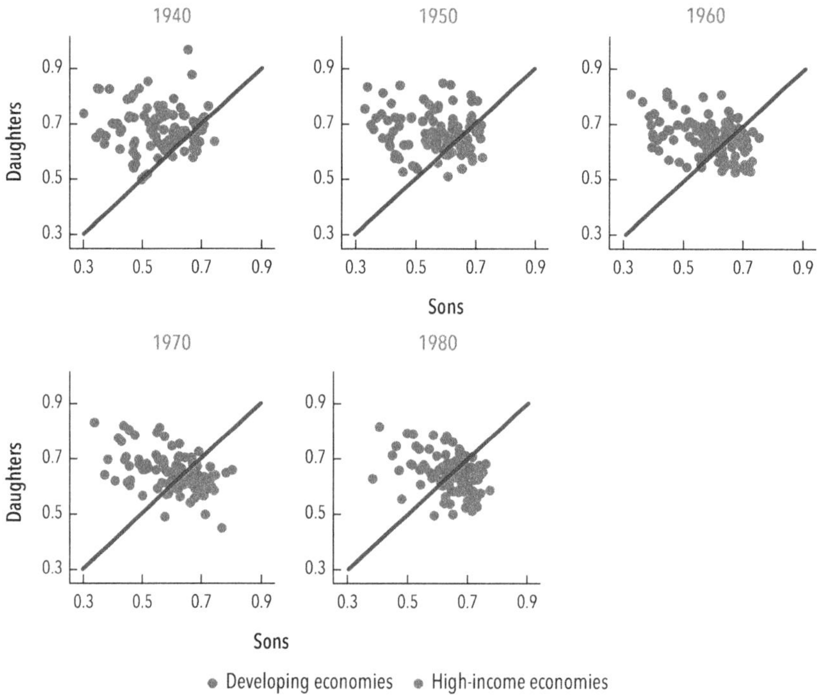

● Developing economies   ● High-income economies

Source: Calculations based on data in the GDIM 2018.
Note: The figure compares intergenerational persistence of poverty among sons and daughters. Each point below the 45-degree line indicates an economy with lower persistence of poverty among daughters than among sons in the same cohort.

Greater Mobility Is Associated with Better Economic Outcomes

Greater Intergenerational Mobility Is Associated with Higher National Income across Economies

Absolute IGM and relative IGM are both greater in the average high-income economy than in the average developing economy (see figure 3.2). Across economies, the difference in averages reflects a consistent pattern: greater mobility is associated with higher levels of gross domestic product (GDP). Figure 3.9, panels a and b, which consider variations both between and within economies, show that relative IGM increases with per capita GDP if the latter exceeds $2,500 per capita (1990 purchasing power parity). This may occur because the policies needed to equalize opportunities may not be affordable at lower levels of national income (chapter 4). Absolute mobility, meanwhile, is positively associated with national income at relatively low levels of income and is unchanged in the case of per capita GDP above $5,000 per capita. This may derive from a convergence effect: raising educational attainment is likely to become more difficult after a certain threshold of attainment has been reached.

Does mobility tend to improve as economies become wealthier? Figure 3.9, panels c and d, track trends in relative mobility and national

FIGURE 3.9   Intergenerational mobility and gross domestic product per capita

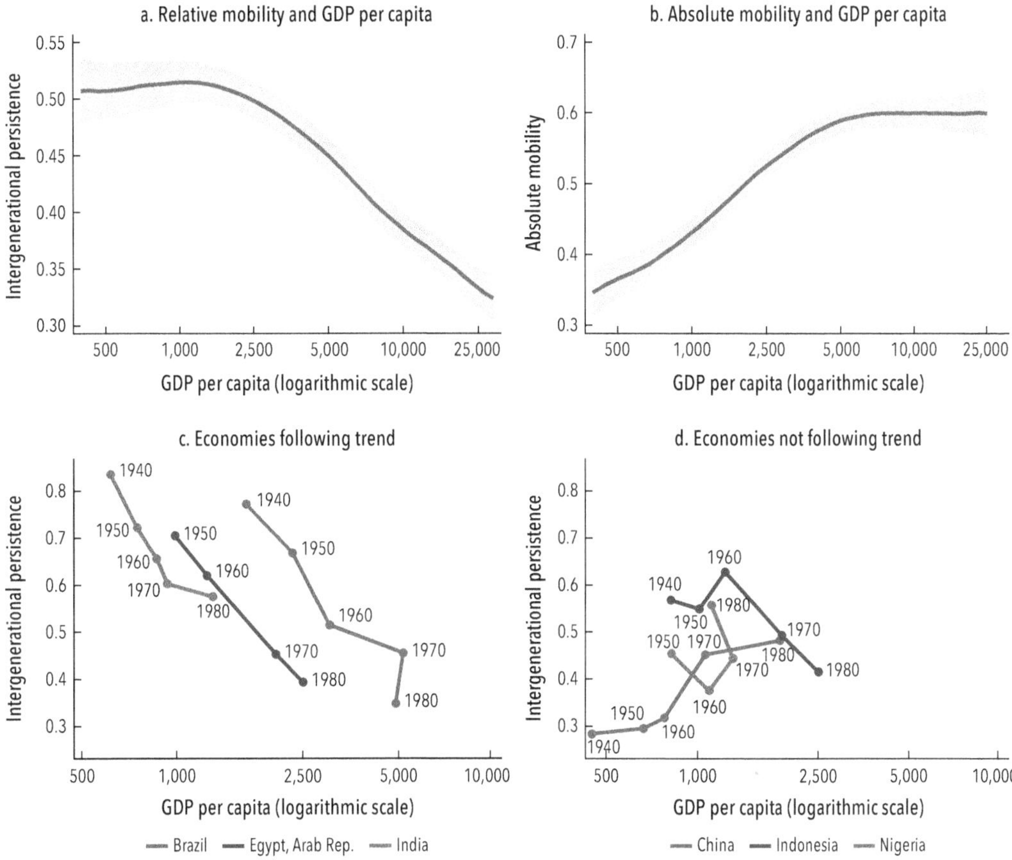

a. Relative mobility and GDP per capita

b. Absolute mobility and GDP per capita

c. Economies following trend

d. Economies not following trend

Brazil — Egypt, Arab Rep. — India

China — Indonesia — Nigeria

Source: Calculations based on data in GDIM 2018.
Note: The shaded areas indicate 95 percent confidence intervals.

income in six large developing economies. In four of these economies, mobility increases with national income. This is not, however, the case of China or, to a lesser extent, Nigeria, which suggests that rising income may not necessarily lead to greater relative mobility.

The positive association between IGM and economic development is consistent with a two-way relationship predicted by the theoretical literature (chapter 1).[9] Greater mobility boosts long-term economic growth because it promotes the accumulation of human capital. Greater relative mobility may also lead to a more efficient allocation of human capital resources, which is good for growth (chapter 1, box 1.3).[10] Economic growth in turn can enhance relative and absolute mobility by lifting credit constraints. Economies with higher income levels also tend to have higher levels of public spending on human capital development, which leads to higher relative mobility if public spending has an equalizing effect on opportunities (chapter 4).

Greater mobility is associated with greater gross domestic product growth and poverty reduction in subsequent years

Greater absolute IGM and relative IGM in education among a generation are both associated with greater economic growth and less poverty when the generation reaches adulthood, using cross-country regressions (figure 3.10). In the case of poverty, the relationship is largely driven by a strong association between the poverty rate and upward mobility among households with little or no education (or by the extent to which individuals born to relatively uneducated parents obtain an education).[11] The economic significance of this relationship can be illustrated by a back-of-the-envelope calculation based on such regressions. The rise of an economy from the bottom quartile

FIGURE 3.10   Greater mobility is associated with greater economic growth and less poverty

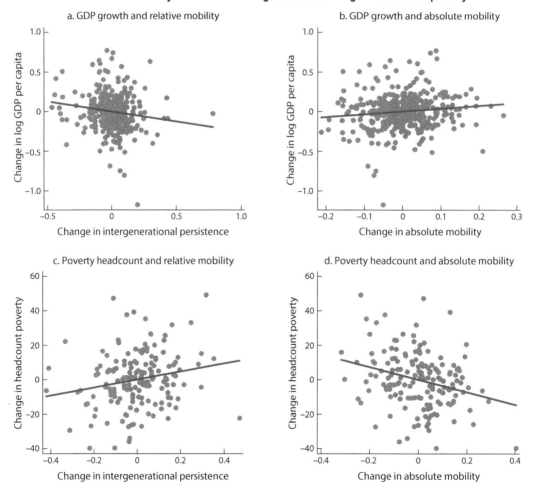

Source: Calculations based on data in the GDIM 2018.
Note: The top (bottom) panel regresses the residual log GDP (headcount poverty at $1.90 purchasing power parity) on residual mobility. The residual variables are obtained by first regressing the corresponding variable on lagged log GDP, cohort and economy (seven regions) fixed effects. GDP is lagged by 20 years; GDP (poverty) data cover 1940–2000 (1980–2000).

of economies according to relative IGM to the top quartile is associated with an increase in GDP per capita of about 10 percent when the generation reaches adulthood.

Even though they are significant, these empirical patterns do not necessarily mean that greater IGM causes greater growth and poverty reduction but, rather, that economies with greater IGM in education are also likely to exhibit higher rates of growth and poverty reduction subsequently. The relationship might be attributable, at least in part, to factors that are not accounted for here. For example, the same conditions that favor mobility in an economy, including public policies, may also be good for economic growth in the longer run; and, conversely, richer economies might be more able to afford public policies and investments that promote mobility.

Given that mobility and economic development reinforce each other, the stalled progress in absolute mobility and relative mobility in the developing world and the large gaps with respect to high-income economies raise important concerns about the prospects for growth and poverty reduction. These concerns are particularly strong in economies where mobility is exceptionally low, many but not all of which are low-income or fragile economies. Nonetheless, the rising absolute IGM among girls—even as progress among boys and girls taken together has been stalled since the 1960s—is a positive sign for economic growth and for reducing inequality of opportunity in developing economies. In high-income economies, meanwhile, the widening in the reverse gender gap since the 1950s suggests that education outcomes among boys need to improve to raise mobility and the prospects for growth.

Greater relative mobility is associated with lower inequality

The relationship between relative IGM and income inequality is mutually reinforcing. Lower relative IGM in income is known to be associated with higher income inequality, as illustrated by the Great Gatsby curve of various researchers (chapter 1). Similar patterns are exhibited by relative mobility in education, particularly in developing economies. Higher education inequality during the schooling years of a cohort is associated with lower relative mobility, which is akin to a Gatsby curve in education (figure 3.11, panels a and b).[12] Lower relative mobility in education among a particular generation is also associated with higher income inequality during the peak earning years of that generation (figure 3.11, panels c and d). Both these correlations are much stronger in developing economies than in high-income economies (figure 3.11, panels b and d). Absolute IGM is not correlated with inequality in education or income in either direction (not shown here).

The Gatsby curve is likely to be the consequence of a two-way relationship: higher inequality tends to limit relative mobility, which worsens inequality over time (chapter 1). This is because higher inequality leads to more unequal parental investments in children and affects the policies, institutions, and balance of power in society that shape opportunities, and unequal opportunities lead in turn to lower relative mobility and more

FIGURE 3.11   Lower relative mobility in education is associated with higher inequality in education and income, particularly in developing economies

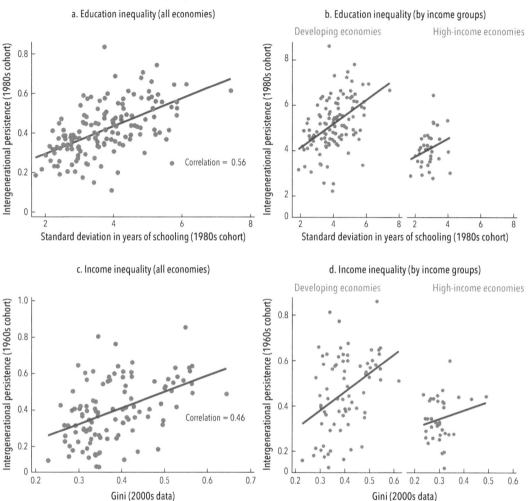

Source: Calculations based on data in the GDIM 2018.
Note: Panels a and b: inequality measured by the standard deviation of education in the same decade. Panels c and d: relative mobility for the 1960s cohort has been chosen so that the inequality data correspond to the prime earning years of the cohort.

inequality in the next generation.[13] The correlations in figure 3.11 hint at this circular relationship. Higher inequality in education is associated with lower relative mobility in education, which is associated with higher income inequality in a subsequent period when the generation has reached peak earning potential.

Mobility in Some of the World's Largest Developing Economies

The trends in mobility reported so far reflect unweighted averages across economies. Results not reported here confirm that population-weighted estimates show similar patterns. Population-weighted averages are largely driven by a small number of the world's largest economies (in terms of population). This section examines six of these giants from the developing and emerging world, namely, Brazil, China, the Arab Republic of Egypt, India, Indonesia, and Nigeria. These economies are sufficiently large to permit a study of subnational trends and patterns in IGM.

Many of the Global Patterns Identified above Carry Over to the Large Developing Economies

Absolute mobility rose in all six large economies from the 1940s to the 1980s; Egypt and Indonesia show the largest increase, and Nigeria exhibits the smallest increase (figure 3.12). The trends in absolute mobility in China and Nigeria largely match the trend in average developing economies: an increase in the early decades, but a leveling off at around 50 percent beginning in the 1960s. In Brazil, Egypt, India, and Indonesia, absolute mobility continued rising until the 1980s, reaching more than 60 percent.

Relative mobility has increased in Brazil, Egypt, India, and Indonesia, while it declined in China and Nigeria (see figure 3.12). The declining trend in relative mobility in China and Nigeria contrasts with the gradually rising trend in the average developing economy. In the case of India, even though relative mobility has continued to improve from one generation to the next, it is still low by international standards and the lowest among the six large developing economies. This is also consistent with the fact that India is among the bottom five economies in upward mobility from the bottom to the top in educational attainment (see figure 3.6).

Greater relative mobility is associated with higher income at the subnational level as well

Provinces with greater relative mobility among the 1980s generation are likely to exhibit higher GDP per capita in five of the six economies (figure 3.13). This is consistent with the finding that mobility and national income trend in the same direction (see figure 3.9). China is the notable exception; there, provinces with greater relative mobility tend to be poorer. Mobility maps drawn for five of the six economies provide a snapshot of IGM among the 1980s generation across states or provinces (map 3A.1). Provinces with greater absolute IGM are also likely to have greater relative IGM in most of these economies, but the correlation is imperfect, and there are several outliers. The correlation is the lowest in China, which is consistent with the fact that China is the single economy in which relative IGM tends to be lower in richer provinces.[14]

Gender convergence in relative mobility has occurred in four of the six economies

The global trends in gender convergence are also evident in four of the six large economies considered here (figure 3A.1). In Brazil, China, Egypt, and

FIGURE 3.12 Absolute mobility and relative mobility in selected developing economies

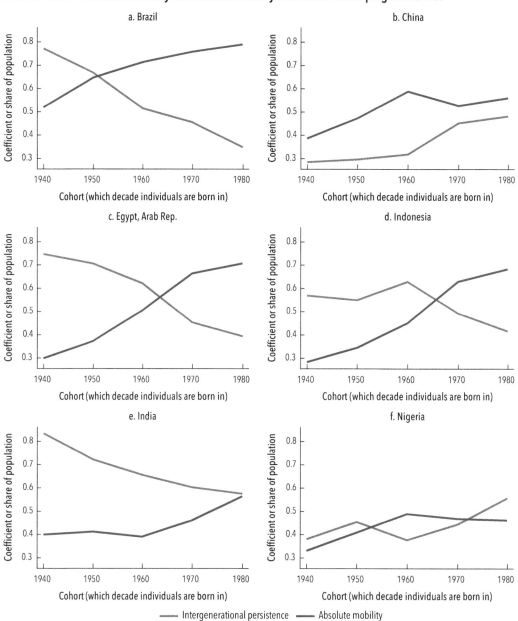

Source: Calculations based on data in GDIM 2018.

FIGURE 3.13   Intergenerational persistence and province-level gross domestic product per capita

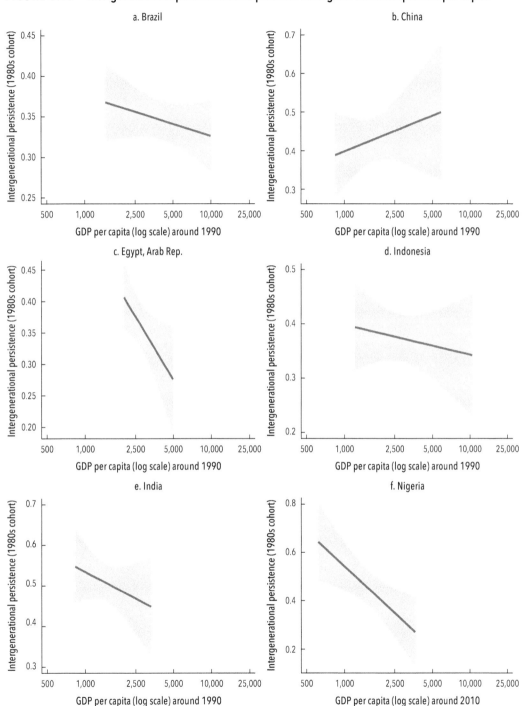

Source: Calculations based on data in GDIM 2018. The shaded areas indicate 95 percent confidence intervals.
Note: GDP = gross domestic product.

Indonesia, the gender gaps are close to zero among the current generation.[15] No such convergence is observed in India and Nigeria, where the gender gaps are almost as large among the 1980s generation as among cohorts born in the 1940 and 1950s.

Mobility across Multiple Generations: Do Grandparents Matter?

To assess long-term mobility in an economy, one needs to consider the persistence of outcomes across not only two, but multiple generations. Consider an economy in which educational attainment among grandparents directly influences the educational attainment of the current generation over and above the effect transmitted through parental education. Such an economy would exhibit more persistence across three generations than an economy in which the education of grandparents matters for the education of the current generation only to the extent it influences the education of the parents of the current generation.

The literature on multigenerational mobility is sparse, possibly because of the data requirements. Some of the early theoretical models of multigenerational mobility provide arguments for a negative effect of grandparents on children, conditional on the outcomes among the parents.[16] However, this prediction can be reversed if grandparents contribute directly through cultural inheritance, if there are group effects such as racial discrimination, or if there is measurement error.[17] A recent summary of the handful of articles written about multigenerational mobility concludes that, in general, grandparents do not have any appreciable direct effect beyond the indirect effects through parents.[18] Only two recent papers—one on rural China and the other on a city in Sweden—seem to suggest otherwise.[19] Apart from the first of these studies, there is little evidence on multigenerational mobility in developing economies.

Grandparents Also Matter, but Not as Much as Parents and Mostly in Developing Economies

The years of schooling of parents and that of grandparents matter for an individual's years of schooling, although the effect is notably smaller in the case of grandparents relative to parents. In regressions with individual years of schooling as the dependent variable in 39 economies in which multigenerational links could be established, the coefficient associated with parental years of schooling is, on average, two to three times larger than the coefficient associated with grandparents (figure 3.14).

Most of the estimated coefficients in figure 3.14, panel a, are located between the diagonal and vertical lines. (The diagonal line corresponds to the 45-degree line, while the vertical line corresponds to a zero effect of grandparents.) This suggests that the educational attainment of parents and grandparents has a positive effect on the education of the current generation, but the effect of parents is stronger than the effect of grandparents. In figure 3.14, panel b, both the coefficients are plotted against

FIGURE 3.14   Persistence in education across three generations tends to be greater in developing economies

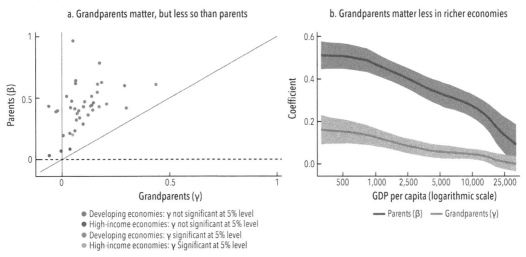

a. Grandparents matter, but less so than parents

b. Grandparents matter less in richer economies

● Developing economies: γ not significant at 5% level
● High-income economies: γ not significant at 5% level
● Developing economies: γ significant at 5% level
● High-income economies: γ Significant at 5% level

— Parents (β)   — Grandparents (γ)

Source: Calculations based on data in the GDIM 2018.
Note: The shaded areas indicate 95 percent confidence intervals. The panels show coefficients of the regression $educ_{child} = \alpha + \beta * educ_{parent} + \gamma * educ_{grandparent} + \varepsilon$. GDP = gross domestic product.

national incomes in the respective economies. Controlling for parental education, one finds that the effect of the education of grandparents is often significant, but the significance tends to be less in richer economies. This might also explain why the empirical literature on multigenerational mobility, which is primarily focused on high-income economies, has not found that the effect of the education of grandparents is crucial in the education of the current generation.

These results imply that longer-term relative mobility in education in developing economies may even be lower than suggested by the estimates here that measure persistence across two generations. Also, the disadvantages of birth in a family with low educational attainment are more likely to persist across several generations in poorer economies than in richer ones.

What Do Today's Enrollments Suggest about Intergenerational Mobility of the Next Generation?

The standard estimates of IGM discussed so far are more a reflection of what has happened in the past. Yet current patterns of child educational outcomes and the ways these are associated with parental socioeconomic status offer a window into future mobility. Even though the economic status of the next generation will depend on more factors than education, such as the efficiency and fairness of factor markets, education is likely to continue to play a key role in economic mobility across generations.

Poverty and Lack of Parental Education Restrict Upward Mobility among Children in Poorer Economies

In low- and lower middle-income economies, the likelihood of enrollment among the 7–11, 12–14, and 15–17 age groups, which roughly correspond to primary, lower-secondary, and upper-secondary school, respectively, rises with parental income and education (figure 3.15). Also, if parental educational attainment is low, the enrollments of older children in secondary education are sensitive to relatively low household income.[20] Given the well-documented problems in learning outcomes that children in economically disadvantaged households experience, inequality of opportunity in education is likely to be higher than suggested by enrollment profiles once the quality of learning is considered (chapter 5).

Across regions, the prospects of relative mobility are lowest among children in Africa and South Asia

Relative IGM among adults born in the 1980s is particularly low in Africa and South Asia (see figure 3.4). Rising enrollments in the last decade in these regions, as public investment in education has expanded, may have enhanced mobility among subsequent generations. But this cannot be verified using available survey data because the cohorts of the 1990s and 2000s were not yet old enough to have completed their education at the time of the surveys. It is feasible, however, to examine an alternative measure of educational attainment among individuals in these more recent cohorts, which may be called the educational shortfall.

The educational shortfall of a child is defined as the difference between the observed years of schooling completed and the years of schooling that should have been completed according to the child's age. This serves as a reasonable proxy for an individual's expected educational attainment.[21] The shortfall is evaluated separately for children aged 6–11 and 12–17, which are roughly the primary- and secondary-school age groups, respectively. Intergenerational persistence in education shortfall among children is measured by the coefficient of a Tobit regression of children's shortfall on parental years of schooling. These estimates of persistence can be considered as a proxy for relative IGM of young cohorts, but they are not directly comparable with persistence in the educational attainment of adults because of obvious differences in methodology.

Figure 3.16 shows average intergenerational persistence in the educational shortfall among cohorts aged 6–11 and 12–17 and in educational attainment among the 1980s generation in five of the six developing regions using only those economies on which the shortfall variable can be constructed.[22] The results indicate that relative mobility among the younger cohorts is the lowest in Africa and South Asia, similar to the case of the 1980s generation. This suggests that the gaps in relative mobility between Africa and South Asia and the other regions are likely to persist among the next generation of adults. Among children aged 5–11, the gaps in persistence between Africa and South Asia and the other regions are smaller but still present.

FIGURE 3.15   Enrollment patterns suggest limited educational mobility among children of poor or less-educated parents

a. Likelihood of being enrolled by parental income, for different age groups

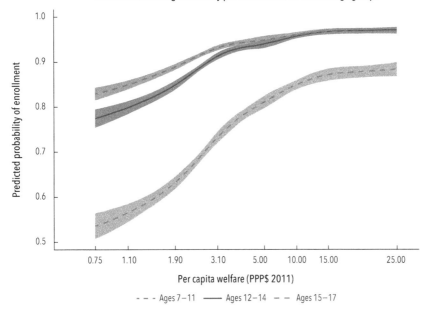

b. Likelihood of being enrolled by parental income, as parental education varies

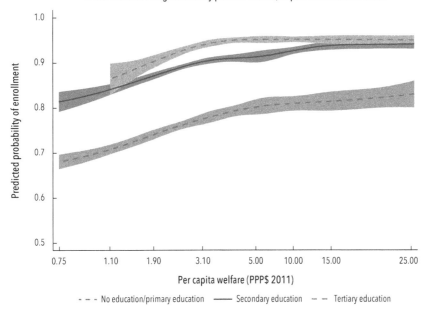

Source: Evans, Newhouse, and Suarez-Becerra (forthcoming).
Note: Estimates refer to 67 low- and lower-middle-income economies and 78 percent of all children in the 7–17 age group. The shaded areas indicate 95 percent confidence intervals.

FIGURE 3.16   Intergenerational persistence among younger children

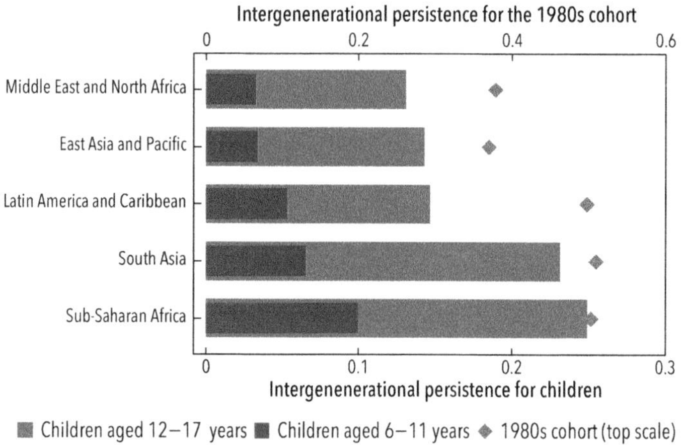

Intergenenerational persistence for the 1980s cohort

| | 0 | 0.2 | 0.4 | 0.6 |

Middle East and North Africa

East Asia and Pacific

Latin America and Caribbean

South Asia

Sub-Saharan Africa

| | 0 | 0.1 | 0.2 | 0.3 |

Intergenenerational persistence for children

■ Children aged 12−17 years   ■ Children aged 6−11 years   ◆ 1980s cohort (top scale)

Source: Calculations based on data in the GDIM 2018.
Note: Intergenerational persistence for children is the regression coefficient of a Tobit regression of children's "education shortfall" on parental years of schooling. Education shortfall: observed years of education−(age of child−5).

Given the current schooling profiles, it therefore appears that the prospects of children will continue to be tied to parental educational attainment more closely in Africa and South Asia than in any other region of the world. Such persistence points to high inequality of opportunity among children in these two regions, which translates to a loss of human potential that harms the prospects for growth. Moreover, high inequality of opportunity that translates to low relative mobility is also likely to perpetuate income inequality across generations (see chapter 1), making growth less inclusive with further adverse consequences for poverty reduction in two regions that are also home to most of the world's poor. Even among the youngest age group, persistence is particularly significant in Africa, which indicates the uphill challenge to promoting upward mobility in the poorest region of the world.

In absolute mobility, Africa may be catching up with other developing regions among younger cohorts

Among adults born in the 1980s, absolute mobility is particularly low in Africa compared to other developing regions, whereas South Asia has almost caught up with the developing world average (figure 3.4). With rising enrollments, the prospects of absolute mobility may have increased in these two regions among younger cohorts. In Africa for example, average enrollment in primary school increased from 73 to 98 percent between 1996 and 2014, which may signal an increase in absolute mobility for the 1990s cohort.[23] Rough predictions of what absolute mobility might look like for the 1990s cohort hint that average absolute IGM in Africa may be improving faster than in the previous two decades and catching up with the developing economy average. Absolute IGM among the 1990s cohort in South Asia may have caught up with or even surpassed the developing economy average (box 3.4).

BOX 3.4 Rough estimates of absolute upward mobility among the 1990s cohort

Using available data, rough predictions of what absolute IGM might look like for the 1990s cohort can be obtained under some strong assumptions. First, given that the completed level of education is unknown for only those individuals who are still enrolled in school, upper and lower bounds on absolute IGM of the 1990s cohort can be obtained by considering two extreme scenarios, respectively: (1) all those who are enrolled will go on to surpass the level of education of their parents, and (2) all those who are enrolled will not complete any education level higher than the level they have already completed. Second, point estimates can be obtained by imposing stricter assumptions to convert "education shortfall" (the number of years a child is behind in school) of each child still enrolled in school into an estimated likelihood he or she will surpass the education of his or her parents (see annex 3A for details). All surveys that cover the 1990s cohort are included in this exercise. This excludes, however, all surveys from the Europe and Central Asia region and half of the surveys from the Latin America and Caribbean region (where data are collected only for individuals above a certain age). In total, this analysis covers 43 developing economies representing 64 percent of the population in the developing world.

FIGURE B3.4.1 Absolute mobility of the 1990s Cohort: Estimates and bounds

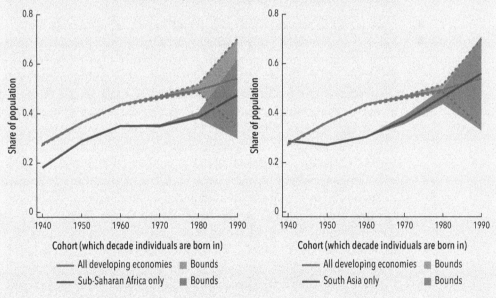

Source: Calculations based on data from the GDIM 2018.
Note: The bounds and point estimate of absolute mobility for the 1990s cohort is estimated under a special set of assumptions, as described above. The averages for developing economies and regions are simple (unweighted by population) across economies in each group.

box continues next page

BOX 3.4   **Rough estimates of absolute mobility among the 1990s cohort (continued)**

Figure B3.4.1 shows the averages for Africa, South Asia, and all developing economies. The predictions of absolute mobility for the 1990s cohort (the solid lines shown inside the bounds) suggest that Africa is showing signs of convergence in absolute mobility toward the developing world average, although there is still a gap. This finding should be treated with caution because the predictions for the 1990s cohorts rest on strong assumptions. The large bounds (the dotted lines) that are obtained underscore the range of predictions that can be made using different assumptions. The predictions suggest that (1) the trend in the developing world average between the 1980s and 1990s cohorts continues the trend over the previous two decades; (2) Africa may be converging in absolute IGM toward the developing world average since the 1980s cohort, although the region is still lagging; and (3) absolute IGM in South Asia may catch up with or surpass the developing economy average for the 1990s cohort.

Although the signs of improving absolute mobility in the two lagging regions provide cause for optimism, these trends are speculative, given the strong assumptions underlying the predictions for the 1990s cohort (box 3.4). Better estimates, comparable with those for the older cohorts, will be possible when new surveys become available corresponding to a period when those born in the 1990s reach an age at which they would have completed their education.

Conclusions and a Summary of Key Findings

This chapter focuses on IGM in education both on its own merits and as one of the determinants of IGM in income, using a database that covers most of the world. Its findings suggest that, among most of the world's population, parental educational attainment is still too decisive in determining the educational success of the offspring. Absolute IGM and relative IGM are greater among richer economies than among developing economies. After rapid gains in education between the 1940s and 1980s, educational mobility in some parts of the developing world, particularly East Asia and the Pacific, Latin America and the Caribbean, and the Middle East and North Africa, has been strong, and absolute mobility in these regions and in high-income economies is comparable. The trends are less encouraging in other regions. Whereas absolute mobility and relative mobility have fallen in Eastern Europe and Central Asia, relative mobility showed almost no change in Africa and in South Asia from the 1950s to the 1980s. Economies with greater absolute mobility in education are also likely on average to exhibit greater relative mobility.

In today's highly heterogeneous developing world, the lack of mobility is most severe in some of the poorest economies, including low-income and fragile economies in parts of Africa and South Asia. Thirteen of the 15 economies in the bottom deciles of absolute and relative mobility among adults born in the 1980s are in these two regions, and several of these economies are in fragile situations. Africa and South Asia are also the regions where the educational prospects of children remain more closely tied to the education of their parents than in other parts of the world, which suggests that relative mobility is likely to remain low among generations born after the 1980s. Current enrollment patterns also suggest that poverty and low parental educational attainment reinforce each other in creating vast inequalities in access to education among children and in entrenching low IGM, limiting prospects for upward mobility in low- and low-middle-income economies.

On a positive note, as enrollments have rapidly expanded in the last two decades, younger generations born after the 1980s in Africa and South Asia are likely to experience increased levels of absolute mobility. Predictions of absolute mobility among those born in the 1990s suggest that the African average is moving closer to the developing economy average, while the average for South Asia may have surpassed the average for developing economies.

Although educational mobility in this report is measured in terms of attainment, the quality of learning is a key factor influencing how mobility in educational attainment relates to economic mobility more broadly. The 2018 World Development Report emphasizes that schooling is not the same as learning, and it shows that the learning crisis is particularly acute in low- and middle-income economies and even more so among children from disadvantaged socioeconomic backgrounds in these economies.[24] Thus, once the quality of education is taken into account, the "true" mobility in education may well be lower than what is shown in this chapter, which indicates an even deeper challenge faced by large parts of the developing world.

Globally, the intergenerational persistence of privilege (at the top quartile of education) and of deprivation (in the bottom half) continues to be significant everywhere and far more common than movements up or down. Developing economies should be especially concerned about growing persistence at the bottom. Among the 50 economies with the lowest rate of mobility from the bottom to the top among the 1980s generation, 46 are developing economies.

Mobility trends and patterns are similar in six of the world's largest emerging economies and in the average developing economy, with a few exceptions. Absolute mobility and relative mobility rose between the 1950s and 1980s in Brazil, Egypt, India, and Indonesia and in the average developing economy. However, relative mobility declined in China over the period. Within economies, relative mobility tends to be greater in richer provinces, though China is an important exception in this pattern. The narrowing of the gender gap in mobility (to almost zero) occurred in four of the six economies, with the notable exceptions of India and Nigeria, where the gender gaps were almost unchanged among cohorts from the 1950s to the 1980s.

Intergenerational effects can persist beyond two generations, particularly in developing economies. The educational attainment of individuals is correlated not only with the education of their parents but also (to a lesser extent) with the education of their grandparents, though the latter effect tends to be smaller in richer economies. The grandparent effect is an additional source of persistence in educational outcomes across multiple generations in developing economies.

Greater absolute IGM and relative IGM among a generation are associated with higher rates of economic growth and poverty reduction when the generation reaches adulthood. Thus, stalled progress in absolute mobility and relative mobility in the developing world raises important concerns about the prospects for growth and poverty reduction. This concern is particularly strong for economies where mobility is exceptionally low, many—but not all—of which are low-income or fragile economies. But rising absolute IGM among girls—even as progress for boys and girls taken together stalled since the 1960s—is a positive sign for economic growth and for reducing inequality of opportunity in developing economies. Girls have overtaken boys in upward mobility in high-income economies, and the gap is closing quickly in the developing world.

Absolute IGM in education is a direct measure of progress in education and has benefits for upward mobility of incomes and for growth through human capital formation. In most economies, absolute mobility is also a necessary condition for meeting the aspirations of society and supporting greater relative mobility. Absolute mobility tends to be greater in a society in which prosperity is expanding and is broadly shared.

But, even if absolute mobility is rising, relative IGM may not necessarily follow. The average economy in South Asia, for example, experienced rising absolute mobility between the 1950s and the 1980s generations, but with no improvement in relative mobility. Substantial absolute mobility in education can coexist with low relative mobility, given the imperfect association between the two. Relative IGM matters intrinsically because it is closely associated with fairness and equality of opportunity (chapter 1). It also matters instrumentally because it supports economic growth, social stability, and narrower income inequality, which are key elements of a sustainable social contract.

Breaking the cycle of low mobility and low rates of economic progress requires expanding opportunities through economic growth, which is a necessary condition for improving both absolute mobility and relative mobility and for a more equitable distribution of the benefits of growth. Improving relative mobility and, more specifically, upward mobility from the bottom of the ladder also requires equalizing opportunities to reduce disadvantages inherited at birth because of circumstances such as parental education or income, gender, or geographic location.

Subsequent chapters of this report focus on the question of how policies, markets, and institutions can contribute to higher mobility by expanding and equalizing opportunities at successive stages of life. The evidence presented in these chapters suggest that a likely explanation for why relative IGM improves with income levels is that richer economies invest, on the average, more public resources on equalizing opportunities. They are also likely to have, on the average, better policies and institutions that lead to better quality of services, more efficient and fair markets, and a higher rate of domestic resource mobilization—all of which are key factors in improving IGM in both education and income.

Annex 3A

Estimating Absolute Mobility among the 1990s Cohort under Strong Assumptions

The point estimates for absolute IGM among the cohorts born in the 1990s are obtained under some strong assumptions, whereby the education shortfall (the difference between the observed years of schooling completed and the years of schooling that should have been completed according to the child's age) for every child is converted into the likelihood that a child still enrolled in school will ultimately surpass the education level of his or her parents. This likelihood, in turn, equals the probability that the child will still be enrolled in school upon reaching the level that would surpass the education of his or her parents. The likelihood that a child is enrolled in school at any given age, for a given level of parental education, is estimated from the survey of every given economy.

The details are best illustrated through an example. Consider a girl who is 18 years old at the time of the survey in an economy, and who is still in school at a level that is two years behind where she should be for her age (the education shortfall). Also, consider that this girl would need to complete a tertiary degree to attain an education level higher than that of her parents. Suppose that, if the education shortfall was zero, one could acquire a tertiary education at the age of 21. Then, on the basis of the girl's observed track record, she is assumed to reach the final year of tertiary education at the age of 23. The likelihood that she will complete tertiary education is computed as the share of 23-year-old girls with matching parental education who are still enrolled in school at the time of the survey, with the assumption that enrollment rates for 23-year-old girls observed at the time of the survey will still apply five years later. For every individual who is still enrolled in school, this procedure yields an estimated probability between 0 and 1 of exceeding the education of her parents. Moreover, a probability of 0 or 1 can be assigned to individuals who have already completed their education at the time of the survey because their completed level of education is known with certainty. The point estimate of absolute mobility is obtained by averaging these over all eligible individuals.

Mobility in Six Large Developing Economies

MAP 3A.1 Mobility maps of five large developing economies

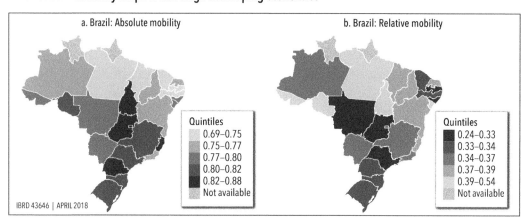

a. Brazil: Absolute mobility

b. Brazil: Relative mobility

Quintiles
0.69–0.75
0.75–0.77
0.77–0.80
0.80–0.82
0.82–0.88
Not available

Quintiles
0.24–0.33
0.33–0.34
0.34–0.37
0.37–0.39
0.39–0.54
Not available

IBRD 43646 | APRIL 2018

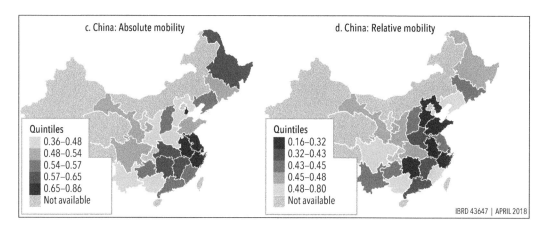

c. China: Absolute mobility

d. China: Relative mobility

Quintiles
0.36–0.48
0.48–0.54
0.54–0.57
0.57–0.65
0.65–0.86
Not available

Quintiles
0.16–0.32
0.32–0.43
0.43–0.45
0.45–0.48
0.48–0.80
Not available

IBRD 43647 | APRIL 2018

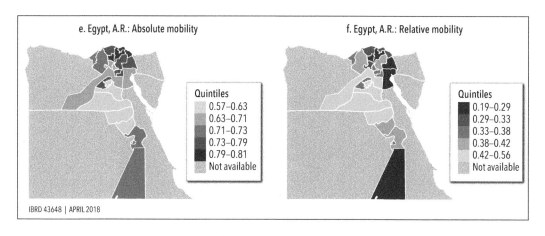

e. Egypt, A.R.: Absolute mobility

f. Egypt, A.R.: Relative mobility

Quintiles
0.57–0.63
0.63–0.71
0.71–0.73
0.73–0.79
0.79–0.81
Not available

Quintiles
0.19–0.29
0.29–0.33
0.33–0.38
0.38–0.42
0.42–0.56
Not available

IBRD 43648 | APRIL 2018

map continues next page

MAP 3A.1   Mobility maps of five large developing economies (continued)

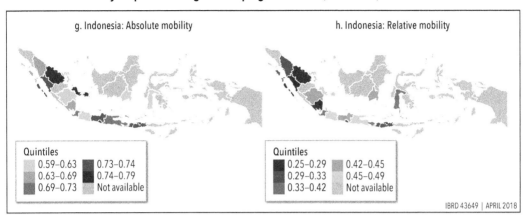

g. Indonesia: Absolute mobility

h. Indonesia: Relative mobility

Quintiles
0.59–0.63	0.73–0.74
0.63–0.69	0.74–0.79
0.69–0.73	Not available

Quintiles
0.25–0.29	0.42–0.45
0.29–0.33	0.45–0.49
0.33–0.42	Not available

IBRD 43649 | APRIL 2018

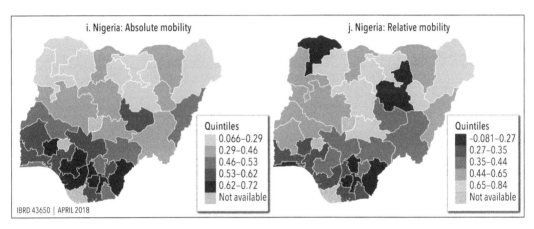

i. Nigeria: Absolute mobility

j. Nigeria: Relative mobility

Quintiles
0.066–0.29
0.29–0.46
0.46–0.53
0.53–0.62
0.62–0.72
Not available

Quintiles
-0.081–0.27
0.27–0.35
0.35–0.44
0.44–0.65
0.65–0.84
Not available

IBRD 43650 | APRIL 2018

Source: Calculations based on data in the GDIM 2018.
Note: Darker shades indicate greater absolute IGM and relative IGM. The IGM estimates are shown only for those provinces or states for which 50 or more observations are available. IGM = intergenerational mobility.

FIGURE 3A.1   Gender differences in intergenerational poverty, intergenerational privilege, and poverty to privilege

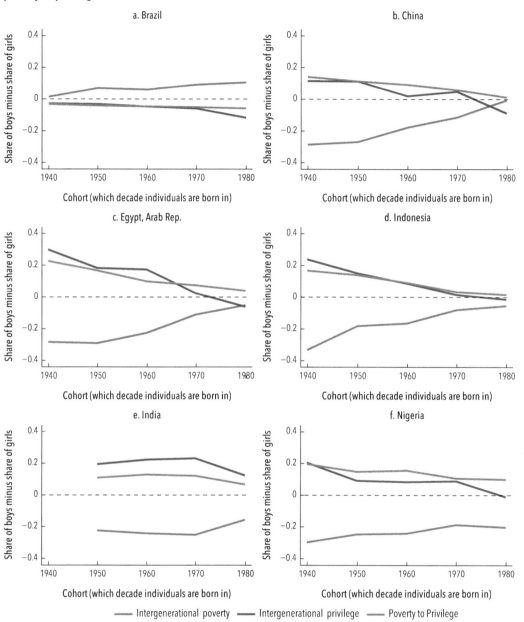

Source: Calculations based on data in the GDIM 2018.

Notes

1. See Hertz et al. (2007), who estimate 50-year trends in the intergenerational persistence of educational attainment in 42 economies: 29 developing or former transition economies, 12 economies in Western Europe, and the United States.

2. The gap in absolute mobility among the 1980s generation between high-income and developing economies is almost as large if the measure of absolute IGM includes individuals whose parents have tertiary educational attainment (instead of dropping them, as in figure 3.2) and considers these individuals as upwardly mobile if they have at least as much education as their parents. The gap reverses, however, if the measure of mobility is the mean difference in education level between the offspring and the parent (figure 2A.1).

3. See, for example, Corak (2016a) for reviews of the evidence.

4. Castello-Climent and Domenech (2017).

5. The trends since the 1960s are a bit more positive if the measure of absolute IGM includes individuals whose parents have tertiary education (instead of dropping them) and considers them upwardly mobile if they have at least as much education as their parents. Absolute IGM then improves slightly in developing economies and declines slightly in high-income economies. If the measure of mobility is the mean difference in educational attainment between the offspring and the parent, then average absolute IGM has declined steeply in both groups of economies since the 1960s (see figure 2A.1).

6. Beegle et al. (2016) estimate relative IGM in education for 10 African economies. The trends and levels are similar to those presented in this report for the cohorts born between 1940 and 1980. One exception is Nigeria. The other key difference is that they measure a drop in intergenerational persistence for many of the economies. But this may be an artifact of the fact that Beegle et al. (2016) extend their analysis to the 1990s cohort. This report decides to omit the 1990s cohort from the analysis because the average individual from this cohort would have been about 15 years old at the time of the survey, and thus will not have had a chance to complete his or her education. Figure 3.16 measures intergenerational persistence for individuals born in the 1990s using shortfall in years of schooling as the outcome variable. By this measure, Africa continues to stand out as a region with relatively low levels of intergenerational mobility.

7. The FCV group of economies is based on the World Bank Group's Harmonized List of Fragile Situations (fiscal year 2018), see http://www.worldbank.org/en/topic/fragilityconflictviolence/brief/harmonized-list-of-fragile-situations. Of the 36 economies in the list, IGM estimates for all cohorts can be computed for seven economies,

which are the Comoros, the Democratic Republic of Congo, Iraq, Kosovo, Liberia, Mali, and Togo.

8. "Poverty to privilege" is identical to the indicator referred to as "rags to riches" in Corak (2016b). The use of the word "poverty" here is just intended to suggest that those with education in the lower half of the distribution are likely to have relatively low levels of well-being, and not imply that they are poor according to any specific income or consumption standard.

9. Maoz and Moav (1999); Owen and Weil (1998). Also see Loury (1981).

10. Owen and Weil (1998)

11. In allowing for a nonlinear relationship between parent and child years of schooling, intergenerational persistence at lower levels of parental educational attainment exhibits a stronger correlation with poverty than intergenerational transmission at higher levels of parental educational attainment.

12. Torul and Oztunali (2017) report a similar relationship between relative IGM and inequality in education in Europe.

13. According to Corak (2013, 98), inequality "heightens the income consequences of innate differences between individuals; it also changes opportunities, incentives, and institutions that form, develop, and transmit characteristics and skills valued in the labor market; and it shifts the balance of power so that some groups are in a position to structure policies or otherwise support their children's achievement independent of talent."

14. The correlation between absolute IGM and intergenerational persistence across provinces among the 1980s cohort is –0.14 in China, –0.34 in India, –0.42 in Indonesia, –0.66 in the Arab Republic of Egypt, and –0.67 in Nigeria. In Brazil, the correlation among the 1980s cohort appears to be in the opposite direction, that is, greater relative mobility is associated with lower absolute mobility. However, the coefficient for Brazil is sensitive to the criteria for including provinces and is –0.64 if a stricter criterion is used.

15. Despite an absence of convergence in Brazil, it is included here because the gender gaps were relatively small from the outset.

16. Becker and Tomes (1979).

17. See Solon (2014) for a discussion of these three extensions to the baseline model.

18. See Solon (2017); also see, for example, Behrman and Taubman (1985); Lucas and Kerr (2013); Peters (1992); Ridge (1974); and Warren and Hauser (1997), all of which are cited in Solon (2017).

19. Lindahl et al. (2015) find parent–child rank correlations of 0.3–0.4 and grandparent–grandchild rank correlations of 0.1–0.2 in Malmö, Sweden. Zeng and Xie (2014) find that co-resident grandparents induce a sizable transmission of advantage in rural China.

20. These findings are reported in Evans, Newhouse, and Suarez-Becerra (forthcoming).

21. The educational shortfall of a child of age T = observed years of education – (T – 5).
22. On the Middle East and North Africa, shortfall estimates are available for 9 of the 10 economies on which there are estimates for the 1980s cohort. For the other regions, the numbers are East Asia and the Pacific, 13 of 16; Latin America and the Caribbean, 6 of 18; South Asia, 7 of 8; Sub-Saharan Africa, 38 of 41; Eastern Europe and Central Asia, none of 29 (excluded from the figure); and industrialized economies, 1 of 25 (also excluded).
23. World Development Indicators (2018). See UIS (2012) for the source of the statistics.
24. World Bank (2018).

References

Becker, Gary S., and Nigel Tomes. 1979. "An Equilibrium Theory of the Distribution of Income and Intergenerational Mobility." *Journal of Political Economy* 87 (6): 1153–89.

Beegle, Kathleen, Luc Christiaensen, Andrew Dabalen, and Isis Gaddis. 2016. *Poverty in a Rising Africa*. Washington, DC: World Bank.

Behrman, Jere, and Paul Taubman. 1985. "Intergenerational Earnings Mobility in the United States: Some Estimates and a Test of Becker's Intergenerational Endowments Model." *The Review of Economics and Statistics* 67 (1): 144–51.

Castello-Climent, Amparo, and Rafael Domenech. 2017. "Human Capital and Income Inequality: New Facts and Some Explanations." BBVA Working Papers. BBVA Research, Spain.

Chetty, Raj, David Grusky, Maximilian Hell, Nathaniel Hendren, Robert Manduca, and Jimmy Narang. 2017. "The Fading American Dream: Trends in Absolute Income Mobility since 1940." *Science* 356 (6336): 398–406.

Corak, Miles. 2013. "Income Inequality, Equality of Opportunity, and Intergenerational Mobility." *Journal of Economic Perspectives* 27 (3): 79–102.

———. 2016a. "Inequality from Generation to Generation: The United States in Comparison." IZA Discussion Paper 9929, Institute for the Study of Labor, Bonn.

———. 2016b. "How Much Social Mobility? More, but Not without Other Things." In *The US Labor Market: Questions and Challenges for Public Policy*, edited by Michael Strain, 2–3. Washington, DC: American Enterprise Institute.

Evans, Martin, David Newhouse, and Pablo Suarez-Becerra. Forthcoming. "Poverty, Schooling, and the Intergenerational Transmission of Educational Disadvantage." Policy Research Working Paper, World Bank, Washington, DC.

GDIM (Global Database on Intergenerational Mobility). 2018. *Global Database on Intergenerational Mobility*. Development Research Group, World Bank. Washington, DC: World Bank.

Hertz, Tom, Tamara Jayasundera, Patrizio Piraino, Sibel Selcuk, Nicole Smith, and Alina Verashchagina. 2007. "The Inheritance of Educational Inequality: International Comparisons and Fifty-Year Trends." *The B.E. Journal of Economic Analysis & Policy* 7 (2): 1–48.

Lindahl, Mikael, Mårten Palme, Sofia Sandgren Massih, and Anna Sjögren. 2015. "Long-Term Intergenerational Persistence of Human Capital: An Empirical Analysis of Four Generations." *Journal of Human Resources* 50 (1): 1–33.

Loury, Glenn C. 1981. "Intergenerational Transfers and the Distribution of Earnings." *Econometrica* 49 (4): 843–67.

Lucas, Robert E. B., and Sari Pekkala Kerr. 2013. "Intergenerational Income Immobility in Finland: Contrasting Roles for Parental Earnings and Family Income." *Journal of Population Economics* 26 (3): 1057–94.

Maoz, Yishay D., and Moav, O. 1999. "Intergenerational Mobility and the Process of Development." *The Economic Journal* 109 (458): 677–97.

Owen, Ann L., and David N. Weil. 1998. "Intergenerational Earnings Mobility, Inequality and Growth." *Journal of Monetary Economics* 41 (1): 71–104.

Peters, H. Elizabeth. 1992. "Patterns of Intergenerational Mobility in Income and Earnings." The *Review of Economics and Statistics* 74: 456–66.

Ridge, John Michael. 1974. "Three Generations." In *Mobility in Britain Reconsidered*, edited by J. M. Ridge. Oxford: Clarendon Press.

Solon, Gary. 2014. "Theoretical Models of Inequality Transmission across Multiple Generations." *Research in Social Stratification and Mobility* 35: 13–18.

———. 2017. "What Do We Know So Far about Multigenerational Mobility?" NBER Working Paper 21053, National Bureau of Economic Research, Cambridge, MA.

Torul, Orhan, and Oguz Oztunali. 2017. "Intergenerational Educational Mobility in Europe." Working Papers 2017/03, Department of Economics, Bogazici University, Istanbul, Turkey.

UIS (Institute for Statistics, United Nations Educational, Scientific, and Cultural Organization). 2012. "International Standard Classification of Education: ISCED 2011." UIS, Montreal. http://uis.unesco.org /sites/default/files/documents/international-standard-classification-of -education-isced-2011-en.pdf.

Warren, John Robert, and Robert M. Hauser. 1997. "Social Stratification across Three Generations: New Evidence from the Wisconsin Longitudinal Study." *American Sociological Review* 62 (4): 561–72.

World Bank. 2018. *World Development Report 2018: Learning to Realize Education's Promise*. Washington, DC: World Bank.

Zeng, Zhen, and Yu Xie. 2014. "The Effects of Grandparents on Children's Schooling: Evidence from Rural China." *Demography* 51 (2): 599–617.

CHAPTER 4
Pathways to Intergenerational Mobility in Education and Income

Economic growth, which increases the size of the economic pie, is important for achieving greater absolute mobility but does not guarantee it; achieving long-term improvements in the living standards of a large section of the population also requires growth to be sustained over time with its benefits distributed more equitably. The example of the United States (see chapter 1) provides a telling example—inadequate distribution of the benefits of growth has contributed much more to the decline in absolute income mobility between the 1940s and the 1980s in the United States than any slowdown in aggregate growth.

But, even if absolute intergenerational mobility (IGM) increases with sustained and inclusive growth, relative IGM may not necessarily follow. Substantial absolute mobility can coexist with low relative mobility (see chapter 3). The importance of improving both types of mobility—absolute and relative—has been discussed at length in chapters 1 and 3. This chapter will make the case that improving relative mobility, which includes increasing upward mobility of individuals at the bottom of the ladder, requires not just inclusive growth sustained over time but also proactive efforts to equalize opportunities to reduce disadvantages that individuals face because of circumstances such as parental education or income, gender, race, or geographic location. Reducing these disadvantages, for the reasons described in chapter 1, is also likely to raise growth and lower income inequality in the long run, which will be beneficial for poverty reduction and for absolute mobility.

Although education mobility—the primary focus of the global story highlighted in chapter 3—is important in its own right, social mobility is largely limited by the persistence of *incomes* across generations, for which persistence of education is an important, but not the only, driving factor. Economies may be successful in providing a level playing field in the accumulation of human capital but not on the labor market, or vice versa. Recognizing this, the chapter starts by exploring the relationship between education mobility and income mobility. Estimates of income mobility are provided for the subset of economies for which they are available, compiled from the existing literature and complemented by additional estimates derived for this report. Decompositions of the coefficient of the intergenerational persistence of income are used to estimate the size of the different channels of income persistence from parent to offspring.

The analysis sheds light on the importance of various channels, including the education channel, in producing income persistence and on any cross-country patterns in these relationships. The results highlight the relevance of the equality of opportunity framework in identifying the drivers of mobility, by pointing to the range of potential circumstances other than parental income and education that also influence the channels of income persistence. The circumstances interact with policies, markets, and institutions to produce inequality of opportunity at different stages of life, which in turn leads to higher persistence in income and education outcomes across generations.

The chapter subsequently discusses the basic concepts and measures of inequality of opportunity and presents aggregate, cross-country evidence on the relationship between inequality of opportunity and relative mobility. A simple life cycle–based framework clarifies in more detail how opportunities are influenced at different stages of life by circumstances, indirectly—because opportunities at every stage of life affect opportunities at subsequent stages—and directly, and the role of public policy in leveling the playing field for individuals who are born with vastly different endowments. The importance of public policy in equalizing opportunities is underscored by evidence that a key reason why relative mobility tends to be higher in richer economies is that these economies invest, on the average, more public resources on equalizing opportunities. The discussion and evidence presented in this chapter set the stage for chapters 5 and 6, which examine the drivers of IGM and the implications thereof for policy, using the life-cycle framework to organize the review of the literature and the analysis of cross-country data.

Relative Mobility in Income around the World

The estimates of relative IGM in income, which are available for 75 economies, should be treated with caution because of the strong assumptions that underlie most of these estimates—regardless of whether they are primary (own estimates) or secondary (taken from other sources)—and the differences in methodology across various sources (annex 4A). Also, these estimates are available only for a single generation of adults who were at their peak earning age, roughly speaking, during the time of the surveys (cohort of 1960s or 1970s), unlike the estimates of educational mobility that are available for all cohorts from the 1940s to the 1980s for most economies (chapter 3). Given these caveats and the widespread gaps in geographic coverage, the income IGM estimates are used primarily to complement the global picture of education mobility, and for comparisons with educational mobility, rather than to present a complete global view of mobility trends and patterns as was done with educational IGM.

Like Educational Mobility, Income Mobility Varies Widely and Tends to Be Low in Developing Economies

When all economies with available estimates are sorted by relative IGM in income, most of the developing economies are clustered at the higher end of income persistence (figure 4.1). A global map of relative IGM of income, despite the many gaps due to lack of estimates, is still useful for comparisons with a similar map of educational mobility (map 4.1, panel a). The map confirms that relative IGM of income tends to be lower in developing regions than in the high-income economies, similar to what is seen for relative mobility in education. Among developing economies, income IGM tends to be relatively low in parts of Africa, Latin America and the Caribbean, and South Asia compared with East Asia and the Pacific and with Eastern Europe and Central Asia. The United States, with income IGM comparable with some developing economies, is less mobile than most high-income economies.

The wide variation in income mobility across countries can be illustrated with a few examples. In countries such as Brazil, India, Nigeria, Peru, and South Africa, if a man earns double the amount earned by another man, his son is on average expected to make somewhere between 60 and 70 percent more than the son of the lower-income man. This gap rises to more than 90 percent in the Arab Republic of Egypt, Morocco, and Panama, and more

FIGURE 4.1   Developing economies tend to have lower relative IGM in income

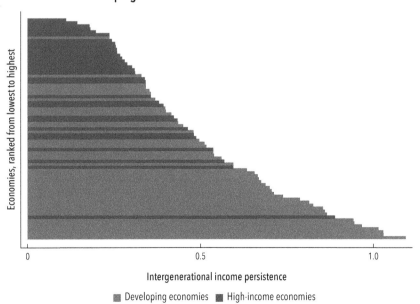

Note: IGM = intergenerational mobility.

MAP 4.1 Relative intergenerational mobility of income across the world

a. IGM for selected economies for which estimates are available

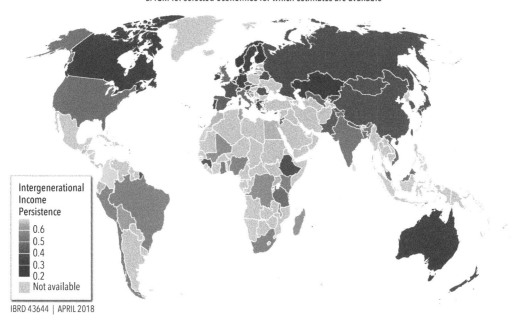

Intergenerational
Income
Persistence

0.6
0.5
0.4
0.3
0.2
Not available

IBRD 43644 | APRIL 2018

b. Difference between relative IGM in income and in education

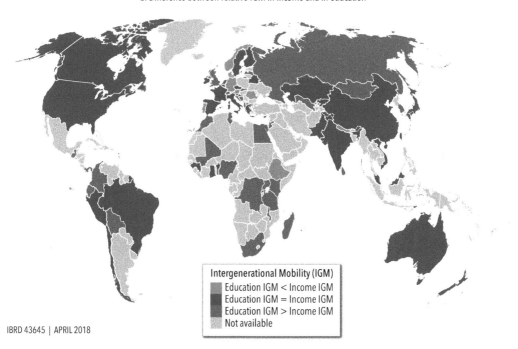

Intergenerational Mobility (IGM)

Education IGM < Income IGM
Education IGM = Income IGM
Education IGM > Income IGM
Not available

IBRD 43645 | APRIL 2018

Source: Estimates based on GDIM 2018; Equalchances 2018 (compiled from multiple studies).
Note: The darker colors in panel a indicate higher relative mobility of income (or lower persistence). Gray indicates economies for which mobility of income or education is not available. Mobility in education is considered equal to mobility in income if the difference in absolute value is less than 0.15. Income persistence estimates are approximately for the 1960s or 1970s cohort. Education persistence estimates are for the cohort best matching the income persistence estimate.

FIGURE 4.2   Higher relative IGM in income is associated with lower income inequality

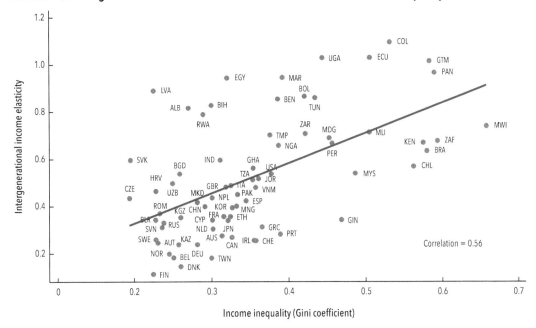

Source: Equalchances 2018, compiled from multiple studies; estimates using GDIM 2018 and World Development Indicators for income inequality.
Note: Higher intergenerational income persistence or elasticity represents lower relative intergenerational mobility (IGM). Income persistence estimates are approximately for the 1960s or 1970s cohort.

than 100 percent in Colombia, Ecuador, Guatemala, and Uganda (figure 4.2). In Colombia, Ecuador, Guatemala, and Panama, high persistence in income is also accompanied by a relatively high persistence in education (figure 4.4). In comparison, the son of the higher-income father is expected to earn about 50 percent more than the son of the lower-income father in countries like Italy, the United Kingdom, the United States, and Vietnam; about 40 percent more in countries such as China, Republic of Korea, Mongolia, and Spain; and less than 20 percent more in Belgium, Denmark, Finland, and Norway.

A look at the differences between relative IGMs in education and in income reveals a few patterns (map 4.1, panel b). First, economies in Africa and in the Middle East and North Africa for which estimates are available tend to exhibit lower income IGM than educational IGM. Second, income IGM and educational IGM line up well in much of the world, such as in parts of East Asia and the Pacific, Eastern Europe and Central Asia, Latin America and the Caribbean, South Asia, and most high-income economies. Thus, South Asia and Sub-Saharan Africa are the regions in which parental background—whether in education or income—matters the most for the prospects of the offspring. Income mobility in the African economies on which estimates are available tends to be low, even compared with the low levels of relative mobility of education shown in chapter 3.

FIGURE 4.3   Economies in the bottom third and in the top third, by relative income mobility

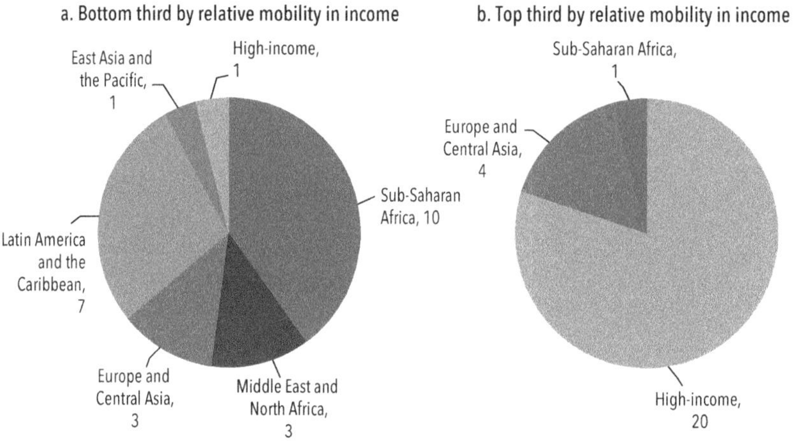

a. Bottom third by relative mobility in income

East Asia and
the Pacific,
1

High-income,
1

Latin America
and the
Caribbean,
7

Sub-Saharan
Africa, 10

Europe and
Central Asia,
3

Middle East and
North Africa,
3

b. Top third by relative mobility in income

Sub-Saharan Africa,
1

Europe and
Central Asia,
4

High-income,
20

Source: Calculations using GDIM 2018.
Note: High-income economies are excluded from the count for developing regions. Income intergenerational mobility estimates are for the 1960s or 1970s cohort.

Economies in the bottom third by income mobility are all developing economies

Among the 25 economies that are in the bottom third by income mobility, with income persistence coefficients between 0.6 and 1.1, 10 are in Africa and 7 are in Latin America and the Caribbean; 24 are developing economies (figure 4.3, panel a). In contrast, out of the 25 economies in the top third by income mobility, with income persistence coefficients ranging between 0.11 and 0.35, 20 are high-income economies, and 4 are in Eastern Europe and Central Asia (figure 4.3, panel b). African economies in the bottom third by mobility include not just those with high incidence of poverty, such as the Democratic Republic of Congo, Mali, Malawi, and Uganda, but also large emerging economies like Kenya, Nigeria, and South Africa. Four of the bottom five economies by income mobility are in Latin America—Colombia, Ecuador, Guatemala, and Panama.

Notably, these figures present an incomplete picture because they are based on just 75 countries for which estimates are available. Also, they may not reflect recent conditions in countries because the mobility of a cohort born in the 1960s or 1970s reflects to some degree the policies and institutions of the past, particularly in human capital development. However, given the importance of relative mobility for long-term improvements in inclusion and growth, these figures are still deeply concerning for parts of the developing world.

The Great Gatsby curve is valid for both income mobility and educational mobility

As discussed in chapter 1, an important reason to care about relative IGM is the mutually reinforcing relationship between the phenomenon and income inequality. Lower relative IGM in income is associated with greater income inequality (figure 4.2), which confirms the relationship known as the Great Gatsby curve that has been shown by earlier studies based on fewer observations.[1] A similar relationship was also observed between relative IGM in education and education inequality in chapter 3. The weight of evidence thus strongly supports the view that lower relative mobility is associated with higher inequality, most likely because of a two-way relationship: more inequality tends to limit relative mobility, which tends to increase inequality over time (see chapter 1).

Income Mobility and Educational Mobility: How They Are Related

Although IGM in earnings and IGM in education are highly correlated, they yield different relative rankings of economies, as seen in chapter 1. In some economies, IGM in income is much lower than the average income mobility given their levels of IGM in education (for example, Colombia, Kenya, Latvia, and Uzbekistan). Meanwhile, economies such as Ethiopia, the former Yugoslav Republic of Macedonia, Nepal, Portugal, and Romania exhibit much higher income mobility than the average for their levels of educational mobility; Brazil, Peru, the Russian Federation, and Vietnam have the average income mobility given their levels of educational mobility. Income IGM in some of the Nordic economies is higher than what might be predicted on the basis of education IGM: these economies are ranked at the top in income mobility, but on a par with several other high-income economies in educational mobility (figure 4.4a). The association between two

FIGURE 4.4   Relative IGMs for education and income are more strongly associated with each other in developing economies than in high-income economies

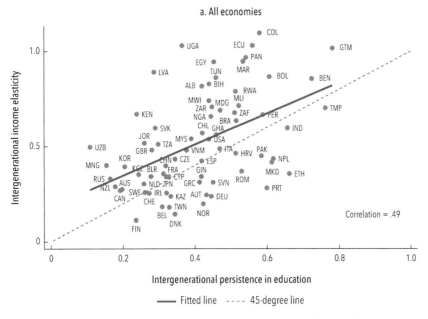

a. All economies

figure continues next page

FIGURE 4.4   Relative IGMs for education and income are more strongly associated with each other in developing economies than in high-income economies (continued)

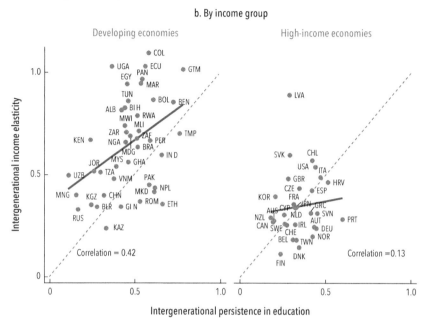

b. By income group

Source: Estimates based on GDIM 2018; Equalchances 2018; compiled from multiple studies.
Note: Higher elasticity (persistence) indicates lower intergenerational mobility (IGM). Data points are limited by the availability of IGM income estimates. Income persistence estimates are for the 1960s or 1970s cohort; education persistence estimates are for the cohort best matching the income persistence estimate.

IGMs is also stronger among developing economies than among high-income economies (figure 4.4b).

If economic opportunities do not keep pace with rising education mobility, societies may come under growing stress. For example, a pattern of expansion in schooling, coupled with weak labor market conditions in recent decades, has been particularly pronounced in the economies that saw upheaval during the Arab Spring.[2] Average IGM in education, both absolute and relative, among the economies of the Middle East and North Africa region is well above the developing economy averages (chapter 3). But income mobility in Egypt, Morocco, and Tunisia, for example, is low relative to what might be expected of an economy at their level of persistence in education (figure 4.4a and 4.4b). As economic opportunities have fallen behind the rising expectations of an increasingly educated population in these economies, the potential for social instability may have grown.[3]

Why Incomes Persist from One Generation to the Next

To understand why incomes persist from one generation to the next and the role that persistence in education plays in income persistence, it is useful

BOX 4.1   Estimating the relationship between IGM in earnings and IGM in education

Intergenerational persistence in earnings (β_y) is related to intergenerational persistence in education (β_s). What connects the two is the Mincer equation for both generations, which describes the income one is expected to earn given one's level of education (and work experience). The relationship between β_y and β_s satisfies

$$\beta_y = R_p^2 \left(\frac{\lambda_c}{\lambda_p} \right) \beta_s + R_p^2 \left(\frac{\delta_s}{\lambda_p} \right) + (1 - R_p^2)\delta_y, \tag{B4.1.1}$$

where R_p^2 captures how much of the variation in earnings (for the parent's generation) is explained by the variation in schooling alone (ranging between 0 and 1, where 1 indicates a situation where years of schooling perfectly predicts earnings), λ_c (λ_p) measures the return to an additional year of schooling in the child (parent) generation, δ_s measures the extent to which parental education matters for noneducational determinants of child earnings, while δ_y measures the extent to which noneducational determinants of parent earnings matter for child earnings. A detailed discussion on the estimation of these parameters for 49 economies is included in the annex 4A.

The decomposition of β_y into the three channels of intergenerational persistence rests on several assumptions. First, it is assumed that linear models provide reasonable approximations to the intergenerational transmission of earnings and education as well as to the Mincer equations that describe the relationship between earnings and education. Second, education is measured by years of schooling, meaning that quality of education is not accounted for. To the extent that quality of education matters for earnings and is subject to variation, R_p^2 will arguably underestimate the degree to which earnings can be explained by education. It should also be noted that this decomposition is implemented for a subset of economies only. Economies for which estimates of persistence in earnings are obtained from existing studies, and for which the database compiled by the authors of this report does not permit for the estimation of persistence in earnings, are excluded.

to examine the different channels through which parental income influences income of the next generation. The channels can be identified by formalizing the statistical relationship between relative IGMs of income and education under some simplifying assumptions, and decomposing the coefficient of intergenerational income persistence (or income elasticity) that measures relative IGM of income. The decompositions, and the underlying assumptions, are described briefly in box 4.1 and in more detail in annex 4A.

Figure 4.5 is a stylized representation of the three channels through which parental incomes influence incomes of the next generation, which reflect the effect of (1) parental educational attainment on the income of offspring through the educational attainment of the offspring (channel 1); (2) parental educational attainment on the determinants of the income of the offspring that are independent of education (channel 2); and (3) parental characteristics, other than education, related to parental income on the income of offspring (channel 3).

FIGURE 4.5   Channels of income persistence across generations

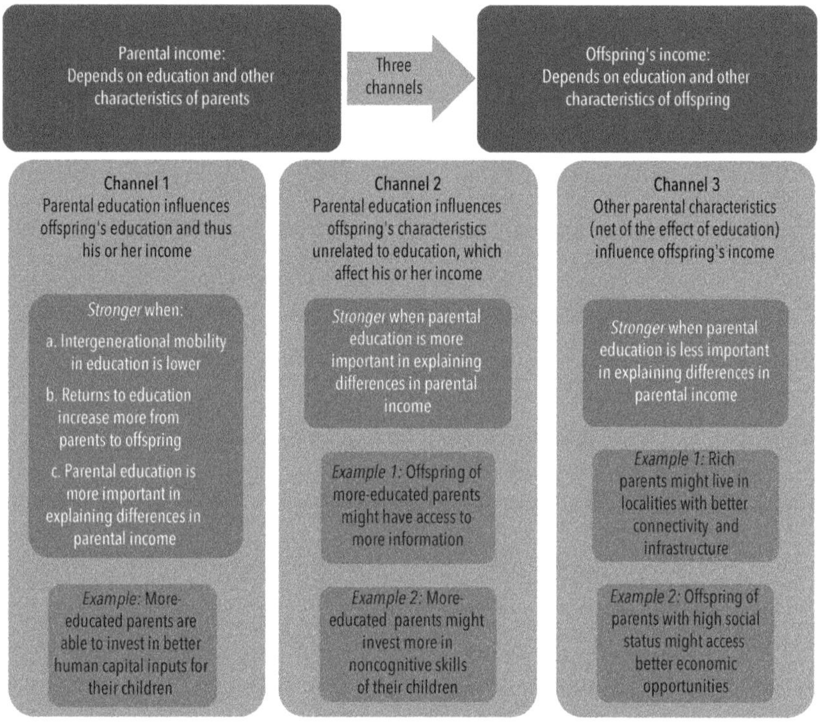

| Parental income: Depends on education and other characteristics of parents | Three channels → | Offspring's income: Depends on education and other characteristics of offspring |

Channel 1	Channel 2	Channel 3
Parental education influences offspring's education and thus his or her income	Parental education influences offspring's characteristics unrelated to education, which affect his or her income	Other parental characteristics (net of the effect of education) influence offspring's income
Stronger when: a. Intergenerational mobility in education is lower b. Returns to education increase more from parents to offspring c. Parental education is more important in explaining differences in parental income	*Stronger* when parental education is more important in explaining differences in parental income	*Stronger* when parental education is less important in explaining differences in parental income
	Example 1: Offspring of more-educated parents might have access to more information	*Example 1:* Rich parents might live in localities with better connectivity and infrastructure
Example: More-educated parents are able to invest in better human capital inputs for their children	*Example 2:* More-educated parents might invest more in noncognitive skills of their children	*Example 2:* Offspring of parents with high social status might access better economic opportunities

Note: The figure is a stylized representation of a complex process.

Channel 1 gets stronger as IGM in education falls, which happens if educated parents make higher investments in their children's human capital development relative to less-educated parents and as returns to education of the offspring's generation rise relative to the parents' generation. This also implies that IGM in education and IGM in income are likely to move in the same direction—consistent with the strongly positive association observed between the two (chapter 1). Channel 2 becomes stronger, for example, if educated parents can provide better access to information or social skills that allow the offspring to earn higher incomes for a given level of education. Channel 3 is strengthened if the offspring enjoys greater privileges due to the social status or wealth of his or her parents, for example, by finding better jobs and credit, or a better quality of education because of parental connections or because they live in richer, better-connected neighborhoods. Also, the weaker the relationship between education and income in the parental generation, the higher the importance of channel 3 and the lower the importance of channels 1 and 2.

These channels are somewhat of an abstraction because they ignore interactions and nonlinearity in the underlying relationships between income and education within and across generations. Thus, it is difficult to disentangle the impacts of the three channels empirically and estimate their relative sizes and impacts in an economy. That said, they are useful to provide a rough sense of the kind of factors, in addition to IGM in education, that drive persistence in incomes, and the direction of these effects.

Parental Characteristics Other Than Education Contribute Strongly to Income Persistence

The decomposition of the coefficient of intergenerational income persistence for 49 of the 148 economies studied in this report—which include 41 developing and 8 high-income economies—suggests that channel 3 tends to be large in most economies, accounting for an average of about 80 percent of the persistence of income (figure 4.6). The size of channel 3 is related to the fact that it reflects the share of income persistence attributable to *all parental characteristics that are associated with income but independent of parental education*—directly through their effect on offspring's earnings through factor markets and indirectly by affecting offspring's education, which then influences their earnings. Channel 1 is on average larger than channel 2, which means that the combined effect of education mobility and returns to education in the offspring's generation is also an important contributor to income persistence, and more so in developing economies than in high-income economies (figure 4.6).

FIGURE 4.6   Parental characteristics other than education contribute strongly to persistence in incomes

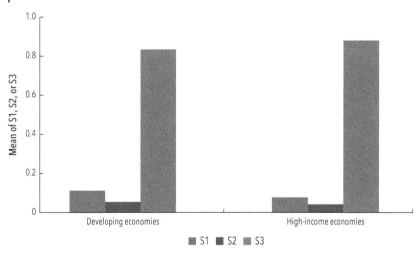

Source: Estimated using GDIM 2018.
Note: S1 = share of income persistence that is the effect of parental education on offspring's income via offspring's education; S2 = share of income persistence that is the effect of parental education on the determinants of offspring's income that are independent of education; S3 = share of income persistence that is the effect of parental characteristics (other than education) that are related to income, on offspring's income.

The aggregate nature of the third transmission channel implies that numerous influences may be in play, though they are impossible to disentangle through this exercise. However, it seems reasonable to argue that three types of effects are likely to be important contributors to channel 3. The first is the effect of distorted factor markets, which reward individuals with parental connections, legacies, social privilege (such as membership in a preferred social group), or political power. The second is the effect of household residence: more well-off parents tend to cluster together in places that allow their children to enjoy better access to information, connectivity to services and jobs, access to networks, and positive spillovers from peer groups and role models. The third effect is related to the offspring of richer parents getting education of higher quality, which is not considered in channel 1. If individuals with richer parents are also likely to get education of a higher quality (for a given level of education), which seems quite plausible, its effect on income persistence will be picked up by channel 3—another reason why the size of this channel tends to be large in most economies.

The Contribution of Parental Education to Income Persistence Falls with Gross Domestic Product

The size of the third channel of persistence increases, and that of the first channel declines relative to the others, with per capita gross domestic product (GDP) (figure 4.7). This is consistent with the association between IGM of income and IGM of education being stronger among developing economies than among high-income economies (figure 4.6, panel b).

FIGURE 4.7   The contribution of parental educational channels to income mobility falls with per capita GDP

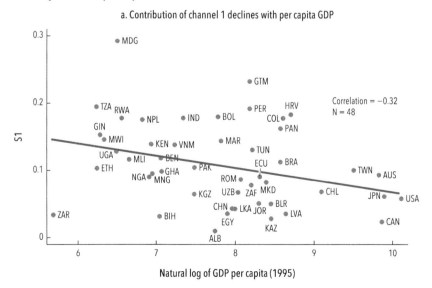

a. Contribution of channel 1 declines with per capita GDP

figure continues next page

FIGURE 4.7 The contribution of parental educational channels to income mobility falls with per capita GDP (continued)

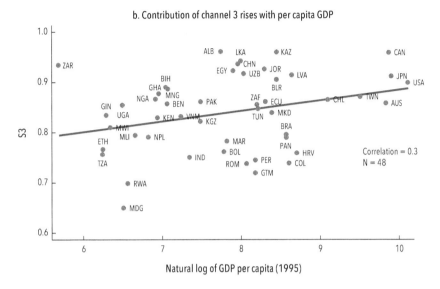

b. Contribution of channel 3 rises with per capita GDP

Source: Estimates based on GDIM 2018.

Note: In panel a, channel 1 is the effect of parental educational attainment on the income of offspring through the educational attainment of the offspring. In panel b, channel 3 is the effect of parental characteristics other than education on the income of offspring. GDP = gross domestic product.

These patterns could be related to the fact that, if GDP is higher, the relative mobility in education tends to be higher; and education tends to be a weaker predictor of income, which weakens the link between education mobility and income persistence.[4] As this occurs, unequal opportunities arising from the effects of distorted factor markets (influenced by parental status and connections) and location (related to the clustering of more well-off parents in advantaged residential areas) contribute more to income persistence across generations. Another factor that might explain this pattern is that the third channel may also include the effect of differences in quality of education. Also, as the general education level in an economy rises with economic progress, children of wealthier parents are more likely to have an advantage in the quality of education they receive rather than in the level of education. And this effect, if it is independent of parental education, would tend to strengthen the contribution of the third channel as economies get richer.

Equality of Opportunity as a Pathway to Greater IGM

The decompositions above confirm the importance of a broader set of circumstances, beyond parental education, as contributors to income persistence across generations; and the contribution of these broader circumstances tends to rise as countries achieve more economic progress. This broader set of circumstances can potentially include a wide range of characteristics related to parental social status and attributes that an individual has no control over, which affect him or her at different stages of life. Where one lives, or one's gender, ethnicity, or other markers of social status, for example, could affect the size of channel 3 through direct or indirect routes, or channel 1 through their impact on returns to education.

Given the above, the inequality of opportunity framework seems well suited to identify the barriers to higher relative mobility, as discussed below. Other studies support this view, one of which characterizes inequality of opportunity as "the missing link between the concepts of income inequality and social mobility; if higher inequality makes IGM more difficult, it is likely because opportunities for economic advancement are more unequally distributed among children" (Brunori, Ferreira, and Peragine 2013, 20).

Inequality of opportunity refers to the extent or share of inequality in outcomes that is attributable to differences in circumstances outside an individual's control, such as parental educational attainment and income, location at birth, gender, ethnicity, and other markers of social status of an individual at birth. Although this definition embodies the same principle of origin independence as in the concept of relative IGM used in this report, the two become equivalent only in the special case where the set of circumstances is limited to parental educational attainment or parental income.

Before introducing a framework to describe how inequality of opportunity can emerge at different stages of life because of the effects of circumstances to limit relative mobility, it is useful to examine whether cross-country data suggest an association between inequality of opportunity and relative IGM.

Measuring Inequality of Opportunity

A wide range of measures of inequality of opportunity is used in the economic literature.[5] Of these, two types of commonly used measures are employed for the analysis in this report. These are a measure of ex ante inequality in income between types, also known as the inequality of economic opportunity (IEO); and the Human Opportunity Index (HOI) (see box 4.2 for a short description of both).

Although the two measures are motivated by similar ideas, they are quite different in nature and thus complement each other. Both start by defining a set of circumstances, such as gender, place of birth, parental education, and so on, but then diverge considerably from each other. IEO estimates inequality of opportunity as the extent (or share) of income inequality attributable to these circumstances. HOI treats a basic service or indicator of well-being (such as attending school or not, or being adequately nourished or not) as an opportunity for a child, and considers the overall coverage of the opportunity and inequality in coverage between children born with different circumstances.

BOX 4.2   Two common measures of inequality of opportunity used in this report

Both inequality of economic opportunity (IEO) and the Human Opportunity Index (HOI) start by defining a set of circumstances, which are attributes individuals cannot be held responsible for, so that any inequality arising from them is considered unfair. The population is segmented into several *types*, such that all individuals of the same type share the same set of circumstances. The IEO measure assigns everyone an "opportunity set" corresponding to the mean income level of his or her type. Inequality *between* these opportunity sets is solely driven by circumstances and hence considered unfair. Denoting the income of an individual as y and the opportunity set assigned to an individual as $\hat{y}$, absolute IEO is the inequality in these opportunity sets, $I(\hat{y})$, and relative IEO is the share of total inequality attributable to differences between types, $I(\hat{y})/I(y)$. Absolute inequality of opportunity is thus the extent to which income inequality is associated with the circumstances into which an individual is born, whereas relative inequality of opportunity is the share of absolute inequality of opportunity in total income inequality. The Gini coefficient and the mean log deviation are frequently used measures of inequality for this purpose.

The HOI is a synthetic measure combining both the level and inequality of opportunities, where opportunities are measured directly through binary variables (such as school attendance or being adequately nourished) rather than inferred from incomes. The measure considers two inputs: the coverage (denoted by C), which is the share of the population that has the opportunity in question, and a dissimilarity index (denoted by D) that measures the differences in coverage between types. To arrive at the HOI, coverage is penalized by the amount of differences in coverage by types, such that HOI = (1-D)*C. Intuitively, the dissimilarity index—which is an inequality of opportunity component—is the fraction of opportunities that need to be redistributed from opportunity-rich to opportunity-deprived people to produce complete equality of opportunity. The HOI is the average coverage of an opportunity discounted by a penalty that increases with inequality in coverage between types.

Source: Brunori, Ferreira, and Peragine 2013; Ferreira and Gignoux 2011; Paes de Barros et al. 2009, 2012.

Economies with Greater Inequality of Opportunity Tend to Have Lower Relative IGM

The Global Database on Intergenerational Mobility (GDIM), merged with estimates of IEO in other studies, confirms the findings of earlier studies: economies with greater inequality of opportunity are likely to show lower relative IGM in education (figure 4.8).[6] In measuring IEO, the set of circumstances varies across countries because the estimates have been compiled from studies relying on different methods. But, in most cases, the circumstances include parental education, geographical location of residence or birth and gender, and, in some cases, race, ethnicity, and religion. The concept of inequality of opportunity based on such a broad set of circumstances and income as the outcome variable is clearly distinct from relative IGM in education. Thus, the correlation between the two cannot be interpreted as an inevitable consequence of the similarity of the two concepts,

FIGURE 4.8 ´ **Greater inequality of opportunity is associated with lower IGM**

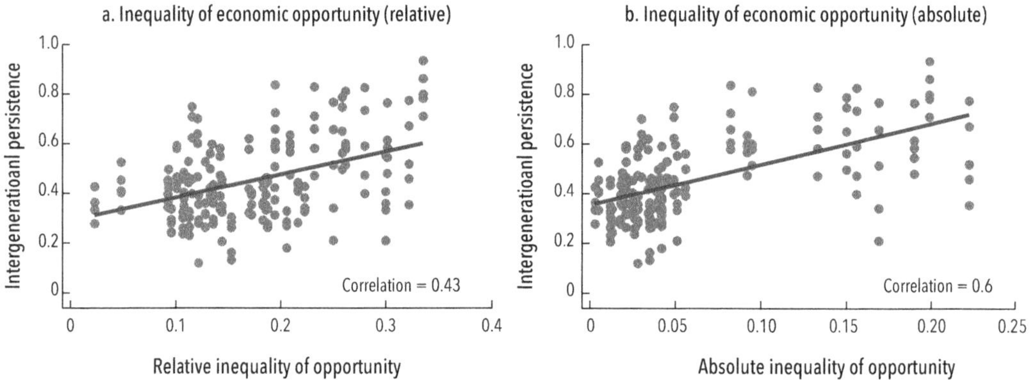

a. Inequality of economic opportunity (relative)

b. Inequality of economic opportunity (absolute)

Correlation = 0.43

Correlation = 0.6

Source: Calculations using data of Brunori, Ferreira, and Peragine 2013 and GDIM 2018.
Note: Higher intergenerational persistence indicates lower relative intergenerational mobility (IGM) in education.

but suggests a deeper relationship. Although correlations do not imply cause and effect, they are consistent with the idea that the path to a more mobile society goes through narrower inequality of opportunity. A similar relationship has also been noted in the literature between inequality of opportunity and relative mobility in *income.*[7]

More evidence on the relationship between inequality of opportunity and IGM is found by looking at HOI and dissimilarity indexes (the inequality of opportunity component of HOI) across the world. These measures are available for only a limited number of economies, primarily in Sub-Saharan Africa and Latin America and the Caribbean regions, for the 1990s—the period that loosely corresponds to the years when the 1980s generation would be attending school.

HOI for primary school completion among children of ages 12–15 years varies widely across economies (figure 4.9, panel a) because of significant differences in coverage as well as inequality in coverage between children with different circumstances (the gap between coverage and HOI). The dissimilarity index—which measures the inequality of opportunity in terms of primary school completion among children of ages 12–15 years—has a strong negative association with absolute IGM and positive association with intergenerational persistence (figure 4.9, panels b and c). In other words, economies with greater inequality of opportunity in primary school completion in the late 1990s are likely to have lower absolute and relative IGM.

Improving Mobility Requires Identifying the Drivers of Inequality of Opportunity

Thus, the path to greater mobility in education and income seems to go through lower inequality of opportunity. Understanding the drivers of inequality of opportunity, which involves expanding the associated set of potential

FIGURE 4.9 IGM in education for the 1980s generation is lower in economies with higher inequality in primary school completion in the late 1990s

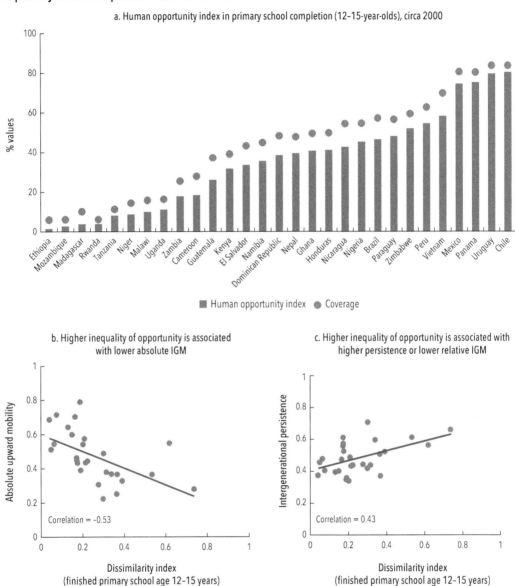

Source: GDIM 2018; Visualize Inequality (World Bank): http://www1.worldbank.org/poverty/visualizeinequality/.
Note: IGM estimates refer to the 1980s generation. HOI and Dissimilarity are for 1994–2001 (median year of 2000). Relative IGM is higher if intergenerational persistence is lower. IGM = intergenerational mobility.

disadvantages beyond low parental income or education, can help uncover the true impediments to higher mobility. This is because the inequality of opportunity framework encompasses all observable circumstances, such as race, social group, or location, which may potentially produce persistence of income inequality across generations. The advantages passed on from

BOX 4.3   **Understanding inequality of opportunity helps identify the barriers to IGM in income in South Africa**

Characterized by high and persistent inequality, South Africa also exhibits high inequality of opportunity. Thus, a recent study finds that inherited circumstances, including the educational attainment, occupation, and race of fathers, explain a significant share of South Africa's earnings inequality (Piraino 2015). The same study also estimates a high intergenerational elasticity of earnings (low mobility), a significant part of which seems to be attributable to differences in earnings by race because of the persistent concentration of the white minority at the top of the earnings distribution. This is similar to what is found in the United States, as reported by Hertz (2008): the persistent presence of African Americans at the lower end of the income distribution generates a high share of the overall degree of intergenerational income persistence. In both countries, what appears to be low IGM of earnings is partly attributable to the deep differences between races that persist across generations, net of the effect of the economic status of parents. Moreover, the persistence of these inequalities, even if there is economic growth for everyone, seems to suggest the existence of inequality traps (Bourguignon, Ferreira, and Walton 2007). These are situations whereby "the various dimensions of inequality (in wealth, power, and social status) interact to protect the rich from downward mobility and to prevent the poor from being upwardly mobile" (Rao 2006, 11).

However, race is far from being the only important factor driving inequality of opportunity at different stages of life in South Africa. Im et al. (2012) find that, if parental educational attainment and the location of the residence of the child (in rural areas, urban townships, informal settlements, or more-well-off urban areas) are considered, race is no longer the most important contributor to the deep inequalities in primary school completion rates and access to improved sanitation, safe water, and health insurance. Race also becomes secondary to the residence location of workers in explaining differences in the likelihood of full-time employment, particularly among younger workers. Thus, although race is still important in perpetuating inequalities across generations, at least as important is where an individual resides—in developed urban areas, urban townships, or rural parts of the country.

generation to generation, even if they are correlated with parental education or income, may be attributable at least in part to these other circumstances. Designing the appropriate sort of policies to raise IGM requires identifying these underlying circumstances and their importance individually and in interaction with each other in restricting opportunities.

The example of South Africa, which has high inequality of opportunity and low relative IGM in earnings, illustrates how the expanded framework of opportunities leads to a better understanding of the factors restricting mobility (box 4.3). Race and location turn out to be important contributors to inequality of opportunity in South Africa, which increases the persistence of income inequality across generations. A framework that ignores these key circumstances in South Africa would have little chance of being useful in identifying the underlying causes of low relative IGM in income.

The circumstances that contribute to inequality of opportunity show some consistent patterns across most economies. Household economic status, parental education, and location of the household are almost always the most important contributors to the component of HOI that measures inequality of opportunity among children. In Sub-Saharan Africa, for example, household wealth, followed by location (urban or rural) and education of the household head, is the most important contributor to inequality of opportunity for one-year-old children (figure 4.10). "Opportunity" is defined here as meeting a few of the universally accepted basic standards, in terms of the child having access to improved sources of water and adequate sanitation, being fully immunized (as appropriate for age), and not being stunted.

The contributions of these circumstances to inequality translate to vast gaps in opportunities among children with contrasting socioeconomic profiles, which vary widely across countries. For example, an urban child living in a household in the highest quintile of wealth and with a household head who has 10 years or more of education has a much higher likelihood of having the basic opportunity at age one than a rural child living in a household in the bottom wealth quintile and with a household head who

FIGURE 4.10   Contributions of different circumstances to inequality of opportunity among one-year-old children (20 countries in Sub-Saharan Africa)

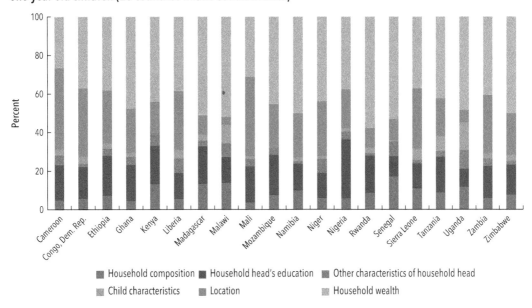

Source: Reproduced from figure 5.3(a), Dabalen et al. 2015.
Note: The figure shows contribution of each group of circumstances to the Dissimilarity Index for the opportunity of a one-year-old child. The child has the opportunity if her household has improved source of water and adequate sanitation, she is fully immunized (for age 1), and she is not stunted.

has no education. The difference in likelihood is larger than 20 percentage points in 19 of the 20 African countries named in figure 4.10, and 50 percentage points or more in 5 of these countries.[8]

Inequality of Opportunity Emerges at Various Stages of the Life Cycle

Identifying the drivers of income mobility requires examining the factors that shape opportunities at different stages of life. Circumstances at birth, such as parental background, ethnicity, and geographic location, influence the opportunities available to an individual and thus IGM of income in two ways: direct effects, at every stage of the life cycle, and indirect effects, because opportunities at each stage of life influence outcomes in subsequent stages. For example, parental incomes influence investments in children's human capital that will in turn affect their incomes later in life, which is the first channel of income persistence shown in figure 4.5. Parental status can also exert a direct influence on adult incomes, through networks and connections in labor and other factor markets, as in the third channel in figure 4.5. Figure 4.11 is a stylized representation of how circumstances of an individual at birth interact with policies, markets, and institutions to shape opportunities at different stages, which determine the individual's adult earnings to a large extent and thus IGM in income.

FIGURE 4.11   Circumstances at birth interact with policies and institutions to shape IGM in income

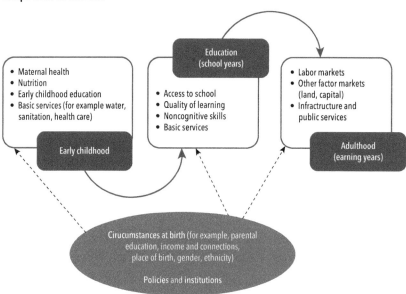

Note: The figure is a stylized representation of a complex process. IGM = intergenerational mobility.

Circumstances Affect Opportunities at Different Stages of Life

Circumstances begin affecting opportunities early in a child's life. They affect the endowments of children at birth, and they affect the critical inputs into human capital development throughout childhood, including nutrition, access to health care, basic services such as safe water and sanitation, and access to quality education. Children's endowments at birth are affected by maternal nutrition and health during gestation, as well as by nonmonetary endowments or traits inherited from parents, all of which are typically associated with circumstances such as parental educational attainment, income, and geographic location.[9]

Consider, for example, the ways in which parental socioeconomic status may influence the educational achievements of children. Monetary investments in children and parental human capital tend to complement or reinforce each other in influencing human capital formation among children. This may occur because richer or more highly educated parents may be more effective at navigating school systems and finding higher-quality schools, may live in neighborhoods with better schools where their children can interact with similarly advantaged children, and may provide their children with complementary inputs, such as educational games and reading time. Indeed, theory predicts that more highly educated parents will invest more in their children relative to less well-educated parents, reducing IGM, even if there were no credit constraints.[10] In the presence of credit constraints, which are common in most countries, the link between parental incomes and parental investments in children becomes stronger because parental investments are constrained by the resources available to the parents (see box 4.3).[11]

The schooling and noncognitive skills attained by children affect incomes later in life through the returns the children obtain as adults for their human capital in the labor market and interactions with other factor markets. In addition to influencing adult earnings indirectly through the channel of human capital, parental status can also exert a direct influence on adult incomes through networks and connections in labor and other factor markets. Other circumstances, such as geographic location, gender, and health endowments at birth can affect the earnings of the next generation through a similar combination of direct and indirect pathways in interaction with parental background.

At each stage of the life cycle, a few actors external to the individual and the parents of the individual are key to mediating the process of equalizing opportunities. These include, for example, the systems of maternal and child health care and early childhood care at the first stage; the school system at the second stage; and the structure and institutions of factor markets—labor, capital, and land—at the third stage. The private sector plays a key role not only in labor markets but also in the provision of services such as infrastructure, education, and health. Governments can influence these external actors in crucial ways, for example, through regulations and policies that affect markets and the provision of services. And public investments have a critical role to play in improving mobility by leveling the playing field at different stages of life.

Although the role of specific public policies and program interventions is discussed in much greater detail in subsequent chapters, the following section examines the extent of evidence offered by aggregate, cross-country data on the importance of public policies in equalizing opportunities to promote IGM, using the level of public spending as an imperfect proxy for the extent of public action.

The Role of Public Investments in Raising Relative Mobility

As seen in chapter 3, relative IGM in education tends to be higher for richer economies, which is to say that it rises with per capita GDP. Theory suggests a variety of channels of intergenerational persistence that can pull relative IGM in different directions as economies get richer. The trajectory of relative IGM in an economy will depend on which of these forces dominate at different stages of development (see box 4.4). In particular, whether relative IGM will rise or decline with GDP, and to what extent, depends on whether government investments to equalize opportunities increase as economies get richer.

Higher public investments may be an important reason why IGM rises with national income

The extent to which public spending can influence the trend in relative IGM in education as economies get richer will depend on the magnitude, nature, and allocation of public spending. If public spending helps equalize opportunities, through investments on poor children that compensate for the gap in private investments between children of rich and poor parents, the effect of parental background on an individual's human capital can be reduced. Existing literature has argued that public investments are more likely to increase mobility when they are sufficiently large;[12] when they are targeted to benefit disadvantaged families or neighborhoods;[13] when they focus on early childhood;[14] and when political power is not captured by the rich unless the rich have the interests of the poor at heart.[15] To the extent that richer economies can invest more, relative IGM can rise as economies get richer. Regressions using the GDIM suggest that higher public spending – on education as well as on aggregate, as a share of GDP – is associated with higher relative IGM in education, after controlling for an economy's per capita GDP. [16]

Figure 4.12 shows that both total public spending and public spending on education (as a share of GDP), which are imperfect proxies of public investments to equalize opportunities, rise with per capita GDP and are associated with higher relative IGM.[17] As economies develop, whether relative IGM rises or falls depends on which effect dominates—the mobility-reducing effect of private investments by optimizing parents (see box 4.4), or the mobility-raising effect of lower credit constraints and higher public

BOX 4.4   As economies get richer, relative IGM in education may rise or decline depending on the relative strength of opposing forces

As an economy gets richer, opposing effects on intergenerational persistence in education may be at work, which can produce a net positive or negative impact on relative IGM at different stages of a country's development process, depending on which effect is stronger.

On the one hand, economic growth may positively affect relative mobility in education through a few channels, the most prominent of which is related to capital market imperfections. These imperfections can be an important reason for intergenerational persistence of education (Piketty 2000). If poorer parents have limited access to credit to invest in their children, then low levels of human capital will be transmitted from one generation to the next. As economies become richer, the effect of credit constraints may decline if incomes of poorer or lower-skilled workers rise and credit markets become more efficient, which would tend to reduce intergenerational persistence in education (see, for example, Maoz and Moav 1999; Owen and Weil 1998).

On the other hand, growth may have an adverse effect on relative mobility in education through other channels. Under the standard assumption that parents seek to optimize the incomes of their children, economic theory predicts that private investments in children's human capital will be an increasing function of both parental income and parental human capital (see, for example, Becker and Tomes 1979, 1986; Becker et al. 2015; Loury 1981). Children born to highly educated parents benefit from exposure to their parents' higher human capital and from the higher (monetary) investments their parents make in their human capital. This is consistent with empirical evidence, such as in Guryan, Hurst, and Kearney (2008); Ramey and Ramey (2010); and Duncan and Murnane (2011). The advantages enjoyed by such children are even stronger when parental human capital and their investments in children act as complements (see, for example, Becker et al. 2015; Heckman and Mosso 2014; Lareau 2011). As economies become richer and average education levels increase, it can be shown that parental investments in their children's education become more "efficient" in terms of producing outcomes. For example, in the stylized model by Becker et al. (2015) that assumes perfect credit markets and no government intervention, an increase in average parental education and income is predicted to raise the level of intergenerational persistence unless inequality in parental education were to decline significantly.

investments to level the playing field. The pattern of relative IGM increasing with GDP, seen in chapter 3, seems to suggest that the second effect dominates when GDP rises above a certain level (see figure 3.10).[18] It also suggests that relative IGM is less likely to rise with GDP if government spending does not act to create a more level playing field in richer economies.[19]

These arguments—and the supporting evidence that is indicative rather than being definitive—have an important implication. Even though relative IGM in education seems to improve with the level of development, this association should not be seen as an inevitable consequence of growth. Rather, relative IGM improves with income levels likely through a combination of two factors: the effects of economic growth, which may (but not necessarily) improve IGM, and the fact that richer economies invest, on the

FIGURE 4.12   **Public spending is higher for richer economies, and associated with higher relative IGM**

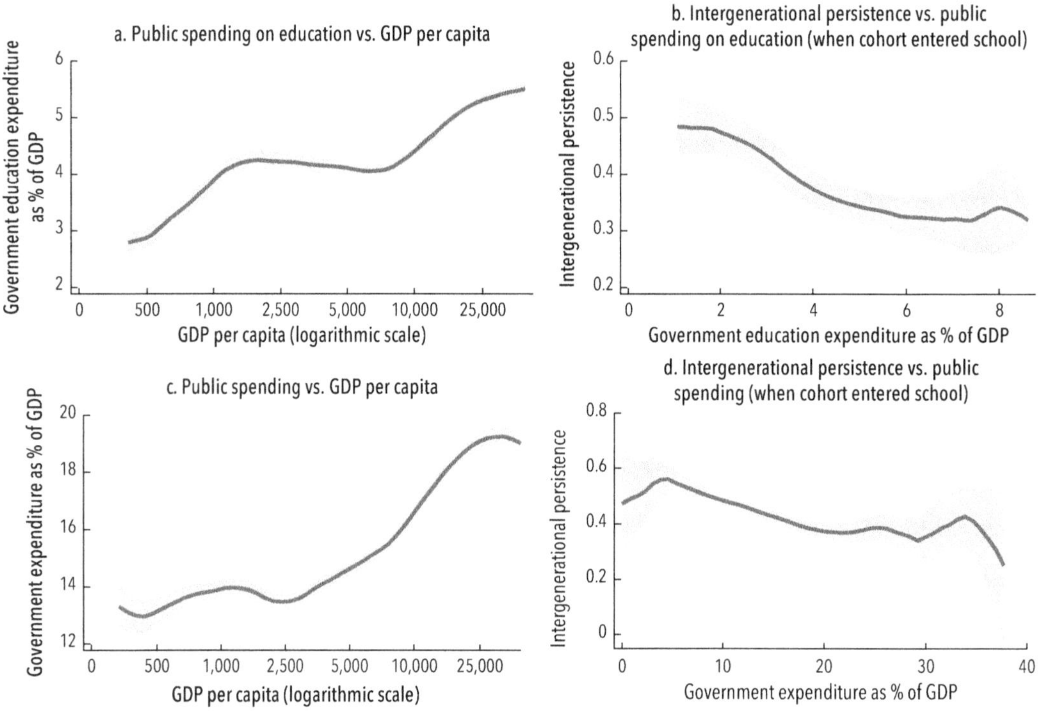

a. Public spending on education vs. GDP per capita

b. Intergenerational persistence vs. public spending on education (when cohort entered school)

c. Public spending vs. GDP per capita

d. Intergenerational persistence vs. public spending (when cohort entered school)

Source: Calculations based on GDIM 2018, the Maddison Project, and UNESCO.
Note: Intergenerational persistence of each cohort is matched to GDP and public spending for the year when the average individual in the cohort is 5 years old (for example, IGM of the 1980s cohort is matched to GDP and public spending in 1990). The shaded areas indicate 95 percent confidence intervals.

average, more public resources relative to the size of their economies on equalizing opportunities.

Thus, economic growth is more likely to lead to a rise in relative mobility in education when it is accompanied by rising public investments to equalize opportunities. This is in turn critical for improving income mobility. If returns to education in the labor market rise over time in an economy, which typically occurs with technological progress, relative IGM in income will tend to decline unless relative IGM in education were to improve. Although public policies can positively influence IGM in education and income, a higher level of public spending by itself is not enough to do so. To improve relative IGM, public policies need to be "progressive" so that the relatively poor benefit more than those who are more well-off. This principle applies not just to direct spending, such as public transfers or public investments in children, but also to all aspects of public actions that can affect the relationship between families and factor markets, including the structure of taxation and regulations.[20]

Equalizing Opportunities at Different Life Stages–Chapters 5 and 6

Given the importance of relative mobility for long-term improvements in inclusion, growth, and social stability, the low levels of mobility in income and education in much of the developing world documented in this report should be a cause for serious concern. These patterns underscore the urgency of proactive policies to reduce inequality of opportunities, which is the underlying reason for low relative mobility. Economic progress alone, in the form of higher growth and reduction in income poverty, is clearly not sufficient to raise relative mobility—17 of the bottom 25 economies by relative income mobility are middle-income economies, including a few that are in the upper-middle-income category with low rates of poverty by international standards.

Although much of the discussion in this chapter is motivated by the need to improve relative mobility, policies guided by the equality of opportunity principle would seek to raise opportunities for the least advantaged groups in a society at every point of time, which will also reduce poverty and improve absolute mobility.[21] To put it differently, equalizing opportunities is about improving upward mobility among poorer families from one generation to the next, which is also likely to lead to greater absolute mobility for the society as a whole.

Labor and other factor markets are critical for income mobility; but ladders to opportunity must be created in childhood, well before an individual enters working age.[22] Chapter 5 deals with this pivotal phase of life, namely, the years of early childhood and schooling, which are the first two stages of the life cycle in figure 4.11. These are also the stages that are most directly relevant to educational mobility, which is the focus of the global trends analyzed in chapter 3. For the developing world, raising IGM in education should be a priority; absolute and relative IGMs in education are lower in the average developing economy than in the average high-income economy, and stronger educational mobility of a generation is associated with higher rates of growth and poverty reduction during the adult years of the generation (chapter 3). Relative mobility of education in turn has a strong influence on relative mobility of income through the first channel of intergenerational income persistence identified in figure 4.5.

The efficiency of labor, capital, and land markets is important for mediating mobility in earnings in adulthood, as is a government's decisions to intervene or participate in these markets. These factors affect the strength of the first and third channels of income persistence across generations identified in figure 4.5. If capital markets do not work well, the poor are unable to borrow against future incomes to become entrepreneurs or to acquire skills outside of formal education. A labor market that rewards a privileged background rather than skills may be a serious obstacle to IGM. Absolute and relative IGMs also depend on robust economic growth that creates more opportunities and helps generate public revenues that can then be used to invest in progressive programs to equalize opportunities. These topics are the focus of chapter 6, which reviews the evidence on the drivers of IGM during the third stage of the life cycle (figure 4.11). This involves an examination of factor markets and government policies that act upon individuals during their adulthood to influence relative and absolute mobility across generations.

The distinction between drivers of income mobility at different stages of life can be blurry at times because they can potentially influence mobility in interrelated ways. For example, policies, markets, and institutions that directly affect the earnings and assets of adults can influence the incentives and ability of parents to invest in the education of their children, affecting education mobility. Given these interrelationships, categorizing the drivers of equal opportunities by life stages, although useful as an organizing framework, can lead to certain ambiguities. The distribution of topics between the two chapters in such cases is a matter of subjective judgment.

The drivers of mobility at different stages of the life cycle complement each other, which calls for a holistic approach toward policies to improve mobility. For example, efficient factor markets and robust economic growth may not be sufficient to raise IGM in income if opportunities are widely unequal at earlier stages of life. Rising economic returns to higher skills can be the outcome of an efficient labor market in a transforming economy, but they can also tighten the association between the incomes of parents and children if opportunities in earlier stages of the lives of the children are widely uneven, which results in low IGM in education.[23]

Conversely, mobility in education by itself is not enough to ensure income mobility in the absence of economic growth and efficient markets that provide rewards commensurate with skills. Thus, improving mobility requires a focus on all stages of the life cycle so that the positive effects at different stages strengthen each other: equalizing opportunities in childhood, to increase IGM in education; addressing market distortions that may limit IGM in income over and above the effect of education on earnings; and reducing gaps in circumstances among children through taxes and transfers that reduce the inequality of income and of wealth among adults.

Annex 4A

Estimation of IGM in Earnings

To expand the number of economies for which IGM in earnings is estimated, different methods of estimations are considered that are tailored to the diverse types of data constraints encountered. Where possible, estimates are borrowed directly from the existing literature. This includes 19 estimates obtained from Equalchances (2018). For the remaining economies, estimates are derived by the authors of this report. An overview of the economies for which IGM in earnings is estimated, and of the methods of estimation used, is shown in table 2A.1 in annex 2A. In all instances, intergenerational persistence in earnings is measured by the regression coefficient (b_y) from the following standard linear intergenerational regression:

$$y_{C,i} = c_y + \beta_y y_{P,i} + \varepsilon_i, \qquad (4A.1)$$

where $y_{C,i}$ and $y_{P,i}$ denote (log) permanent income (that is, lifetime earnings) of individual i and his or her parents, respectively. The estimation of β_y involves a number of challenges. The first challenge is that data on permanent incomes are rarely available. Surveys typically collect data on current income earned (over a certain reference period, such as over the last 12 months) and current wages. A commonly adopted solution is to evaluate wage earnings at a reference age; income earned around the age of 40 is found to provide a reasonable approximation to permanent income (Haider and Solon 2006).

Restricting the survey sample to individuals whose age is around the reference age severely reduces the number of observations that can be used for estimation, which poses a second challenge. This can be dealt with by accounting for age in the regression model, such that all income earners (between the ages of 20 and 60, say) can be included in the regression analysis (Lee and Solon 2009). Because age is now part of the model, β_y at a choice of reference age can be inferred. This still denotes an approximation and hence does not fully resolve the life-cycle bias problem (see, for example, Nybom and Stuhler 2016a, 2016b).

The third challenge is that retrospective data on parental income are often not available. Although in some cases data on parental earnings can be extracted from long panel surveys, these are rare exceptions. If these data are in fact available, then β_y can be estimated by means of ordinary least squares (OLS). Retrospective data on parental education and age (and sometimes occupation) are more common and denote the type of data used in this report. These parental characteristics can be used to predict parental earnings. The resulting predicted earnings can then be used as an instrument in the intergenerational earnings regression. This approach, which is referred to as two-sample two-stage least squares (TSTSLS), involves the following steps (see, for example, Björklund and Jäntti 1997): (1) estimate an income equation from an older sample that is representative of the current population of parents (when they were younger, that is, pseudo-parents), (2) use the estimated model coefficients (that is, return to education and experience) to predict parental earnings at the reference age using the retrospective data on parental age and education as predictors (explanatory variables), and (3) regress child earnings at the reference age on predicted parental earnings at the reference age.

Formally, the income equation that accounts for the age of the respondent (pseudo-parent) takes the following form:

$$y_{P,i} = \alpha_P + \gamma S_{P,i} + \sum_k \alpha_{P,k} \left(A_{P,i} - \overline{A} \right)^k + \sum_k \tau_{P,k} \left(A_{P,i} - \overline{A} \right)^k S_{P,i} + e_{P,i}, \quad (4A.2)$$

where $S_{P,i}$ denotes education of the respondent (either years of schooling or a vector indicating grade completed), $A_{P,i}$ and $\bar{A}$ denote age of the respondent and a choice of reference age, respectively, and γ denotes the coefficient of interest ($\alpha_{P,k}$ and $\tau_{P,k}$ are also estimated but do not feature in the prediction of parental earnings). The degree of the polynomial of age is set by the modeler, and may vary with the number of observations available for the regression (more observations allow for higher-degree polynomials). In the present analysis, a second-degree polynomial is used. Because the polynomial equals zero for $A_{P,i} = \bar{A}$, predicted earnings at the reference age solve $\hat{y}_{P,i} = \hat{a}_P + \hat{\gamma}S_{P,i}$. Note that $\hat{a}_P$ may be omitted because it will get absorbed by the intercept in the intergenerational earnings regression. Given this predictor of parental income, an estimate of intergenerational persistence in earnings (β_y) can be obtained by means of the following TSTSLS regression:

$$y_{C,i} = c_y + \beta_y \hat{y}_{P,i} + \sum_k \alpha_{C,k}\left(A_{C,i} - \bar{A}\right)^k + \sum_k \tau_{C,k}\left(A_{C,i} - \bar{A}\right)^k \hat{y}_{P,i} + \tilde{\varepsilon}_i. \quad (4A.3)$$

For selected economies (mostly developing economies), all regressions are conducted using the same survey (including estimation of the income equation for pseudo-parents). The sample, in that case, is divided into two subsamples, one representing the child generation that is used for the intergenerational earnings regression (respondents between the ages of 20 and 40) and one representing the parent generation that is used to estimate the income equation (respondents between the ages of 35 and 55), which in turn is used for the prediction of parental income. For both generations, the reference age is set at 37.

The adopted estimation approach relies on a variety of assumptions: (1) income earnings at the chosen reference age provide an accurate approximation of permanent income, (2) the residual from the intergenerational earnings regression is uncorrelated with predicted parental earnings, and (3) for economies where a single survey is used, it is implicitly assumed that income shocks pseudo-parents incurred in years prior to the survey year have carried over (that is, are reflected in income earnings observed at the time of survey). Finally, note that any earnings data are observed for a select subset of the population, as it excludes individuals that do not engage in waged employment (that is, it excludes self-employed, unemployed, and individuals who are not part of the labor force). This excluded group tends to be larger in low-income economies.

The Relationship between IGM in Earnings and IGM in Education

Recall that intergenerational persistence in income earnings (β_y) and education (β_s) are measured by the regression coefficients from the following standard linear regression equations:

$$y_{C,i} = c_y + \beta_y y_{P,i} + \varepsilon_i, \quad (4A.4)$$

and:

$$S_{C,i} = c_s + \beta_s S_{P,i} + u_i, \tag{4A.5}$$

where $y_{C,i}$ and $y_{P,i}$ denote (log) earnings at a reference age for individual i and his or her parents, respectively, and where $S_{C,i}$ and $S_{P,i}$ denote years of schooling. To establish the relationship between β_y and β_s, consider the linear Mincer equation for both generations, which describes how education determines income earnings:

$$y_{C,i} = \alpha_C + \lambda_C S_{C,i} + e_{C,i}, \tag{4A.6}$$

and:

$$y_{P,i} = \alpha_P + \lambda_P S_{P,i} + e_{P,i}, \tag{4A.7}$$

where $S_{C,i}$ and $S_{P,i}$ denote education (years of schooling completed) for the child and parent generation, and where λ_C and λ_P represent the returns to education.

Intergenerational persistence in earnings satisfies $\beta_y = cov[y_{C,i}, y_{P,i}]/var[y_{P,i}]$. It can be verified that substituting the intergenerational transmission equations and the Mincer equations solves the following statistical accounting equation:

$$\beta_y = R_p^2 \left(\frac{\lambda_c}{\lambda_p} \right) \beta_s + R_p^2 \left(\frac{\delta_s}{\lambda_p} \right) + \left(1 - R_p^2 \right) \delta_y, \tag{4A.8}$$

where R_p^2 denotes the R-squared (measuring goodness-of-fit) from the parent's Mincer equation, $\delta_s = cov\left[e_{C,i}, S_{P,i} \right] / var\left[S_{P,i} \right]$ is the slope coefficient from the regression of noneducational determinants of child earnings $e_{C,i}$ on parental schooling $S_{p,i}$, and $\delta_y = cov\left[y_{C,i}, e_{P,i} \right] / var\left[e_{P,i} \right]$ is the slope coefficient from the regression of child earnings $y_{C,i}$ on noneducational determinants of parent earnings $e_{P,i}$. Note that R_p^2 captures how much of the variation in earnings is explained by the variation in schooling alone (for the parent's generation).

Estimates of λ_C and λ_P, as well as an estimate of R_p^2, are readily obtained from the Mincer equation regressions. The residuals from the child's Mincer equation can be used to obtain an estimate of δ_s by regressing $e_{C,i}$ on $S_{p,i}$. Because parental earnings are not directly observed, it is not possible to obtain an estimate of δ_y by regressing $y_{C,i}$ on $e_{P,i}$. Instead, δ_y will be estimated indirectly by solving the statistical accounting equation, where δ_y denotes the only remaining unknown variable. Given estimates of all the parameters, the share of β_y that may be attributed to each of the three additive components from the accounting equation can be obtained by dividing the estimated value of each component by the estimate of β_y.

The decomposition of β_y into the three channels of intergenerational persistence rests on some assumptions. Most notably, it is assumed that the linear regression models provide reasonable approximations to the intergenerational transmission of earnings and education as well as to the Mincer equations that describe the relationship between earnings and education. Furthermore, note that in all regression equations the age of the respective individual is also accounted. This is omitted from the presentation for ease of exposition. Finally, this decomposition is implemented for a subset of economies only. Economies for which estimates of IGM in earnings are obtained from existing studies, and for which the database compiled by the authors of this report does not permit for the estimation of IGM in earnings, are excluded.

Notes

1. See Corak (2016).
2. Campante and Chor (2012).
3. Some observers highlighted the potential risks of this combination of factors at the time; see Campante and Chor (2012).
4. Even though education is a weaker predictor of income if GDP is higher, the returns to education do not show any relationship with per capita GDP across the 49 economies.
5. See Ramos and Van de Gaer (2016) for a recent review.
6. The estimates of IEO are taken from Brunori, Ferreira, and Peragine et al. (2013), who compiled them from multiple studies.
7. Brunori, Ferreira, and Peragine (2013).
8. See chapter 5, figure 5.5 in Dabalen et al. (2015).
9. Becker and Tomes (1979, 1986); Currie (2009).
10. For example, see Becker et al. (2015).
11. See Piketty (2000) for an overview of the literature.
12. Iyigun (1999).
13. Mayer and Lopoo (2008), Herrington (2015), and Blankenou and Youderian (2015).
14. Herrington (2015), and Blankenou and Youderian (2015).
15. Uchida (2017).
16. These are linear regressions of intergenerational persistence in education on public spending on education or total public spending (as a share of GDP) and (the logarithm of) per capita GDP, pooling cohorts from the 1960s to the 1980s and including cohort fixed effects. The coefficients on public spending on education and total public spending, as well as on per capita GDP, are negative and strongly significant. Intergenerational persistence of each cohort is matched to GDP and public spending for the year when the average individual in the cohort is five years old.
17. That public spending as a share of GDP increases with national income is a well-known fact, known as Wagner's Law.
18. Relative IGM rises with per capita GDP after it reaches about 2000 USD (at 1990 purchasing power parity), as shown in figure 3.10.

19. An alternative explanation would have to rely on a large mobility-increasing effect of the lowering of credit constraints. This seems like a less likely explanation for rising mobility than rising public investments, because the poor tend to be credit-constrained in most economies, particularly if the impact of public policies (such as social assistance) is netted out, which must be done so that the effects of lower credit constraints are not conflated with those of higher public investments.
20. Solon (2004) and Corak (2016).
21. Bourguignon, Ferreira, and Walton et al (2007), as cited in Ferreira and Peragine (2016). Ferreira and Peragine (2016, 37) also put forth two principles as ethical limits to the pursuit of these objectives: "This objective should be pursued subject to two constraints: first, that policies employed should belong to a permissible set, defined not only by standard feasibility constraints, but also in terms of the ethical acceptability of the policies themselves. Second, along the future path of the economy, no individual is ever below an absolute minimum income level, to be socially agreed upon."
22. As noted by Chetty (2016), among many others.
23. Solon (2004).

References

Becker, Gary Stanley, Scott Duke Kominers, Kevin M. Murphy, and Jörg L. Spenkuch. 2015. "A Theory of Intergenerational Mobility." Managerial Economics and Decision Sciences Working Paper, Northwestern University, Evanston, IL.

Becker, Gary S., and Nigel Tomes. 1979. "An Equilibrium Theory of the Distribution of Income and Intergenerational Mobility." *Journal of Political Economy* 87 (6): 1153–89.

———. 1986. "Human Capital and the Rise and Fall of Families." *Journal of Labor Economics* 4 (3), Part 2: S1–39.

Björklund, Anders, and Markus Jäntti. 1997. "Intergenerational Income Mobility in Sweden Compared to the United States." *The American Economic Review* 87 (5): 1009–18.

Blankenau, William, and Xiaoyan Youderian. 2015. "Early Childhood Education Expenditures and the Intergenerational Persistence of Income." *Review of Economic Dynamics* 18 (2): 334–49.

Bourguignon, François, Francisco H.G. Ferreira, and Michael Walton. 2007. "Equity, Efficiency and Inequality Traps: A Research Agenda." *The Journal of Economic Inequality* 5 (2): 235–56.

Brunori, Paolo, Francisco H.G. Ferreira, and Vito Peragine. 2013. "Inequality of Opportunity, Income Inequality, and Economic Mobility: Some International Comparisons." In *Getting Development Right*, edited by Eva Paus, 85–115. New York: Palgrave Macmillan.

Campante, Filipe R., and Davin Chor. 2012. "Why Was the Arab World Poised for Revolution? Schooling, Economic Opportunities, and the Arab Spring." *Journal of Economic Perspectives* 26 (2): 167–88.

Corak, Miles. 2016. "Inequality from Generation to Generation: The United States in Comparison." IZA Discussion Paper 9929, Institute for the Study of Labor, Bonn.

Chetty, Raj. 2016. "Improving Opportunities for Economic Mobility: New Evidence and Policy Lessons." In *Economic Mobility: Research & Ideas on Strengthening Families, Communities & the Economy,* edited by the Federal Reserve Bank of St. Louis and the Board of Governors of the Federal Reserve System, 35–43. St. Louis, MO:. Federal Reserve Bank of St. Louis.

Currie, Janet. 2009. "Healthy, Wealthy, and Wise: Socioeconomic Status, Poor Health in Childhood, and Human Capital Development." *Journal of Economic Literature* 47 (1): 87–122.

Dabalen, Andrew, Ambar Narayan, Jaime Saavedra-Chanduvi, Alejandro Hoyos Suarez, Ana Abras, and Sailesh Tiwari. 2015. *Do African Children Have an Equal Chance?: A Human Opportunity Report for Sub-Saharan Africa.* Directions in Development. Washington, DC: World Bank.

Duncan, Greg J., and Richard J. Murnane, eds. 2011. *Whither Opportunity?: Rising Inequality, Schools, and Children's Life Chances.* New York: Russell Sage Foundation.

Equalchances. 2018. "International Database on Inequality of Opportunity and Social Mobility." University of Bari, Italy.

Ferreira, Francisco H. G., and Jérémie Gignoux. 2011. "The Measurement of Inequality of Opportunity: Theory and an Application to Latin America." *Review of Income and Wealth* 57 (4): 622–57.

Ferreira, Francisco H. G., and Vito Peragine. 2016. "Individual Responsibility and Equality of Opportunity." In *The Oxford Handbook of Well-Being and Public Policy,* edited by Matthew D. Adler and Marc Fleurbaey, 745–84. Oxford, UK: Oxford University Press.

GDIM (Global Database on Intergenerational Mobility). 2018. *Global Database on Intergenerational Mobility.* Development Research Group, World Bank. Washington, DC: World Bank.

Guryan, Jonathan, Erik Hurst, and Melissa Kearney. 2008. "Parental Education and Parental Time with Children." *Journal of Economic Perspectives* 22 (3): 23–46.

Haider, Steven, and Gary Solon. 2006. "Life-Cycle Variation in the Association between Current and Lifetime Earnings." *American Economic Review* 96 (4): 1308–20.

Heckman, James J., and Stefano Mosso. 2014. "The Economics of Human Development and Social Mobility." *Annual Review of Economics* 6 (1): 689–733.

Herrington, Christopher M. 2015. "Public Education Financing, Earnings Inequality, and Intergenerational Mobility." *Review of Economic Dynamics* 18 (4): 822–42.

Hertz, Tom. 2008. "A Group-Specific Measure of Intergenerational Persistence." *Economics Letters* 100 (3): 415–17.

Im, Fernando, Sandeep Mahajan, Allen Dennis, Sailesh Tiwari, Alejandro Hoyos Suarez, Shabana Mitra, Phindile Ngwenya, and Ambar Narayan. 2012. *South Africa Economic Update: Focus on Inequality of Opportunity (English)*. South Africa Economic Update, Issue 3. Washington, DC: World Bank.

Iyigun, Murat F. 1999. "Public Education and Intergenerational Economic Mobility." *International Economic Review* 40 (3): 697–710.

Lareau, Annette. 2011. *Unequal Childhoods: Class, Race, and Family Life.* Oakland: University of California Press.

Lee, Chul-In, and Gary Solon. 2009. "Trends in Intergenerational Income Mobility." *The Review of Economics and Statistics* 91 (4): 766–72.

Loury, Glenn C. 1981. "Intergenerational Transfers and the Distribution of Earnings." *Econometrica: Journal of the Econometric Society* 49 (4): 843–67.

Maddison Historical Statistics (database), Groningen Growth and Development Centre, Faculty of Economics and Business, University of Groningen, Groningen, The Netherlands, https://www.rug.nl/ggdc/historicaldevelopment/maddison/.

Mayer, Susan E., and Leonard M. Lopoo. 2008. "Government Spending and Intergenerational Mobility." *Journal of Public Economics* 92 (1–2): 139–58.

Maoz, Yishay D., and Moav, O. 1999. "Intergenerational Mobility and the Process of Development." *The Economic Journal* 109 (458): 677–97.

Nybom, Martin, and Jan Stuhler. 2016a. "Heterogeneous Income Profiles and Lifecycle Bias in Intergenerational Mobility Estimation." *Journal of Human Resources* 51 (1): 239–68.

———. 2016b. "Biases in Standard Measures of Intergenerational Income Dependence." *Journal of Human Resources* 51 (1): 0715-7290R.

Owen, Ann L., and David N. Weil. 1998. "Intergenerational Earnings Mobility, Inequality and Growth." *Journal of Monetary Economics* 41 (1): 71–104.

Paes de Barros, Ricardo, Francisco H.G. Ferreira, Jose R. Molinas Vega, Jaime Saavedra Chanduvi. 2009. *Measuring Inequality of Opportunities in Latin America and the Caribbean.* Washington, DC: World Bank; New York: Palgrave Macmillan.

Paes de Barros, Ricardo, José R. Molinas Vega, Jaime Saavedra Chanduvi, Marcelo Giugale, Louise J. Cord, Carola Pessino, and Amer Hasan. 2012. *Do Our Children Have a Chance? A Human Opportunity Report for Latin America and the Caribbean.* Washington, DC: World Bank.

Piketty, Thomas. 2000. "Theories of Persistent Inequality and Intergenerational Mobility." In *Handbook of Income Distribution*, vol. 1, edited by A. B. Atkinson and F. Bourguignon, 429–76. North Holland.

Piraino, Patrizio. 2015. "Intergenerational Earnings Mobility and Equality of Opportunity in South Africa." *World Development* 67: 396–405.

Ramey, Garey, and Valerie A. Ramey. 2010. "The Rug Rat Race." *Brookings Papers on Economic Activity* 41 (1): 129–99.

Ramos, Xavier, and Dirk Van de Gaer. 2016. "Approaches to Inequality of Opportunity: Principles, Measures and Evidence." *Journal of Economic Surveys* 30 (5): 855–83.

Rao, Vijayendra. 2006. "On 'Inequality Traps' and Development Policy." Africa Region Findings & Good Practice Infobriefs 268, World Bank, Washington, DC.

Solon, Gary. 2004. "A Model of Intergenerational Mobility Variation over Time and Place." In *Generational Income Mobility in North America and Europe*, edited by Miles Corak, 38–47. Cambridge, UK: Cambridge University Press.

Uchida, Yuki. 2017. "Education, Social Mobility, and the Mismatch of Talents." *Economic Theory* 63 (1): 1–33.

World Bank. 2012. *South Africa Economic Update: focus on Inequality of Opportunity*. South Africa Economic Update Issue No. 3. Washington, DC: World Bank.

CHAPTER 5
Equalizing Opportunities for Children to Achieve Fair Progress

Building ladders to opportunity among children through investments and policies aimed at the first two stages of an individual's life cycle is critical in promoting economic mobility across generations (see chapter 4, figure 4.11). Fostering equality of opportunity in childhood typically requires interventions that compensate for the disadvantages suffered by children who are born into adverse circumstances. These circumstances include endowments inherited from parents and attributes such as race, gender, location, family composition, and so on.

This chapter combines evidence from the economic literature and an analysis of cross-country patterns using the Global Database on Intergenerational Mobility (GDIM), and attempts to extract lessons that are relevant to developing economies. The chapter highlights the importance of a few key policy drivers in the effort to equalize opportunities in childhood and youth, but only if the evidence appears strong. It does not attempt to be exhaustive or definitive. One of these drivers is education policy, a topic that the *World Development Report 2018* (World Bank 2018), which focuses on the quality of learning, covers in much more detail.

Theory predicts that the progressivity of public investments in human capital is one of the drivers of greater intergenerational mobility (IGM) in education and income.[1] Although empirical evidence, including some of the findings presented in this chapter, confirm this prediction, the question that is most relevant for policy makers is what form should these equalizing investments take? And what exactly does it mean to compensate for disadvantages that are attributable to the circumstances of birth? The question of which circumstances should be offset by policy steps requires value judgments that may be different across countries, depending on the nature of inequalities and their drivers, and societal preferences.

Although absolute and relative IGM are treated as separate concepts in the measurement of mobility earlier in this report, the two objectives are likely to be compatible from a policy perspective (see chapter 4). Equalizing opportunities in childhood and youth is important for improving relative mobility in education and for raising upward mobility among poor and disadvantaged families, which would generate greater absolute mobility throughout the economy. This is also a reason why absolute and relative IGM are positively correlated across the world (chapter 3).

Inequality of Opportunity among Children in the Developing World

An assessment of the extent of inequality of opportunity among children in the developing world and the key attributes or circumstances that contribute to inequality is useful. One measure of the opportunities available to children is the widely applied synthetic measure, the human opportunity index (HOI), which is the average coverage of an indicator (such as the school enrollment rate), discounted by a penalty that increases with inequality in coverage across children experiencing different key circumstances (see chapter 4, box 4.2).[2]

The HOIs estimated for indicators such as school enrollment and completion, nutrition, immunization, and access to basic infrastructure show varying degrees of deprivation and inequality in developing countries across the world. In large parts of Sub-Saharan Africa and South Asia, which exhibit the least IGM of education (chapter 3), the HOIs for some of the most basic indicators tend to be low because of low coverage rates and wide inequality between children with substantial differences in circumstances.[3] Figure 5.1 illustrates the low levels and wide inequality in access to critical inputs for human development among one-year-olds in 20 African countries around the year 2008. The opportunities available among this age group are defined to meet the most basic standard, whereby children are considered opportunity deprived if they lack access to improved sources of water, lack access to adequate sanitation, are not fully immunized as appropriate for their age, or are not adequately nourished (stunted).

Even using this minimal standard, which some might consider highly inadequate, the HOI is low in most countries (the bars in figure 5.1). This is because of the low coverage of opportunities (the circles in figure 5.1) and substantial inequality across children experiencing different circumstances in most cases (the gap between the circles and the bars). In five countries, fewer than 10 percent of one-year-olds enjoy these opportunities. The HOI, which adds a penalty for the inequality in coverage between children with different circumstances, is 10 percent or lower in nine countries and does not exceed 30 percent in any country. In Senegal, which has the highest HOI among these countries, just 35 percent of one-year-olds meet all four

FIGURE 5.1   Opportunity deprivation among one-year-olds, Sub-Saharan Africa, circa 2008

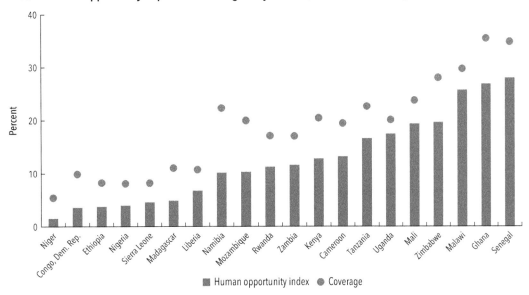

■ Human opportunity index   ● Coverage

Source: Dabalen et al. 2015.
Note: HOI and coverage rates measure the extent to which one-year-olds in a country are not opportunity deprived. Children are opportunity deprived if they lack access to an improved source of water (piped, well, or rainwater), lack access to adequate sanitation (pit or flush toilet), are not fully immunized (for age 1), or if they are stunted. A higher HOI indicates a lower deprivation of opportunity. The gaps between the circles and bars indicate the penalty because of inequality of opportunity for a given set of circumstances. Countries are sorted in increasing order by HOI. HOI = human opportunity index.

thresholds of human development. The HOI of 28 means that there is considerable inequality in coverage among children facing different circumstances.[4] As shown in chapter 4, the circumstances that contribute to inequality of opportunity in childhood show a consistent pattern. Household economic status, parental educational attainment, and the location of the household are almost always the most important contributors to the component of HOI that measures inequality of opportunity.[5]

The Importance of Improving the Early Life Environment

Improving the early life environment represents the low-hanging fruit for policy makers looking to equalize opportunities and increase mobility.[6] Efforts to equalize opportunities by removing or compensating for disadvantages associated with circumstances of birth must start even before a child is born. These efforts must prioritize children whose circumstances put them at a disadvantage, which are most commonly related to low incomes and assets among families, low parental educational attainment, and location in underserved or poor areas. The early life environment of a child is also affected by the health of the mother, which is influenced by the circumstances of the mother and the child.

Maternal health is a critical determinant of a child's health at birth, which is an important predictor of long-term outcomes in education, income, and disability. Research has shown that children with lower birthweight exhibit substantially worse outcomes as adults relative to outcomes among their twins or closely spaced siblings in schooling attainment, test scores, employment, reliance on disability programs, wages, and adult health.[7] Maternal disadvantage associated with the socioeconomic status (SES) of mothers related to differences in education, income, and other circumstances such as race and marital status leads to poorer health among the children at birth through four key channels: poor health behaviors during the prenatal period; greater exposure to harmful environmental factors; lower access to medical care, including family planning services; and poorer maternal health, including nutrition (box 5.1).[8]

Disadvantages inherited at birth may be difficult to overcome through postnatal investments. Children with poorer initial health endowments might benefit from fewer postnatal investments, and the investments that

---

BOX 5.1   **Maternal disadvantages adversely affect long-term outcomes of the next generation**

Mounting evidence suggests that maternal disadvantages associated with SES during the prenatal period have a substantial impact on infant health, which affects long-term outcomes among the children. Research, largely based on sibling comparisons or natural experiments (to avoid confounding factors such as unfavorable genetically inherited traits that could conceivably affect both maternal and infant health) identify four main domains of maternal disadvantage: poor health behaviors during the prenatal period (for example, tobacco consumption and neglect of prenatal care); greater exposure to harmful environmental factors, including the direct effect of toxic pollutants, violence, and stress; poorer access to medical care, including contraception, leading to a greater likelihood of unplanned pregnancy; and poorer underlying health conditions, including chronic diseases and undernutrition (Aizer and Currie 2014).

Although some of these areas of disadvantage are well known, a few examples are worth highlighting. A study of all births in five large states in the United States found that African-American and less-educated women are more likely to live in environmentally hazardous sites and less likely to move to cleaner areas between births. In addition to experiencing poorer health because of conditions such as diabetes or hypertension, disadvantaged women in the United States might also be disproportionately affected by contagious diseases such as influenza, which can negatively affect fetal development. A recent report on inequalities in the health of women and girls in Sub-Saharan Africa finds that reproductive and maternal health services for women and girls are scarce—half of women and girls are not receiving the most essential care—and distributed highly unequally within countries. Maternity care packages and delivery attended by skilled personnel are among the most unevenly distributed health services, primarily linked to differences in family wealth, educational attainment among women, and location of residence (ISGlobal and World Bank 2016).

Sources: Aizer and Currie 2014; ISGlobal and World Bank 2016.

they do receive may be less effective.[9] Research seems to support the view that health investments among newborns and postnatal investments are complementary. One example is offered by the Infant Health and Development Program (IHDP) in the United States, a randomized intervention with an intensive preschool program on low-birthweight infants, whereby the treatment is compared against a less-intensive program among a control group. The intensive preschool program had a significant and sustained (to age 18 years) positive impact on cognitive test scores, but only among children at the higher end of the low birthweight spectrum and almost no impact among children at the other end of the spectrum.[10] Such complementarity can potentially explain why the long-term impact of low birthweight is greater if children are born into poverty. It also underscores the importance of the health endowments of children at birth, and this calls for a focus on the health of mothers from disadvantaged backgrounds.

Child malnutrition, which is often the combined effect of prenatal and postnatal disadvantages in the nutritional and health environment, can generate learning difficulties, poor health, and lower productivity and earnings over a lifetime.[11] A study in Norway finds that, even among twins, higher birthweight is associated with greater height later in life, higher intelligent quotients, greater likelihood of secondary school completion, and higher earnings.[12] Evidence from the United Kingdom and the United States shows that individuals who are taller also have higher cognitive ability.[13] Adult height is determined by growth in childhood, and growth deprivation in early childhood, in particular, cannot be offset. If the same environmental conditions in early childhood—primarily nutrition and disease incidence—affect the likelihood that individuals meet their full height potential and cognitive potential, it is logical that those who are taller would have, on average, greater cognitive ability.[14]

In the GDIM, economies with lower rates of stunted growth and wasting (low weight for height) among five-year-olds are also likely to have higher relative and absolute IGM in education, which is consistent with the notion that better nourishment and health at an early age lead to better education outcomes and, thus, higher educational mobility. The relationship with IGM is particularly strong in the case of stunting (figure 5.2), which seems intuitive because a high rate of stunting in a population is associated with "poor socioeconomic conditions and increased risk of frequent and early exposure to adverse conditions such as illness and/or inappropriate feeding practices," according to the World Health Organization.[15]

The importance of childhood nutrition is also indirectly shown by research on the long-term impact of childhood disadvantages on adult outcomes. Rainfall is an exogenous shock, which affects agricultural production and therefore household income, food consumption, and nutrition. A study of the impact of rainfall in rural Indonesia finds that women who

FIGURE 5.2   Greater mobility is associated with lower rates of stunting and wasting

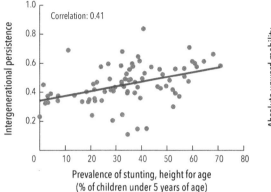

a. Relative mobility and stunting rate

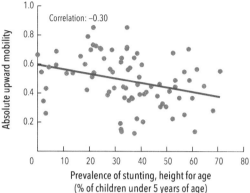

b. Absolute mobility and stunting rate

Source: GDIM 2018; Institute for Statistics, United Nations Educational, Scientific and Cultural Organization; World Development Indicators (database), World Bank, Washington, DC, http://data.worldbank.org/products/wdi.
Note: The figure shows IGM estimates for cohorts born in the 1980s. The rates of stunting, height for age (% of children under 5 years of age), refer to averages in 1986–95, including economies with at least one observation during this period. The period is chosen roughly to match the early childhood years of the 1980s cohorts.

had been exposed to 20 percent more than average rainfall in their early childhood years are almost 4 percentage points less likely to self-report poor health, complete nearly quarter of a year more of school, and have more assets as adults.[16] Similar effects are not found among boys, which suggests that exposure to economic shocks in the early years can increase the inequality of opportunity among girls relative to boys.

Lost opportunities during childhood, regardless of whether they emerge out of prenatal or postnatal conditions, are hard to offset through interventions later in life. At a general policy level, investments to improve access to and quality of basic services and reduce the related inequalities—including in prenatal care, nutrition among mothers, immunization, health care, and safe water, sanitation, and other basic infrastructure—are critical to equalizing opportunities at birth and in early childhood. Low quality of infrastructure and health care affect all, but they disproportionately affect children from disadvantaged backgrounds, who are more likely to be born with poorer health.

The importance of targeting maternal health and early childhood improvements among disadvantaged families is well known. However, much of the research measures the average impact of programs on short-term indicators, rather than on relative or absolute mobility. To assess the effectiveness of programs in improving IGM, one needs to look at the long-term outcomes of programs among the most opportunity-deprived individuals. If the effects are positive, then the program will likely increase both absolute and relative IGM. The review of the evidence on program interventions below has such a long-term focus, particularly on impacts among children born under conditions of socioeconomic disadvantage.

Targeting Mothers in the Prenatal Period

Evidence from the United States suggests that policy measures aimed at disadvantaged women of childbearing age, including health insurance, measures to curb domestic violence, and family-planning services, can have positive impacts on infant health and longer-term outcomes among children.[17] Food supplementation programs also appear to show benefits. For example, studies have found positive impacts of the introduction of the Special Supplemental Nutrition Program for Women, Infants, and Children and the Supplemental Nutrition Assistance Program on the incidence of low-birthweight babies among disadvantaged mothers in the United States.[18]

Randomized controlled trials (RCTs) of nutritional supplementation during pregnancy in developing countries have shown that relatively inexpensive nutritional supplements can increase birthweight and, in some cases, other, longer-term outcomes.[19] For example, in Tanzania, children who were likely to be exposed to iodine supplements during their first trimester in utero attained an average of 0.35 more years of schooling than nonexposed children.[20] Iodine is known to be important for human growth and brain development. About 1 billion people worldwide are at risk of brain damage from iodine deficiency disorders, signifying that programs successfully boosting iodine supplementation can be of great value.

Programs to build the awareness and knowledge of mothers provide additional examples of successful prenatal interventions. The Nurse-Family Partnership Program in the United States provides home visits by nurses to poor, unmarried young women who are pregnant for the first time. Nurses visit monthly during the pregnancy and during the first two years of the child's life and provide guidance to pregnant women and new mothers on healthy behaviors, competent care of children, and personal maternal development. The program has been found to reduce child abuse and adolescent criminal activity and improve academic achievement among the children; the greatest improvements are among children with mothers with cognitive and mental health disadvantages.[21]

Program Interventions in Early Childhood

Although the deprivations suffered in utero can reduce the effectiveness of postnatal investments, intervening in the postnatal period can also be effective, particularly if the interventions occur early in a child's life. Evidence shows that early childhood education programs can have a positive impact on long-term outcomes among children of low-income families.[22] There is also some evidence of successful programs targeting nutritional and health improvements in early childhood.

Nutritional interventions

Available evidence highlights the critical importance of nutritional interventions early in life, before a child turns age 3 (box 5.2). Evidence on Guatemala

BOX 5.2   Evidence on long-term impacts of nutritional and health interventions in early childhood

Hoddinott et al. (2008) have researched the long-term impacts of nutritional supplements among nearly 2,400 children in four villages in Guatemala in 1969–77. In two of the villages, a nutritious liquid supplement, high in protein, was provided twice a day to children ages 0–7. Between 2002 and 2004, economic data on 60 percent of the original sample were obtained. Exposure to the nutritional supplement before age 3 had caused a substantial rise in hourly wages. Among children exposed between ages 0 and 2, the impact was equivalent to a 46 percent increase in average wages. Hoddinott et al. (2013) estimate benefit–cost ratios of reducing stunting through such programs and find these estimates to range from 3.6 in the Democratic Republic of Congo to 48.0 in Indonesia. In all cases, the benefits greatly outweigh the cost of implementation.

Bharadwaj, Løken, and Neilson (2013) study the impact of early childhood health interventions on long-run educational achievements, exploiting the fact that children in Chile and Norway with a birthweight below 1,500 grams receive special medical attention. Because children slightly above or below this cutoff are similar in all other respects, the impact of extra medical attention can be studied causally. In both countries, the extra medical attention among infants below the cutoff involved the treatment of respiratory distress syndrome. In Chile, in addition, it involved specialized nutritional supplements. The authors tracked the treatment children years later, when they were in school. In Chile and Norway, children slightly below the cutoff performed 0.15 and 0.22 standard deviations better in mathematics test scores than children slightly above the cutoff, respectively. Providing extra medical attention to children suffering from disadvantage at birth has thus been shown to help improve later-in-life outcomes.

shows that nutritional supplements provided to children lead to a significant increase in hourly wages as adults; the strongest effect occurs if the supplements are given to children ages 2 or less.[23] In Guatemala, the nutritional supplements had no effect on adult outcomes if they were given to children above age 3.

Estimates quantifying the returns to investing in nutritional supplement programs suggest that the benefits of such programs greatly outweigh the cost of implementation. Evidence on Chile and Norway demonstrates that extra medical attention to infants suffering from health disadvantages at birth (indicated by low birthweight) leads to better learning achievements in the long run.[24] Although early interventions are crucial, interventions at a later stage can also be effective in addressing specific causes of poor health among children. Evidence on Kenya reveals the positive impact of school deworming programs on adult outcomes, including secondary school attendance among women and hours worked among men.[25]

Learning, noncognitive skills, and childcare
Preschool programs can play an important equalizing role in early childhood because skill formation is a dynamic process in which early inputs strongly affect the productivity of later inputs.[26] Early childhood education

has strong long-term impacts. Preschoolers with low levels of cognitive development exhibit lower school achievement and earn lower wages in adulthood.[27] A study conducted in Tennessee finds a high correlation between kindergarten test scores and adult outcomes such as earnings at age 27, college attendance, home ownership, and retirement savings.[28] Reviews of the evidence indicate that intervening during preschool years is more effective than postschool interventions, and only programs that start before children reach age 3 seem to have long-lasting effects on cognitive abilities.[29]

Cognitive skills are not the only determinants of long-term outcomes. Intensive preschool programs such as the Perry Preschool and Abecedarian projects had large long-term effects mainly because they improved noncognitive skills among children, starting around age 3 (box 5.3).[30] Although most of the research on the long-term impacts of early childhood programs has been conducted in high-income countries, the Jamaica Study provides

---

BOX 5.3   Long-term impacts of early childhood interventions to improve cognitive and noncognitive skills

Substantial research has been carried out on the long-run impacts of programs that change early learning environments. Although most of the research has been done in high-income economies, the Jamaica Study highlights the importance of developing socioemotional skills in early childhood in a developing economy. In the study, 129 toddlers suffering from stunting were randomly assigned to four treatment groups involving weekly visits from community health workers for two years (1986–87). One treatment group underwent sessions during which the community workers sought to help develop the children's cognitive, language, and psychosocial skills; another group was given a nutritional intervention; and a third group was given both interventions. Relative to the control group (the fourth group), the children who had received the psychosocial treatment (with or without the nutritional supplement) had 25 percent higher labor market earnings 20 years later (Gertler et al. 2014).[a]

The Perry Preschool Project was conducted in the mid-1960s in Michigan and targeted low-income, low-intelligent quotient African-American children ages 3–4. Among the participants, 127 were randomly divided into treatment and control groups. The treatment group was provided active participatory learning for 2.5 hours five days a week during the school year and 1.5-hour home visits focused on socioemotional development. Data collected at different ages during adulthood show that the program fostered long-term gains in personality skills, healthy behavior, and economic outcomes and reductions in criminal activity. The program raised high school graduation among girls by 56 percent and employment at age 40 among men by 29 percent (Heckman, Pinto, and Savelyev 2013).

Two randomized controlled trials conducted in North Carolina in the 1970s—the Carolina Approach to Responsive Education and the Carolina Abecedarian Project—aimed to improve early life skills among disadvantaged, primarily African-American children by supplying

box continues next page

BOX 5.3   Long-term impacts of early childhood interventions to improve cognitive and noncognitive skills (continued)

center-based childcare. The centers received the children 6.50–9.75 hours a day, 50 weeks a year from the time they were eight weeks old until they reached age 5. The Carolina Approach program included home visits. Garcia et al. (2016) find that the treated children exhibited a higher lifetime income, lower crime rates, and better health and calculate the rate of return on the programs at about 14 percent a year, equivalent to a benefit–cost ratio of more than 7.

The much larger Head Start Program in the United States was launched in 1965 and provides early childhood education, health care, nutrition, and parent involvement services to low-income children ages 5 or below, benefitting millions of children since its inception. Bauer and Schanzenbach (2016) find that Head Start boosts the likelihood that a participating child will complete high school and receive a postsecondary degree, diploma, or certification and has positive impacts on measures of self-control, self-esteem, and parenting practices (among the parents of participants). Other studies have found beneficial impacts of the program on education and health outcomes and in reducing criminal activities and idleness among young adults (Carneiro and Ginja 2014; Garces, Thomas, and Currie 2002). Deming (2009) finds significant impacts of the program on a summary index of young adult outcomes (high school graduation, college attendance, idleness, crime, teen parenthood, and health status) and larger impacts among African-Americans and relatively disadvantaged children. These occur even though gains in test scores at ages 5–6 fade among many Head Start children by age 14 (middle school age), particularly among the groups that gain the most in the long run. This seems to suggest that the long-term impacts of such programs are due in large part to their contributions to noncognitive development among children. Moreover, relying on test score gains alone to assess the future benefits of such programs could greatly understate their impacts. This is important in making cost–benefit calculations to guide decisions on whether to invest in such programs.

a. That the nutritional treatment had no significant impact on earnings does not necessarily contradict the findings of Hoddinott et al. (2008) reported in box 5.2. Nutritional intake in the early years may affect future productivity in the form of wages, but not necessarily earnings.

an important example in a developing-country setting. It finds that interventions to improve children's socioemotional skills during the first three years of life can have a positive and significant impact on labor earnings in adulthood.

While small, intensive, model programs such as the Perry Preschool Project demonstrate the frontier of possibilities with early childhood development, research on the long-term impacts of the Head Start Program in the United States—one of the longest-running and largest preschool programs targeting low-income children in the world—offers key insights on what might be possible if such programs were to be scaled up to national coverage (see box 5.3). Despite all the challenges of implementation and the inefficiencies associated with scaling up, the benefits of a program such as Head Start can still be substantial: as much as 80 percent of the gains in young adult outcomes induced by the model programs such as Perry, according to one study.[31] With scale also comes the need for experimentation, flexibility to adapt to local circumstances within a country, and timely analysis of results to create a feedback loop to induce program administrators to engineer improvements.

Subsidized childcare is another policy instrument available to governments, distinct from interventions through specific programs on early childhood development. A reform in Norway in 1975 that greatly expanded subsidized childcare offers a rare opportunity to study the long-run impacts of a countrywide childcare reform. In the four years following the reform, childcare coverage rose from 10 percent to 28 percent among three- to six-year-olds. The responsibility for expanding the childcare system was assigned to local communities, which implemented the reform at different times, creating spatial and time variation that make it possible to estimate impacts. One study has found that the program led to a reduction in crime, an increase in life-cycle labor income, and a rise in educational attainment. The largest effects occurred among girls and the children of less well-educated mothers.[32] Another recent paper suggests that the childcare expansion significantly equalized opportunities between children from most family backgrounds.[33] These impacts show that reforms aimed at making childcare more accessible could improve both absolute and relative mobility.

School meal programs

School meal programs have been widely adopted by governments to improve childhood nutrition and school attendance and performance. There is little evidence on the long-run impacts of school meals except for two examples in Scandinavian countries that show small positive effects. In Norway, a nutritious breakfast program implemented in 26 cities in the 1920s and 1930s increased educational attainment by 0.1 years and earnings by 2–4 percent.[34] A similar program in Sweden in the 1960s raised long-run incomes by about 4 percent.[35]

Given the scarcity of direct evidence on the long-run impacts of school meal programs, studies of more near-term effects on school attendance and learning outcomes can help identify the potential for long-term impacts. Evidence on the short-run impacts of school meals is mixed in developing countries, probably because the effects depend on the characteristics of the program, such as the quality of the food provided. In India, after the country's Supreme Court issued a directive requiring that midday meals be served in schools, one study estimated that the program had a positive impact of 13 percent on school enrollments.[36] A school meal program in Kenya increased school participation and student test scores.[37] However, a program in Chile that targeted high-calorie meals among rural public schools had no such effect.[38] Evidence is more consistently positive among programs in high-income countries. In the United Kingdom, a change in the health composition of free school meals, which is part of a means-tested program, led to better learning outcomes in mathematics, English, and science and reduced school absences related to illness and health.[39] In the United States, the School Breakfast Program has raised learning achievements in mathematics and reading.[40]

Reducing Opportunity Gaps in Education Can Improve Mobility

Education policies that reduce gaps in enrollment and in the quality of learning are key tools for equalizing opportunities in the second stage of the life cycle (chapter 4, figure 4.11). Cross-country correlations hint at the importance of investments that improve enrollments and the quality of learning. Economies with higher absolute and relative IGM in education among the 1980s cohorts were likely to have lower shares of children out of school during the 1990s, a period that roughly matches the school years of those cohorts (figure 5.3, panels a and b).

Enrollments are only part of the story, however, because enrollment does not necessarily imply that the child receives an education of the quality that is needed to promote upward mobility. Economies showing higher average primary-school test scores—a rough indicator of the quality of education provided by the school system—are likely to exhibit greater absolute and relative IGM in education (figure 5.3, panels c and d).

Moreover, average learning outcomes obscure the large disparities across the children of parents with different levels of income and education. For example, socioeconomically disadvantaged students across the countries of the Organisation for Economic Co-operation and Development (OECD) are almost three times more likely than advantaged students not to attain the baseline level of proficiency in science in the relevant Program for International Student Assessment (PISA) tests among 15-year-old students.[41] The SES of a child, followed by parental educational attainment and location of residence, is the most important contributor to inequality in the attainment of basic levels of proficiency in reading, mathematics, and science in the 2012 round of the PISA.[42]

Learning outcomes tend to be particularly low in developing economies. According to the 2018 *World Development Report*, leading international assessments of literacy and numeracy show that the average student in low-income countries performs worse than 95 percent of the students in high-income countries. Even in middle-income countries, many students who are in the top quarter of their cohorts would rank in the bottom quarter in a wealthier country.[43]

The differences in learning outcomes between the haves and have-nots are particularly acute in developing economies. For example, large gaps between urban and rural children and between children with high and low SES in basic reading and numeracy skills have been observed among sixth-grade students in eight countries in Sub-Saharan Africa that participated in the Southern and Eastern Africa Consortium for Monitoring Educational Quality SACMEQ-III project in 2007.[44] Inequality of opportunity—the share of total inequality attributable to circumstances such as gender, parental education, family background,

FIGURE 5.3   Economies with better learning outcomes and smaller shares of children out of school show greater mobility, on average

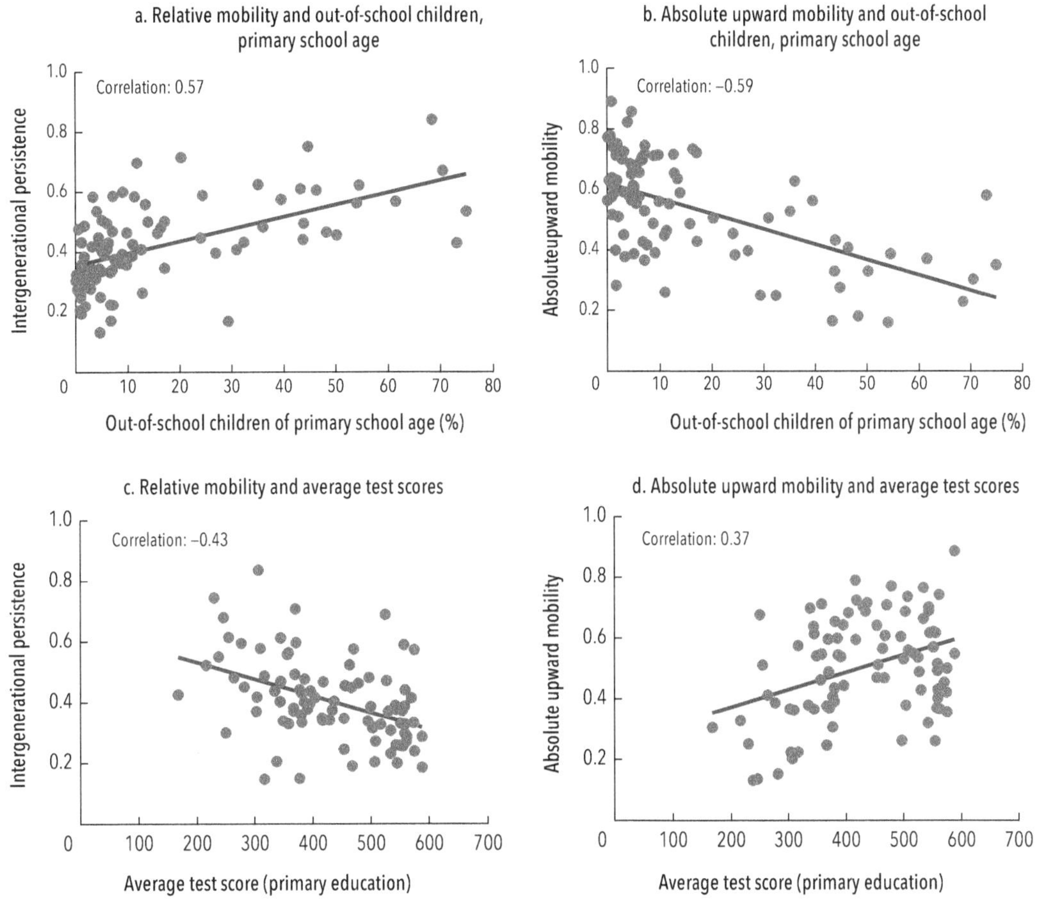

a. Relative mobility and out-of-school children, primary school age

Correlation: 0.57

Intergenerational persistence (y-axis, 0 to 1.0)
Out-of-school children of primary school age (%) (x-axis, 0 to 80)

b. Absolute upward mobility and out-of-school children, primary school age

Correlation: −0.59

Absolute upward mobility (y-axis, 0 to 1.0)
Out-of-school children of primary school age (%) (x-axis, 0 to 80)

c. Relative mobility and average test scores

Correlation: −0.43

Intergenerational persistence (y-axis, 0 to 1.0)
Average test score (primary education) (x-axis, 0 to 700)

d. Absolute upward mobility and average test scores

Correlation: 0.37

Absolute upward mobility (y-axis, 0 to 1.0)
Average test score (primary education) (x-axis, 0 to 700)

Source: GDIM 2018; Institute for Statistics, United Nations Educational, Scientific and Cultural Organization; Altinok, Diebolt, and Demeulemeester 2014.
Note: The figure shows intergenerational mobility estimates for cohorts born in the 1980s. The share of out-of-school children of primary school age refers to the average in 1991–2000, including only economies with at least three observations during this period. The average test scores refer to the average in primary schools in 1964–2010, including economies with at least one observation.

and location—accounts for a sizable share (between 9 percent and 35 percent) of total inequality in mathematics and science test scores across nine countries in the Middle East and North Africa region.[45]

Public Spending on Education Can Promote Relative Mobility

Enrollments and quality of learning depend on a range of factors, including policy choices. Investment in public education is widely considered to promote equality of opportunity, a view that is confirmed by cross-country correlations. Economies with higher public spending on education (as a share of gross domestic product [GDP]) in the 1990s, the period roughly

FIGURE 5.4   Higher relative mobility in education is associated with more public spending on education, particularly in developing economies

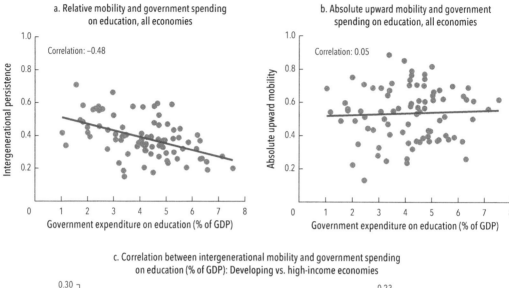

a. Relative mobility and government spending on education, all economies

b. Absolute upward mobility and government spending on education, all economies

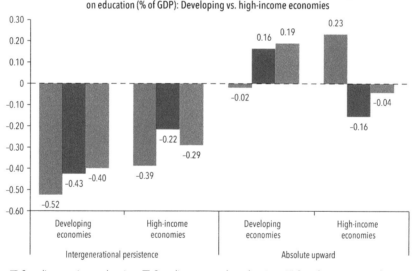

c. Correlation between intergenerational mobility and government spending on education (% of GDP): Developing vs. high-income economies

Source: GDIM 2018; Institute for Statistics, United Nations Educational, Scientific and Cultural Organization.
Note: The figure shows intergenerational mobility (IGM) estimates for cohorts born in the 1980s. Higher intergenerational persistence implies lower relative IGM. Government expenditure on education as a % of gross domestic product (GDP) refers to the average in 1991–2000, including only economies with at least four observations during this period (and excluding Lesotho as an extreme outlier). Spending on primary, secondary, and tertiary education as a % of GDP refers to the average in 1991–2000, including economies with at least one observation.

corresponding to the schooling years of cohorts of the 1980s, are also likely to have higher relative IGM among those cohorts (figure 5.4, panel a). No such pattern is observed for absolute IGM, which may result because equality of opportunity is more closely associated with relative IGM than with absolute IGM (figure 5.4, panel b).

The association between relative IGM and public spending on education related to cohorts of the 1980s is much stronger in developing economies than in high-income economies, possibly reflecting greater variation across the developing world in the amount of resources going to public education (figure 5.4, panel c). Although public spending on all levels of education in the two groups of economies is associated with higher relative IGM, the strongest associations are observed in spending on primary education. Higher absolute mobility is also weakly associated with higher public spending on secondary and tertiary education in developing economies and on primary education in high-income economies.

These correlations should not necessarily be interpreted as cause and effect because they might be explained by other factors that affect both. That said, the correlations show that economies with higher public investment in education also tend to exhibit greater relative mobility in education, probably because such spending is generally progressive and promotes a more level playing field among children across various socioeconomic characteristics in society.[46] Developing economies showing greater relative and absolute mobility seem to have invested more public resources not only in primary education but also in secondary and tertiary education.

Higher public spending may not necessarily lead to better learning outcomes

Higher public spending does not necessarily lead to better quality of education, which matters for economic mobility. Public spending is only weakly correlated with average learning outcomes across countries and statistically insignificant after controlling for the country's income level. For any given level of spending, a wide range of outcomes can be observed, even among countries at a similar level of development.[47] On the other hand, there is some evidence that higher public spending in primary and secondary education is associated with lower inequality in learning achievement.[48] Another study suggests that higher education spending is associated with better learning outcomes only among education systems that spend below a certain threshold per student.

Furthermore, high public spending on education does not necessarily lead to better access and higher quality in education among disadvantaged groups. What also matters is how efficient the spending is in producing the key inputs into education and how equitable the allocation of spending is across groups and space. The availability and quality of teachers are such critical inputs into education. Economies with a higher teacher–student ratio in primary education are also likely to exhibit higher relative and absolute IGM (figure 5.5). The association with IGM is weaker in the case of the teacher–student ratio in secondary education, which is consistent with the notion that smaller class sizes are more important for the quality of the education provided to younger children. However, this is not the entire explanation, given the other factors that

FIGURE 5.5 Greater absolute and relative IGM is associated with better teacher-student ratios in primary school

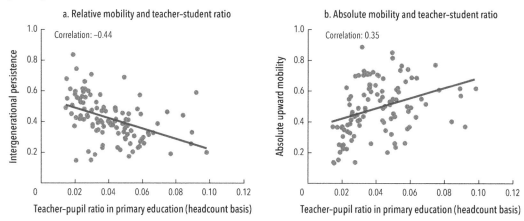

Source: GDIM 2018; Institute for Statistics, United Nations Educational, Scientific and Cultural Organization.
Note: The figure shows intergenerational mobility (IGM) estimates for cohorts born in the 1980s. Government expenditure on education as a % of GDP refers to the average in 1991–2000, including only economies with at least four observations during this period. The teacher-pupil ratio in primary education refers to the average in 1991–2000, including only economies with at least four observations.

are key to the quality of education, such as the quality of teachers, the instruction they provide, curricula, and other critical inputs, which are highlighted and discussed in detail in *World Development Report 2018* (World Bank 2018).

Education Policies that Promote Mobility: The Evidence

The evidence on the impact of education policies on relative mobility or equality of opportunity all points in the same direction: relative mobility improves if policy changes improve the accessibility of education among disadvantaged students. There is a variety of ways in which education can become more accessible to the disadvantaged indirectly through changes in the tracking, duration, cost, or intensity of an education program or directly by expanding the number of years of compulsory education.

The practice of tracking—separating pupils according to academic ability by following different curricula within a school or placing them in different schools—is prevalent in many education systems to varying degrees. Given the key role tracking plays in the education profiles of generations of students, the practice has been studied extensively because of its impacts on equality of opportunity. Most of the research finds that reforms that weaken the practice or postpone it until students are older promote equality of opportunity (box 5.4). This suggests that tracking, which appeals to a notion of meritocracy in many societies, tends to reinforce the (dis)advantages associated with family background. One study encourages a more nuanced view, arguing with some empirical support that, although reforms that reduce tracking might improve IGM among the next generation, the

BOX 5.4   Reforms that reduce tracking in the education system might promote equality of opportunity

Ferreira and Gignoux (2014) find that inequality of opportunity is positively associated with tracking into general or technical/vocational schooling at the secondary level. The study of an educational reform in the 1960s in England and Wales provides causal evidence on the impact of tracking on inequality of opportunity (Jones, Roemer, and Dias 2014). Prior to the reform, 11-year-old students took a test that determined whether they would proceed to a seven-year academically oriented grammar school or to a modern five-year secondary school. The reform introduced unified mixed-ability secondary schools. Because only some respondents were exposed to the new system, the authors could estimate the impact of the reform on equality of opportunity in self-assessed health care and educational qualifications using the dissimilarity index as a measure. Switching to a less differentiated (or tracked) system was found to have a small but positive systematic impact on equality of opportunity. However, the reform was not always opportunity enhancing, suggesting that it may have improved relative mobility, but not necessarily absolute mobility. Another study finds similar results using cross-country evidence on OECD countries. It determined tracking reinforces the impact of family background on earnings, thus lowering relative mobility (Brunello and Checchi 2007).

Studies relying on administrative data in Nordic countries also find positive impacts of reforms that weaken tracking on relative IGM. In Finland, postponing tracking from age 11 to age 16 has been found to reduce intergenerational persistence of income by 23 percent (Pekkarinen, Uusitalo, and Kerr 2009). In Norway, a reform postponing tracking and extending compulsory education from seven to nine years moderated the influence of family background on educational attainment (Aakvik, Salvanes, and Vaage 2010). In Sweden, a similar reform has been found to increase the earnings of children (as adults) with unskilled fathers, while the earnings of the children (as adults) of highly skilled parents might have decreased (Meghir and Palme 2005). A somewhat contrary view is provided by one study on Sweden, which argues that, although reforms that weaken tracking often improve IGM in the next generation, mobility might partly revert to the pre-reform level for the generation that follows. The study builds a theoretical model underlying this claim and shows that the model has empirical validity in Sweden (Nybom and Stuhler 2016).

improvements might fade among subsequent generations.[49] In some countries, narrowing inequality of opportunity has been linked to reforms in tracking, complemented by other reforms, such as raising the duration of compulsory education.

Other policy changes, such as changes in the duration and intensity of educational programs, can also influence equality of opportunity by affecting the implicit or explicit costs of education. There are limited opportunities to study the impact of such broad policy changes. One example is a study of an education reform in Italy that reduced the length of the first tertiary degree from four to six years to three years and introduced two-year master's degrees with the intent of reducing dropout rates and expanding the prevalence of university education. The study finds that the reform enhanced fairness in the form of equality of opportunity in access to tertiary education.[50]

A study of IGM in Norway after World War II finds the influence of childhood location on adult outcomes to have declined by half between the 1946–55 and 1956–65 birth cohorts, in part because of school reforms in the 1960s that aimed at increasing equality of opportunity. These reforms increased compulsory schooling from seven to nine years, introduced a common curriculum for all schools, provided access to the same number of teaching hours across the country, increased access to student grants, and redistributed resources across municipalities through central grants.[51]

Germany offers an example of a reform that changed the intensity of an education program by reducing the duration of secondary schooling from nine to eight years at different points in time across federal states between 2001 and 2008.[52] The curriculum was maintained unchanged for the first affected cohorts, who then experienced a sharp increase in learning intensity. A study exploits the variation in the duration of secondary school across cohorts and across federal states to evaluate the impact of learning intensity on the equality of educational opportunity, which is measured as the share of inequality in cognitive skills explained by circumstances.[53] The reform widened inequality of educational opportunity in the medium term, suggesting that making education more intense has a relatively adverse impact on disadvantaged students.

As primary school enrollment approaches 100 percent in many developing economies and policy attention shifts to secondary education, making secondary school more affordable for low-income students should increasingly take priority. Although evidence on long-term impacts of such programs in developing economies is scarce, a policy experiment in Ghana—in the form of an RCT—to evaluate the impact of free secondary school on education, labor market, and social outcomes of young adults has produced encouraging results (box 5.5).

These studies confirm the intuition that reforms making educational programs more accessible and affordable to disadvantaged students are more likely to reduce the inequality of opportunity in education. The instruments for accomplishing this are varied and context-specific, such as reducing the number of years one needs to invest in university education to obtain a degree, as in the case of Italy; comprehensive education reforms to promote equality of opportunity, as in Norway; or providing secondary schooling for free to deserving low-income students, as in the Ghanaian experiment.

Although educational mobility in this report is measured in terms of attainment, the purpose of improving educational mobility is defeated if higher attainment does not translate to better skills. The 2018 *World Development Report* describes a "learning crisis" and identifies its proximate causes—such as children arriving to school unprepared to learn, teachers lacking the skills or motivation to teach, inputs that are

BOX 5.5   A randomized experiment with free secondary education in Ghana

Duflo, Dupas, and Kremer (2017) report the results of a policy experiment in rural Ghana, where a random subset of qualified but financially constrained students were awarded secondary school scholarships, and detailed outcomes data collected after five, seven, and eight years. In 2008, full scholarships were awarded to 682 adolescents, randomly selected among a sample of 2,064 rural youth who had gained admission to a specific track in a public high school but did not immediately enroll, most of whom cited lack of funds as the reason. By age 25, scholarship winners were 55 percent more likely to complete secondary school, had more than an extra year of secondary education, scored significantly higher on a reading and math test, adopted more preventative health behavior, and had fewer children (for women). The scholarship also significantly increased enrollment in tertiary education, from 8 percent to 11 percent. And even though scholarship winners were more likely to be enrolled in school at the time of the endline survey, they were reporting higher earnings and more likely to be earning a positive income. Treatment effects for women were greater relative to men on multiple dimensions, including learning, tertiary enrollment, and labor market outcomes. The effects differed by education track as well—by age 25, treatment effects on labor market outcomes were significantly larger for the vocational track students than for the academic track students, which is to some extent driven by larger tertiary school enrollment among scholarship winners admitted into academic tracks.

unavailable or of inferior quality, and poor management and governance of schools—as well as the deeper systemic causes. The policy actions identified to address the causes of the learning crisis are grouped into three broad categories: (1) assess learning through better measurement and tracking; (2) act on evidence to make schools work for all learners, using evidence to guide innovation and practice; and (3) align actors to make the entire system work for learning, by tackling the barriers to learning at scale.[54] These strategies, which are discussed in detail in that report, are perfectly aligned with the objective of reducing inequality of opportunity in education among children in order to promote economic mobility.

Breaking the Cycle of Low Aspirations and Low Mobility

Low aspirations interacting with social hierarchies and norms can be both a consequence of and an impediment to IGM. This has policy implications. Inequalities embedded in social hierarchies and norms can impede IGM by reducing the aspirations of individuals in disadvantaged groups, which influences their actions and beliefs in a way that perpetuates the disadvantages across generations. The poor and the disadvantaged who live in societies with low mobility may come to think of their places in the social order as unchangeable.[55] Interventions that act upon social norms and aspirations often involve incorporating behavioral insights and seem to offer a way to improve the effectiveness of social policies and to break the cycle of low aspirations and low mobility.

How Aspirations and Social Environments Shape Ladders to Opportunities

Breaking the cycle of low aspirations and mobility requires first understanding how beliefs or perceptions about mobility are formed, how they
are related to actual mobility, and how they influence aspirations that affect
mobility.

*Perceptions of mobility vary widely across countries and are only
partially related to mobility*

Although the extent of the IGM is obviously important, it is the perceptions
of mobility that often drive individual attitudes and decisions. Actual direct
evidence on perceptions of mobility is sparse, however, and primarily relates
to absolute upward mobility rather than relative mobility (annex 5A).

Evidence on perceptions of absolute mobility reveals considerable
heterogeneity across countries, even within the same geographical region.
In Eastern Europe and Central Asia, on the basis of data from the Life
in Transition surveys, the share of adults who think they have done better in
life than their parents ranges from roughly two-thirds or more in Uzbekistan
and Tajikistan to only a quarter in Armenia (figure 5.6).[56] There is also a
wide range of expectations about the future: most adults in countries such
as the Kyrgyz Republic, Tajikistan, or Uzbekistan believe that children born
today will do better in life than the current generation, whereas similar
views are expressed by only 12 percent of adults in Slovenia and less than a
quarter of adults in Cyprus, Greece, and Italy (figure 5.7).

Perceived past mobility need not be indicative of perceived future mobility. Although in several countries in Eastern Europe and Central Asia
(Kazakhstan, the Kyrgyz Republic, Tajikistan, and Uzbekistan) respondents
hold strongly positive views with respect to past and future mobility, these
views diverge in many countries. For example, the Czech Republic ranks
high on perceptions of past absolute mobility, but low on expectations of
future mobility; whereas Georgians perceive limited past mobility, but are
optimistic about the future of their children (figure 5A.1).

How far are perceptions of mobility aligned with actual mobility? The
limited evidence available indicates that actual mobility influences perceptions to some extent. Indeed, actual occupational mobility may be an
important predictor of perceived occupational mobility, although other factors (income, educational attainment, educational attainment of parents)
are also crucial.[57] Other research shows that people who have experienced
upward mobility directly are more optimistic that children born in the bottom quintile of the income distribution will be able to reach the fourth or
fifth quintiles when they grow up.[58]

However, there are notable inconsistencies between actual and perceived mobility, especially in comparisons across countries. For example,
respondents in the United States perceive greater future relative mobility
relative to respondents in France, Italy, Sweden, and the United Kingdom
and are overoptimistic in their perceptions of mobility compared with

FIGURE 5.6   Perceived absolute mobility compared with the parents of respondents

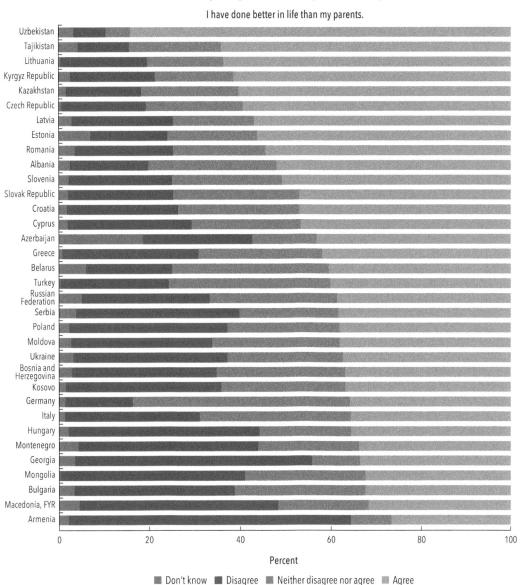

Source: Estimates based on data from the Life in Transition III survey, 2016 wave, European Bank for Reconstruction and Development, London, http://www.ebrd.com/what-we-do/economic-research-and-data/data/lits.html.

actual mobility estimates, which show lower mobility in the United States relative to European countries.[59]

The relationship between actual mobility and perceptions thereof can be affected by multiple factors, including how the perception question is phrased, which affects how the question is likely to be interpreted by the respondents. Data in the GDIM, combined with Gallup data, show that, in economies with greater relative educational mobility, a larger share of

FIGURE 5.7   Perceived future absolute mobility among individuals born today

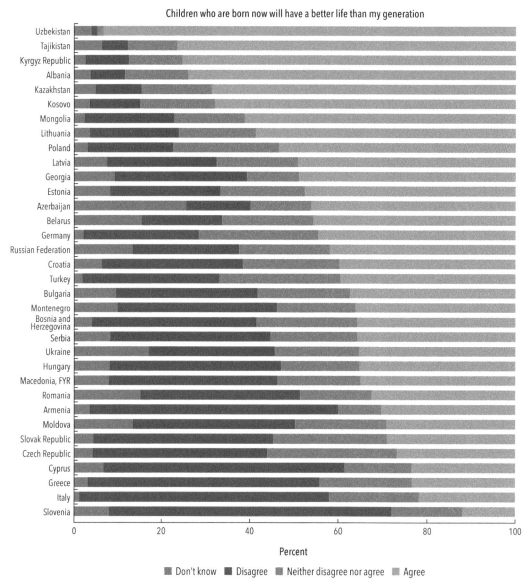

Children who are born now will have a better life than my generation

Percent

⬛ Don't know   ⬛ Disagree   ⬛ Neither disagree nor agree   ⬛ Agree

Source: Estimates based on data from the Life in Transition III survey, 2016 wave, European Bank for Reconstruction and Development, London, http://www.ebrd.com/what-we-do/economic-research-and-data/data/lits.html.

parents tend to believe that their children have the opportunities to learn and grow (figure 5.8, panel a). But no such relationship is observed for responses to a question about whether hard work can help people in their country to get ahead, even though this question seems to hint at perceptions of fairness and equality of opportunity (figure 5.8, panel b). Whether this implies that actual mobility influences individuals' perceptions of optimism (or lack thereof) for their children's future more than their

FIGURE 5.8   In economies with greater mobility, parents are more optimistic about children's opportunities to learn and grow

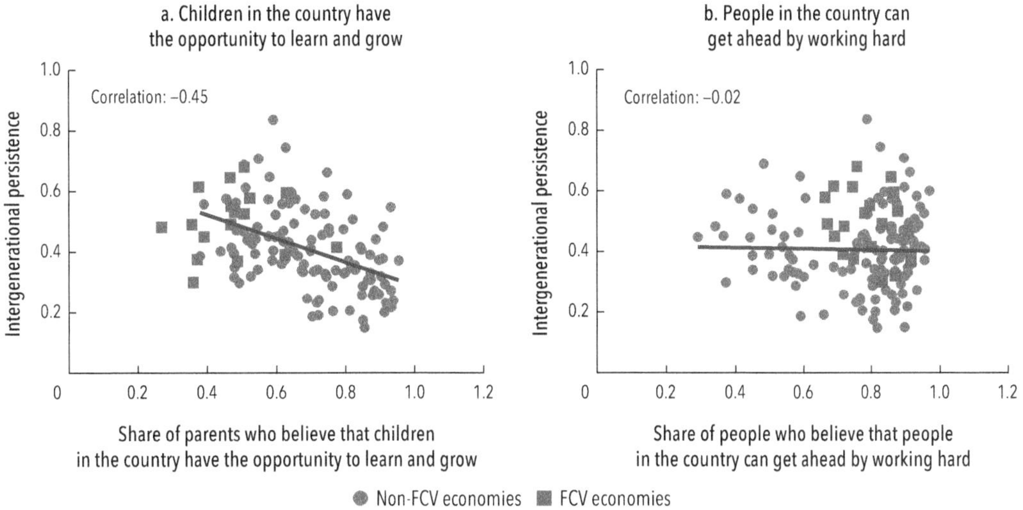

a. Children in the country have the opportunity to learn and grow

Correlation: −0.45

Intergenerational persistence

Share of parents who believe that children in the country have the opportunity to learn and grow

b. People in the country can get ahead by working hard

Correlation: −0.02

Intergenerational persistence

Share of people who believe that people in the country can get ahead by working hard

● Non-FCV economies   ■ FCV economies

Source: GDIM 2018; Gallup, Washington, DC, http://www.gallup.com/home.aspx.
Note: Intergenerational persistence refers to the coefficient from regressions of children's years of education on the education of their parents among cohorts born in 1980–89. Higher values indicate greater persistence and lower relative mobility. The share of individuals or parents with these beliefs refers to the average in 2008–16, including only economies with at least four observations from this period. The group in this figure affected by fragility, conflict, and violence (FCV) (marked in orange) includes 20 economies.

perceptions of fairness in society may be an important question for future research to explore.

Other conditions in the country clearly matter for perceptions and how they correlate with actual mobility. For example, in economies affected by fragility, conflict, and violence (FCV), social and economic conditions can be quite different from other developing economies, which leads to a different relationship between actual mobility and perceptions thereof. Perceptions about children's opportunities to thrive tend to be lower in FCV economies compared to other developing economies, and uncorrelated with relative IGM (figure 5.8, panel a). In contrast, perceptions on the value of hard work in FCV economies are more positive on the average than in other developing economies, and shows some association with relative IGM (figure 5.8, panel b).[60]

Perceptions of absolute mobility may be associated with actual relative mobility

In Eastern Europe and Central Asia, the perceptions of past and future absolute mobility are strongly correlated with actual relative mobility in education (figure 5A.2). Thus, countries with lower relative educational mobility are likely to have a smaller share of adults who view their lives as better than the lives of their parents or who expect the lives of children born today to be better than their own lives. These perceptions are not correlated with estimates of absolute educational mobility in the same group of countries.[61]

Although there may be several explanations for this apparent paradox, one plausible theory is that an individual's perceptions about mobility are likely to conflate the concepts of absolute and relative mobility. For example, even though the question about whether one is doing better in life than his or her parents is worded to elicit information about absolute upward mobility, an individual responding to the question might implicitly consider his or her position in society relative to the corresponding position of the parents, rather than comparing the absolute level of welfare across generations.[62] If this were true, it would imply that, in regard to perceptions, the distinction between different types of mobility may be misleading. Furthermore, it would mean that actual relative mobility in a society is important not only for its own sake but also because of how it may influence the perceptions of relative and absolute mobility.

Beliefs about mobility influence the aspirations window of individuals

Beliefs about mobility and aspirations influence each other because the behavior of individuals depends on the belief systems impressed upon them by society, and actual mobility contributes to the formation of these belief systems.[63] Evidence suggests that mobility trajectories and long-run beliefs can be determined jointly and thus depend on each other. This may occur, according to one theory, because the experimentation needed to learn the returns to effort is costly, which leads to a reliance on dynastic learning or learning from one's own experience.[64] According to this theory, individuals can share the same beliefs initially and put in the same amount of effort, but, over time, those who receive shocks because of pure bad luck may become discouraged and supply less effort. Beliefs and social norms, once established, may also be difficult to change.[65]

To explain how perceptions of mobility shape aspirations, a well-known theory refers to an *aspirations window*, or the set of similar (or attainable) individuals whose lives and achievements help form one's future goals, which is broadened by higher (perceived) mobility.[66] The aspirations window, or the lived reality, is shaped by multiple reference groups, including fellow family members, peers, neighbors, and others with whom one interacts on a regular basis, such as teachers and doctors. The composition of these reference groups is influenced by the individual's SES and the associated rigidities imposed by social hierarchies and norms.

Aspirations are critical to mobility

There is compelling evidence that aspirations are critical to mobility. For example, in Mexico, poor youth ages 12–22 with higher mobility aspirations—measured as the difference between the future and current positions on a 10-rung ladder—have been found to stay in school longer, exhibit better health behavior, and engage less in self-destructive behavior.[67] The higher aspirations of 12-year-olds in Telangana and Andhra Pradesh in India are positively associated with the amount of time devoted to education, with forward-looking views, and, ultimately, with educational outcomes at age 19.[68] Students with higher educational aspirations at the beginning of ninth grade in Parisian schools are found to have better test results at the end of the grade and a higher probability of assignment to an academic track rather than a vocational track in grade 10.[69]

But the link between aspirations and educational attainment is not necessarily monotonic. Defining the aspirations gap as the difference between the current standard of living and the standard of living that is the focus of aspirations, one may show that, whereas a small aspirations gap provides little incentive to seek to achieve a better situation, an aspirations gap that is too big also supplies few incentives because potential investments may be insufficient to bridge the gap, which leads to frustration.[70] This implies an inverse U-shaped relationship between the size of the aspirations gap and educational outcomes or investments. This representation finds support in recent data on India and Nepal.[71] The tension generated by the gap can also lead to differences in behaviors between groups with similar aspirations. For example, the aspirations of indigenous and nonindigenous children in Peru are quite similar, but indigenous children exhibit a much wider aspirations gap, which impedes them in adopting forward-looking behavior such as investing in education.[72] Whether aspirations that are too high relative to current reality can discourage investments to improve mobility is an important question that needs to be investigated more thoroughly.

Low aspirations constrain future mobility among the children of the socially disadvantaged

The aspirations window for socially disadvantaged children is likely to be narrow because of two main factors that are interrelated. The household economic conditions in which a child grows up and, related to these, the social environment outside the home may directly influence the aspirations of children and youth. Parental aspirations, which can be influenced by the social environment, also influence the aspirations of children and the investment of parents in the education of the child.

Evidence suggests that children of low SES are likely to have lower aspirations, which is associated with lower educational achievement. For example, students of low SES in schools in France are much more likely to mention the vocational track as relevant, attainable, and preferable, compared with students of high SES who perform similarly in education.[73] A panel study of cohorts of children born in the United Kingdom in 1958 and in 1970 finds that parental social class exerts a large influence on teenage aspirations, which are the strongest predictor of adult occupational attainment.[74] Another study in the United Kingdom reports that nearly 80 percent of teenagers in the top socioeconomic quintile expect to apply to and be accepted at a university, compared with fewer than half of teenagers in the bottom quintile.[75] The material well-being of the family correlates with indicators of self-efficacy, self-esteem, and educational aspirations among 12-year-olds in Peru.[76] Most low-income students scoring well on standardized tests, such as the ACT and SAT tests, in the United States do not apply to selective colleges although such colleges are often more affordable because of generous financial aid.[77]

Parental aspirations influence the mobility of their offspring indirectly by shaping the aspirations of children and youth and directly through parental investments (box 5.6). Parental aspirations are also likely to be lower among families of low SES because the individuals in poor households may have less favorable perceptions of mobility or access to fewer positive examples.[78] Wealthier individuals in Ethiopia have been found to

---

BOX 5.6   Parental aspirations and social environment are crucial to the aspirations and education of children

Parental aspirations influence the educational achievements of children in two ways: indirectly by affecting the aspirations of children and youth and directly through parental investments. Several studies have found that parental aspirations and attitudes are important in children's education. For example, in Andhra Pradesh, India, parental aspirations have been associated with greater parental investment in education and a higher probability that a child is enrolled in private school and will exhibit better educational achievement at age 15 (Galab et al. 2013; Serneels and Dercon 2014). A study in the United Kingdom finds that parental aspirations are among the best predictors of educational achievement of youth, second only to household material conditions (Schoon and Parsons 2002). Another study in the United Kingdom finds that parental attitudes—primarily the hopes of mothers about the university education of their children—account for about 12 percent of the education gap at age 11 between poor and rich families, after controlling for prior ability at age 7 and for about a third of the progress made between ages 7 and 11 (Gregg and Washbrook 2010). Some of these impacts may be explained by the indirect route of the influence of parental aspirations on children's aspirations and attitudes. The evidence has been provided by study findings in the United Kingdom and the United States that parental aspirations are an important determinant of aspirations among teenagers or adolescents (Schoon and Parsons 2002; Zhang et al. 2011).

The social environment outside the home also affects the aspirations of children (and of their parents); it is also linked to parental social status and the economic situation of the household. Consistent with the theory of multiple reference groups, the social environment in which children grow up, including the interaction of the children with peers, teachers, and role models, helps determine the shape of the window of aspirations. The social environment can adversely affect the aspirations of children of low SES. For instance, the educational aspirations of children in Nepal are positively correlated with educational attainment in the children's reference groups (Janzen et al. 2017). Peer effects on educational attainment have been widely documented, although causal interpretations can be contentious.[a]

a. See Sacerdote 2011 for a review of the literature.

have higher aspirations in income for themselves and higher educational aspirations for their children.[79] Mothers in wealthier households and mothers with greater educational attainment in Andhra Pradesh, India, have been found to have higher educational aspirations for their children.[80] The link between low SES and low aspirations is not, however, always close. One study finds that low caste status does not appear to dampen parental aspirations for their children in rural Pakistan.[81] A study in the United Kingdom does not find a positive gradient between children's aspirations and the economic background of the family.[82]

The social environment outside the home, often associated with the economic condition of the household, is also important for the aspirations of children and their parents and for children's educational achievement (box 5.6). Children in families of low SES are likely to grow up in a social environment that contributes to the closing of their aspirations window. The educational decisions of children of low SES are influenced by the pessimism of their teachers.[83] High-achieving low-income students in the United States who do not apply to selective colleges are less likely to meet a teacher, high school counselor, or schoolmate in an older cohort who has attended a selective college.[84] Data on the United Kingdom show that 63 percent of teenagers in the bottom welfare quintile say that most of their friends are likely to stay in school through the age of 16, compared with 86 percent of teenagers in the top quintile.[85]

Rigid social hierarchies may contribute to or compound the effects of low aspirations among children of low SES. An experiment in India shows that providing cues to one's place in the caste order influences the ability of low caste boys to learn and the willingness of high caste boys to expend effort.[86] Research in Pakistan suggests that long-standing social hierarchies discourage school enrollment among children, especially girls, in lower-status social groups.[87] Parental aspirations may also reflect and reinforce social hierarchies. Parental aspirations have been found to favor boys in Ethiopia and India and girls in Vietnam, biases that are mirrored in the aspirations of boys and girls in these countries.[88]

Evidence on Interventions to Improve Mobility by Expanding Aspirations

Several channels appear to influence the formation of aspirations among children and youth. These include household economic conditions, parental aspirations, and the influence of other individuals, such as peers, who may close or open the aspirations window. On the basis of the nature of these channels, a broad range of policies and programs—anything that improves the economic conditions of families and the social environments—can also expand aspirations indirectly. While recognizing the role of broader policies, this subsection will focus on reviewing the evidence on policy interventions that *directly* act upon the aspirations of parents and children, to improve the educational outcomes of the next generation and their prospects for mobility.

How can policy interventions open the aspirations window? One possibility is to expose children and parents to information, experiences, and role models that influence the shaping of aspirations. For convenience, such policy interventions may be grouped into two categories: (1) interventions aimed at providing information and (2) interventions aimed at altering the set of individuals that children and parents encounter. Although evidence is available on the potential of such interventions to improve educational outcomes and mobility, it is not sufficiently robust to provide definitive answers about the impacts of such interventions. There is thus a need to build a systematic body of evidence through experimentation and evaluation.

Providing information can boost aspirations

A few recent studies point to the important effects of providing information that may aid in the formulation of goals. For example, providing information on the returns to education to students in the Dominican Republic at the end of compulsory schooling significantly improves their perceptions of the returns to schooling relative to similar schoolchildren in a control group.[89] In the United Kingdom, a program that involved outreach to universities and that focused on talented young people in deprived urban schools was found to exert a positive impact on the secondary school examination scores and the reported intentions to participate in higher education among students (box 5.7). One study argues that, among the reasons high-achieving low-income students do not apply to selective colleges in the United States is because the usual information and recruitment campaigns do not reach these students frequently enough.[90]

Interventions can address not only low aspirations but also aspirations that are unreasonably high and that lead to a large aspirations gap. Low-achieving students in schools in France often overestimate their chances of success in academic courses of study and undervalue the returns to vocational courses of study. Providing information on alternative courses of study and employment opportunities thereafter has a significant effect on reducing repetition and dropout rates.[91]

The role of information is not limited to improving children's aspirations: it also raises aspirations among their parents to achieve broader impacts, including in children's education. Showing hour-long documentaries to poor farmers in Ethiopia about individuals from their communities who had succeeded in business or agriculture was found to have a significant effect on aspirations, as well as on savings behavior, educational spending, and work-leisure choices.[92] The introduction of cable television in rural India is associated with greater autonomy among women and higher school enrollment, likely through the exposure of rural households to urban lifestyles and behaviors, which they begin to emulate.[93]

BOX 5.7   Limited evidence to link direct interventions to raise aspirations with educational outcomes

Empirical evidence is partial and inconclusive on the full causal chain linking interventions aimed at affecting aspirations and improved educational or occupational outcomes. Goodman and Gregg (2010) review the evidence on several recent, mainly school-centered, policy interventions in the United Kingdom aimed at improving aspirations, attitudes, and behaviors among school-age children. They find little evidence of effectiveness, partly because robust evaluations of some of the programs have not yet been conducted. In one successful case, an additional year of exposure at ages 15–16 to a program—the Excellence Challenge component of the AimHigher intervention focusing on talented young people in deprived urban schools—raised General Certificate of Secondary Education scores among students by 2.5 points and the reported intentions of the students to participate in higher education by 3.9 percentage points.

On the basis of a comprehensive review, Gorard, See, and Davies (2012) find that, although there is evidence of positive associations between parental expectations and aspirations and the educational attainment of children, no successful interventions have influenced outcomes through parental aspirations. Across four domains—parental expectations, parental involvement, parental substance abuse, and parenting style—they conclude that "parental involvement in their child's learning was the only area reviewed with sufficient evidence to meet the four criteria for a robust causal model" (Gorard, See, and Davies 2012, 7). They similarly find weak, mostly positive links between the aspirations of individuals and educational attainment and participation, but little evidence of successful interventions linking individual aspirations and educational attainment.

Exposure to role models and social interactions can open the aspirations window wider

Interventions involving social interactions, including the identification of role models, can help raise aspirations. A random assignment of women leaders in selected village councils in West Bengal in India has been associated with a 20 percent reduction in the gender aspirations gap among parents, particularly the aspirations of mothers for the education and occupational choices of their children. It has also led to a 32 percent reduction in the gender aspirations gap among adolescents ages 11–15 because of higher aspirations among girls in villages with women leaders. The gender gap in adolescent educational attainment was eliminated completely. Given no simultaneous changes in labor market opportunities among young women, the authors of the study ascribe the impact of women leaders to a role model effect.[94] Social interactions can help magnify the impact of the provision of information. The field experiment in Ethiopia mentioned earlier finds that providing information through documentaries featuring success stories of escaping from poverty has a positive impact, even among those people who were not in the treatment group but whose peers saw the documentaries.[95]

Direct interventions on aspirations can raise educational mobility,
but the evidence is still limited

Although there is much evidence highlighting the importance of aspirations for mobility, there is limited knowledge to date on how effective interventions aimed purely at affecting aspirations among children or parents are in producing sustainable improvements in educational outcomes (see box 5.7). Interventions to improve aspirations and attitudes among school-age children have shown positive impacts, but more robust evidence is needed. Evidence is weaker on the impacts of interventions to raise parental aspirations.[96]

The lack of direct evidence is in part because some of the behavioral interventions are recent and the available evaluations are not sufficiently rigorous. Moreover, some evidence suggests that many youths from disadvantaged backgrounds may not necessarily lack high aspirations. Rather, they lack informed support through various stages of their lives and opportunities to fulfill their ambitions, including better schools and teachers who pay more attention to the lived experience of young people and better career advice and other types of support to keep aspirations on track.[97] One study concludes that the existing evidence need not point to a general conclusion that children and parents in families of low SES have low aspirations that need to rise. But, rather, high aspirations among disadvantaged youth become stalled in the context in which they are living; thus, young people's horizons can be expanded by better opportunities, jobs, and training and education.[98] Consistent with this view is evidence that shows the importance of improved neighborhoods and local environments in the long-term outcomes among children.[99]

The Importance of Neighborhoods and Local Environments

Evidence on local drivers of mobility indicates that neighborhoods and social environments are critical in shaping aspirations, investment in human capital, and outcomes. The Moving to Opportunity Project (MTO) in the United States has highlighted the important effect of better neighborhoods and local environments on long-term outcomes among children, including their incomes as adults, if the change occurs at an early age.[100] The project shows that the earlier a child is exposed to better neighborhoods and more stable circumstances, the more long-lasting the effects will be, including the greater likelihood of more upward mobility. A large body of multidisciplinary research provides evidence on the importance and complexity of neighborhood factors to the education and health of children.[101] Some have used such evidence to argue for policies, such as housing policies, that seek to reduce segregation.[102]

Neighborhood characteristics, such as income segregation and concentrated poverty, inequality, racial segregation, school quality, crime rates, and the share of two-parent families, are key determinants of IGM in the United States.[103] Estimates suggest that at least half the variance in IGM across areas in the United States is attributable to the effects of location.[104] The same study also shows that the effect of neighborhoods on mobility depends on the length of exposure in childhood and is thus more likely to derive from peer effects and local resource investments, rather than factors such as access to jobs in adulthood. Another study finds children in low-income households in U.S. counties with high mobility to have better developmental trajectories between the ages of 3 and 9.[105]

Other studies have suggested the importance neighborhood-level peer effects. Low-income high-achieving students in the United States are highly concentrated; they come from a small number of schools with a high share of high-achieving students.[106] Educational aspirations of children have been found to be positively correlated with the education levels in the children's reference groups in Nepal.[107] Recent research finds that children in the United States who grow up in areas with more inventors and who thus enjoy more exposure to innovation are much more likely to become inventors themselves, and children in families of low SES are less likely to benefit from such exposure (box 5.8).

BOX 5.8   Children who grow up in areas with more inventors are more likely to become inventors

Bell et al. (2017) study the lives of more than 1 million inventors in the United States to identify the key factors that determine who becomes an inventor, as measured by the filing of a patent. They find that children from the top income percentile families are 10 times as likely to become inventors as children in families below the median income, and the gaps by race and gender are similarly large. Differences in innate ability as measured by test scores in early childhood explain relatively little of these gaps. Children at the top of their third-grade mathematics class are much more likely to become inventors, but only if they live in high-income families. In explaining the differences, the authors explain that children who grow up in areas with more inventors and who are thus more exposed to innovation are much more likely to become inventors. Children in low-income families or minority families are less likely to enjoy such exposure through their families and neighborhoods. Exposure influences not only whether children grow up to become inventors but also the type of inventions they produce, and this is influenced by gender. Girls are more likely to become inventors in a class of technology if they grow up in an area in which there are more women inventors in that class of technology, while the converse is true for men. The authors argue that such exposure effects are more likely to be driven by mechanisms such as mentoring, the transmission of information, and networks rather than, say, neighborhood differences in the quality of schools.

On the basis of their findings, the authors call for a greater focus on policies that provide lagging groups with greater exposure to innovation, such as mentoring programs, internships, and interventions through social networks. Although the analysis does not shed light on which types of exposure programs are likely to be most effective, it provides some advice on how such programs should be targeted. Targeting might be focused on children in less privileged groups who excel in mathematics and science at early ages, and interventions might be tailored to the backgrounds of participants. Women are, for example, more readily influenced by women inventors than men inventors.

Although the causal pathways are not yet fully understood, opening the aspirations window could be one of the ways in which a better neighborhood social environment can improve the prospects for mobility. Neighborhoods have been described as important building blocks of the aspirations window among individuals; a highly segregated neighborhood, for instance, may only offer a limited set of experiences upon which individuals may draw.[108] Studies have found that the income aspirations of individuals tend to increase as the average income of the communities in which they reside increase.[109] A study in Andhra Pradesh, India, finds that the highest grade attained by any village inhabitant has a large effect on the educational aspirations of mothers for their children.[110]

How Neighborhoods Matter for Long-Term Outcomes: Evidence from the Literature

The causal pathways between neighborhood characteristics and long-term outcomes are not yet well documented, particularly in developing countries. This is because people living in proximity will have correlated outcomes not only because of shared neighborhood characteristics but also because family backgrounds inside a neighborhood will tend to be similar.[111] Disentangling the causal effect of neighborhood characteristics on IGM or other outcomes is a demanding task in terms of the data requirement and econometric identification issues.

Moreover, much of the evidence in the literature on neighborhood effects does not measure directly the effects on IGM. Rather, the empirical evidence, mostly from developed economies, highlights the importance of neighborhood-level characteristics such as institutional resources, peers, and social norms, for developmental outcomes of children. This type of empirical evidence is relevant for relative IGM because neighborhood characteristics that affect children and youth, and hence their chances in life, are not distributed uniformly across income groups. Children from low-income households, or minority groups, are more likely to reside in disadvantaged neighborhoods, compared to neighborhoods where better-off families live. The differential access to resources and exposure to good peers and mentors contributes to the intergenerational persistence documented in this report.

A fair amount of theoretical work has examined the possible mediating channels through which neighborhood characteristics causally influence development outcomes of children. Many theoretical models focus on neighborhood institutional resources (for example, childcare, schools, medical facilities, recreational facilities, and employment opportunities) as mediating factors and on pathways such as relationships (for example, parental characteristics and support networks available to parents), norms (neighborhood formal and informal institutions, and peer effects), or relative deprivation (for example, the well-being or behavioral effects of having higher-income neighbors).[112] The influence of neighborhoods on outcomes operates through multiple channels, and the relative importance of a given channel may vary across different points in the life cycle.

Early childhood

Although the family environment is a crucial determinant of child development in early childhood, neighborhoods can influence children even at this early age through multiple pathways. An analysis of cognitive development of low birthweight infants in the IHDP data in the United States shows that the presence of affluent neighbors is associated with higher cognitive development among preschool children (ages 3–4) and early school-age children (ages 5–6), after accounting for differences in several family characteristics including mother's education and family income.[113] Similar findings are also reported among children in the National Longitudinal Survey of Youth (NLSY) in the United States and by several recent studies based on data from Canada.[114]

Studies also find that the neighborhood SES influences developmental health outcomes in young children, primarily the incidence of internalizing (depressive) and externalizing (aggressive) behavioral problems and antisocial behavior.[115] For example, a study in the United Kingdom found residence in a lower-deprivation neighborhood to be associated with fewer emotional and behavioral problems among children of age 3–16 two years later, after controlling for child and family characteristics, and maternal psychological distress.[116] The effect of neighborhood SES on developmental outcomes need not be monotonic, however. A large study spanning the Canadian province of British Columbia found that greater neighborhood affluence is associated with higher scores on an Early Development Instrument composed of five scales; but, for four out of five scales, the relationship is nonlinear, so that the best child outcomes are recorded in locations with relatively equal proportions of affluent and disadvantaged families.[117]

Several mechanisms have been found to mediate the relationship between quality of neighborhoods and the developmental outcomes for children of preschool and early school age. The associations found in the IHDP and NLSY data are consistent with the mediating pathway of neighborhood resources—higher prevalence of affluent neighbors translates to greater availability of public and private services in the neighborhood, as well as greater opportunities for enrichment.[118] For preschool age children from low-income households, the lack of availability and low quality of childcare has been found to have long-term cognitive and socioemotional outcomes.[119]

Social-interactive resources or their absence (social capital, social cohesion or disorder, collective efficacy) have also been found to be important for developmental health outcomes of young children. In particular, lack of safety, higher levels of neighborhood social disorder, lower social cohesion, and lower potential for community involvement have been associated with lower outcomes on indicators such as language acquisition, as well as emotional and behavioral outcomes.[120]

School years and adolescence
The impact of neighborhoods on cognitive and behavioral outcomes of children gets accentuated with age, as older children and young adolescents spend relatively more time outside of the home. A study of children ranging from elementary school ages to high school ages in urban school districts in four U.S. cities finds that the influence of neighborhood characteristics on educational outcomes is weak in elementary school ages and becomes stronger during middle and high school ages.[121] Several studies based on the Panel Study of Income Dynamics (PSID) in the United States find high neighborhood SES to be associated with higher school completion rates, higher number of years of schooling completed, and greater college attendance. For example, the youths from low-income minority families residing in public housing in Chicago who moved to more affluent neighborhoods as part of the Gautreaux Project were more likely to stay in school or to continue onto college, compared to their peers who did not move.[122]

The early assessment of the New York City MTO Program compared the outcomes among families who moved out of public housing in high-poverty neighborhoods into low-poverty neighborhoods with the outcomes among those who stayed in public housing in high-poverty neighborhoods. The study found notable effects of moving on behavioral problems and some modest effects on school participation and substance use, after just two years of exposure. In particular, children of age 8–13 years who moved to low-poverty neighborhoods displayed superior emotional health, and more than a 30 percent reduction in behavioral problems compared to stayers.[123] The mid-term evaluation across all of the participating cities suggested that there were significant improvements in mental health and lower rates of psychological distress, depression, and anxiety.[124]

For youth in particular, exposure to peers and social norms, including formal and informal institutions that can mentor and monitor the behavior of adolescents, have been found to be an important mediator of the effect of more advantaged neighborhoods on developmental outcomes. In the MTO project, neighborhood safety, rather than employment opportunities, was one of the key reasons for relocating, whereas some of the improvements in the reported behavioral problems were attributed to lower delinquency rates among the new peers.

Although data from developing economies do not allow for neighborhood-level determinants of mobility to be identified, correlations at a more aggregated level offer a few hints about the importance of subnational or local-level drivers of mobility, as briefly outlined below.

*In the global data, greater relative mobility is associated with
lower levels of segregation*

Globally, IGM in education seems to be associated with the extent of segregation: economies with lower levels of spatial segregation by education levels tend to have higher IGM, both absolute and relative (figure 5.9).[125] This
association is also visible within six large developing economies—relative
mobility tends to be higher in provinces or states with lower levels of educational segregation (figure 5.10). Lower levels of segregation might benefit
mobility because children from disadvantaged backgrounds get a chance to
share the same public services as children from richer backgrounds, and
they benefit from positive spillovers and role models, thereby reducing the
significance of parental background.

*Upward mobility is greater in areas with higher concentration
of privilege*

In the six large developing economies, the rate of upward mobility is higher
in areas with a greater concentration of highly educated (figure 5A.3). This
is similar to the patterns for Canada and the United States found by an
existing study—mobility from the bottom to the top tends to be higher
in regions with higher concentrations of the highly educated and intergenerational privilege in both countries.[126] At the same time, in areas with a
greater concentration of the more educated, those born into the bottom half
also appear to be at more disadvantage compared to others, as far as reaching the top quartile of education is concerned.[127]

Thus, in areas with higher concentration of "privilege," those at the
bottom of the ladder have higher odds of making it to the top; but they also

FIGURE 5.9   Economies with higher educational mobility tend to have lower levels of spatial
segregation by education

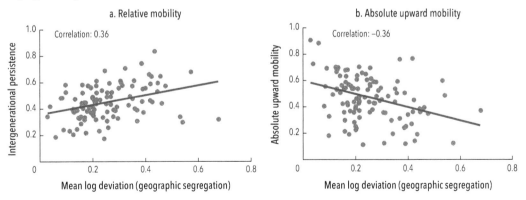

Source: Calculations using GDIM 2018.
Note: Intergenerational mobility estimates for cohort born in the 1980s. Mean log deviation refers to segregation measured by the share of
between-primary sample unit inequality in education out of total inequality, using sample of all adults from surveys underlying GDIM
(World Bank).

FIGURE 5.10   In six large developing economies, relative mobility in education is higher in areas with lower levels of segregation (by education levels)

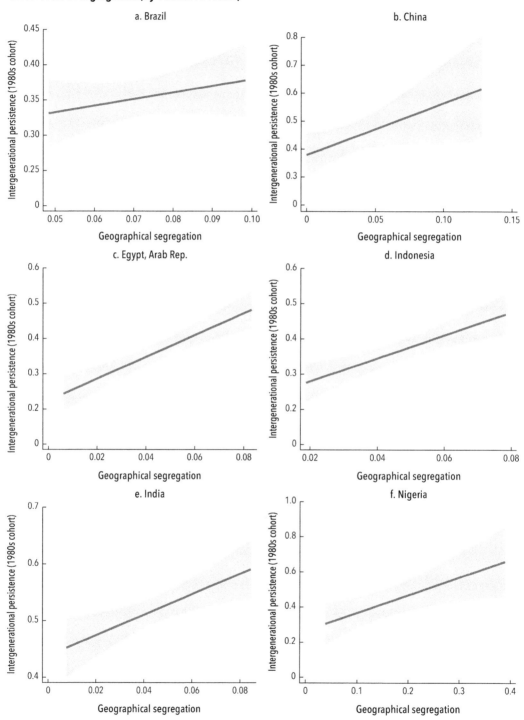

Source: Calculations based on data in the GDIM 2018.
Note: Intergenerational mobility estimates for cohort born in the 1980s. Geographical segregation at the province/state level is measured by the share of between-PSU inequality in education out of total inequality. PSU = primary sampling unit.

have a greater disadvantage relative to others living in the same geographical area in terms of their chances of reaching the top. These areas may be acting as mobility poles, possibly because of more economic dynamism, better services, and other positive spillovers from the highly educated that aid upward mobility among the disadvantaged.[128] But the higher *inequality* in upward mobility in these areas suggests that those in the bottom half face enormous barriers in accessing the opportunities available in these areas.

Therefore, for mobility and opportunity, it matters *where* one is born within a country, in addition to the social status of the family one is born into. Although much more research is needed, the combined evidence so far underscores the importance of focusing locally—at the level of provinces, regions, and neighborhoods—for improving IGM.

Public Policies to Strengthen Local Drivers of IGM

Although many of the studies highlighted here have found the effect of neighborhoods on outcomes to be smaller than the effect of household-level characteristics such as income or education, neighborhoods nevertheless have been found to affect both young children and adolescents, both directly and through their effect on parental behavior. Many of the neighborhood characteristics that form the key mediating pathways for neighborhood effects can be influenced through policy levers. For example, improving neighborhood characteristics such as neighborhood safety or accessibility, the quality of childcare and educational institutions, or the availability of recreational facilities in the neighborhood, are policy interventions that are likely to be universally important.

Neighborhood-level characteristics are not just the domain of local-level policies and interventions. For example, policies aimed at poverty reduction, income support, or improving the design of social safety nets, even if these operate at the national level, will have neighborhood-level effects. Nevertheless, it is important to tackle social mobility not only at the national but also at the local level. This is especially the case in light of the evidence that the earlier a child is exposed to better neighborhoods and stable family circumstances, the greater the likelihood of upward mobility.

Improving the quality of local schools is critical, but may not be sufficient. For all the reasons discussed earlier, interventions to improve neighborhoods and social environments, in particular those aimed at reducing neighborhood (and school) socioeconomic segregation and concentrated poverty, can be particularly beneficial for mobility. Programs such as mandatory inclusionary zones and community land trusts, which provide affordable housing for low-income families, can be effective in some cases. For example, a recent study found that, in neighborhoods of St. Louis, Missouri, that have managed to "rebound" during the 1970–2010 period, subsidized housing played an important role in supporting socioeconomic diversity by sustaining affordability.[129] The analysis of differences in innovation rates across neighborhoods in the United States suggests the role of mentoring programs, interventions through social networks, and internships at local companies as ways to motivate and help children from disadvantaged backgrounds to pursue certain career paths (see box 5.7).[130]

Given the empirical evidence on the importance of social norms and connections within neighborhoods for child outcomes and for IGM, there is increasing recognition of the need for more comprehensive approaches to building neighborhood social capital. Such approaches, rather than focusing on housing provision, or on jobs, in isolation, adopt an integrated approach that combines service delivery, housing, public and private investment, and building resident governance structures (box 5.8).[131] Comprehensive neighborhood initiatives recognize the interrelatedness of multiple neighborhood aspects for promoting healthy development for children and families. Such initiatives present significant challenges to evaluations; existing evidence on the effectiveness of comprehensive approaches to building community social capital is primarily from developed countries like the United States.[132]

Conclusion

Increasing education mobility requires the promotion of equality of opportunity in childhood through investments and behavioral interventions. Evidence in the literature and preliminary cross-country patterns reviewed in this chapter provide insights on a few broad policy directions.

First, interventions early in life are critical because gaps that emerge early in life are difficult to offset through interventions later. Interventions to equalize opportunities must begin even before a child is born because maternal health is a key determinant of a child's health at birth, and the deprivations suffered in utero can reduce the effectiveness of postnatal investments. Policy measures aimed at disadvantaged women of childbearing age can have a positive impact on infant health and longer-term outcomes of children. These include food supplementation programs that might involve relatively inexpensive nutritional supplements for mothers and programs to build awareness and knowledge among mothers, for example through visits by health workers.

Intervening in the postnatal period can also be effective, particularly if this is accomplished early in a child's life. Programs targeting nutritional and health improvements in early childhood can yield long-term benefits in education outcomes and wages. Early childhood education programs, particularly those that combine cognitive and noncognitive skill development, can improve long-term outcomes among children in low-income households. Noncognitive development among children accounts for some of the long-term impacts, which also means that assessing the value of such programs by tracking cognitive test scores only may well understate the long-term benefits.

The evidence on the long-term benefits of other types of programs and policies that could potentially equalize opportunities in childhood is somewhat thin. One example is subsidized childcare, a key policy instrument the impacts of which on long-term outcomes are less well understood. Evidence on Norway suggests that making childcare more accessible could improve absolute and relative mobility. Although school meal programs have been widely adopted by governments to improve nutrition and educational outcomes, evidence on relatively small long-run impacts is available only in two Scandinavian countries.

Second, closing the gaps in the access to and quality of education between the haves and have-nots is clearly important for mobility. Economies with higher absolute and relative IGM in education among cohorts of the 1980s were likely to exhibit smaller shares of children who were out of school and higher average test scores in primary education during the school years of these cohorts. Within countries, the gaps in learning outcomes across children of parents at different levels of income and education tend to be even larger than the gaps in access.

Consistent with the view that public spending on education promotes a more level playing field among children in households with different socio-economic characteristics, economies in which there is more public investment in education also tend to exhibit higher relative mobility in education. This relationship is particularly strong for developing economies, and stronger for primary education, which is known to be highly progressive, than for other levels of education. That said, developing economies showing greater relative and absolute mobility seem to invest more public resources in all levels of education.

However, high public spending on education is likely to improve mobility only if it improves the quality of key inputs in education and supports policies that level the playing field for disadvantaged groups. Absolute and relative mobility tend to be greater in economies with a higher teacher–student ratio in primary education, which is a broad measure of one of the inputs that are crucial to the quality of education.[133] Relative mobility also tends to improve if policy changes enhance the accessibility of education among disadvantaged students, for example through changes in the tracking, duration, or intensity of an education program or by expanding the years of compulsory education. For example, reforms that weaken or postpone the practice of tracking until students are older seem to promote equality of opportunity, as seen from examples of such reforms in three Nordic countries.

In many developing economies, as primary school enrollments approach 100 percent, improving access to secondary schooling should take priority. A recent RCT in Ghana found large impacts of secondary school scholarships for low-income students on their education and labor market outcomes. It highlights the potential benefits of free secondary schooling, as well as the need for developing economies to consider such policy experiments to build the evidence that shapes future education reforms.

Improving the quality of learning and reducing vast inequalities in learning outcomes requires education policies that address the proximate and systemic causes of the learning crisis (World Bank 2018). Policy actions to address this crisis can be summarized under three broad categories: assessing learning through better measurement and tracking, acting on evidence to make schools work for all learners, and aligning actors to make the entire education system work for learning.

Third, social norms interact with aspirations, which are influenced by perceptions of mobility, and this may limit mobility. Several channels affect the formation of aspirations among children and youth, including household economic conditions, parental aspirations, and the surrounding social environment, including peers. This means that a wide range of policies and programs that affect material well-being or improve general economic conditions can also indirectly raise aspirations. Interventions that directly act upon aspirations, including interventions that often involve incorporating behavioral insights, might also offer a way to break the cycle of low aspirations and limited mobility. For example, providing information to aid in the formulation of goals and aspirations appears to have positive impacts in some settings.

Evidence is scarce, however, on whether interventions primarily aimed at raising the aspirations of children or parents can improve education outcomes. Interventions to enhance aspirations and attitudes among school-age children have shown positive impacts. However, more evidence is needed before policy conclusions can be established, which points to the need for experimentation with behavioral interventions that target aspirations. Given the dynamic ways in which aspirations are formed and sustained, interventions that aim directly at raising aspirations are not the only answer. Young people who have high aspirations and who are from socially disadvantaged backgrounds also require support to maintain their aspirations through the various stages of life, through opportunities to realize their ambitions, including better schools and teachers, better career advice, and so on.

Fourth, how policies and investments are applied locally is important because neighborhoods and social environments shape opportunities, aspirations, and outcomes among young people. The earlier a child is exposed to better neighborhoods and more stable circumstances, the more long-lasting the effects seem to be, with a greater likelihood of upward mobility. Globally, lower levels of spatial segregation by education levels are associated with higher absolute and relative educational mobility, both within and across countries. All of these suggest the importance of local-level drivers of mobility, be it at the level of neighborhoods, counties, or provinces.

Several characteristics that influence the key pathways for local effects on mobility can be influenced using policy levers, such as safety, accessibility, infrastructure, the quality of child care, health care and educational institutions, and the availability of recreational facilities. Interventions aimed at reducing the concentration of poverty and the socioeconomic segregation of neighborhood and schools can be particularly beneficial for mobility. Given the empirical evidence on the importance of social norms and connections within neighborhoods for child outcomes and for IGM, there is also increasing recognition of the need for more comprehensive approaches to build neighborhood social capital.

In some large developing economies, areas with higher concentration of educated people seem to offer a greater chance of upward mobility to the disadvantaged, possibly because of positive economic and social spillovers from the highly educated; but these areas also have greater inequality in upward mobility. To ensure that the advantages offered by these "mobility poles" are available more equitably, policies need to focus on narrowing the opportunity gaps between children born with different parental backgrounds living in these areas.

This chapter focuses on broad policy directions that affect opportunities among children. It does not cover the range of fiscal, social, and regulatory policy tools that may be effective in reducing the gaps in circumstances, addressing entrenched inequities, or promoting efficiency and fairness in markets. Although such policies act on the earnings and assets of adults, they can also affect educational mobility by influencing the incentives and ability of parents to invest in the education of their children.

Annex 5A

Perceptions of Mobility: What Type of Direct Evidence Is Available?

Data on perceptions of inter- and intragenerational mobility are typically gathered through attitudinal and other household surveys that include questions to respondents about their lives or the lives of others, such as parents and children. These questions often solicit information on subjective comparisons of the job or financial status of respondents with the jobs or financial status of their parents or, in the case of perceptions of future mobility, comparisons between the lives of the current generation with the lives of children born now (table 5A.1; figures 5A.1 and 5A.2).

Survey questions related to fairness provide additional indirect evidence on perceived opportunities for mobility. For example, the Life in Transition Survey asks respondents about the most important factors of success in life now: effort and hard work, intelligence and skills, political connections, or breaking the law. The World Values Survey enquires about the opinions of respondents on a scale of 1 to 10, where 1 is "in the long run, hard work usually brings a better life" and 10 is "hard work doesn't generally bring success; it's more a matter of luck and connections."[134] The British Social Attitudes Survey asks respondents whether they agree with the statement "In a fair society, every person should have an equal opportunity to get ahead."

TABLE 5A.1   Questions in attitudinal surveys

Source	Question
International Social Survey Program; British Social Attitudes Survey	"Please think of your present job (or your last one if you don't have one now). If you compare this job with the job your father had when you were 16, would you say that the level or status of your job is (or was)." (much lower, much higher)
Life in Transition Survey	"I have done better in life than my parents." (strongly agree, strongly disagree)
	"Children who are born now will have a better life than my generation." (strongly agree, strongly disagree)
General Social Survey (the United States)	"Compared to your parents when they were the age you are now, do you think your own standard of living is much better, somewhat better, about the same, somewhat worse, or much worse than theirs was?"

Sources: British Social Attitudes (database), NatCen Social Research, London, http://www.bsa.natcen.ac.uk/; GSS (General Social Survey) (database), National Opinion Research Center, University of Chicago, Chicago, http://gss.norc.org/Get-The-Data; ISSP (International Social Survey Program) (database), Mannheim, http://issp.org/data-download/by-year/; LITS (Life in Transition Survey) (database), European Bank for Reconstruction and Development, London, http://www.ebrd.com/what-we-do/economic-research-and-data/data/lits.html.

FIGURE 5A.1   Perceptions of past and future IGM are positively but imperfectly correlated

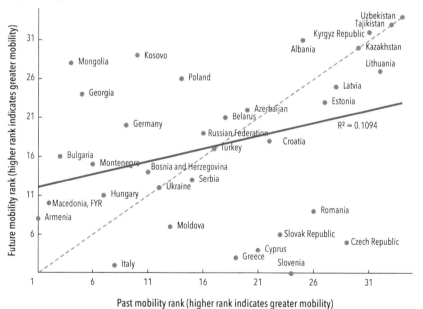

Past mobility rank (higher rank indicates greater mobility)

Source: Estimates based on data from the Life in Transition III survey, 2016 wave, European Bank for Reconstruction and Development, London, http://www.ebrd.com/what-we-do/economic-research-and-data/data/lits.html.
Note: Past mobility refers to the share of respondents agreeing with the statement "I have done better in life than my parents." Future mobility refers to the share of respondents agreeing with the statement "Children who are born now will have a better life than my generation." Rank refers to rank in perceived mobility (past/future) among countries in the Eastern Europe and Central Asia region; a higher rank indicates greater mobility.

FIGURE 5A.2   In economies with greater relative mobility, adults perceive past and future expected upward mobility to be greater

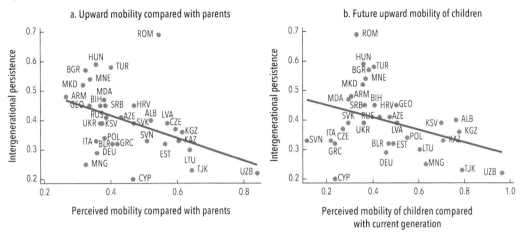

Source: Estimates based on GDIM 2018; Life in Transition III survey, 2016 wave, European Bank for Reconstruction and Development, London, http://www.ebrd.com/what-we-do/economic-research-and-data/data/lits.html.
Note: Intergenerational persistence refers to the coefficient from regressions of children's years of education on the education of their parents among cohorts born in 1980–89. Higher values indicate greater persistence and lower relative mobility. Perceived mobility among parents is based on the share of adults who agree or strongly agree with the statement "Children who are born now will have a better life than my generation."

FIGURE 5A.3   Poverty to privilege vs. share of children in national top quartile

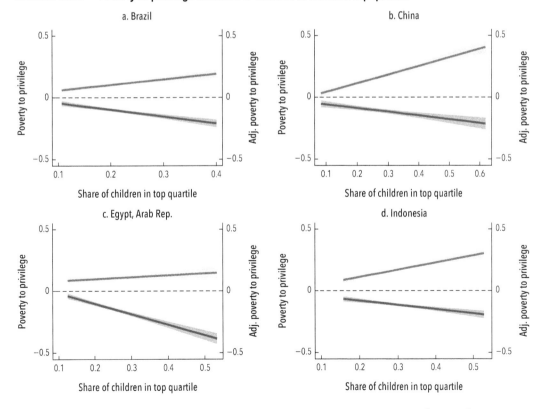

figure continues next page

FIGURE 5A.3   **Poverty to privilege vs. share of children in national top quartile (continued)**

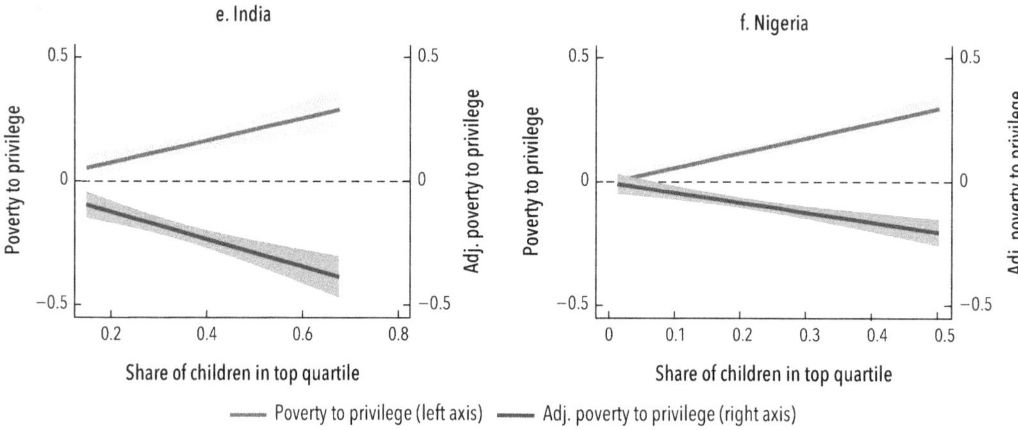

Source: Calculations based on data in the GDIM 2018.
Note: The blue lines indicate the rate of upward mobility from the bottom half to the top quartile of the education distribution. The red lines indicate the degree to which being born into the bottom half acts as a disadvantage as measured by the difference between the conditional and unconditional probability of reaching the top quartile of the national distribution.

Notes

1. Solon (2004).
2. Also see Paes de Barros et al. (2009, 2012).
3. Dabalen et al (2015a); and Rama et al (2015).
4. The numbers in this case imply that one-fifth of the opportunities would need to be redistributed to ensure that every circumstance group has the same coverage rate. The HOI would then be equal to the coverage rate.
5. Known also as the dissimilarity index, the inequality of opportunity component of the HOI is the ratio of the penalty for inequality (between groups differentiated by circumstances) to the coverage rate. This index can be interpreted as the share of opportunities that needs to be redistributed from opportunity-rich to opportunity-deprived people to produce complete equality of opportunity (Paes de Barros et al. 2012).
6. Mazumder (2016).
7. Aizer and Currie (2014).
8. For example, see Aizer and Currie (2014).
9. Aizer and Currie (2014).
10. McCormick et al. (2006).
11. Alderman, Hoddinott, and Kinsey 2006; Hoddinott et al. 2008.
12. Black, Devereux, and Salvanes 2007.
13. Case and Paxson (2008).
14. This discussion is based on Butcher (2017).

15. See "Health Situation and Trend Assessment," World Health Organization, Geneva, http://www.searo.who.int/entity/health_situation _trends/data/nutrition_stunting-in-children/en/. According to the World Health Organization, although wasting may also be the result of a chronic illness, it typically indicates "a recent and severe process of weight loss, which is often associated with acute starvation and/or severe disease." See "Global Database on Child Growth and Malnutrition," World Health Organization, Geneva, http://www.who.int/nutgrowthdb /about/introduction/en/index2.html.
16. Maccini and Yang (2009).
17. Aizer and Currie (2014).
18. See Aizer and Currie (2014), who report the findings of Almond, Hoynes, and Schanzenbach (2011); Hoynes, Page, and Stevens (2011); Hoynes and Schanzenbach (2012); Rossin-Slater (2013).
19. Abu-Saad and Fraser (2010).
20. Between 1986 and 1997, iodine supplements were distributed in several districts of Tanzania. Field, Robles, and Torero (2009) exploit time and spatial variation in the distribution of these supplements to study the impact of in-utero exposure to iodine supplements on educational attainment 10–14 years later.
21. Eckenrode et al. (2010); Olds et al. (2007), as reported by Aizer and Currie (2014).
22. Campbell et al. 2014; Heckman, Pinto, and Savelyev 2013.
23. Hoddinott et al. (2008).
24. Bharadwaj, Løken, and Neilson (2013).
25. Baird et al. (2016).
26. Heckman (2006).
27. Case and Paxson (2006); Currie and Thomas (2001).
28. Chetty et al. (2011).
29. Heckman, Pinto, and Savelyev (2013).
30. Heckman and Kautz (2014).
31. See Deming (2009), who compares the gains of Head Start with the gains of the Perry and Abecedarian projects.
32. Havnes and Mogstad (2011).
33. Andreoli, Havnes, and Lefranc, (forthcoming).
34. Butikofer, Mølland, and Salvanes (2016).
35. Alex-Petersen, Lundborg, and Rooth (2016).
36. Jayaraman and Simroth (2015).
37. Vermeersch and Kremer (2005).
38. McEwan (2013).
39. Belot and James (2011).
40. The program offers breakfast to any student who attends a school participating in the program. Children from households with incomes below 130 percent and 185 percent of the poverty rate receive free meals and subsidized prices, respectively. Many states mandate that schools with a specified share of eligible students participate in the

program. Frisvold (2015) exploits the variation in this share across states and the inherent discontinuity to estimate impacts on mathematics and reading test scores.

41. OECD (2016).
42. See Balcazar, Narayan, and Tiwari (2015), who use PISA 2012 test scores for 15-year-old students across 65 countries. Basic proficiency is defined as level 2 proficiency; parental education is the maximum educational attainment among parents or guardians; and location refers to city, large or small town, or village categorized by population. The contributions of each circumstance to inequality is measured by decomposing the dissimilarity index of attaining level 2 proficiency in reading, mathematics, and science.
43. World Bank (2018)
44. For example, see Dabalen, Parinduri, and Paul (2015b); Hungi et al (2010).
45. Salehi-Isfahani, Hassine, and Assaad (2014), as reported in Krishnan et al. (2016).
46. Ferreira and Gignoux (2014); Sahn and Younger (2000).
47. World Bank (2018).
48. Vegas and Coffin (2015) find that controlling for GDP per capita and income inequality, higher education spending has a significant association with increased student performance only among education systems that spend less than US$8,000 per student annually (in purchasing power parity). Mean student achievement is approximately 14 points higher on the PISA scale for every additional US$1,000 spent. Regardless of how strong the relationship is between the level of public spending and learning outcomes, it seems intuitive that just spending more is not enough to improve the quality of learning and that the quality of spending matters significantly.
49. Nybom and Stuhler (2016).
50. Brunori, Peragine, and Serlenga (2012).
51. Raaum (2006)
52. Aside from improving Germany's general educational performance, the purpose of the reform was to make the German educational system more aligned with the rest of Europe and decrease the age of university graduates.
53. Camarero Garcia (2017).
54. World Bank (2018).
55. Hoff (2012).
56. See LITS (Life in Transition Survey) (database), European Bank for Reconstruction and Development, London, http://www.ebrd.com/what-we-do/economic-research-and-data/data/lits.html.
57. Kelley and Kelley (2009).
58. Alesina, Stantcheva, and Teso (2017).
59. Alesina, Stantcheva, and Teso (2017).

60. The FCV economies included in these figures are Afghanistan, Chad, the Central African Republic, the Comoros, the Democratic Republic of Congo, the Republic of Congo, Côte d'Ivoire, Djibouti, Iraq, Kosovo, Lebanon, Liberia, Mali, Mozambique, Sudan, Sierra Leone, South Sudan, Togo, West Bank and Gaza, and the Republic of Yemen.

61. This is consistent with the fact that, unlike the situation at the global level, where there is a negative correlation between absolute and relative mobility, the same relationship is not observed within the sample of countries in Eastern Europe and Central Asia.

62. Another factor specific to Eastern Europe and Central Asia might be contributing to this paradox. Educational attainment in the generation of parents was relatively higher in many of the economies with a socialist past than in developing economies generally, which may mean that absolute educational mobility is not a good predictor of absolute income mobility in this region. In contrast, relative educational mobility is likely to be correlated with relative mobility in income, which may influence perceptions of absolute upward mobility.

63. As argued in *World Development Report 2006* (World Bank 2005).

64. Piketty (1995)

65. For example, see Alesina and Angeletos (2005) for a theoretical explanation of how multiple, self-sustaining equilibriums at different levels of taxation and redistribution can lead to a society in which income is a function of talent, investment, effort, and luck (noise) if agents derive disutility from unfair social outcomes and support a social demand for fairness.

66. See Ray (2006), who is inspired by the work of Appadurai (2002) on the capacity to aspire. This work argues that aspirations are socially determined and that the poor may lack the aspirational resources to contest or alter the conditions of their own poverty.

67. Ritterman Weintraub et al. (2015).

68. Ross (2017).

69. Guyon and Huillery (2016).

70. Ray (2006).

71. Janzen et al. (2017); Ross (2017).

72. Pasquier-Doumer and Brandon (2015).

73. See Guyon and Huillery (2016), who find that, compared with students of high SES who perform similarly in school, students of low SES exhibit a greater probability of reporting that the vocational track is salient (by 7 percent), more attainable (by 45 percent), and preferable (by 120 percent).

74. Schoon and Parsons (2002).

75. Chowdry et al. (2010).

76. Dercon and Krishnan (2009).

77. Hoxby and Avery (2013).

78. Appadurai (2004).

79. Tanguy et al. (2014).

80. Serneels and Dercon (2014).
81. Jacoby and Mansuri (2012).
82. Kintrea, Clair, and Houston (2011).
83. Flechtner (2014).
84. Hoxby and Avery (2013).
85. Chowdry et al. (2010).
86. Hoff and Pandey (2014).
87. Jacoby and Mansuri (2015).
88. Dercon and Singh (2013).
89. Jensen (2010).
90. Hoxby and Avery (2013).
91. Goux, Gurgand, and Maurin (2017).
92. Tanguy et al. (2014).
93. Jensen and Oster (2009).
94. Beaman et al. (2011)
95. Tanguy et al. (2014).
96. Gorard, See, and Davies (2012).
97. Cummings et al. (2012); Kintrea Clair, and Houston (2011).
98. Cummings et al. (2012).
99. Chetty and Hendren (2018a).
100. Chetty, Hendren, and Katz (2016).
101. See Leventhal and Brooks-Gunn (2000); Martens et al. (2014).
102. For example, see Chetty (2016); Chetty, Hendren, and Katz (2016).
103. Chetty et al. (2014).
104. Chetty and Hendren (2018b).
105. Donnelly et al. (2017).
106. Hoxby and Avery (2013)
107. Janzen et al. (2017).
108. Ray (2006).
109. Cojocaru (2014a); Cojocaru (2014b); Knight and Gunatilaka (2012); Stutzer (2004).
110. Serneels and Dercon (2014).
111. Solon (1999).
112. See Leventhal and Brooks-Gunn (2000) for more details and a thorough review of the literature. Additional reviews of theoretical and empirical studies can also be found in Brooks-Gunn, Duncan, and Aber (1997), Jencks and Mayer (1990), and Solon (1999).
113. Chase-Lansdale et al. (1997).
114. Cushon et al. (2011); Kershaw and Forer (2010); Kohen, Oliver, and Pierre (2009).
115. See Minh et al. (2017) for a recent review of the literature.
116. Flouri, Mavroveli, and Midouhas (2013)
117. Carpiano, Lloyd, and Hertzman (2009)

118. Chase-Lansdale et al. (1997).
119. See Leventhal and Brooks-Gunn (2000) and references therein.
120. See Minh et al. (2017) and references therein.
121. Halpern-Felsher et al. (1997).
122. See discussion in Leventhal and Brooks-Gunn (2000).
123. Leventhal and Brooks-Gunn (2002).
124. Orr et al (2003).
125. Segregation is measured by the share of between-PSU (primary sampling unit) inequality in education out of total inequality, as the average for 1986–95.
126. Corak (2017).
127. That a higher concentration of privilege is associated with both higher rates of upward mobility and greater disadvantage of being born into the bottom half might seem paradoxical. The intuition of how this happens is that, in areas that have relatively low shares of the highly educated of the country, the unconditional probability of reaching the top quartile is low for everyone, compared to an area with a sizeable population of the highly educated. But in areas where the highly educated are concentrated, the *difference* between the unconditional probability and the probability of reaching the top quartile conditional on being born in the bottom half, which is the "disadvantage" of being born in the bottom half, is also high.
128. These patterns can also occur because of the migration of high-potential individuals from disadvantaged backgrounds to provinces with high levels of education. However, preliminary analysis suggests that such migration sorting is unlikely to be the main driver of the pattern seen in these countries.
129. Swanstrom, Webber, and Metzger (2015).
130. Bell et al (2017).
131. Brown and Richman (1997).
132. An evaluation of the social impact of most prominent and mature Community Development Corporations (CDCs) in the United States found that, in addition to improved housing conditions, residents in CDC neighborhoods experienced increased actual and perceived safety, through the community organizing efforts of CDCs and by way of building acquaintanceship ties in the neighborhood (Briggs, Mueller, and Sullivan 1997).
133. Quality of teachers is one of the critical inputs that is not captured by the teacher–student ratio. For example, Araujo et al. (2016) find significant impacts of teacher quality on learning outcomes among kindergarten children in Ecuador.
134. See WVS (World Values Survey) (database), King's College, Old Aberdeen, United Kingdom, http://www.worldvaluessurvey.org/wvs.jsp.

References

Aakvik, Arild, Kjell G. Salvanes, and Kjell Vaage. 2010. "Measuring Heterogeneity in the Returns to Education Using an Education Reform." *European Economic Review* 54 (4): 483–500.

Abu-Saad, Kathleen, and Drora Fraser. 2010. "Maternal Nutrition and Birth Outcomes." *Epidemiologic Reviews* 32 (1): 5–25.

Aizer, Anna, and Janet Currie. 2014. "The Intergenerational Transmission of Inequality: Maternal Disadvantage and Health at Birth." *Science* 344 (6186): 856–61.

Alderman, Harold, John Hoddinott, and Bill Kinsey. 2006. "Long Term Consequences of Early Childhood Malnutrition." *Oxford Economic Papers* 58 (3): 450–74.

Alesina, Alberto, and George-Marios Angeletos. 2005. "Fairness and Redistribution." *American Economic Review* 95 (4): 960–80.

Alesina, Alberto, Stefanie Stantcheva, Edoardo Teso. 2017. "Intergenerational Mobility and Support for Redistribution." NBER Working Paper No. 23027, National Bureau of Economic Research, Cambridge, MA.

Alesina, Alberto, Stelios Michalopoulos, and Elias Papaioannou. 2016. "Ethnic Inequality." *Journal of Political Economy* 124 (2): 428–88.

Alex-Petersen, Jesper, Petter Lundborg, and Dan-Olof Rooth. 2017. "Long-Term Effects of Childhood Nutrition: Evidence from a School Lunch Reform." IZA DP 11234, Discussion Paper Series, Institute for the Study of Labor, Bonn.

Almond, Douglas, Hilary W. Hoynes, and Diane Whitmore Schanzenbach. 2011. "Inside the War on Poverty: The Impact of Food Stamps on Birth Outcomes." *The Review of Economics and Statistics* 93 (2): 387–403.

Altinok, Nadir, Claude Diebolt, and Jean-Luc Demeulemeester. 2014. "A New International Database on Education Quality: 1965–2010." *Applied Economics* 46 (11): 1212–47.

Andreoli, Francesco, Tarjei Havnes, and Arnaud Lefranc. Forthcoming. "Equalization of Opportunity: Definitions, Implementable Conditions and Application to Early-Childhood Policy Evaluation."

Appadurai, Arjun. 2002. "Grassroots Globalization and the Research Imagination." *The Anthropology of Politics: A Reader in Ethnography, Theory, and Critique*, edited by Joan Vincent, 271–84. Hoboken, NJ: Wiley-Blackwell.

———. 2004. "The Capacity to Aspire: Culture and the Terms of Recognition." In *Culture and Public Action*, edited by Vijayendra Rao and Michael Walton, 59–84. Palo Alto, CA: Stanford University Press.

Araujo, M. Caridad, Pedro Carneiro, Yyannú Cruz-Aguayo, and Norbert Schady. 2016. "Teacher Quality and Learning Outcomes in Kindergarten." *The Quarterly Journal of Economics* 131 (3): 1415–53.

Baird, Sarah, Joan Hamory Hicks, Michael Kremer, and Edward Miguel. 2016. "Worms at Work: Long-Run Impacts of a Child Health Investment." *The Quarterly Journal of Economics* 131 (4): 1637–80.

Balcazar, Carlos Felipe, Ambar Narayan, and Sailesh Tiwari. 2015. "Born with a Silver Spoon: Inequality in Educational Achievement across the World." Policy Research Working Paper 7152, World Bank, Washington, DC.

Bauer, Lauren, and Diane Whitmore Schanzenbach. 2016. "The Long-Term Impact of the Head Start Program." The Hamilton Project. Brookings Institution, Washington, DC.

Beaman, Lori, Esther Duflo, Rohini Pande, and Petia Topalova. 2011. "Female Leadership Raises Aspirations and Educational Attainment for Girls: A Policy Experiment in India." *Science* 335 (6068): 582–86.

Bell, Alexander M., Raj Chetty, Xavier Jaravel, Neviana Petkova, and John Van Reenen. 2017. "Who Becomes an Inventor in America? The Importance of Exposure to Innovation." NBER Working Paper 24062, National Bureau of Economic Research, Cambridge, MA.

Belot, Michèle, and Jonathan James. 2011. "Healthy School Meals and Educational Outcomes." *Journal of Health Economics* 30 (3): 489–504.

Bharadwaj, Prashant, Katrine Vellesen Løken, and Christopher Neilson. 2013. "Early Life Health Interventions and Academic Achievement." *American Economic Review* 103 (5): 1862–91.

Black, Sandra E., Paul J. Devereux, and Kjell G. Salvanes. 2007. "From the Cradle to the Labor Market? The Effect of Birth Weight on Adult Outcomes." *The Quarterly Journal of Economics* 122 (1): 409–39.

Briggs, Xavier de Souza, Elizabeth J. Mueller, and Mercer L. Sullivan. 1997. *From Neighborhood to Community: Evidence on the Social Effects of Community Development.* New York: Community Development Research Center, Graduate School of Management and Urban Policy, New School for Social Research.

Brooks-Gunn, Jeanne, Greg J. Duncan, and Lawrence J. Aber. 1997. *Neighborhood Poverty, Volume 1: Context and Consequences for Children.* New York: Russell Sage Foundation.

Brown, Prudence, and Harold A. Richman. 1997. "Neighborhood Effects and State and Local Policy." *Neighborhood Poverty* 2: 164–81.

Brunello, Giorgio, and Daniele Checchi. 2007. "Does School Tracking Affect Equality of Opportunity? New International Evidence." *Economic Policy* 22 (52): 782–861.

Brunori, Paolo, Vito Peragine, and Laura Serlenga. 2012. "Fairness in Education: The Italian University before and after the Reform." *Economics of Education Review* 31 (5): 764–77.

Butcher, Kristin. 2017. "Assessing the Long-Run Benefits of Transfers to Low-Income Families." Paper presented at the Hutchins Center on Fiscal and Monetary Policy at Brookings' Conference "From Bridges to Education: Best Bets for Public Investment," Washington, DC, January 9.

Butikofer, Aline, Eirin Mølland, and Kjell G. Salvanes. 2016. "Childhood Nutrition and Labor Market Outcomes: Evidence from a School Breakfast Program." No. 15/2016, Discussion Paper Series in Economics, Norwegian School of Economics, Bergen, Norway.

Campbell, Frances, Gabriella Conti, James J. Heckman, Seong Hyeok Moon, Rodrigo Pinto, Elizabeth Pungello, and Yi Pan. 2014. "Early Childhood Investments Substantially Boost Adult Health." *Science* 343 (6178): 1478–85.

Carneiro, Pedro, and Rita Ginja. 2014. "Long-Term Impacts of Compensatory Preschool on Health and Behavior: Evidence from Head Start." *American Economic Journal: Economic Policy* 6 (4): 135–73.

Carpiano, Richard M., Jennifer E. V. Lloyd, and Clyde Hertzman. 2009. "Concentrated Affluence, Concentrated Disadvantage, and Children's Readiness for School: A Population-Based, Multi-Level Investigation." *Social Science & Medicine* 69 (3): 420–32.

Case, Anne, and Christina Paxson. 2006. "Children's Health and Social Mobility." *The Future of Children.* 16 (2): 151–73.

———. 2008. "Stature and Status: Height, Ability, and Labor Market Outcomes." *Journal of Political Economy* 116 (3): 499–532.

Camarero Garcia, Sebastian. 2017. "Equality of Opportunity of Education in Germany. Evidence from a Quasi-Natural Experiment." Graduate School of Economics and Social Sciences Working Paper, University of Mannheim, Mannheim, Germany.

Chase-Lansdale, P. Lindsay, Rachel A. Gordon, Jeanne Brooks-Gunn, and Pamela K. Klebanov. 1997. "Neighborhood and Family Influences on the Intellectual and Behavioral Competence of Preschool and Early School-Age Children." *Neighborhood Poverty* 1: 79–118.

Chetty, Raj. 2016. "Improving Opportunities for Economic Mobility: New Evidence and Policy Lessons." In *Economic Mobility: Research & Ideas on Strengthening Families, Communities & the Economy*, edited by the Federal Reserve Bank of St. Louis and the Board of Governors of the Federal Reserve System, 35–43. St. Louis, MO: Federal Reserve Bank of St. Louis.

Chetty, Raj, John N. Friedman, Nathaniel Hilger, Emmanuel Saez, Diane Whitmore Schanzenbach, and Danny Yagan. 2011. "How Does Your Kindergarten Classroom Affect Your Earnings? Evidence from Project STAR." *Quarterly Journal of Economics* 126 (4): 1593–660.

Chetty, Raj, and Nathaniel Hendren. 2018a. "The Impacts of Neighborhoods on Intergenerational Mobility I: Childhood Exposure Effects." *Quarterly Journal of Economics.* qjy007. https://doi.org/10.1093/qje/qjy007.

———. 2018b. "The Impacts of Neighborhoods on Intergenerational Mobility II: County-Level Estimates." *Quarterly Journal of Economics.* qjy006. https://doi.org/10.1093/qje/qjy006.

Chetty, Raj, Nathaniel Hendren, and Lawrence F. Katz. 2016. "The Effects of Exposure to Better Neighborhoods on Children: New Evidence from the Moving to Opportunity Experiment." *American Economic Review* 106 (4): 855–902.

Chetty, Raj, Nathaniel Hendren, Patrick Kline, and Emmanuel Saez. 2014. "Where Is the Land of Opportunity? The Geography of Intergenerational Mobility in the United States." *The Quarterly Journal of Economics* 129 (4): 1553–623.

Chowdry, Haroon, Claire Crawford, Lorraine Dearden, Robert Joyce, Luke Sibieta, Kathy Sylva, and Elizabeth Washbrook. 2010. "Poorer Children's Educational Attainment: How Important Are Attitudes and Behaviour?", edited by Alissa Goodman and Paul Gregg, 1–72. Joseph Rowntree Foundation, York, UK.

Cojocaru, Alexandru. 2014a. "Prospects of Upward Mobility and Preferences for Redistribution: Evidence from the Life in Transition Survey." *European Journal of Political Economy* 34: 300–14.

———. 2014b. "Fairness and Inequality Tolerance: Evidence from the Life in Transition survey." *Journal of Comparative Economics* 42 (3): 590–608.

Corak, Miles. 2017. "Divided Landscapes of Economic Opportunity: The Canadian Geography of Intergenerational Income Mobility." Working Papers 2017-043, Human Capital and Economic Opportunity Working Group, University of Chicago, Chicago, IL.

Cummings, Colleen, Karen Laing, James Law, Janice McLaughlin, Ivy Papps, Liz Todd, and Pam Woolner. 2012. *Can Changing Aspirations and Attitudes Impact on Educational Attainment?* New York: Joseph Rowntree Foundation.

Currie, Janet, and Duncan Thomas. 2001. "Early Test Scores, School Quality and SES: Long Run Effects on Wage and Employment Outcomes." *Research in Labor Economics*, 20: 103–32.

Cushon, Jennifer A., Lan T. H. Vu, Bonnie L. Janzen, and Nazeem Muhajarine. 2011. "Neighborhood Poverty Impacts Children's Physical Health and Well-Being over Time: Evidence from the Early Development Instrument." *Early Education and Development* 22 (2): 183–205.

Dabalen, Andrew, Ambar Narayan, Jaime Saavedra-Chanduvi, Alejandro Hoyos Suarez, Ana Abras, Sailesh Tiwari. 2015. *Do African Children Have an Equal Chance? A Human Opportunity Report for Sub-Saharan Africa.* Washington, DC: World Bank.

Dabalen, Andrew, Rasyad A. Parinduri, and Saumik Paul. 2015. "The Effects of the Intensity, Timing and Persistence of Personal History of Mobility on Support for Redistribution in Transition Countries." *Economics of Transition* 23 (3): 565–95.

Deming, David. 2009. "Early Childhood Intervention and Life-Cycle Skill Development: Evidence from Head Start." *American Economic Journal: Applied Economics* 1 (3): 111–34.

Dercon, Stefan, and Pramila Krishnan. 2009. "Poverty and the Psychosocial Competencies of Children: Evidence from the Young Lives Sample in Four Developing Countries." *Children Youth and Environments* 19 (2): 138–63.

Dercon, Stefan, and Abhijeet Singh. 2013. "From Nutrition to Aspirations and Self-Efficacy: Gender Bias over Time among Children in Four Countries." *World Development* 45: 31–50.

Donnelly, Louis, Irwin Garfinkel, Jeanne Brooks-Gunn, Brandon G. Wagner, Sarah James, and Sara McLanahan. 2017. "Geography of Intergenerational Mobility and Child Development." *Proceedings of the National Academy of Sciences* 114 (35): 9320–25.

Duflo, Esther, Pascaline Dupas, and Michael Kremer. 2017. "The Impact of Free Secondary Education: Experimental Evidence from Ghana." Massachusetts Institute of Technology Working Paper, Cambridge, MA.

Eckenrode, John, Mary Campa, Dennis W. Luckey, Charles R. Henderson, Robert Cole, Harriet Kitzman, Elizabeth Anson, Kimberly Sidora-Arcoleo, Jane Powers, and David Olds. 2010. "Long-Term Effects of Prenatal and Infancy Nurse Home Visitation on the Life Course of Youths: 19-Year Follow-Up of a Randomized Trial." *Archives of Pediatrics & Adolescent Medicine* 164 (1) 9–15.

Ferreira, Francisco H. G. and Jérémie Gignoux. 2014. "The Measurement of Educational Inequality: Achievement and Opportunity." *The World Bank Economic Review* 28 (2): 210–46.

Field, Erica, Omar Robles, and Maximo Torero. 2009. "Iodine Deficiency and Schooling Attainment in Tanzania." *American Economic Journal: Applied Economics* 1 (4): 140–69.

Flechtner, Svenja. 2014. "Aspiration Traps: When Poverty Stifles Hope." *Inequality in Focus* 2 (4): 1–4.

Flouri, Eirini, Stella Mavroveli, and Emily Midouhas. 2013. "Residential Mobility, Neighbourhood Deprivation and Children's Behaviour in the UK." *Health & Place* 20: 25–31.

Frisvold, David E. 2015. "Nutrition and Cognitive Achievement: An Evaluation of the School Breakfast Program." *Journal of Public Economics* 124: 91–104.

Galab, Shaik, Uma Vennam, Anuradha Komanduri, Liza Benny, and Andreas Georgiadis. 2013. "The Impact of Parental Aspirations on Private School Enrolment: Evidence from Andhra Pradesh, India." Young Lives Working Paper 97, Oxford Department of International Development (ODID), University of Oxford, Oxford, UK.

Garces, Eliana, Duncan Thomas, and Janet Currie. 2002. "Longer-Term Effects of Head Start." *American Economic Review* 92 (4): 999–1012.

Garcia, Jorge Luis, James J. Heckman, Duncan Ermini Leaf, and María José Prados. 2016. "The Life-Cycle Benefits of an Influential Early Childhood Program." NBER Working Paper 22993, National Bureau of Economic Research, Cambridge, MA.

GDIM (Global Database on Intergenerational Mobility). 2018. *Global Database on Intergenerational Mobility.* Development Research Group, World Bank. Washington, DC: World Bank.

Gertler, Paul, James Heckman, Rodrigo Pinto, Arianna Zanolini, Christel Vermeersch, Susan Walker, Susan M. Chang, and Sally Grantham-McGregor. 2014. "Labor Market Returns to an Early Childhood Stimulation Intervention in Jamaica." *Science* 344 (6187): 998–1001.

Goodman, Alissa, and Paul Gregg, eds. 2010. *Poorer Children's Educational Attainment: How Important Are Attitudes and Behaviour?* New York: Joseph Rowntree Foundation.

Gorard, Stephen, Beng Huat See, and Peter Davies. 2012. *The Impact of Attitudes and Aspirations on Educational Attainment and Participation.* April. New York: Joseph Rowntree Foundation.

Goux, Dominique, Marc Gurgand, and Eric Maurin. 2017. "Adjusting Your Dreams? High School Plans and Dropout Behaviour." *The Economic Journal* 127 (602): 1025–46.

Gregg, Paul, and Elizabeth Washbrook. 2010. "From Birth through Primary School: Evidence from the Avon Longitudinal Study of Parents and Children." In *Poorer Children's Educational Attainment: How Important Are Attitudes and Behavior?*, edited by Alissa Goodman and Paul Gregg, 26–33. York, UK: Joseph Rowntree Foundation.

Guyon, Nina, and Elise Huillery. 2016. "Aspirations and the Perpetuation of Social Inequalities." Proceedings of the Seoul National University Economic Research Institute, 1–30, May 26.

Halpern-Felsher, Bonnie L., James P. Connell, Margaret Beale Spencer, J. Lawrence Aber, Greg J. Duncan, Elizabeth Clifford, Warren E. Crichlow, Peter A. Usinger, Steven P. Cole, LaRue Allen, and Edward Seidman. 1997. "Neighborhood and Family Factors Predicting Educational Risk and Attainment in African American and White Children and Adolescents." *Neighborhood Poverty* 1: 146–73.

Havnes, Tarjei, and Magne Mogstad. 2011. "No Child Left Behind: Subsidized Child Care and Children's Long-Run Outcomes." *American Economic Journal: Economic Policy* 3 (2): 97–129.

Heckman, James J. 2006. "Skill Formation and the Economics of Investing in Disadvantaged Children." *Science* 312 (5782): 1900–02.

Heckman, James J., and Tim Kautz. 2014. "Fostering and Measuring Skills: Interventions that Improve Character and Cognition." In *The Myth of*

Achievement Tests: The GED and the Role of Character in American Life, 341–430, edited by J. Heckman, J.E. Humphries and T. Kautz. Chicago, IL: University of Chicago Press.

Heckman, James J., Rodrigo Pinto, and Peter Savelyev. 2013. "Understanding the Mechanisms through which an Influential Early Childhood Program Boosted Adult Outcomes." *American Economic Review* 103 (6): 2052–86.

Hoddinott, John, Harold Alderman, Jere R. Behrman, Lawrence Haddad, and Susan Horton. 2013. "The Economic Rationale for Investing in Stunting Reduction." *Maternal & Child Nutrition* 9 (S2): 69–82.

Hoddinott, John, John A. Maluccio, Jere R. Behrman, Rafael Flores, and Reynaldo Martorell. 2008. "Effect of a Nutrition Intervention during Early Childhood on Economic Productivity in Guatemalan Adults." *The Lancet* 371 (9610): 411–16.

Hoff, Karla. 2012. "The Effect of Inequality on Aspirations." Background paper for *Addressing Inequality in South Asia*, edited by M. Rama, T. Béteille, Y. Li, P. Mitra, and J. Newman. Washington, DC: World Bank.

Hoff, Karla, and Priyanka Pandey. 2014. "Making up People—The Effect of Identity on Performance in a Modernizing Society." *Journal of Development Economics* 106: 118–31.

Hoxby, Caroline, and Christopher Avery. 2013. "The Missing 'One-Offs': The Hidden Supply of High-Achieving, Low-Income Students." *Brookings Papers on Economic Activity* 2013 (1): 1–65.

Hoynes, Hilary W., Marianne E. Page, and Ann Huff Stevens. 2011. "Can Targeted Transfers Improve Birth Outcomes?: Evidence from the Introduction of the WIC program." *Journal of Public Economics* 95: 813–27.

Hoynes, Hilary W., and Diane Whitmore Schanzenbach. 2012. "Work Incentives and the Food Stamp Program." *Journal of Public Economics* 96 (1–2): 151–62.

Hungi, Njora, Demus Makuwa, Kenneth Ross, Mioko Saito, Stéphanie Dolata, Frank Van Cappelle, Laura Paviot, and Jocelyne Vellien. 2010. "SACMEQ III Project Results: Pupil Achievement Levels in Reading and Mathematics." Working Document 1, SEACMEQ. Gaborone, Botswana.

ISGlobal and World Bank. 2016. *Inequalities in Women's and Girls' Health Opportunities and Outcomes: A Report from Sub-Saharan Africa.* Barcelona, Spain, and Washington, DC.

Jacoby, Hanan G., and Ghazala Mansuri. 2011. *Crossing Boundaries: Gender, Caste and Schooling in Rural Pakistan.* Policy Research Working Paper 5710, World Bank, Washington, DC.

———. 2015. "Crossing Boundaries: How Social Hierarchy Impedes Economic Mobility." *Journal of Economic Behavior & Organization* 117: 135–54.

Janzen, Sarah A., Nicholas Magnan, Sudhindra Sharma, and William M. Thompson. 2017. "Aspirations Failure and Formation in Rural Nepal." *Journal of Economic Behavior & Organization* 139: 1–25.

Jayaraman, Rajshri, and Dora Simroth. 2015. "The Impact of School Lunches on Primary School Enrollment: Evidence from India's Midday Meal Scheme." *The Scandinavian Journal of Economics* 117 (4): 1176–203.

Jencks, Christopher, and Susan E. Mayer. 1990. "The Social Consequences of Growing up in a Poor Neighborhood." *Inner-City Poverty in the United States* 111: 186.

Jensen, Robert. 2010. "The (Perceived) Returns to Education and the Demand for Schooling." *The Quarterly Journal of Economics* 125 (2): 515–48.

Jensen, Robert, and Emily Oster. 2009. "The Power of TV: Cable Television and Women's Status in India." *The Quarterly Journal of Economics* 124 (3): 1057–94.

Jones, Andrew M., John E. Roemer, and Pedro Rosa Dias. 2014. "Equalising Opportunities in Health through Educational Policy." *Social Choice and Welfare* 43 (3): 521–45.

Kelley, Sarah M. C., and Claire G. E. Kelley. 2009. "Subjective Social Mobility: Data from 30 Nations." In *Charting the Globe: The International Social Survey Programme 1984–2004*, 106–24, edited by Max Hallier, Roger Jowell and Tom W. Smith. London: Routledge.

Kershaw, Paul, and Barry Forer. 2010. "Selection of Area-Level Variables from Administrative Data: An Intersectional Approach to the Study of Place and Child Development." *Health & Place* 16 (3): 500–11.

Kintrea, Keith, Ralf St. Clair, and Muir Houston. 2011. *The Influence of Parents, Places and Poverty on Educational Attitudes and Aspirations.* York, UK: Joseph Rowntree Foundation.

Knight, John, and Ramani Gunatilaka. 2012. "Income, Aspirations and the Hedonic Treadmill in a Poor Society." *Journal of Economic Behavior & Organization* 82 (1): 67–81.

Kohen, Dafna, Lisa Oliver, and Fritz Pierre. 2009. "Examining the Effects of Schools and Neighbourhoods on the Outcomes of Kindergarten Children in Canada." *International Journal of Speech-Language Pathology* 11 (5): 404–18.

Krishnan, Nandini, Gabriel Lara Ibarra, Ambar Narayan, Sailesh Tiwari, and Tara Vishwanath. 2016. *Uneven Odds, Unequal Outcomes: Inequality of Opportunity in the Middle East and North Africa.* Directions in Development Series. Washington, DC: World Bank.

Leventhal, Tama, and Jeanne Brooks-Gunn. 2000. "The Neighborhoods They Live In: The Effects of Neighborhood Residence on Child and Adolescent Outcomes." *Psychological Bulletin* 126 (2): 309.

————. 2003. "Moving to Opportunity: An Experimental Study of Neighborhood Effects on Mental Health." *American Journal of Public Health* 93 (9): 1576–82.

Maccini, Sharon, and Dean Yang. 2009. "Under the Weather: Health, Schooling, and Economic Consequences of Early-Life Rainfall." *American Economic Review* 99 (3): 1006–26.

Martens, Patricia J., Daniel G. Chateau, Elaine M. J. Burland, Gregory S. Finlayson, Mark J. Smith, Carole R. Taylor, Marni D. Brownell, Nathan C. Nickel, Alan Katz, James M. Bolton, and the PATHS Equity Team. 2014. "The Effect of Neighborhood Socioeconomic Status on Education and Health Outcomes for Children Living in Social Housing." *American Journal of Public Health* 104 (11): 2103–13.

Mazumder, Bhashkar. 2016. "What Should Be Done to Increase Intergenerational Mobility in the US?" In *The US Labor Market: Questions and Challenges for Public Policy*, edited by Michael Strain. Washington, DC: American Enterprise Institute.

McCormick, Marie C., Jeanne Brooks-Gunn, Stephen L. Buka, Julie Goldman, Jennifer Yu, Mikhail Salganik, David T. Scott, Forrest C. Bennett, Libby L. Kay, Judy C. Bernbaum, Charles R. Bauer, Camilia Martin, Elizabeth R. Woods, Anne Martin, and Patrick H. Casey. 2006. "Early Intervention in Low Birth Weight Premature Infants: Results at 18 Years of Age for the Infant Health and Development Program." *Pediatrics* 117 (3): 771–80.

McEwan, Patrick J. 2013. "The Impact of Chile's School Feeding Program on Education Outcomes." *Economics of Education Review* 32: 122–39.

Meghir, Costas, and Mårten Palme. 2005. "Educational Reform, Ability, and Family Background." *American Economic Review* 95 (1): 414–24.

Minh, Anita, Nazeem Muhajarine, Magdalena Janus, Marni Brownell, and Martin Guhn. 2017. "A Review of Neighborhood Effects and Early Child Development: How, Where, and For Whom, Do Neighborhoods Matter?" *Health & Place* 46: 155–74.

Nybom, Martin, and Jan Stuhler. 2016. "Heterogeneous Income Profiles and Lifecycle Bias in Intergenerational Mobility Estimation." *Journal of Human Resources* 51 (1): 239–68.

OECD (Organisation for Economic Co-operation and Development). 2016. *PISA 2015 Results (Volume I): Excellence and Equity in Education.* Paris: OECD Publishing.

Olds, David L., Harriet Kitzman, Carole Hanks, Robert Cole, Elizabeth Anson, Kimberly Sidora-Arcoleo, Dennis W. Luckey, Charles R. Henderson, Jr., John Holmberg, Robin A. Tutt, Amanda J. Stevenson, and Jessica Bondy. 2007. "Effects of Nurse Home Visiting on Maternal and Child Functioning: Age-9 Follow-Up of a Randomized Trial." *Pediatrics* 120 (4): e832–45.

Orr, Larry, Judith Feins, Robin Jacob, Eric Beecroft, Lisa Sanbonmatsu, Lawrence F. Katz, Jeffrey B. Liebman, and Jeffrey R. Kling. 2003. "Moving to Opportunity: Interim Impacts Evaluation." Office of Policy Development and Research, US Department of Housing and Urban Development.

Paes de Barros, Ricardo, Francisco H. G. Ferreira, Jose R. Molinas Vega, Jaime Saavedra Chanduvi. 2009. *Measuring Inequality of Opportunities in Latin America and the Caribbean.* Washington, DC: World Bank; New York: Palgrave Macmillan.

Paes de Barros, Ricardo, José R. Molinas Vega, Jaime Saavedra Chanduvi, Marcelo Giugale, Louise J. Cord, Carola Pessino, and Amer Hasan. 2012. *Do Our Children Have a Chance? A Human Opportunity Report for Latin America and the Caribbean.* Directions in Development; Poverty. Washington, DC: World Bank.

Pasquier-Doumer, Laure, and Fiorella Risso Brandon. 2015. "Aspiration Failure: A Poverty Trap for Indigenous Children in Peru?" *World Development* 72: 208–23.

Pekkarinen, Tuomas, Roope Uusitalo, and Sari Kerr. 2009. "School Tracking and Intergenerational Income Mobility: Evidence from the Finnish Comprehensive School Reform." *Journal of Public Economics* 93 (7–8): 965–73.

Piketty, Thomas. 1995. "Social Mobility and Redistributive Politics." *The Quarterly Journal of Economics* 110 (3): 551–84.

Raaum, Oddbjørn, Kjell G. Salvanes, and Erik Ø. Sørensen. 2006. "The Neighbourhood Is Not What It Used To Be." *The Economic Journal* 116 (508): 200–22.

Rama, Martin, Tara Béteille, Yue Li, Pradeep K. Mitra, and John Lincoln Newman. 2015. *Addressing Inequality in South Asia.* Washington, DC: World Bank.

Ray, Debraj. 2006. "Aspirations, Poverty, and Economic Change." *In Understanding Poverty,* edited by Abhijit Vinayak Banerjee, Roland Bénabou, and Dilip Mookherjee, chapter 28. Oxford, UK: Oxford University Press.

Ritterman Weintraub, Miranda Lucia, Lia C. H. Fernald, Nancy Adler, Stefano Bertozzi, and S. Leonard Syme. 2015. "Perceptions of Social Mobility: Development of a New Psychosocial Indicator Associated with Adolescent Risk Behaviors." *Frontiers in Public Health* 3: 62.

Ross, Phillip H. 2016. "Aspirations and Human Capital Investment: Evidence from Indian Adolescents." Boston University Working Paper, Boston, MA.

Rossin-Slater, Maya. 2013. "WIC in Your Neighborhood: New Evidence on the Impacts of Geographic Access to Clinics." *Journal of Public Economics* 102: 51–69.

Sacerdote, Bruce. 2011. "Peer Effects in Education: How Might They Work, How Big Are They and How Much Do We Know Thus Far?" In *Handbook of the Economics of Education*, vol. 3, edited by Eric A. Hanushek, Stephen Machin, and Ludger Woessmann, 249–77. New York: Elsevier.

Sahn, David E., and Stephen D. Younger. 2000. "Expenditure Incidence in Africa: Microeconomic Evidence." *Fiscal Studies* 21 (3): 329–47.

Salehi-Isfahani, Djavad, Nadia Belhaj Hassine, and Ragui Assaad. 2014. "Equality of Opportunity in Educational Achievement in the Middle East and North Africa." *Journal of Economic Inequality* 12 (4): 489–515.

Schoon, Ingrid, and Samantha Parsons. 2002. "Teenage Aspirations for Future Careers and Occupational Outcomes." *Journal of Vocational Behavior* 60 (2): 262–88.

Serneels, Pieter, and Stefan Dercon. 2014. "Aspirations, Poverty and Education: Evidence from India." Young Lives Working Paper 125. Oxford Department of International Development, University of Oxford, Oxford, UK.

Solon, Gary. 1999. "Intergenerational Mobility in the Labor Market." In *Handbook of Labor Economics*, vol. 3, 1761–800. New York: Elsevier.

———. 2004. "A Model of Intergenerational Mobility Variation over Time and Place." In *Generational Income Mobility in North America and Europe*, edited by Miles Corak, 38–47. Cambridge, U.K. Cambridge University Press.

Stutzer, Alois. 2004. "The Role of Income Aspirations in Individual Happiness." *Journal of Economic Behavior & Organization* 54 (1): 89–109.

Swanstrom, Todd, Hank Webber, and Molly Metzger. 2015. "Rebound Neighborhoods in Older Industrial Cities: The Case of St. Louis." In *Federal Reserve System Community Development Conference*, 2–3.

Tanguy, Bernard, Stefan Dercon, Kate Orkin, and Alemayehu Taffesse. 2014. "The Future in Mind: Aspirations and Forward-Looking Behaviour in Rural Ethiopia." CEPR Discussion Paper DP10224. Centre for Economic Policy Research, London, UK.

Vegas, Emiliana, and Chelsea Coffin. "When Education Expenditure Matters: An Empirical Analysis of Recent International Data." *Comparative Education Review* 59 (2): 289–304.

Vermeersch, Christel and Michael Kremer. 2005. "School Meals, Educational Achievement and School Competition: Evidence from a Randomized Evaluation." Policy Research Working Paper 3523, World Bank, Washington, DC.

World Bank. 2005. *World Development Report 2006: Equity and Development*. Washington, DC: World Bank; New York: Oxford University Press.

————. 2018. *World Development Report 2018: Learning to Realize Education's Promise.* Washington, DC: World Bank.

Zhang, Yanyan, Eileen Haddad, Bernadeth Torres, and Chuansheng Chen. 2011. "The Reciprocal Relationships among Parents' Expectations, Adolescents' Expectations, and Adolescents' Achievement: A Two-Wave Longitudinal Analysis of the NELS Data." *Journal of Youth and Adolescence* 40 (4): 479–89.

CHAPTER 6

Promoting Intergenerational Mobility: The Role of Factor Markets and Policies

This chapter focuses on the drivers of intergenerational mobility (IGM) that act upon individuals primarily during adulthood, which is the third stage of the life-cycle framework (chapter 4, figure 4.11). Factor markets, institutions, and government policies interact with an individual's circumstances to influence the extent to which the individual's human capital, acquired primarily at an earlier stage of life, translates into income mobility. But the impacts of these drivers of mobility are not limited to adults; barriers to income mobility that affect adults also influence the incentives and the ability of parents to invest in the education of their children, exerting an impact on the education mobility and income mobility of the next generation.

The efficiency of markets and the productivity of the private sector are key to IGM by determining the returns to human capital and creating demand for jobs. A labor market that produces inadequate demand for labor or that is inefficient and unfair because it rewards the advantages of a privileged background above skills can be a strong barrier to IGM in income in addition to the factors that limit educational mobility. The capital market can also play a constraining role: in credit-constrained environments, the poor are unable to borrow to finance the education of their children, to acquire skills outside formal education, or to become entrepreneurs. Market distortions can also lead to increased market concentration that produces more economic rents, generating rising inequality and exerting an adverse impact on IGM. This chapter unpacks the role of markets in limiting mobility across generations. It focuses especially on the labor market, given the critical influence of the labor market in raising incomes and reducing poverty in developing economies.[1]

Economic growth and the pace of economic transformation are important drivers of IGM in income in developing economies. This is because absolute IGM requires expansion in the size of the economic pie, which also helps generate public revenue to finance investments that equalize the opportunities to raise relative IGM. Transformation and global trends in technology and integration can also induce important shifts, such as raising productivity and the returns to skills, reducing barriers to geographic mobility, and changing incentives and norms. The chapter looks at the evidence in the literature to examine briefly how the process of economic transformation might benefit IGM in a developing economy and the factors that might act as barriers and lead to uneven impacts locally within an economy. Unpacking the relationship between key features of IGM and economic transformation—such as urbanization, structural adjustments in the labor market, and spatial mobility—empirically on a global scale is beyond the scope of this report and must remain a subject for future research.

This chapter also analyzes the role of fiscal policy, which is the most common and flexible among the redistributive tools available to a government and is thus critical for IGM in both education and income. Public investments are key to equalizing the opportunities at various stages of life. Fiscal policy may affect IGM through other avenues as well, such as by reducing inequality of wealth and income. In addition to the impacts of individual taxes and spending policies, consideration of the overall impact of the fiscal system is important, particularly in achieving a balance between efficiency and equity objectives.

The chapter then examines briefly the question of why policies to promote fair progress are not adopted or implemented effectively often enough by governments. The lack of evidence on what policies work provides a partial explanation; reports like this one can play a role in filling these evidence gaps. However, the extent of evidence and experience that do exist and yet fail to influence policy decisions suggests that knowledge may not be the binding constraint in many cases. Rather, the likely explanation for why good policies can be hard to adopt and implement is political economy constraints, which prevent institutions from functioning well enough to support a process of policy making that supports the greater good of a society.

The chapter focuses primarily on relative mobility. In developing economies, the distinction between absolute mobility and relative mobility is often not important from a policy perspective: equalizing opportunities is mainly about raising upward mobility among poorer families, which generates greater absolute mobility for the society overall (chapter 4). This means that the two concepts of mobility are complementary in many policies. But, even if this is not the case, such as in directly redistributive policies that seek to reduce income inequality, the argument for prioritizing relative mobility can be compelling, given the significance of relative mobility for long-term growth, equality, and social cohesion. Relative mobility may even influence perceptions on absolute mobility. Given these reasons, absolute mobility is referred to in this chapter only on the few occasions in which the policy drivers of absolute mobility merit emphasis separately from the drivers of relative mobility, such as in the context of trade-offs between efficiency and equity.

The chapter concludes by summarizing some high-level policy messages on improving IGM that emerge from the report. These represent an attempt to summarize the broad policy areas that a review of the literature and the patterns in the global data suggest as crucial. While there is some degree of selectivity—based on theory and evidence—in the choice of policy ideas that are highlighted, no attempt has been made to provide an explicit ranking of policies. Such an attempt would not have been useful, because the ranking of policy priorities for any economy should depend on the constraints to IGM in its own specific context and thus cannot be generalized. Instead, the discussion is intended to provide a broad range of candidate policies informed by economic theory and evidence, which policy makers can assess to identify the package of priorities that may be effective and feasible in their own contexts.

Labor Markets and Intergenerational Mobility

Among factor markets, labor markets are especially significant in shaping the persistence of income inequality across generations. In the context of the decomposition results shown in chapter 4, the functioning of the labor market influences the size of the first channel through returns to education and the size of the third channel through the effect of parental circumstances other than education on the earnings of offspring. Both these effects may be influenced by other circumstances associated with individuals, such as gender and race.

Although the labor market directly affects individuals in the adult stage of life, it can have a feedback effect on human capital formation as well. Investments in human capital are priced on the labor market, and such investments are, to a large extent, motivated by the ability of individuals with higher educational attainment to obtain better jobs. Thus, all opportunities, incentives, and institutional factors influencing how such prices are formed have a feedback effect on the investment decisions parents make on their children's education and on the decisions made by the children themselves as they approach adulthood.

A healthy labor market is a precondition for inclusive growth and IGM. A labor market in which job creation is sufficient to accommodate the labor force and in which competition among firms contributes to the efficient allocation of talent across jobs is one that maximizes the returns to intergenerational investments on human capital. Conversely, a labor market in which jobs are rationed, labor mobility is limited, and human capital investments are priced differently on the basis of characteristics unrelated to a worker's productivity is one in which earnings inequality is more likely to persist across generations. Such a labor market produces inequality of economic opportunities, which introduces a wedge between IGM of education and IGM of income. Moreover, labor market distortions can lead to inefficient investments in human capital and a subsequent loss in human potential that ultimately dampens economic growth.

Labor Market Health and Intergenerational Mobility

Low labor force participation rates and high unemployment are the most obvious signs of labor market imbalances, such as excess labor supply and rigidities like barriers to labor mobility, job-matching frictions, and so on. The inability to find a job or losing a job if the likelihood of obtaining a new one is slim are among the most pressing concerns of households all over the world (figure 6.1). The challenge is particularly severe in economies lacking unemployment insurance or other forms of last resort income support and among poorer households that rely the most on labor income for livelihoods and lack access to credit or insurance to smooth consumption in times of hardship.

An economy characterized by low labor force participation or high unemployment is one in which investments in human capital are more difficult to monetize and a wedge is more likely to exist between educational and income mobility across generations. The relationship between education IGM and income IGM is much weaker in economies with low labor force participation (lower than the median) than in economies with high participation (figure 6.2). Regressions show that the relationship between educational IGM and income IGM is affected significantly by the labor force participation rate and is stronger if the rate is higher.[2] It seems

FIGURE 6.1 Unemployment is a serious concern worldwide

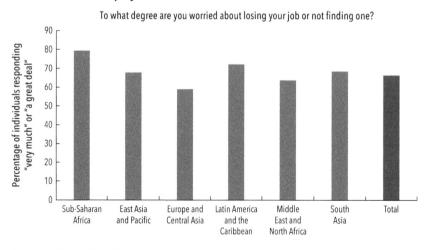

Source: Data from WVS (World Values Survey), Wave 6 (2010–2014) (database), King's College, Old Aberdeen, the United Kingdom, http://www.worldvaluessurvey.org/WVSDocumentationWV6.jsp.

FIGURE 6.2   If labor force participation is higher, relative mobility in income and in education are more closely associated

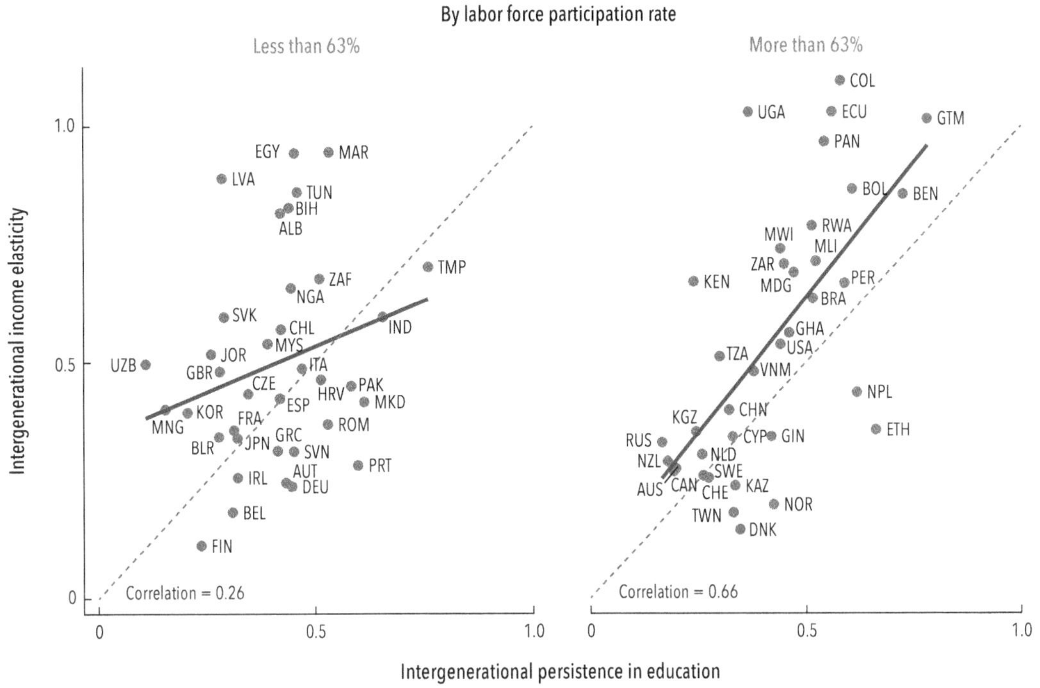

By labor force participation rate

Sources: GDIM 2018; Equalchances 2018; ILOSTAT Database, International Labour Organization, Geneva, http://www.ilo.org/ilostat/.
Note: The median labor force participation rate is 63 percent in economies for which estimates of income mobility and educational mobility are available. Higher persistence or elasticity indicates lower relative mobility.

intuitive that, if a smaller share of working-age adults are in the labor market, educational mobility is less likely to track income mobility.

The unemployment rate does not have such an effect probably because unemployment is not a reliable indicator of the overall health of the labor market in developing economies with relatively low incomes, inadequate safety nets, and large informal sectors.[3] Once the effect of labor force participation is considered, the economy's per capita gross domestic product (GDP) does not have a strong impact on the relationship between education and income IGMs, which suggests that, for this relationship, an economy's labor market conditions matter more than its overall level of development.

How does the overall health of the labor market affect IGM? Consider two young individuals who are perfectly identical in age, education, and ability, but who enter the labor market at different points of the business cycle. One enters during a boom when jobs are being created, whereas the other enters during a recession when jobs are being destroyed and unemployment is high, which discourages participation in the labor market among some of this generation. Would these two individuals face different prospects of IGM? Moreover, would two equally productive individuals from different socioeconomic backgrounds experience the same economic opportunities during a recession?

The evidence on advanced economies suggests that the individual who enters the labor market during a recession is likely to face a long-term disadvantage, that is, unemployment at the time of entry may have an impact on future labor market outcomes.[4] First, if few jobs are available and the probability of a match between labor supply and the characteristics of labor needs is scarce, job seekers may be obliged to lower their reservation wages and accept suboptimal offers, which can adversely affect lifetime growth in earnings. Second, if the entrant is unable to find a job for some time, unemployment may have a long-lasting impact on lifetime earnings through its influence on the accumulation of experience, skills depreciation, psychological discouragement, and scarring effects.[5] Thus, otherwise identical individuals may end up with different lifetime earnings depending on labor market conditions at the time and place of entry. Labor market conditions at entry can affect absolute IGM directly by reducing the lifetime earnings of the generation experiencing high unemployment and indirectly by altering the expectations of the returns to human capital and thereby the incentives to invest in the education of the next generation.

Unfavorable labor market conditions can also strengthen intergenerational persistence: the impact of a crisis on workers living in different circumstances can be quite uneven because of differences in their ability to cope with a crisis. Evidence on the financial crises in Mexico and Southeast Asia in the 1990s shows that poorer, credit-constrained households are more likely to withdraw children from school in response to unemployment shocks.[6] One study finds that Brazilian youth adjust their school and labor force behavior in response to an unexpected economic shock to their households.[7] Unemployment among household heads leads to higher labor force participation and a decline in school performance among youth.

The income effect of unemployment is particularly severe among poor or credit-constrained households. Youth from disadvantaged backgrounds may be forced to enter the labor market at a time when few economic opportunities are available, compared with youth in households that are more well off or enjoy better access to credit, who are more likely to postpone labor market entry, accumulate more schooling or unpaid work experience, and improve their prospects of upward mobility.[8] More generally, the higher risk of unemployment among less-skilled workers and the higher risk of job displacement in low-skilled sectors can contribute to low mobility among the most vulnerable segments of the workforce.

The impact of youth unemployment on IGM adds to the already conspicuous social costs. By the most recent estimates, 71 million youth were unemployed worldwide in 2017, of whom about 63 million were living in developed or emerging economies.[9] If technological progress leads to increasingly jobless growth as feared by some, youth unemployment is likely to remain a challenge, which would limit the prospects of income mobility globally. Economic shocks such as the 2008–09 financial crisis that disproportionately affected younger workers in many high-income and emerging economies can also have a permanent impact on the mobility of a generation, which may not be offset by subsequent periods of recovery. The consequences of these global trends and shocks for relative IGM are evident, given that unemployment has uneven impacts on the income mobility of workers with differing circumstances. But absolute IGM would suffer as well because the extent of absolute mobility of a society depends on the share of the current generation that is doing better than their parents in absolute terms.

The Distribution of Labor Market Opportunities and Intergenerational Mobility

The way in which jobs are allocated affects economic growth and overall market efficiency, as well as IGM. If the distribution of jobs is not based on the productive attributes of workers, but is mediated by social connections (such as family networks) or by circumstances beyond the control of an individual (such as race, caste, and gender), the link between investments in human capital and returns in the labor market is weakened.

Family networks and the intergenerational transmission of labor market opportunities

Social networks are important for obtaining information about jobs and in the referral process for available jobs. Friends and relatives are instrumental in the job search throughout the occupational spectrum and in a multitude of geographically defined labor markets.[10] Informal job search methods appear to be more important for low-skill jobs and in markets or neighborhoods characterized by high poverty rates.[11] In general, the effectiveness of social networks in facilitating job searches and matching supply to demand depends on the structure of the ties in the network, the availability and functioning of formal job search alternatives, and the conditions of the markets in which the network operates.[12] Social networks contribute to the persistence of labor market outcomes and, ultimately, to inefficient investments in human capital and poverty traps.[13] For example, networks characterized by widespread unemployment and substantial likelihood of dropping out of the labor force might adjust investments in education in response to weak employment prospects.[14]

Social networks may represent a barrier to IGM if they are inherited across generations and are not the result of contacts developed over the academic career of individuals or through community interactions and early occupational experiences. Parents who belong to influential networks can provide their offspring with job information, referrals, and access to their connections, which can put those without such connections at a considerable disadvantage. Strong reliance on such networks can also lead to inefficiencies that slow absolute mobility in society. This can occur if connections are not a good vehicle for objective information on the productivity of prospective workers or if the lack of competition among employers curbs their incentives to increase the productivity of the workforce.

The role of parental social networks can be a particularly important barrier to relative mobility if jobs are rationed and unemployment is high.[15] A study of young adults in Cape Town finds that the occupational networks of fathers can have a strong effect on the labor market outcomes among sons and can account for most of the labor market disadvantage suffered by black and colored young men, many of whose fathers are absent, unemployed, or deceased.[16] A recent World Bank report finds that, in the Middle East and North Africa region, circumstances at birth, including the occupation of fathers, account for a sizable portion of inequality in labor market outcomes among young adults, as measured by the likelihood of full-time employment, formal employment, and public sector employment. Personal connections or the culture of *wasta* (Arabic for "connections"; literally a middleman) plays a substantial role in compounding the effects of weak job creation on IGM in the region (box 6.1).[17]

BOX 6.1   Social networks compound the effects of weak job creation on intergenerational mobility in the Middle East and North Africa

The influence of social networks and, specifically, family networks in curtailing IGM is heightened whenever jobs or good-quality jobs are in limited supply. Evidence on the intergenerational transmission of privilege through rationed labor market access in the economies of the Middle East and North Africa is abundant. Decades of progress in educational outcomes and growing youth aspirations have clashed with an endemic lack of labor market opportunities. Figure B6.1.1 shows that, in most of these economies, employment as a share of the population is low, despite the rapid gains in educational attainment that have led to relatively high IGM in education (chapter 3). The lack of a dynamic private sector, the predominance of informal and low-productivity jobs, and the reliance on a capital-intensive extractive sector in many economies of the region are most often cited as reasons for weak job creation. The public sector has historically played an important compensating role. In recent years, however, growing wage bills and fiscal constraints have led to public sector hiring freezes in some economies. Conflict, geopolitical tension, and population displacement have added to the strains.

The lack of jobs is compounded by a widespread perception of unfairness in labor market opportunities, which might also have contributed to social and political instability. The Arab Democracy Barometer Wave II, 2010–11, finds that most individuals believe that knowing people in high places is important in obtaining government jobs.[a] In 6 of the 10 economies surveyed, most citizens felt that political affiliations or family and tribal identities were more important than

box continues next page

BOX 6.1 Social networks compound the effects of weak job creation on intergenerational mobility in the Middle East and North Africa (continued)

FIGURE B6.1.1 Employment has not kept up with rising educational attainment throughout the Middle East and North Africa

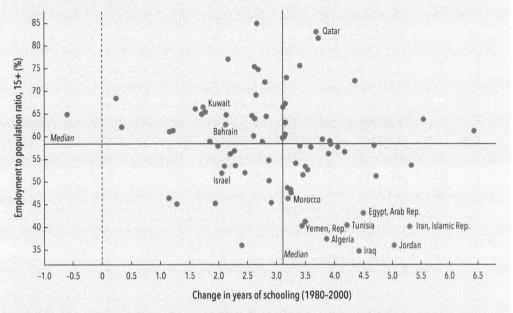

Sources: Estimates based on Barro and Lee 2010 and the World Bank World Development Indicators, adapted from Campante and Chor 2012.

or as important as qualifications and experience in obtaining a job in the public sector. Disappointed youth aspirations are described in *World Development Report 2013: Jobs* (World Bank 2012a). "To work in a big company, you've got to have *wasta*," commented a young person in the Arab Republic of Egypt. "Regardless of your qualifications, you must search for someone to secure the job for you. In some cases, you have to pay money" (World Bank 2012a, 137).

Sources: ILO 2016; Krishnan et al. 2016; World Bank 2012a.
a. See Arab Barometer II (database), Inter-university Consortium for Political and Social Research, Institute for Social Research, University of Michigan, Ann Arbor, MI, http://www.arabbarometer.org/content/arab-barometer-ii.

Social networks can distort labor markets even in economies with healthy, growing labor demand. In China, social networks or *guanxi* are critical in the allocation of nonfarm labor opportunities.[18] Social networks acquired through the marriage market have also been shown to improve labor market outcomes among young men in China.[19] Parental networks are an important reason why privilege persists across generations at the top end of the income distribution even in relatively mobile societies. In Canada, a study finds that sons inheriting the employers of their fathers is one way in which parental advantage in the labor market is passed on to the next generation.[20] By the age of 30, approximately 40 percent of sons have worked for an employer who had also employed their fathers in the past. This is much more common among the rich: close to 70 percent of the sons of top percentile fathers had the same employers as their fathers at some point. Other studies provide evidence on the inheritance of jobs from self-employed fathers and on the family-based succession of chief executive officers.[21]

Labor market discrimination and intergenerational mobility

The impact of networks on labor market outcomes and IGM is compounded by labor market discrimination based on inherited circumstances. Labor market discrimination refers to a situation whereby individuals who are identical in terms of productivity (determined by education and ability) show different labor market outcomes because of characteristics, such as gender, race, caste, or religion, that are unrelated to productivity. Evidence suggests that labor market discrimination can lead to labor market segregation, greater risk of unemployment, longer unemployment spells, and lower wages among individuals in groups that experience discrimination and thus tends to perpetuate inequalities across generations.

Several theories have been developed to account for the emergence of discrimination in wages and the level and duration of employment across demographic groups.[22] The empirical literature on labor market discrimination is extensive, although it focuses mostly on high-income economies. The objective of such research is to estimate differences in the career paths of two individuals who are identical in all respects other than their demographic characteristics so that the resulting wage gap does not reflect productivity differences. Because ability is largely unobservable and productivity difficult to measure, significant effort has gone into trying to identify the extent of discrimination using decomposition techniques, audits, correspondence studies, and laboratory experiments or by restricting the analysis to occupations where productivity is more easily observable. In the United States, for example, most studies conclude that minorities and women are victims of significant wage discrimination.[23]

Discrimination has also been shown to interact with social networks in transmitting disadvantage across generations. This contributes to a high degree of inertia so that discrimination can persist in labor markets long after legislative interventions, such as affirmative action programs, have been launched to offset the effects, as in the case of caste-based discrimination in India or apartheid in South Africa (box 6.2).

Discrimination in labor markets hinders the upward mobility of individuals belonging to groups experiencing discrimination. Discrimination inserts a wedge between educational investments and labor market returns, which weakens the link between educational mobility and income mobility. It can also reduce the incentives for parents to invest in human capital,

---

BOX 6.2   Discrimination in labor markets can persist: Two examples

Caste-based discrimination in the labor market has been found to persist in India despite laws banning such discrimination and decades of affirmative action policies. Banerjee and Knight (1985) provide evidence of job and wage discrimination in New Delhi's labor market whereby individuals belonging to scheduled castes receive lower wages and work in lower-paying occupations compared with individuals with the same characteristics but from nonscheduled castes. An important component of job discrimination against scheduled castes is imputed to the role of contacts and networks in the recruitment for low-skilled manual jobs, which contributes to the transmission of labor market discrimination across generations. Résumé-based correspondence studies provide evidence on the barriers faced by workers belonging to historically disadvantaged caste groups, even if hiring involves a formal application process as in the case of call center jobs or entry-level white-collar jobs (Banerjee et al. 2009; Siddique 2011). Less discrimination seems to be associated with jobs entailing more technical skills and formal qualifications or if the scale of operations of a firm is large, which may derive from corporate ethics standards or the likelihood that normative antidiscriminatory provisions cover small employers less.[a]

In the case of South Africa, the legacy of decades of apartheid is still evident in the labor market despite post-1994 normative interventions to "redress the disadvantages in employment experienced by designated groups [or] to ensure their equitable representation in all occupational categories and levels in the workforce."[b] Using various decomposition techniques, Burger and Jafta (2006) provide evidence of the persistent disadvantages of the average black worker, as captured by the race gap in employment, occupational attainment, and wages that remains unexplained after controlling for differences in observable characteristics. Meanwhile, black workers at the top of the wage distribution have seen their wage gap decrease over time, which seems to suggest that labor market discrimination reinforces pre–labor market inequalities.

a. For similar evidence in the United States, see, for example, Chay (1998); Holzer (1998).
b. Employment Equity Act 55 of 1998, Republic of South Africa.

---

which widens the inequality of opportunity among children in different circumstances and reduces the relative IGM of education and of income.

Labor market discrimination is often associated with residential segregation, which can reinforce the effects of discrimination on IGM. In South Africa, for example, where an individual resides—in developed urban areas, urban townships, or rural parts of the country—compounds the role of race in explaining differences in the likelihood of full-time employment, particularly among younger workers (chapter 4). As in the case of network effects, discrimination and the associated inefficient allocation of talents to jobs are more likely to exist in labor markets where competition is limited, such as cases in which there is a high degree of monopsony power or labor market frictions.

Women in the Labor Market and Intergenerational Mobility

In both developed and developing economies, women are less likely to participate actively in the labor market. Moreover, among women who choose to work outside the household, labor market disparities persist in wages, occupation, and sector of employment.[24] The persistence of labor market disparities affecting women contrasts with the progress achieved in narrowing the gender education gap (chapter 3).

A recent review of the literature shows a substantial reduction of the gender wage gap, an increase in female labor force participation, and a reduction in occupational segregation in the United States; the biggest gains occurred during the 1980s.[25] Still, in 2014, among full-time workers, women earned about 79 percent of the earnings of men on an annual basis and about 83 percent on a weekly basis. In many developing economies, although women have been entering the labor force in large numbers, the increase in participation has not translated into equal employment opportunities or equal earnings relative to men. In general, women are more likely than men to work in low-productivity activities, to be involved in informal, unpaid family employment, and to be active in agriculture, where they tend to manage smaller and less-productive plots. Similarly, if women become entrepreneurs, they tend to manage smaller firms in less-productive sectors compared with men.[26]

Several factors contribute to the gender disparities in the labor market, including differences in time use, social networks, and gender roles between women and men and discrimination by employers (box 6.3). As in the case of social networks and discrimination based on demographic characteristics, social norms can influence the reproduction of gender disparities in the labor market from one generation to the next.

BOX 6.3   Why gender disparities in labor markets persist across generations

The persistence of gender disparities in labor market outcomes among individuals with equivalent educational attainment has been explained for the most part by differences in time use. First, because women traditionally devote more time to household work and the provision of care in the home, their employment history is more likely to be characterized by work interruptions, lower accumulated experience, and lower investment in job-specific training (Acemoglu and Pischke 1999). Second, women tend to prefer more flexible work arrangements that are generally associated with a severe wage penalty, particularly in higher-paying professional jobs (Goldin 2014). Third, women are more likely to sort into occupations and industries that allow them to reconcile livelihoods and family obligations and that tend to pay less than the average.

The gender wage gap has also been explained by differences in social networks between men and women, differences in gender roles, and employer discrimination. Women have lower

box continues next page

BOX 6.3   Why gender disparities in labor markets persist across generations (continued)

FIGURE B6.3.1   Attitudes toward gender roles

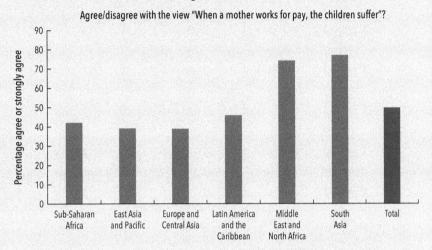

Source: Data of WVS (World Values Survey), Wave 6 (2010–2014) (database), King's College, Old Aberdeen, the United Kingdom, http://www.worldvaluessurvey.org/WVSDocumentationWV6.jsp.

access to professional networks compared with men and are less likely than men to rely on friends and relatives during job searches. Moreover, the use of gender-based professional networks might reinforce any preexisting occupational segregation.[a]

Labor market inequalities are also reproduced through the transmission of social norms related to gender roles. Data from the World Values Survey identify a widespread belief that the employment of women is incompatible with motherhood: 50 percent of the respondents in the 59 economies included in the sample agreed or strongly agreed with the statement that, "when a mother works for pay, the children suffer." Figure B6.3.1 shows this belief to be especially prevalent in the Middle East and North Africa and in South Asia, which are also the regions in which female labor force participation is particularly low in most economies. Traditional gender roles also have implications for wages. Several studies provide evidence of a motherhood wage penalty because of self-selection into less-demanding child-friendly jobs, lower investments by employers in firm-specific training among women of childbearing age, and changes in productivity because of constraints on work schedules and travel (Blau and Kahn 2017). Mothers also face discrimination because they are perceived as less productive (Correll, Benard, and Paik 2007).

a. For example, Mencken and Winfield (2000) show that women who find jobs through contacts who are men are less likely to work in women-dominated occupations. Similarly, Beggs and Hurlbert (1997) provide evidence that the gender aspect of social ties affects occupational status and that women whose contacts are with other women work in occupations with lower socioeconomic index scores.

In economies with large gender disparities in labor markets, rising educational mobility among women is unlikely to translate into a commensurate rise of income mobility. Greater shares of women are becoming better educated than their parents and their brothers, but many of these women are unlikely to earn more than their parents or their brothers because of the disadvantages they face in the labor market.

Some of the implications of gender disparities in the labor market for IGM are similar to those discussed in the context of labor market discrimination based on other demographic attributes, such as race or caste. Lower economic opportunities among women can adversely affect household earnings, thereby influencing investments in human capital among the next generation, particularly in low-income or single-parent households. Less favorable labor market prospects among women might also reduce investments in the education of girls and increase the labor market disadvantages of women.[27]

Employment outcomes among women can affect IGM through additional channels. Better labor market outcomes may increase women's bargaining power within households, thereby exerting a positive impact on investment in children and the educational mobility of both boys and girls.[28] Maternal employment, especially if it occurs early during a child's life, might also have a negative impact on children's cognitive and behavioral development, which can reduce IGM. The evidence is inconclusive; findings vary depending on the country context, the quality of formal care, and on how soon the mother returns to work after childbirth.[29] In general, the impact of maternal employment on cognitive development and on breastfeeding rates and duration in the first year of a child's life seems to be negative, albeit small.[30] It also seems to be stronger among children in two-parent households and in high-income or highly educated households. After the first year of a child's life, participation in formal childcare may have a positive impact on cognitive and behavioral development, unless the child receives inferior-quality care or is in care for long hours. Irrespective of the age of the child, participation in high-quality formal childcare appears to be most beneficial among children of disadvantaged backgrounds.

Maternal employment may also affect IGM by influencing the labor market decisions of daughters. One study finds that maternal employment during children's high school years is correlated with the future labor market supply decisions of daughters. Daughters of working mothers are more likely to make similar labor market choices as adults, which appears to increase the correlation in intergenerational earnings (or reduce relative IGM).[31]

Labor Market Policies, Institutions, and Intergenerational Mobility

The labor market can clearly limit economic mobility across generations by compounding any preexisting inequality, namely, the inequality of opportunities that affect individuals prior to their entry into the labor market. The labor market is more likely to be a barrier to IGM if it fails to generate sufficient jobs, if the jobs are unfairly allocated among individuals based on unproductive circumstances, or if differences in earnings are related to discrimination or inherited privilege rather than productivity differences. Weak labor market conditions among young entrants, as seen during the 2008–09 financial crisis, have long-lasting effects on the productivity, incomes, and prospects for upward mobility of these individuals.

Labor market institutions and policies can generally support greater IGM by limiting the extent or impact of unemployment spells, easing the labor market access of vulnerable categories of a population and youth, improving the extent of competition among employers, and by increasing the protection of workers who are discriminated against. The less segmented and more competitive a labor market, the less likely are distortionary practices such as discrimination to survive in equilibrium. Furthermore, in advanced economies, the erosion of labor market institutions, such as minimum wages and unions, have been associated with an observed rise in earnings inequality.[32]

A combination of active and passive labor market policies can help reduce the negative, long-run consequences of unemployment, particularly in advanced economies. The income effect of job loss can be minimized by unemployment benefits or, in informal labor markets, by social assistance measures aimed at reducing the likelihood of disinvestment in children's human capital. For workers in less stable jobs, such as unskilled wage employment, better access to social protection systems might soften the impacts of unemployment without reducing labor market flexibility.

Facilitating the integration of youth into the labor market is essential to diminishing the chances of lifetime income losses due to a poor start in the labor market. This could involve, for example, giving incentives to employers to hire young people, such as through targeted reductions in the labor tax wedge or tax credits at the lower end of the wage scale.[33] Programs aimed at improving the human capital or the labor market experience of the workforce, such as training or subsidized employment, could be beneficial for youth, especially during a recession.[34] Wage subsidies and reductions in payroll taxes have been suggested as ways to address the impact of a crisis on youth unemployment.[35] Such interventions aim at increasing the incentives among firms to hire young workers, thereby offsetting the disadvantages of youth in labor market experience.

Active labor market policies might be helpful in smoothing the frictions associated with the job search and improving the employment prospects of marginalized workers. For example, wage subsidies and employability skills training have been used in Jordan to raise the labor force participation of women college graduates. Although the program has generated a significant rise in employment, there is no evidence that the interventions will have longer-term impacts once the subsidies are removed.[36] Active labor market policies might be generally limited in what they can achieve in developing economies; a recent study finds that the impact of active labor market policies in developing economies is relatively small and tends to be offset by the associated costs.[37]

Some economies have chosen to address labor market discrimination by adopting affirmative action programs, particularly to counteract discrimination that is historical and deeply structural. Evidence on the impact of affirmative action is difficult to find. However, a recent review of the theoretical and empirical literature in the United States suggests that, at relatively small cost, if any, in efficiency, affirmative action may have important redistributive labor market effects that act to the advantage of workers experiencing discrimination.[38] Such findings hinge, however, on the possibility of effectively enforcing affirmative action. Labor market discrimination can have effects that persist despite affirmative action, especially if the discrimination is perpetuated through social networks or residential segregation (see box 6.2).

Labor market and social policies such as parental leave, flexible workplace arrangements, and the provision of affordable, high-quality childcare can have a positive impact on women's labor force participation. Moreover, reserving some part of parental leaves for fathers, an increasingly common practice in more advanced economies, can not only limit the gendered impact of family-related interruptions in employment but also reduce differences in time use between men and women, thereby potentially exerting a long-lasting impact on the equality of opportunity between genders.[39]

Capital Markets as a Barrier to Intergenerational Mobility

Capital market imperfections, manifested in credit constraints and lack of insurance, provide an intuitive explanation for why income differences persist across generations and often result in poverty traps. Credit and insurance constraints are particularly likely to pose a crucial barrier to upward mobility among the poor in developing economies, where capital markets tend to be underdeveloped. Such constraints can lead to poverty traps. "If credit markets are imperfect, then dynasties with little initial wealth face limited investment opportunities, and they remain poor," notes Piketty (2000, 453). They also provide an additional incentive for wealth transfers to the next generation, which increases persistence in earning differentials across generations because only individuals with access to inherited wealth can finance investments that may potentially enhance their earnings.

Empirical Evidence on Credit Constraints as a Barrier to Intergenerational Mobility

Nonlinearities in the intergenerational persistence of earnings—when the degree of persistence varies between different points of the distribution of parental income—hints indirectly at the presence of credit constraints.[40] For example, a concave profile of persistence with respect to parental incomes is consistent with theories of IGM that predict that the mobility of income is greater among richer families because richer families are less likely to be constrained.[41] One study shows that relative IGM of income in Brazil rises, on average, with the wages of fathers and is substantially lower among the sons of fathers with wages below the median.[42] Such a profile of mobility does not, however, prove conclusively the existence of credit constraints. Whether persistence declines with the wages of fathers also depends on the nature of the wage function, which implies that credit constraints may even coexist with a convex mobility profile. Moreover, concave patterns may also be explained by other factors and do not necessarily indicate credit constraints.[43]

Direct empirical evidence on the amount of the contribution of capital market imperfections to (the lack of) IGM is difficult to find because of the difficulty of separating the differences in IGM between any two groups into the effects of unobservable credit constraints versus the effects of all the other potential factors. For this reason, the few available studies mostly involve high-income economies where suitable data are available. Studies seeking to estimate the role of credit constraints by identifying groups that are more likely to be constrained find that credit constraints are not particularly important in high-income economies like the United States and Canada.[44] Because capital markets are likely to be much more imperfect in the developing world, where poverty traps are also much more common, the evidence from high-income economies cannot be taken as an indication for how important credit constraints might be as a barrier to IGM in the developing world.

What Do Capital Market Imperfections Imply about Policies to Improve Intergenerational Mobility?

Given the role of credit constraints, broadening access to financial services is likely to improve IGM, especially at the lower end of the income distribution. A similar argument can be made on the benefits of conditional and unconditional cash transfer programs that provide targeted assistance to poorer families and on tax credits for the working poor, such as earned income tax credit programs. Furthermore, in the presence of credit constraints, the lack of collateral among the poor becomes a critical barrier to investments. This seems to suggest that policies aimed at facilitating the legalization of existing assets by conferring property rights or at the broader ownership of assets can be both equity and efficiency enhancing. In this context, the lack of equal rights among women to inherit assets and property in several economies can pose an additional barrier to the economic mobility of women (box 6.4). Equalizing legal rights among women and men would be a necessary first step but may not be sufficient to ensure that women receive fair shares of inheritances, given the nature of social norms in many economies.

In the presence of credit constraints, redistributive programs can also be efficiency enhancing, which strengthens the case for the implementation of such programs to improve both absolute and relative mobility. This is because, if capital market imperfections are taken into account, the distribution of wealth among a generation has important effects not only on the

BOX 6.4   Unequal inheritance rights among women can pose an additional barrier to mobility among girls

Unequal inheritance rights among women and men in several countries can be a barrier to IGM among women by affecting the opportunities provided to girls, including investments in their education. In 39 of 185 countries on which data are available, daughters do not have the same rights to inherit assets and property as sons if there is no will (World Bank 2015). The problem is most severe in the Middle East and North Africa, where no country grants equal rights, but it also applies to half the countries in South Asia and about a fifth of countries in East Asia and Sub-Saharan Africa. Eastern Europe and Central Asia and Latin America and the Caribbean are the only two developing regions in which daughters and sons have equal inheritance rights in all countries. This statistic does not capture how parents allocate inheritances among daughters and sons if there is a will. Thus, there should be no presumption that boys and girls receive equal inheritances even in countries where the law does not systematically discriminate in the absence of a will. World Bank (2015) examines legal restrictions affecting women across a broad range of domains, including property rights more broadly. It also reports on whether the inheritance rights of surviving spouses differ by gender, which has been shown to have important effects on the opportunities available to girls (Deininger, Goyal, and Nagarajan 2013, 2014).

BOX 6.5   In a context of imperfect capital markets, redistributive policies may be efficiency enhancing

Credit constraints in an environment of unequal distribution of wealth may prevent some investments with high potential returns, which would lead to a loss of aggregate efficiency and output. Several authors have suggested that, in a context of imperfect capital markets, the distribution of wealth is important for the level and composition of aggregate investment and, hence, total output levels (see, for example, Galor and Zeira 1993). This is an argument in favor of redistributive policies, such as public funding of education, which, by allowing more individuals to invest in education and skills, entrepreneurship, and so on would help reduce inequality, raise IGM of income, and increase aggregate output at the same time (Loury 1981, cited by Piketty 2000). Differences in initial wealth distribution could also affect occupational choice—who becomes a wage earner, who becomes an entrepreneur, and so on—even if wealth distribution were unrelated to how productive abilities are distributed (Banerjee and Newman 1993). The initial wealth distribution in this model can affect the output, the relative supply of and demand for labor, the trajectories of wages, and the overall development path of an economy. This implies that the usual notions of trade-offs between redistribution and growth need to be reevaluated when capital markets are imperfect.

distribution of income but also on aggregate efficiency and output. The economic literature offers several theories about the channels through which unequal wealth distribution can reduce economic efficiency and output if credit markets or insurance markets fail to work properly (box 6.5). These theories imply that redistributive policies can improve both distribution and efficiency, when the dynamic effects of wealth inequality in the presence of credit constraints are considered. These arguments also strengthen the arguments for taxation of capital income and property, which are discussed in a subsequent section of this chapter.

Economic Transformation and Intergenerational Mobility

In most developing economies, the process of economic transformation greatly influences the operation of factor markets. Economic transformation can induce important changes, such as increasing the returns to skills, reducing barriers to geographic mobility, and changing incentives and norms, with varying impacts on absolute and relative mobility across generations.[45] For example, a recent World Bank study finds that, in three of five economies in Sub-Saharan Africa on which recent data are available, occupational mobility has been rising rapidly, in part because of shifts in the structure of occupations that can be traced to ongoing economic transformation.[46]

The forces of economic transformation can push and pull IGM in different directions. Many of the usual forces—such as employment shifts toward more productive sectors, rising productivity and geographic mobility, higher rates of urbanization and agglomeration, and the weakening of restrictive social norms—likely improve IGM. But skill-biased technological change can reduce relative mobility by raising the returns to education and, consequently, wages at the top. Recent research finds that income inequality has not narrowed at a rate commensurate with a significant reduction in educational inequality around the world, partly because of countervailing forces, such as skill-biased technological change.[47] As labor markets reward higher skills more generously, improving educational IGM becomes even more important to lowering the persistence of income inequality across generations and to ensuring that future generations will be more well off than their parents.

Economic Transformation May Not Improve the Mobility of All

The positive effects of transformation can be muted by existing factor market distortions. Rigidities in land and labor markets, for example, can restrict the processes through which economic transformation may enhance IGM. Land market distortions can constrain spatial mobility, which slows the rate of upward mobility. Distortions in land and labor markets can also interact with restrictive social norms to curb economic transformation. For example, in India, labor mobility across generations may be constrained by limited land markets and a cultural obligation that makes abandoning land costly.[48]

As economic transformation progresses, the trajectories of economic mobility can vary widely across groups and geographic areas within the same economy. For example, in China, IGM in both education and earnings has fallen more among women and residents of economically disadvantaged regions since the beginning of the economic transition. The persistence of incomes is also greater in China among people with higher than average incomes.[49] In Brazil, mobility is higher in the richer Southeast than in the poorer Northeast.[50] In India, IGM among scheduled castes and tribes might have increased and converged toward the IGM of other groups as economic transformation has accelerated. This may be an effect of changing social norms and the growth in competition induced by economic liberalization that started in the early 1990s, which might have made discriminatory labor practices more expensive for businesses.[51]

The differences across groups and regions can be understood more accurately by focusing on nonlinearities in persistence, namely, how persistence varies by parental income. In Brazil, for example, the difference in mobility between the Northeast and the Southeast regions is mainly derived from a much greater persistence in the lowest quintile of income in the Northeast than in the Southeast. Although mobility is also higher among blacks than whites in Brazil, persistence at low wages is much higher among blacks than whites, and the reverse is true of persistence at high wages.[52]

One reason for the wide variation in mobility trends across groups and regions within a country is the significant adjustment costs workers face in changing locations or industries, which can prevent them from exploiting new opportunities in an economy that is transforming and integrating with the rest of the world.[53] A recent World Bank study on the effect of exports on labor outcomes in South Asia finds that the gains are localized, consistent with the presence of significant worker-level adjustment costs. In India and Sri Lanka, rising export demand benefits workers in export-producing locations, but has minimal impacts on other labor markets. These gains are also unevenly distributed in favor of men over women, more educated workers over the less educated, and older workers over younger workers.[54] Worker adjustment costs are also a reason why rising imports in some high-income economies have led to adverse impacts on workers in specific locations and industries.[55] In all these cases, the path to greater economic mobility seems to pass through policies and investments that promote higher mobility across space and industries.

Excessive Market Concentration Can Reduce Income Mobility in a Transforming Economy

As economies transform, promoting competitive markets becomes key to moderating inequality and the persistence of inequality across generations. Higher market concentration typically leads to higher economic rents, which result in higher inequality and an adverse impact on IGM. Although there is little evidence in developing economies on the relationship among economic rents, inequality, and economic mobility, research on high-income economies provides hints on what these effects could be. A recent hypothesis, supported by research in the United States, suggests that the rising prevalence of economic rents and a shift in the rents away from labor to capital have been important in the rise of inequality.[56]

With rising economic rents, people who enjoy privileged connections to rent-providing assets or jobs tend to become more well off. This expands the incentives among parents to pass on such connections to their offspring. This may be a reason why the intergenerational persistence of incomes is high at the top end of the distribution even in relatively mobile societies such as Canada and Sweden.[57] Thus, the concentration of intergenerational privilege is high even in those societies in which public policies are effective in equalizing opportunities and inducing mobility among a large segment of the population.

The Role of Fiscal Policy in Promoting Intergenerational Mobility

There are two main channels through which fiscal policy affects IGM. First, governments make different choices on how many resources to spend on equalizing opportunities among children and how to allocate these resources. Second, because parents spend a portion of their net incomes on their children, taxation influences how many resources can be passed from one generation to the next. Thus, the design and timing of various components of fiscal policy can affect IGM in multiple ways, ranging from the income effect of reducing credit constraints to behavioral effects among workers and parents (box 6.6).

"No advanced economy achieved a low level of inequality with a low level of social spending, regardless of how well that country performed on other dimensions that matter for poverty, notably employment," write Atkinson and Bourguignon (2015, 205). Some estimates suggest that, in advanced economies, direct taxes and transfers reduce income inequality on average by about one-third, and three-quarters of this reduction is achieved through transfers.[58] Expenditures and taxes are obviously connected as policy tools. Government investments to equalize opportunities among children to enhance mobility are constrained by the resources that can be raised through taxation. This is especially true in developing economies, which typically mobilize less revenue relative to high-income economies.[59]

In developing economies, the limited levels of taxation and spending, as well as the composition of revenues, limit fiscal redistribution relative to advanced economies.[60] Developing economies rely heavily on indirect taxation, which has a limited redistributive impact compared with direct taxes, which translates into a lower impact on enhancing IGM.[61] Economies with lower tax revenues and smaller shares of direct taxes in total revenue tend to exhibit lower relative and absolute mobility in education (figure 6.3).[62] Meanwhile, economies with higher public spending relative to the size of the economy tend to exhibit greater relative mobility, which is a reason why mobility is higher in richer economies (chapter 4).

Enhancing redistribution in developing economies requires raising the tax-to-GDP ratio, while addressing competing public spending needs. Recent work conducted by the Commitment to Equity project has

---

BOX 6.6 **The design of fiscal policy can affect intergenerational mobility in multiple ways**

There are multiple avenues through which fiscal policies, including the design and timing of various policy components, can affect IGM. First, fiscal policies have a direct income effect, whereby additional resources going to low-income households can improve long-run outcomes, including among the children. Fiscal policies can reduce persistence in education and in income across generations if poor parents who cannot borrow because of credit constraints are unable to invest optimally in the human capital development of their children (Mayer and Lopoo 2008). Second, fiscal policies can have behavioral effects. Targeted transfer programs might discourage work and therefore have a limited impact on living standards, although the evidence does not seem to support this in the case of developing economies (Banerjee et al. 2017). Tax credits have been shown to increase labor supply in the United States, leading to additional income, but potentially less time spent with children at home, which could have a negative influence on educational outcomes if the quality of care that children receive declines because their parents are working (Bastian and Michelmore forthcoming; Meyer and Rosenbaum 2001). Third, the effects of fiscal policy on parental investment are crucial, including the extent to which taxes lower parental investment and to which transfers crowd out parental investments and the efficiency of public investments in improving children's human capital compared with direct investments by parents (Mayer and Lopoo 2008).

The timing of fiscal policies, that is, the stage in the lives of individuals at which they intervene, is also important. Early childhood interventions can be effective in improving the life outcomes of young children growing up in poverty. Among older children, fiscal policies can improve educational attainment by alleviating credit constraints in payments for college (Manoli and Turner 2016). The optimal timing of policies can differ significantly across economies, depending, for example, on the existence of credit constraints and the location of bottlenecks in the education system.

The data requirements for the credible assessment of whether fiscal policies can help children escape an intergenerational poverty trap are steep. Ideally, the assessment requires panel data that follow children from the time their parents were exposed to fiscal policies to adolescence or adulthood, and such data are only infrequently available (Molina-Millan et al. 2016).

---

highlighted that it is important to consider the entire fiscal system, both taxes and transfers, in judging the progressivity of fiscal policy.[63] For example, a value added tax may be slightly regressive by itself, but, if it generates substantial revenues that can be spent on a pro-poor transfer, the overall effect may be progressive.

Redistributive Transfers to Improve Endowments and Address Credit Constraints

Some types of fiscal spending are clearly associated with higher levels of mobility. More public spending on education is associated with higher relative mobility (chapter 5), which is consistent with the notion that investment in public education promotes equality of opportunity. Research in the United States finds that higher total direct government spending is

FIGURE 6.3   **Economies with higher tax revenue and higher shares of direct taxes in total revenue tend to exhibit greater relative mobility in education**

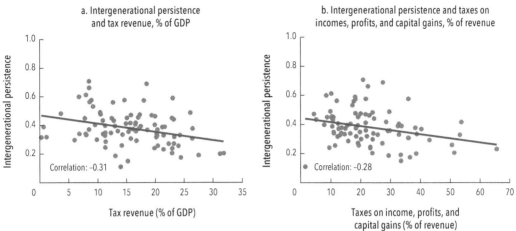

Sources: GDIM 2018; GFS (Government Finance Statistics) (database), International Monetary Fund, Washington, DC, http://data.imf .org/?sk=a0867067-d23c-4ebc-ad23-d3b015045405.
Note: Intergenerational mobility estimates for the 1980s cohort. Tax revenue (% of GDP [gross domestic product]) and taxes on income, profits, and capital gains (% of revenue) refer to the average in 1991–2000, including only economies with at least four observations during the period.

associated with greater relative IGM of income; similar results are found using per child public expenditures on elementary and secondary schooling.[64] Public spending has an equalizing effect: the difference in mobility between advantaged and disadvantaged children is smaller in high-spending states than in low-spending states in the United States, and expenditures aimed at low-income populations increase the future income of low-income, but not high-income children.

Large-scale public investments in early childhood development, in particular, can be a highly effective and cost-efficient way of improving IGM. The long-run effects of such a policy can be significant even after considering the general equilibrium effects of such interventions on labor and capital markets and the deadweight loss of raising taxes to finance the policies, which is often used as an argument against large-scale policies with high fiscal costs (box 6.7).

Chapter 5 sheds some light on the kind of policy interventions and investments that can be effective in reducing inequality of opportunity at various stages of childhood and youth. To complement that discussion, this section now focuses on directly redistributive transfers that are targeted to households to help them meet their basic needs, protect them against income shocks, and allow them to build productive assets.[65] These transfers can be critical to improving IGM by raising the endowments of households in a credit-constrained environment, so that they can invest more in the human capital development of their children.[66]

BOX 6.7 Large investments in early childhood development can raise intergenerational mobility in a general equilibrium setting

Daruich (2018) combines a macroeconomic model with findings on the impacts of an early childhood program. This is done by introducing parental investment in the skills of children into a standard macroeconomic life-cycle general-equilibrium model. Parents build children's skills by investing both time and money during multiple periods. These skills make education easier and are also rewarded by the labor market.

Daruich shows that inequality and social mobility can be improved by introducing universal government investments in early childhood development (for example, mandatory schools for children under age 4). In the United States, a simulation of such a large-scale, permanent early childhood development program, the partial equilibrium impacts of which are validated by evaluations of a small-scale government program, estimates that the relative IGM of income would be improved by as much as 30 percent and that welfare would be raised and inequality reduced sufficiently for the United States to achieve the mobility and inequality levels of Australia or Canada. Although general equilibrium and taxation effects reduce the short-term gains, the long-run change in the distribution of parental characteristics induced by the permanent, large-scale program more than compensates for the reductions. This is so because investments in children not only improve their skills, but also creates better parents for the next generation. Although earlier generations gain less if general equilibrium and taxation effects are considered, the welfare gains are positive across every new generation and grow rapidly during the transition. The second generation to receive the government investments would already obtain over two-thirds of the final welfare gains.

Cash transfer programs produce strong short-run benefits

Cash transfer programs can take two forms: conditional cash transfer programs that provide welfare payments, usually to women in a targeted segment of the population, and are conditional on the actions of potential beneficiaries and unconditional cash transfer programs that provide targeted benefits without mandating any action from beneficiaries. The criteria for receiving the transfers in a conditional program might include enrolling children in schools, undergoing regular checkups at a doctor's office, receiving vaccinations, and so on. These programs seek to combine the dual objectives of reducing poverty and vulnerability among the current generation in poverty and breaking the cycle of poverty by improving the human capital of the next generation. These objectives make conditional cash transfers a potentially direct policy instrument for raising absolute and relative IGM. Unconditional cash transfer programs are primarily intended to reduce poverty and vulnerability, but even these can improve IGM in the presence of credit constraints that are common in developing economies.

Conditional and unconditional cash transfers are used worldwide. Some of the most well-known and longest-running programs are in economies as diverse as Bangladesh, Brazil, Indonesia, Jamaica, Mexico, and South Africa. Many of these programs have been studied extensively and have been shown to produce impacts on consumption, poverty, vulnerability, human capital inputs, women's empowerment, and even psychological well-being to a varying extent depending on the country and the program (box 6.8).

BOX 6.8   Cash transfers can have large immediate benefits, even on psychological well-being

Taking stock of the extensive available research, Fiszbein et al. (2009) find that conditional cash transfers have increased consumption and reduced poverty and the vulnerability to shocks, particularly if the transfers are generous, well targeted, and designed not to discourage recipients from undertaking actions to escape poverty. To a varying extent and depending on the nature of the program, conditional cash transfers have also led to increases in inputs in children's human capital and the narrowing of gender and rich–poor gaps in such inputs, including school enrollment, visiting health providers for preventive checkups, having children weighed and measured, and completing vaccinations. They also may have increased the bargaining power of women in some cases.

Some of these beneficial impacts have been found in unconditional cash transfer programs as well. A notable example is offered by a recent randomized evaluation in Rarieda, a predominantly poor rural district in western Kenya, that finds significant impacts of cash transfers on household consumption, investments in assets, and psychological well-being among recipients (Haushofer and Shapiro 2016). The transfers, provided by the nongovernmental organization GiveDirectly through a mobile phone–based money transfer service, were unconditional, large, and concentrated in time. Transfer recipients experienced large increases in psychological well-being, mostly driven by increases in happiness and life satisfaction and reductions in stress and depression. The psychological improvements were greater among households with women recipients than among households with men recipients. They were driven largely by lower stress levels in the former. This may be related to the improvement of women's empowerment among these households, which was measured by indicators such as reduced domestic violence and increased decision-making power among women.

A study of education grants provided through Mexico's Prospera Program is one of the few cases where the impact of transfers on inequality of opportunity has been directly assessed (Figueroa and Van de Gaer 2015). Prospera education grants are provided to poor rural families, conditional on children being enrolled in school and attending at least 85 percent of classes. The study uses circumstances, that is, factors beyond the control of parents, to predict children's school attendance with and without the cash transfers. Inequality in the predicted values can be considered an estimate of inequality of opportunity in education because the predicted values are solely driven by factors outside individual control. Inequality in the predicted values is found to decrease if families participate in the program. Although these findings suggest that targeted education grants can help reduce inequality of opportunity as measured by school attendance, the effects on longer-term outcomes, including quality of learning, are not known yet. An education grant can get children to school, but what they learn in school also depends on the quality of the inputs provided by the school for the children's education.

Long-term impacts of transfers: Limited evidence so far, but considerable potential

Short-term welfare gains from cash transfer programs can conceivably improve long-term outcomes. However, the evidence on the long-term impacts of such programs, which is necessary for improvements in IGM, is not as extensive or conclusive given the scarcity of data on children from the time their parents receive the transfers to the children's adolescence or adulthood. The limited evidence that does exist suggests a mixed impact of conditional cash transfers on outcomes in health and education as opposed to inputs, for example, on learning achievement and cognitive development rather than school enrollment, or on child height for age rather than growth monitoring.[67] Another recent review concludes that cash transfer programs have had positive impacts on schooling outcomes, whereas the evidence on employment and income impacts is mixed.[68]

Some programs are found to have significant long-term impacts. For example, children ages 9–12 who benefitted from a conditional cash transfer program in Nicaragua experienced a significant increase in learning outcomes and labor market earnings, relative to children who had benefitted when the outcomes were measured at ages 19–22.[69] Exposure to the programs at ages 9–12 may be particularly relevant because this is the age when school dropout rates are high. The program's effects are also the largest among the most disadvantaged households, which would lead directly to a reduction in inequality of opportunity.

The evidence on the long-term impacts of other programs has been less encouraging. In Mexico, three years of cash transfers is found to have induced some increase in schooling but no increase in performance on tests of reading, writing, and math.[70] In Cambodia, transfers to the families of girls in middle school increased educational attainment, but did not improve test scores, employment, or earnings three years after the program had ended.[71] In Ecuador, generous cash transfers provided by the Bono de Desarrollo Humano (human development benefit) Program have small effects on IGM among poor households.[72] Transfers received in early childhood did not improve learning outcomes in late childhood. Transfers received in late childhood, at an age when decisions about secondary-school enrollment were being made, modestly increased the share of young women who completed secondary school but did not affect the education and work choices of these women after graduation.

Taken together, the evidence on the impact of cash transfers on long-term outcomes in developing economies is inconclusive, and more long-term research is needed to build a robust body of evidence on the impacts. This should not imply, however, that such programs have limited potential to improve long-term outcomes. Indeed, the research in some high-income economies has demonstrated what may be achieved through such programs given the appropriate conditions.

A recent study of the Mother's Pension Program, a cash transfer program in the United States between 1911 and 1935, finds that men who received the transfer as children lived about one year longer on average. These men were also less likely by about half to be underweight; they had more years of education; and they had about 14 percent higher earnings in early adulthood, channels that account for about three-quarters of the increase in longevity.[73] In the United States, the earned income tax credit—a tax benefit targeted on low-income households—is one of the largest transfer programs in the country. A recent study finds that an additional $1,000 in exposure to the tax credit as a teenager increases the likelihood an individual will complete high school, complete college, and find employment and earnings as a young adult.[74] Other studies have found a positive impact of the transfer on children's test scores.[75]

It is important to recognize the complementary actions that are necessary to ensure that cash transfer programs have the desired impact on the longer-term outcomes that drive IGM. Possible complementary actions can be broadly divided into two categories: policies that improve the quality of the supply of health care and education services and policies that help promote healthier and more stimulating environments for children in their homes, such as by providing cognitive and noncognitive inputs in early childhood.[76] Realizing the long-term potential of cash transfers requires coordinating the delivery and targeting of such programs with cash transfers, as well as improving the quality of public services.

Redistributive Taxes to Promote Intergenerational Mobility

"If we are concerned about equality of opportunity tomorrow, we need to be concerned about inequality of outcome today," wrote the late Tony Atkinson (2015, 11), expressing a view shared by many welfare economists. If children grow up in vastly different circumstances, they will face vastly different chances in life, which will translate into low upward mobility among those at the bottom of the distribution and continued privilege at the top: today's inequality is tomorrow's immobility.[77]

The discussion now focuses on progressive direct taxation because of the direct link with the resources parents can spend on their children and bequeath to their children, which come from after-tax income.[78] Besides being an important policy tool to reduce the persistence of inequality across generations, progressive direct taxes can also be an important source of revenue for pro-poor social spending. In considering progressive taxation, potential trade-offs with growth that can also adversely affect absolute mobility are also important to take into account. On the basis of simulations, one study shows that progressive taxation, compared with proportional taxation, reduces inequality and income persistence across generations, but at some cost to output growth.[79] Another study posits a theory to explain the persistence of wealth at the top and show, using simulations for the United States, that capital income taxes significantly decrease wealth inequality under various levels of exogenously set mobility parameters.[80]

Income tax systems can be rendered more progressive without harming growth

Income taxes have become less progressive in the economies of the Organisation for Economic Co-operation and Development over the past three decades.[81] As top marginal tax rates declined and exemption thresholds were raised, an increasing share of the tax burden was shifted toward the middle. The evidence on developing economies is more limited, but one factor restricting the effective progressivity in these economies is the high threshold of the top marginal tax rate, about 18 times the per capita income in upper-middle-income economies and 83 times the per capita income in low-income economies.[82]

Any proposal to raise tax progressivity needs to address the potential adverse consequences for growth and therefore for absolute mobility because higher taxes may lower the incentives on high earners to work, invest, or create jobs. However, in a recent analysis, the International Monetary Fund (IMF 2017) found no clear evidence that progressivity—at least at the levels observed since the 1980s—has been harmful for growth.[83] Thus, it may be possible to make income tax systems more progressive without hurting growth, such as by increasing taxes at the top in economies with low levels of progressivity. That said, the evidence presented by the IMF applies only to the levels of progressivity observed since the 1980s, which does not rule out the possibility that highly progressive tax systems, as observed in some advanced economies in the 1970s and earlier, may have negative growth impacts. Conceptually, whether higher taxes at the top increase revenues depends on the size of the top tail to which the rate is applied and on the elasticity of labor supply.[84] There is considerable uncertainty about the range of the elasticity estimates.[85]

Broadening the tax base, such as through the taxation of capital incomes and capital gains can also enhance tax progressivity. Warren Buffett has famously said that he faces a lower tax rate than his receptionist, which can be explained by the fact that most of his income is in the form of dividends and capital gains.[86] Closely related are taxes on property, which currently produce negligible revenues in many economies.[87] Taxing real estate and land can be relatively equitable, and relatively efficient because real estate and land cannot be easily moved across borders.[88] The administrative challenges for implementing such taxes, however, can be severe, and, given these, a gradual approach to raising the progressivity of direct taxes seems to be advisable in low-income economies (box 6.9).

Inheritance taxes as a potential policy tool to raise resources and enhance mobility

Inheritance taxes directly address the transmission of (monetary) advantage from one generation to the next. In developed economies, the revenues raised from these taxes have declined, and they represent a small source of revenue today.[89] This is because tax rates are low, and there are multiple opportunities for avoidance through exemptions and

---

BOX 6.9 **Implementing progressive direct taxes in low-income economies with low capacity**

Implementing progressive income and property taxes requires considerable administrative capacity, which may not exist in some low-income economies. For example, an effective property tax requires an up-to-date cadaster, which is a comprehensive register of all real estate or property boundaries within a country, and regular updating of property valuations. The International Monetary Fund advises low-income economies to start with a relatively high tax-exempt threshold, especially if administrative capacity is low and the informal sector is large (IMF 2017). Personal income tax coverage can be expanded by lowering the threshold as administrative capacity improves. Currently, many of these economies do not have a personal income tax threshold; introducing a threshold reduces the administrative burden and enhances progressivity by targeting enforcement on more well-off taxpayers (IMF 2014). These economies may also benefit from new digital technologies that could simplify the formulation, design, and implementation of fiscal policy (Gupta et al. 2017).

---

special arrangements.[90] Most developing economies do not have significant inheritance taxes.[91]

Inheritance taxes are politically sensitive, which might be linked more with the perceived or actual imperfections of the existing systems rather than the nature of the tax itself. Some oppose inheritance taxes by arguing that they amount to double taxation because bequests are accumulated out of net earnings. However, given that some incomes are seldom taxed, such as a portion of capital gains, inheritance taxes can be seen as imposing a minimum tax on these types of earnings. Furthermore, the double taxation argument equally applies to other taxes, such as sales taxes.

The efficiency cost of inheritance taxes, namely, whether they discourage savings or effort and thus reduce growth, is difficult to assess because it depends on the motives of the parents in making bequests.[92] Although there are several measurement difficulties, evidence in the United States indicates that inheritance taxes reduce wealth accumulation by parents, although the effect is small.[93] But there is also evidence that recipients of inheritances reduce their labor force participation; so inheritance taxes may increase work effort by the next generation.[94]

An effective inheritance tax should incorporate the taxation of inter vivos transfers, or gifts between living people. This is because inheritance taxes can be viewed as falling disproportionately on the moderately rich. The rich may be able to avoid taxes by transferring wealth as gifts while they are still alive, but the wealth of the moderately rich is more likely to be tied up in homes and other assets that are difficult to transfer inter vivos.[95] Although inheritance taxes can be challenging to implement, some economies are more successful at raising revenues (for example, Belgium and France), providing some cause for optimism.[96] Now might also be an opportune moment to consider expanding such taxes because annual inheritance flows have recently increased in some rich economies.[97]

BOX 6.10   A proposal to use a progressive capital receipt tax to fund a grant for all young adults

Some economists have proposed the provision of a one-time grant for all young adults, which has the potential for creating a level playing field and improving mobility across generations. Atkinson (2015) presented a detailed proposal of a lifetime capital receipt tax in the United Kingdom, with a personal lifetime exemption and a progressive rate structure. The revenues would be used to fund a minimum inheritance or stakeholder grants for all young adults when they turn 18. Such a grant would reduce inequalities in capital endowments and relieve credit constraints that pose a barrier to IGM. Although capital receipt taxes are not without implementation issues (for example, technical capacity, political resistance, and international mobility), emerging economies could benefit from the financial innovations that will make it easier to trace financial flows (Bourguignon 2015). Stakeholder grants are also an alternative to the universal basic income, a concept that is now the subject of vigorous debate in many economies (for a recent discussion, see IMF 2017). The argument in favor of a minimum inheritance or stakeholder grant is that it places a greater weight on individual responsibility than a universal basic income because it is a one-time payment that provides an endowment instead of a continuous income stream that provides insurance. Some also argue that, if equality of opportunity is the main justification for redistribution, stakeholder grants might be preferable to a universal basic income (Wright 2006).

Although similar data are not available on developing economies, some developing regions are also likely to see an increase in inheritance flows as their populations become older.

The extra revenues from expanding such taxes could be used to fund investments in children in innovative ways. One proposal, for example, considers using resources from a lifetime capital receipts tax to fund stakeholder grants that would reduce the inequality in endowments among young adults (box 6.10). Although ideas like these might appear impractical, they should be a part of the policy debate in economies because of their potential, at least in theory, to increase IGM and reduce income inequality with relatively low efficiency costs.

Why Are Mobility-Enhancing Policies Not Adopted or Implemented Effectively Often Enough?

Policies that are likely to promote IGM are in most cases well-known because they are also aligned with the objectives of promoting poverty reduction and inclusive growth. The discussion in this report has attempted to examine these policies through the lens of IGM, which may help governments to prioritize from the perspective of long-term improvements in welfare and fairness. But a key question remains: why do governments find it hard to adopt or implement effectively many of the policy solutions that are likely to achieve fair progress? For example, property or inheritance taxes have proven hard to adopt; not enough economies prioritize early childhood development as much as they should; and education reforms to improve the quality of learning are often not adopted or implemented effectively. Conversely, policies that fail to promote inclusive development endure across economies and over time. For example, subsidies that are inefficient and benefit the wealthy more than the poor have proven difficult to eliminate in many developing economies.

Data and Evidence Can Be Obstacles to Effective Policy Making

Lack of evidence about what works, and how, may sometimes be a reason why policies that promote long-term inclusive growth are not adopted. Inadequate data and evidence on IGM are obstacles to policy making in many developing economies. Even monitoring IGM at the national level is difficult in some economies, which can be improved by simple, low-cost solutions such as adding a few questions asking for retrospective information about the parents of adults to existing household surveys (chapter 2). For setting policy priorities, policy makers also need to know more about the correlates and drivers of mobility, evidence on which can be generated using a combination of surveys and "big data" from a variety of possible sources, depending on the country context. Such information needs to be complemented with evidence on the potential impact of specific policy interventions on IGM, which can then be tested in relevant contexts through pilots that, in turn, inform the design of policies (box 6.11). Evidence of this type is typically generated by academic research, which highlights the need for more research in developing economies on how policies can influence the long-term outcomes that determine IGM.

Political Economy Constraints Often Prevent the Adoption of Optimal Policies

In many cases, however, the evidence on "what works" is convincing or at least compelling enough to encourage experimentation. For many of these policies, a wealth of experience also exists to offer lessons on the "how." Given this, the explanation for why the right policies are often not adopted or implemented effectively is likely to be something more fundamental, linked to the political economy constraints created by power asymmetries in society, as argued by the 2017 *World Development Report* (World Bank 2017).[98]

Consider the role that "social separatism," which is a consequence of excessive inequality, can play as an obstacle to the adoption of mobility-enhancing policies.[99] Social separatism is the phenomenon whereby the rich prefer to opt out of publicly provided services because private services may be of better quality and signal the status of those who can afford them. This can lead to vastly different policy preferences between the rich and the rest of the population.[100] And often the preferences of the rich have a stronger influence on public policy than the preferences of the poor or even that of the majority.[101] The combination of these factors means that, with social separatism, the quality of public services can deteriorate because of lack of interest on the part of

BOX 6.11   Evidence to inform the design of mobility-enhancing policies can come from a variety of sources

To design better policies, policy makers need to know more about the evolution, correlates, and drivers of IGM, evidence on which can come from a combination of surveys and different sources of "big data." Long-term longitudinal surveys collecting income information from the same individuals over time, like the Panel Study of Income Dynamics (PSID) in the United States, can be an important source, provided the panel runs for a long enough time. Given the importance of localized patterns and drivers of IGM in most economies, analyzing IGM at a geographically disaggregated level, from regions and provinces down to the level of districts, counties, and even smaller areas can be greatly valuable. Administrative data such as historical tax records, linked to other types of data on households, individuals, or firms, can enable a rich analysis of patterns and drivers of IGM (for example, Corak and Heisz 1999; Corak and Piraino 2011 for Canada, and Chetty et al. 2014 for the United States). The power of such data is also demonstrated by the most recent research by Chetty et al. (2018), who use longitudinal data from the U.S. Census Bureau that covers virtually the entire American population from 1989 to 2015, where anonymized data from the 2000 and 2010 censuses are linked to data from federal income tax returns and household surveys to obtain information on income, race, parental characteristics, and other variables. Although the prospects of having such data are low in most developing economies, greater use of administrative data to examine the drivers of mobility can be a pragmatic, medium-term goal to pursue in many middle-income economies, given the possibilities of technology and the improvement of data management systems. The use of such data comes with important concerns about security and privacy, which need to be addressed as a priority in linking and creating such databases. The sources of such big data may differ by the availability of administrative and census data in an economy and the type of economy—tax records, for example, may be of little use in a highly informal economy. But the broader point about the possibilities of technology to generate and link such data, even within the framework of existing systems, seems applicable to most economies.

Such evidence can provide the impetus for setting priorities and directions for policies, but then needs to be complemented with evidence on specific interventions or investments to promote mobility. The process of evidence-based policy making can be broadly characterized by the following stylized steps. *First*, after the priorities and directions of policies are set on the basis of available evidence, a policy intervention can be designed based on (1) a theory of change, (2) the state of knowledge about the potential impact of interventions that apply the theory of change, and (3) an ex ante analysis of potential impacts using existing data. *Second*, the policy can then be tested through pilots and evaluated for impacts, considering alternative designs as appropriate. *Third*, the pilots can be scaled up, supported by a strong monitoring and evaluation system to enable feedback and inform course corrections during implementation. *Fourth*, the impacts of the policy on outcomes can be evaluated to inform future program adjustments or design. The real process of evidence-based policy making is likely to be much more complex, iterative, and unbalanced across the different steps, because the evidence base and ability to test and experiment with pilots may vary greatly across different policy instruments (see box 6.13). But the stylized version above is a useful benchmark because, in many cases, the "ideal" route to effective policy making would fit at least loosely within this framework.

the rich, which expands the quality gap between private and public services, deepening inequality of opportunity and further limiting mobility of those at the bottom of the distribution.[102]

Persistence of outcomes across generations can often be traced to policies being influenced more by the preferences of the rich rather than by those of the poor and the disadvantaged. To see why policies can be skewed in this manner, one needs to first recognize that inequality in a society often reflects power asymmetries, in the form of "a differential ability of certain actors and groups to influence policy making and the allocation of resources in society" (World Bank 2017, 167). Persistence of outcomes across generations in turn reflects the transmission of power asymmetries through the status inherited by a child from his or her parents.[103] Policies that promote the greater good, including mobility, may be difficult to introduce and implement because groups in society who benefit from the status quo may be powerful enough to resist reforms (box 6.12). This in turn is likely to adversely affect the poorest and most marginalized groups the most because of their limited bargaining power.

Development can take place within a variety of institutional trajectories, including many unorthodox institutional arrangements. World Bank (2017) argues that what matters for policy effectiveness is whether those institutional forms can perform their intended functions in a particular setting; it identifies commitment, coordination, and cooperation as the

---

BOX 6.12   Power asymmetries can undermine the choice of mobility-promoting policies and their effectiveness

Policy making takes place in complex political and social settings in which individuals and groups with unequal power interact. The space in which these interactions take place, which is the policy arena, can take many different, overlapping forms—ranging from formal arenas (such as parliaments, courts, and government agencies), to traditional arenas (councils of elders), to more informal arenas (old boys' networks). The entry barriers and the distribution of power among actors in this space determine who gets a seat at the table and who is excluded. Who participates in the decision-making process fundamentally matters for the selection and implementation of policies—and, consequently, their impact on development outcomes.

If the incentives of powerful actors from the perspective of maintaining their relative power, current or in the future, is at odds with the "greater good," they may attempt to block adoption or undermine implementation. In such cases, unequal distributions of power can distort and undermine the institutions in the policy arena. Individuals or groups, who are often likely to be poor or socially disadvantaged, may find themselves systematically sidelined from policy decisions that affect their interests (exclusion). Influential groups can often capture policies and make those policies serve their narrow interests (capture). In some settings, short-term benefits are exchanged in return for political support (clientelism).

Source: World Bank 2017.

three core functions of institutions that determine policy effectiveness. Effective policies have devices that guarantee a credible commitment over time, even in the face of changing circumstances and incentives. Effective policies—often through rules, standards, and regulations—help coordinate actors' actions according to shared expectations. And effective policies help promote cooperation between various groups and actors by limiting opportunistic behavior, often through credible mechanisms of rewards or penalties.

Concluding Thoughts: Policy Drivers of Intergenerational Mobility

This report argues that both types of mobility across generations, absolute IGM and relative IGM, are important for economic progress and for addressing the aspirations of society. Policies are crucial to influencing economic mobility across generations, and policies that achieve success in this can create a positive feedback loop because perceptions of higher mobility can lead to a social consensus that improves the environment for policies of the future.

As mentioned earlier, this report does not attempt to provide a ranking or clear prioritization of policies to promote IGM, which must depend on the constraints to mobility in the context of individual economies. The discussion in chapters 5 and 6 identifies certain policy directions that are informed in part by the evidence reviewed in this report so far. Evidence, however, tends to favor policies that are more amenable to being evaluated and have a longer history, which is a disadvantage for policies that are less evaluable or that reflect newer ideas. To minimize this potential bias, the implicit selection of policies highlighted below is guided not only by the quality and strength of the evidence but also by the mobility-enhancing *potential* of every policy intervention on the basis of its underlying theory of change (box 6.13).

The Role of the State

In broad terms, policies that support the drivers of economic growth, such as promoting macroeconomic stability, a better investment climate, and greater integration with global markets, are key to improving mobility. Higher absolute mobility requires more rapid growth that is sustained over a long period and that leads to improvements in living standards among a large number of families from one generation to the next. Higher economic growth is also necessary to support public policies that reduce inequality of opportunities to boost relative mobility. Conversely, higher relative and absolute mobility produces a positive feedback on growth in the long run by increasing the stock of human capital and innovation and building support for a social consensus around policies that contribute to the greater good.

However, greater growth even of the kind that leads to improvements in the living standards of everyone in society is not sufficient to ensure

BOX 6.13   Identifying policies that matter for mobility

There are many ways in which evidence can inform policy making (box 6.11), but the quality of evidence varies widely across different types of policies and programs. Some types of program interventions benefit from a rich experience of implementation and research, and by their very nature are more amenable to causal studies of impact. Broadly speaking, program interventions targeting individuals, households or communities are more likely to fall into this category. Examples of such programs in this report include interventions to improve maternal care, early childhood development, and learning outcomes, and some categories of education reforms, transfer programs, active labor market policies, and neighborhood-level interventions. The evidence on such programs provides policy makers with candidates for policies to improve long-term outcomes, depending on the nature of constraints to mobility that are most binding in a an economy.

For making policy choices, it is also important to consider the potential impacts of policies whose effects on IGM have been less studied because they are less amenable to rigorous evaluations, even when these policies have larger budgetary allocations or potential impacts than policies that are more evaluation-friendly. Some economists are concerned, for example, about a "randomization bias" in policy research, which they fear "has skewed research towards smaller policy questions and given short-shrift to larger, macroeconomic questions" (Tollefson 2015, 153). Macroeconomic, fiscal and regulatory reforms or large-scale investment projects, for example, can be critical for improving IGM and closing gaps between educational and income mobility, but less amenable to rigorous evaluations. There may also be a lack of awareness about the impact of some of these policies on IGM because they are often designed with other proximate development objectives in mind. For such policies, identifying with some rigor the underlying economic theory of change can help assess their potential impact on IGM. When rigorous evaluations are unavailable, less robust empirical methods—such as descriptive analysis of patterns in the existing data, and ex ante simulations—can help test the theoretical arguments to some extent. And rigorous monitoring of key outcomes that are likely to be influenced by a policy change can help policy makers make necessary course corrections in a timely manner.

relative mobility. Higher inequality, which is typically associated with higher inequality of opportunity, leads to lower relative mobility, which then leads to inequality in outcomes and opportunities, and so on as the cycle perpetuates across generations. This implies that drivers of inequality in outcomes and opportunities are likely to be barriers to relative mobility as well. Therefore, policies that promote the objectives of growth with greater inclusion arguably also support the drivers of relative and absolute mobility.

Going beyond the broad principles of supporting the drivers of economic growth and promoting fairness by reducing inequality of opportunity, policies to promote mobility can be conceptualized according to three overlapping roles that a state is expected to perform. The first role is that of an *investor* in public goods that support growth and help level the playing field at all stages of life. Although the investments can be at the local, regional, or national level, a national policy is usually needed for coordination and for the optimal allocation of resources across space. The second role is that of a *regulator* to make markets work more efficiently and more equitably. This involves setting the appropriate regulatory and competition policies in factor (labor, land, and capital) and product markets by recognizing that distortions because of discrimination, anticompetitive behavior, and concentration contribute to conditions that limit mobility at different stages of life. The third role of the state in improving mobility is *redistributive*. This involves establishing tax and spending policies that balance efficiency with equity, which can be complementary if a longer view is taken, given the virtuous cycle between growth and higher relative and absolute IGM.

To promote relative mobility, the objective of the state in its various roles can be to prioritize policies that equalize opportunities at different stages of life. This report shows that circumstances associated with one's birth, such as differences in parental background, race, and gender and where one lives, appear to be increasingly important for an individual's prospects for upward economic mobility. The state can play a proactive role in compensating for differences in individual and family starting points to level the playing field in opportunities. In addition to targeting interventions on individuals and households, policies should also aim to equalize opportunities across space, given the contribution of location to inequalities in most economies. Fiscal policy is the most effective public policy tool for realizing these objectives by raising resources for investment in public goods and reducing inequality through redistribution.

Reducing Opportunity Gaps Attributable to Individual Circumstances

Efforts to level the playing field can take several forms, depending on a country's context and stage of development. In practical terms, erasing all parental advantages that are passed on to children is not feasible or even desirable because the question of which circumstances should be offset by policy interventions requires value judgments about the precise notion of equality of opportunity that one seeks to promote. This value judgment is subjective and may well differ across societies or change over time in the same economy.

In most developing economies, where relative mobility in education is low, equalizing opportunities in childhood should be a priority through interventions and policies that seek to influence the behavior and the decisions of households in ways that lead to improvements in children's long-term outcomes that affect mobility (chapter 5). These include interventions to improve maternal care and early childhood development, and education reforms to improve the learning outcomes and accessibility of education for disadvantaged children. The effectiveness of interventions can sometimes be enhanced by paying attention to the role of aspirations and norms in influencing the decisions of households and individuals to break the cycle of low aspirations and low mobility.

Policy interventions to equalize opportunities in adulthood should aim to ensure that individuals with similar skills and talent are able to access similar economic opportunities, regardless of their parental status, connections, or legacies. Promoting competition in markets is generally helpful for reducing the distortions that lead to unequal opportunities. In addition, active labor market policies can help reduce labor market frictions and improve the employment prospects of marginalized workers. A combination of active and passive labor market policies can help reduce the long-run consequences of unemployment among workers, including youth. Social policies such as parental leave, flexible workplace arrangements, and the provision of affordable, high-quality childcare may not only improve women's labor force participation but also enhance the prospects for the mobility of the next generation, particularly girls.

Policies to equalize opportunities may sometimes involve recognizing and promoting, first, the most basic rights of groups that are discriminated against, such as providing equal rights to inherit property by women. Although legal reforms in such instances are necessary, the realization of real changes can be slow because of the inertia created by social norms.

Equalizing Opportunities across Space

Global patterns of educational mobility suggest that differences in mobility within an economy are related to location-specific factors, such as the extent of segregation in education across space and differences in local economic conditions (chapter 5). Evidence in the United States suggests that the earlier a child is exposed to better neighborhoods and stable family circumstances, the greater the likelihood the child will be upwardly mobile as an adult. Such evidence points to the need for policies to equalize opportunities across space to ensure that where one is born does not determine one's life chances. The policy levers are context specific and may vary across economies and across regions and localities in the same economy. Notably, the cost–benefit calculations to inform decisions about making such investments must consider not only the short-term welfare impacts on communities but also the long-term benefits for the children and youth living in these communities, which have a positive impact on the next generation and so on.

Investments in local schools and early childhood services, the quality of which often vary significantly across locations, are likely to be universally important in developing economies. Location-specific investments in housing and infrastructure might also be a priority in many economies to reduce segregation among communities by income levels and improve market connectivity. Local incentives and subsidies to promote the creation of jobs in distressed neighborhoods may help reduce the spatial clustering of poverty and improve the social environment in some settings, which would benefit the mobility of current and future generations.[104]

Equalizing opportunities across locations also involves reducing the barriers to spatial mobility so that people may freely move to take better jobs and benefit from services and opportunities wherever these exist. Barriers to

worker mobility can reduce the diffusion of the benefits of economic transformation and trade across locations and industries. Policies to improve
connectivity by investing in infrastructure, ranging from transport to tele-
communication, and reducing the explicit or implicit costs of internal
migration are likely to favor economic mobility as well.

A Fiscal System to Balance Efficiency with Equity in Developing Economies

In the effort to enhance mobility across generations in developing economies, the importance of public investments to equalize opportunities cannot
be overstated. One of the reasons why relative IGM in education is positively associated with GDP is that richer economies invest, on average, more
public resources on equalizing opportunities relative to the size of their
economies. Relative mobility is more likely to rise if growth is accompanied
by rising public investments to equalize opportunities. Moreover, the strong
association between income and educational IGM in developing economies
suggests that public investments to raise educational mobility are also likely
to raise income mobility.

A fiscal system that raises sufficient resources to support such public
investments in developing economies must balance efficiency and equity
objectives. Redistribution can be compatible with boosting economic
growth, for example, by preventing disadvantaged children from becoming
stuck in inequality traps.[105] Developing economies need to take a comprehensive approach that considers the combined redistributive and efficiency
impacts of taxes and spending and that addresses both design and administration issues.[106]

Enhancing redistribution requires that developing economies raise more
fiscal resources through taxation. A policy strategy could therefore aim to
broaden the income tax base, increase progressivity, and strengthen tax
compliance as a prerequisite. Such a strategy would also contribute to
moderating current inequality in outcomes, which would help reduce
inequality of opportunity and raise relative mobility tomorrow. Property
taxes can provide a relatively efficient and equitable way of enhancing the
progressivity of taxes and raising revenues if the necessary investments in
administrative capacity are undertaken. In principle, inheritance taxes are
a direct way to address intergenerational inequalities and raise resources.
But they add little to fiscal revenue despite a rising flow of inheritances in
many economies, which suggests that there may be considerable scope for
expanding these taxes.

On spending to improve IGM, the case is compelling in most developing
economies to prioritize investments that equalize opportunities among children and mothers. This includes in-kind spending on systems and programs
aimed at improving maternal and child health, education, nutrition, and
early childhood development and well-targeted transfer programs that benefit long-term outcomes among children. The expansion of in-kind spending can reduce opportunity gaps and raise IGM if it raises the access of
low-income groups to high-quality services. Well-designed transfer

programs can mitigate the effects of credit constraints on investments in children. Although the evidence on the long-term impacts of conditional and unconditional cash transfers in developing economies is limited, the successes of programs such as the earned income tax credit in high-income economies show the potential of transfers to raise mobility. Recent experimental evidence also suggests that scholarships or stipends for secondary school students could be an important policy tool to improve educational mobility in developing economies.

In contrast to these priorities, fiscally expensive universal price subsidy schemes, which represent an inefficient approach to protecting the poor, show limited redistributive impacts in the short and long run. For example, the top income quintile is estimated to benefit six times more than the bottom quintile from fuel subsidies, indicating that the subsidies are distribution neutral in the short run, and there is no reason to expect better results in the long run.[107]

Spending priorities of an economy would vary due to different reasons including the extent to which barriers to income mobility and barriers to educational mobility are different. For example, public spending on infrastructure may be a priority in improving income mobility in economies where the lack of spatial mobility and connectivity prevent workers from accessing jobs and block firms and entrepreneurs from accessing credit and markets. In economies with high unemployment, investments in active labor market programs and social protection systems for workers might be crucial to enhancing relative mobility and hindering downward mobility among workers. Economies with narrower regional disparities or less segregation in educational attainment tend to exhibit higher absolute and relative IGM. Thus, how public resources are distributed across geographic areas appears to matter for IGM as well.

Although the priorities may vary across economies and change within an economy, all investments designed to improve relative mobility among workers must share a common principle: improving economic opportunities among disadvantaged workers by raising worker productivity and earnings or by leveling the playing field among workers with different circumstances. The successful application of this principle would lead to higher upward mobility among workers in the lower part of the income distribution, which would also almost always increase the extent of absolute mobility in a society.

Adopting the Right Policies Requires Not Just Evidence but also Better Governance

Lack of data and evidence on IGM and its policy drivers are obstacles to policy making in most of the developing world. At a minimum, simple steps like adding questions on parental education and occupation to existing household surveys can help economies monitor their IGM, so that citizens can then hold their governments accountable for fair progress or lack thereof. To inform policy priorities, a variety of possible sources, including "big data" from administrative records and censuses, can be of use as technological progress opens new frontiers. Such data can then be complemented by evidence on the potential impacts of specific interventions, for which policy makers can draw on international experiences and test the insights they gain from studying these experiences through carefully evaluated pilots.

But too often governments find it hard to adopt or implement many of the policy solutions to achieve fair progress, even when evidence and experience provide clear indications of which policies are likely to succeed. To solve this conundrum, it is important to recognize first that the adoption and implementation of effective policies is influenced by who has a place at the bargaining table during the process of designing and implementing policy. That process, which can be termed *governance*, underlies how institutions in a country function to support policies that promote long-term prosperity and fairness.

Inequities in the ability of actors to influence policy decisions and make the policy-making system more responsive to their needs can lead to cycles of ineffective policies, low aspirations and lack of trust in institutions, and intergenerational persistence of inequality that strengthen power asymmetries and perpetuate the cycle. Successful reforms require adopting and adjusting institutional forms in ways that solve the specific commitment and collective action problems that stand in the way of pursuing further development.

How can the cycle of power asymmetries, ineffective policy making, and persistence of low and inequitable outcomes be disrupted? Governance can mitigate power asymmetries that are partly determined by history, and bring about more effective policy interventions. History offers numerous examples in which rules, institutions, and processes have improved in societies, often incrementally, and existing institutions have been adapted to deliver effective policy solutions. World Bank (2017) identifies incentives, preferences and beliefs, and contestability as levers for positive change. Positive change happens by shifting the incentives of those with power, reshaping their preferences and beliefs to support positive outcomes, and considering the interests of previously excluded participants in the policy arena, thereby increasing contestability. The same report argues that these changes can be brought about through bargains among elites and greater citizen engagement; and the efforts of international actors can help as well by influencing the ability of domestic coalitions to advocate for reforms.

Such changes can catalyze reforms that unlock the human potential among the poor and the disadvantaged and set in motion a virtuous cycle, as this report has shown. Higher intergenerational mobility can lead to greater efficiency and economic growth and lower inequality, which is likely to promote a more level playing field and reduce asymmetries in power. This in turn is likely to boost the mobility of future generations and put an economy on a higher, more self-sustaining path of long-term development.

Notes

1. Inchauste et al. (2014) show that labor income growth—because of the growth in income per worker rather than an increase in the number of employed workers—was the largest contributor to a reduction in moderate poverty in 21 economies experiencing substantial reductions in poverty during the first decade of the 2000s.
2. In regressions of education IGM on income IGM, the labor force participation rate has a significant effect on the slope, namely, the relationship between the two types of mobility. The unemployment rate has no effect on the slope, and per capita GDP has only a weakly significant effect. If both the labor force participation rate and per capita GDP are included in the regression, the former is clearly more crucial to the relationship between the two types of mobility than per capita GDP.
3. Labor force participation is arguably a better indicator of the overall health of the labor market than unemployment rates in developing economies with lower incomes and large informal sectors. In such economies, people cannot afford to remain unemployed, making the labor force participation rate a more meaningful indicator of the health of the labor market. In high-income economies as well, the rate can sometimes be a good indicator of labor demand if the changes in the rate are a result of decisions by workers with higher reservation wages to participate in the labor market only if labor demand is sufficiently high to drive up wages.
4. Altonji, Kahn, and Speer (2016); Faber (2009); Guvenen, Ozkan, and Song (2014); Von Wachter, Song, and Manchester (2009).
5. Arulampalam, Gregg, and Gregory (2001); Clark, Georgellis, and Sanfey (2001); Pissarides (1992); Raaum and Røed (2006).
6. Fallon and Lucas (2002); Funkhouser (1999); Thomas et al. (2004); Rucci (2004).
7. See Duryea, Lam, and Levison (2007), who use longitudinal data from the Brazil Monthly Employment Survey.
8. See Clark (2011) for a discussion of continued investments in education in response to weak labor market conditions.
9. ILO (2016).
10. Jackson (2008).
11. Elliott (1999) looks at search methods among workers with no more than 12 years of schooling and finds that informal job search methods are used to allocate 73 percent of jobs in neighborhoods with poverty rates of 40 percent or more compared with 52 percent of jobs in neighborhoods with poverty rates below 20 percent.
12. Granovetter (1974; 1995); Ioannides and Loury (2004).
13. Calvo-Armengol and Jackson (2007).
14. Ioannides and Loury (2004).

15. Evidence is also available about the role of parental networks in the intergenerational transmission of unemployment. See Macmillan (2014).
16. Magruder (2010).
17. Krishnan et al. (2016).
18. Zhang and Li (2003).
19. Wang (2013).
20. Corak and Piraino (2011).
21. Bennedsen et al. (2007); Dunn and Holtz-Eakin (2000); Perez-Gonzalez (2006).
22. See, for example, Becker (1957); Arrow (1973); and Phelps (1972).
23. See Altonji and Blank (1999); Bertrand and Mullainathan (2004); Darity and Mason (1998); Goldin and Rouse (2000); Lang and Lehmann (2012); Neal and Johnson (1996); O'Neill and O'Neill (2006).
24. World Bank (2012).
25. Blau and Kahn (2017).
26. World Bank (2012b).
27. The negative feedback effect on women is likely to occur unless such investments generate returns on other markets, notably on the marriage market (Lefgren and McIntyre 2006).
28. Duflo (2003); Rangel (2006).
29. Del Carmen Huerta et al (2011).
30. Gregg et al (2005); Hawkins et al (2007); Joshi, Cooksey, and Verropoulou (2009).
31. See Stinson and Gottschalk (2016), who use a linked administrative–longitudinal survey dataset.
32. Jaumotte and Osorio Buitron (2015).
33. Chen et al. (2018).
34. O'Higgins (2010).
35. See Coenjaerts et al. (2009). On the impacts of wage subsidies in different economies and settings, see, for example, Betcherman, Daysal, and Pagés (2010); Groh et al. (2016); and Katz (1998).
36. Groh et al. (2016).
37. McKenzie (2017).
38. Holzer and Neumark (2000).
39. Patnaik (2016).
40. See, for instance, Corak and Heisz (1999), Mulligan (1997), and Solon (1992).
41. See, for example, Grawe (2001); Piketty (2000).
42. Ferreira and Veloso (2006).
43. Grawe (2001).
44. See, for example, Mulligan (1997) and Mazumder (2005).
45. See, for example, Hnatkovska, Lahiri, and Paul (2012) on India.
46. Beegle et al. (2016).
47. Castello-Climent and Domenech (2017).

48. Fernando (2016).
49. Fan, Yi, and Zhang (2015).
50. Ferreira and Veloso (2006).
51. Hnatkovska, Lahiri, and Paul (2012). Sinha (2018) finds a modest convergence in educational mobility between men from scheduled castes and tribes and other men in India between 1983 and 2009, but finds no significant convergence in occupational mobility between these groups.
52. Ferreira and Veloso (2006).
53. Several economic studies point out that workers bear costs of adjustment that are different than the corresponding costs that firms bear, and new estimates suggest that the costs among workers can be as high as seven times the annual earnings of the workers (World Bank 2018).
54. World Bank (2018).
55. See, for example, Autor et al. (2013), who find that rising imports cause higher unemployment, lower labor force participation, and reduced wages in local labor markets that house import-competing manufacturing industries in the United States.
56. Furman and Orszag (2015); Stiglitz (2012).
57. Bjorklund, Roine, and Waldenström (2012); Corak and Heisz (1999).
58. IMF (2017).
59. For instance, see Bastagli, Coady, and Gupta (2015).
60. Clements et al (2015); Lustig (2017).
61. For instance, see Bastagli, Coady, and Gupta (2015).
62. The correlations of tax revenue and of the share of direct taxes in total revenue with absolute IGM in education are weaker than the corresponding correlations with relative IGM, though they are still significant.
63. Inchauste and Lustig (2017); Lustig (2017).
64. Mayer and Lopoo (2008).
65. Gill, Revenga, and Zeballos (2016).
66. World Bank (2016a, 2016b).
67. Fiszbein et al. (2009).
68. Molina-Millan et al. (2016).
69. Barham, Macours, and Maluccio (2017).
70. Behrman, Parker, and Todd (2009, 2011).
71. Filmer and Schady (2014).
72. Araujo, Bosch, and Schady (2016).
73. Aizer et al. (2016).
74. Bastian and Michelmore (forthcoming).
75. Chetty, Friedman, and Rockoff (2011); Dahl and Lochner (2012).
76. Fiszbein et al. (2009).
77. See IMF (2017); World Bank (2016a).
78. The extent to which fiscal policies will reduce intergenerational persistence will depend on the extent to which taxes lower parental

investment (Mayer and Lopoo 2008). Transfers might also crowd out parental investments.

79. See Erosa and Koreshkova (2007). In their model, a progressive tax system has two opposite effects on IGM. First, it reduces persistence because high earners face higher marginal tax rates. Second, it also creates strong incentives for parents who are richer because of their greater luck on the market to invest more in the human capital of their children. These parents expect their children to experience less luck on the market and thus be subject to lower marginal tax rates, which will increase persistence. Simulations indicate that the first effect, which is mobility enhancing, is likely to be more important.

80. Benhabib, Bisin, and Zhu (2011) look at the distribution of wealth, particularly at the top end, and posit that the more persistent the process associated with the rate of return on wealth (the higher are the frictions to social mobility), the thicker is the tail of the wealth distribution (there will be more wealth inequality at the top).

81. IMF (2017).

82. See Peter, Buttrick, and Duncan (2010).

83. This confirms earlier evidence by Piketty, Saez, and Stantcheva (2014).

84. Saez (2001).

85. The uncertainties about the range of the elasticities are such that "views of most politicians [on the top tax rate] could be encompassed" (Atkinson 2015, 185). Atkinson refers to the range observed in the United Kingdom, but this would be applicable to other economies as well.

86. As quoted by Mankiw (2013). As Mankiw points out, this comparison does not account for corporate taxes. The incidence of corporate taxes on capital or labor incomes depends on how mobile these factors are across sectors and economies (Auerbach 2006). In the long term, between 45 percent and 75 percent of corporate taxes fall on wages (Bastagli, Coady, and Gupta 2015).

87. In the 2000s, the 65 economies on which data are available raised about 1 percent of GDP in property tax revenues (Coady, de Mooij, and Shang 2015). Developing economies tend to raise less property taxes as a share of GDP relative to economies of the Organisation for Economic Co-operation and Development (Norregaard 2015).

88. IMF (2017).

89. Atkinson (2015); Eyraud (2015).

90. IMF (2013).

91. Bourguignon (2015).

92. See Boadway, Chamberlain, and Emmerson (2010); Eyraud (2015).

93. Mirrlees et al. (2011).

94. Holtz-Eakin, Joulfaian, and Rosen (1993).

95. Boadway, Chamberlain, and Emmerson (2010).
96. Eyraud (2015).
97. See Piketty (2014). Piketty (2011) shows that the annual flow of inheritances in France rose from less than 5 percent in 1950 to about 15 percent in 2010, reaching 20–25 percent by 2050 under plausible assumptions. Atkinson (2013) finds that inherited wealth increased from 4.8 percent of national income in 1977 to 8.2 percent in 2006.
98. The discussion that follows draws extensively from the Overview of World Bank (2017).
99. Van der Weide and Milanovic (forthcoming).
100. In the United States, for example, the rich (the top 1 percent) and the rest of the population have vastly different preferences when it comes to the cuts in Medicare, education, and infrastructure spending as a way to reduce the federal deficit: 58 percent of the rich are in favor of such cuts versus only 21 percent among the rest of the population (Van der Weide and Milanovic 2017, citing Page et al. 2011).
101. For example, controlling for the preferences of economic elites and the stands of organized interest groups, the preferences of the average American have only a minuscule, statistically nonsignificant impact on public policy (Gilens and Page 2014, as reported in van der Weide and Milanovic 2017).
102. See the model proposed by Bénabou (2000) of a society where high inequality, combined with credit constraint and influence of the rich on the political process, results in a steady-state of low government spending and persistent high inequality. See also, for example, Bénabou (1996).
103. Coleman (1974), who discusses the notions of "ascription versus achievement." Ascription refers to status. Every child born—even though he or she does not have any achievement yet that is a consequence of her own effort—has a position in the distribution of power in society, as determined by the status of his or her parent or parents (World Bank 2017).
104. One example is the Empowerment Zones Program in the United States, which provides a combination of block grants and tax credits to firms on the wages paid to employees who work and live in distressed urban communities. Kline and Moretti (2014) find that these programs have boosted employment and earnings in the targeted communities, without raising the local cost of living.
105. World Bank (2006, 2016a).
106. For example, see Lustig (2017).
107. Del Granado, Coady, and Gillingham (2012).

References

Acemoglu, Daron, and Jorn-Steffen Pischke. 1999. "Beyond Becker: Training in Imperfect Labour Markets." *The Economic Journal* 109 (453): 112–42.

Aizer, Anna, Shari Eli, Joseph Ferrie, and Adriana Lleras-Muney. 2016. "The Long-Run Impact of Cash Transfers to Poor Families." *American Economic Review* 106 (4): 935–71.

Altonji, Joseph G., and Rebecca M. Blank. 1999. "Race and Gender in the Labor Market." *Handbook of Labor Economics* 3: 3143–259.

Altonji, Joseph G., Lisa B. Kahn, and Jamin D. Speer. 2016. "Cashier or Consultant? Entry Labor Market Conditions, Field of Study, and Career Success." *Journal of Labor Economics* 34 (Suppl 1): S361–401.

Araujo, M. Caridad, Mariano Bosch, and Norbert Schady. 2017. "Can Cash Transfers Help Households Escape an Inter-Generational Poverty Trap?" In *The Economics of Poverty Traps,* edited by Christopher B. Barrett, Michael R. Carter, and Jean-Paul Chavas, chapter 10. Chicago, IL:. University of Chicago Press.

Arrow, Kenneth. 1973. "The Theory of Discrimination." *Discrimination in Labor Markets* 3 (10): 3–33.

Arulampalam, Wiji, Paul Gregg, and Mary Gregory. 2001. "Unemployment Scarring." *The Economic Journal* 111 (475): 577–84.

Atkinson, Anthony B. 2013. "Wealth and Inheritance in Britain from 1896 to the Present." CASEpaper, 178, Centre for Analysis of Social Exclusion, The London School of Economics and Political Science, London.

———. 2015. *Inequality.* Cambridge, MA: Harvard University Press.

Atkinson, Anthony B., and François Bourguignon. 2015. "Introduction: Income Distribution Today." In *Handbook of Income Distribution*, vol. 2A, edited by Anthony B. Atkinson and Ivi François Bourguignon. Handbooks in Economics Series. Amsterdam: North-Holland.

Auerbach, Alan J. 2006. "Who Bears the Corporate Tax? A Review of What We Know." *Tax Policy and the Economy* 20: 1–40.

Autor, David H., David Dorn, Gordon H. Hanson, and Jae Song. 2014. "Trade Adjustment: Worker-Level Evidence." *The Quarterly Journal of Economics* 129 (4): 1799–860.

Banerjee, Abhijit V., and Andrew F. Newman. 1993. "Occupational Choice and the Process of Development." *Journal of Political Economy* 101 (2): 274–98.

Banerjee, Abhijit V., Marianne Bertrand, Saugato Datta, and Sendhil Mullainathan. 2009. "Labor Market Discrimination in Delhi: Evidence from a Field Experiment." *Journal of Comparative Economics* 37 (1): 14–27.

Banerjee, Abhijit V., Rema Hanna, Gabriel E. Kreindler, and Benjamin A. Olken. 2017. "Debunking the Stereotype of the Lazy Welfare Recipient: Evidence from Cash Transfer Programs." *The World Bank Research Observer* 32 (2): 155–84.

Banerjee, Biswajit, and John B. Knight. 1985. "Caste Discrimination in the Indian Urban Labour Market." *Journal of Development Economics* 17 (3): 277–307.

Barham, Tania, Karen Macours, and John A. Maluccio. 2017. "Are Conditional Cash Transfers Fulfilling their Promise? Schooling, Learning, and Earnings after 10 Years." CEPR Discussion Paper DP11937. https://ssrn.com/abstract=2941523.

Bastagli, Francesca, David Coady, and Sanjeev Gupta. 2015. "Fiscal Redistribution in Developing Countries: Policy Issues and Options." In *Inequality and Fiscal Policy*, edited by Benedict J. Clements, Ruud A. de Mooij, Sanjeev Gupta, and Michael Keen. 57-76. Washington, DC:. International Monetary Fund.

Bastian, Jacob, and Katherine Michelmore. Forthcoming. "The Long-Term Impact of the Earned Income Tax Credit on Children's Education and Employment Outcomes." *Journal of Labor Economics*.

Becker, Gary S. 1957. *The Economics of Discrimination: An Economic View of Racial Discrimination.* Chicago, IL: University of Chicago.

Beegle, Kathleen, Luc Christiaensen, Andrew Dabalen, and Isis Gaddis. 2016. *Poverty in a Rising Africa.* Washington, DC: World Bank.

Beggs, John J., and Jeanne S. Hurlbert. 1997. "The Social Context of Men's and Women's Job Search Ties: Membership in Voluntary Organizations, Social Resources, and Job Search Outcomes." *Sociological Perspectives* 40 (4): 601–22.

Behrman, Jere R., Susan W. Parker, and Petra E. Todd. 2009. "Schooling Impacts of Conditional Cash Transfers on Young Children: Evidence from Mexico." *Economic Development and Cultural Change* 57 (3): 439–77.

———. 2011. "Do Conditional Cash Transfers for Schooling Generate Lasting Benefits? A Five-Year Followup of PROGRESA/Oportunidades." *Journal of Human Resources* 46 (1): 93–122.

Benabou, Roland. 1996. "Heterogeneity, Stratification, and Growth: Macroeconomic Implications of Community Structure and School Finance." *American Economic Review* 86 (3): 584–609.

———. 2000. "Unequal Societies: Income Distribution and the Social Contract." *American Economic Review* 90 (1): 96–129.

Benhabib, Jess, Alberto Bisin, and Shenghao Zhu. 2011. "The Distribution of Wealth and Fiscal Policy in Economies with Finitely Lived Agents." *Econometrica* 79 (1): 123–57.

Bennedsen, Morten, Kasper Meisner Nielsen, Francisco Pérez-González, and Daniel Wolfenzon. 2007. "Inside the Family Firm: The Role of Families in Succession Decisions and Performance." *The Quarterly Journal of Economics* 122 (2): 647–91.

Bertrand, Marianne, and Sendhil Mullainathan. 2004. "Are Emily and Greg More Employable than Lakisha and Jamal? A Field Experiment on Labor Market Discrimination." *American Economic Review* 94 (4): 991–1013.

Betcherman, Gordon, N. Meltem Daysal, and Carmen Pagés. 2010. "Do Employment Subsidies Work? Evidence from Regionally Targeted Subsidies in Turkey." *Labour Economics* 17 (4): 710–22.

Björklund, Anders, Jesper Roine, and Daniel Waldenström. 2012. "Intergenerational Top Income Mobility in Sweden: Capitalist Dynasties in the Land of Equal Opportunity?" *Journal of Public Economics* 96 (5–6): 474–84.

Blau, Francine D., and Lawrence M. Kahn. 2017. "The Gender Wage Gap: Extent, Trends, and Explanations." *Journal of Economic Literature* 55 (3): 789–865.

Boadway, Robin, Emma Chamberlain, and Carl Emmerson. 2010. "Taxation of Wealth and Wealth Transfers." In *Dimensions of Tax Design: The Mirrlees Review*, edited by Institute for Fiscal Studies, 737–814. Oxford, UK: Oxford University Press.

Bourguignon, François. 2015. *The Globalization of Inequality*. Princeton, NJ: Princeton University Press.

Burger, Rulof, and Rachel Jafta. 2006. "Returns to Race: Labour Market Discrimination in Post-Apartheid South Africa." University of Stellenbosch Economic Working Papers 4, 06, Stellenbosch University, Department of Economics Working Papers. Stellenbosch, South Africa.

Calvo-Armengol, Antoni, and Matthew O. Jackson. 2007. "Networks in Labor Markets: Wage and Employment Dynamics and Inequality." *Journal of Economic Theory* 132 (1): 27–46.

Castello-Climent, Amparo, and Rafael Domenech. 2017. "Human Capital and Income Inequality: Some Facts and Some Puzzles." Working Paper 12/28. BBVA Research Working Paper, Banco Bilbao Vizcaya Argentaria. Madrid, Spain.

Chay, Kenneth Y. 1998. "The Impact of Federal Civil Rights Policy on Black Economic Progress: Evidence from the Equal Employment Opportunity Act of 1972." *ILR Review* 51 (4): 608–32.

Chen, Tingyun, Jean-Jacques Hallaert, Alexander Pitt, Haonan Qu, Maximilien Queyranne, Alaina Rhee, Anna Shabunina, Jérôme Vandenbussche, and Irene Yackovlev. 2018. "Inequality and Poverty across Generations in the European Union." IMF Staff Discussion Note 18/01 (January 24), International Monetary Fund, Washington, DC.

Chetty, Raj, John N. Friedman, and Jonah E. Rockoff. 2011. "New Evidence on the Long-term Impacts of Tax Credits." IRS Statistics of Income White Paper, National Tax Association. Washington, DC.

Chetty, Raj, Nathaniel Hendren, Patrick Kline, and Emmanuel Saez. 2014. "Where Is the Land of Opportunity? The Geography of Intergenerational Mobility in the United States." *The Quarterly Journal of Economics* 129 (4): 1553–623.

Chetty, Raj, Nathaniel Hendren, Maggie Jones, and Sonya Porter. 2018. "Race and Economic Opportunity in the United States: An Intergenerational Perspective." Mimeo. http://www.equality-of-opportu nity.org/assets/documents/race_paper.pdf.

Clark, Andrew E., Yannis Georgellis, and Peter Sanfey. 2001. "Scarring: The Psychological Impact of Past Unemployment." *Economica* 68 (270): 221–41.

Clark, Damon. 2011. "Do Recessions Keep Students in School? The Impact of Youth Unemployment on Enrolment in Post-compulsory Education in England." *Economica* 78 (311): 523–45.

Clements, Benedict J., Ruud A. de Mooij, Sanjeev Gupta, and Michael Keen. 2015. *Inequality and Fiscal Policy*. Washington, DC: International Monetary Fund.

Coady, David, Ruud de Mooij, and Baoping Shang. 2015. "Inequality and Fiscal Redistribution in Advanced Economies" In *Inequality and Fiscal Policy*, edited by Benedict J. Clements, Ruud A. de Mooij, Sanjeev Gupta, and Michael Keen, chapter 3, 37–56. Washington, DC: International Monetary Fund.

Coenjaerts, Claudia, Christoph Ernst, Mariangels Fortuny, Diego Rei, and ILO Markus Pilgrim. 2009. "Youth Employment." In *Promoting Propoor Growth: Employment*, edited by OECD, 119–31. Paris: OECD.

Coleman, James S. 1974. "Inequality, Sociology, and Moral Philosophy." *American Journal of Sociology* 80 (3): 739–64.

Corak, Miles, and Andrew Heisz. 1999. "The Intergenerational Earnings and Income Mobility of Canadian Men: Evidence from Longitudinal Income Tax Data." *Journal of Human Resources* 34 (3): 504–33.

Corak, Miles, and Patrizio Piraino. 2011. "The Intergenerational Transmission of Employers." *Journal of Labor Economics* 29 (1): 37–68.

Correll, Shelley J., Stephen Benard, and In Paik. 2007. "Getting a Job: Is There a Motherhood Penalty?" *American Journal of Sociology* 112 (5): 1297–338.

Dahl, Gordon B., and Lance Lochner. 2012. "The Impact of Family Income on Child Achievement: Evidence from the Earned Income Tax Credit." *American Economic Review* 102 (5): 1927–56.

Darity, William A., and Patrick L. Mason. 1998. "Evidence on Discrimination in Employment: Codes of Color, Codes of Gender." *Journal of Economic Perspectives* 12 (2): 63–90.

Daruich, Diego. 2018. *The Macroeconomic Consequences of Early Childhood Development Policies.* Human Capital and Economic Opportunity Global Working Group, Department of Economics, University of Chicago, Chicago, IL.

Deininger, Klaus, Aparajita Goyal, and Hari Nagarajan. 2013. "Women's Inheritance Rights and Intergenerational Transmission of Resources in India." *Journal of Human Resources* 48 (1): 114–41.

Deininger, Klaus, Thea Hilhorst, and Vera Songwe. 2014. "Identifying and Addressing Land Governance Constraints to Support Intensification and Land Market Operation: Evidence from 10 African Countries." *Food Policy* 48: 76–87.

Del Carmen Huerta, Maria, Willem Adema, Jennifer Baxter, Miles Corak, Mette Deding, Matthew C. Gray, Wen-Jui Han, and Jane Waldfogel. 2011. "Early Maternal Employment and Child Development in Five OECD Countries." OECD Social, Employment and Migration Working Papers, 118, OECD Publishing, Paris.

Del Granado, Francisco Javier Arze, David Coady, and Robert Gillingham. 2012. "The Unequal Benefits of Fuel Subsidies: A Review of Evidence for Developing Countries." *World Development* 40 (11): 2234–48.

Duflo, Esther. 2003. "Grandmothers and Granddaughters: Old-age Pensions and Intrahousehold Allocation in South Africa." *The World Bank Economic Review* 17 (1): 1–25.

Dunn, Thomas, and Douglas Holtz-Eakin. 2000. "Financial Capital, Human Capital, and the Transition to Self-employment: Evidence from Intergenerational Links." *Journal of Labor Economics* 18 (2): 282–305.

Duryea, Suzanne, David Lam, and Deborah Levison. 2007. "Effects of Economic Shocks on Children's Employment and Schooling in Brazil." *Journal of Development Economics* 84 (1): 188–214.

Elliott, James R. 1999. "Social Isolation and Labor Market Insulation." *The Sociological Quarterly* 40 (2): 199–216.

Equalchances. 2018. *International Database on Inequality of Opportunity and Social Mobility.* Bari, Italy: University of Bari.

Erosa, Andres, and Tatyana Koreshkova. 2007. "Progressive Taxation in a Dynastic Model of Human Capital." *Journal of Monetary Economics* 54 (3): 667–85.

Eyraud, Luc. 2015. "The Wealth of Nations: Stylized Facts and Options for Taxation." In *Inequality and Fiscal Policy*, edited by Benedict J Clements, Ruud A. de Mooij, Sanjeev Gupta, and Michael Keen, 121–37. Washington, DC: International Monetary Fund.

Faber, Jacob W. 2009. "Cashing in on Distress: The Expansion of Fringe Financial Institutions during the Great Recession." *Urban Affairs Review* 1078087416684037.

Fallon, Peter R., and Robert E. B. Lucas. 2002. "The Impact of Financial Crises on Labor Markets, Household Incomes, and Poverty: A Review of Evidence." *The World Bank Research Observer* 17 (1): 21–45.

Fan, Yi, Junjian Yi, and Junsen Zhang. 2015. "The Great Gatsby Curve in China: Cross-Sectional Inequality and Intergenerational Mobility." Working Paper, CUHK, Hong Kong.

Fernando, A. Nilesh. 2016. "Shackled to the Soil: The Long-Term Effects of Inheriting Agricultural Land in India." Harvard University Working Paper, Department of Economics, Harvard University, Cambridge, MA.

Ferreira, Sergio Guimaraes, and Fernando A. Veloso. 2006. "Intergenerational Mobility of Wages in Brazil." *Brazilian Review of Econometrics* 26 (2): 181–211.

Figueroa, José Luis, and Dirk Van de Gaer. 2015. "Did Progresa Reduce Inequality of Opportunity for School Re-enrollment?" Preliminary Version, Working Paper, Laboratoire d'Economie Appliquée au Développement (LEAD), University of Toulon, Toulon, France.

Filmer, Deon, and Norbert Schady. 2014. "The Medium-Term Effects of Scholarships in a Low-Income Country." *Journal of Human Resources* 49 (3): 663–94.

Fiszbein, Ariel, Norbert Schady, Francisco H. G. Ferreira, Margaret Grosh, Niall Keleher, Pedro Olinto, and Emmanuel Skoufias. 2009. *Conditional Cash Transfers: Reducing Present and Future Poverty*. World Bank Policy Research Report. Washington, DC: World Bank.

Funkhouser, Edward. 1999. "Cyclical Economic Conditions and School Attendance in Costa Rica." *Economics of Education Review* 18 (1): 31–50.

Furman, Jason, and Peter Orszag. 2015. "A Firm-Level Perspective on the Role of Rents in the Rise in Inequality." Presentation at "A Just Society" Centennial Event in Honor of Joseph Stiglitz, Columbia University, New York, NY, October 23.

Galor, Oded, and Joseph Zeira. 1993. "Income Distribution and Macroeconomics." *Review of Economic Studies* 60 (1): 35–52.

GDIM (Global Database on Intergenerational Mobility). 2018. *Global Database on Intergenerational Mobility*. Development Research Group, World Bank. Washington, DC: World Bank.

Gilens, Martin, and Benjamin I. Page. 2014. "Testing Theories of American Politics: Elites, Interest Groups, and Average Citizens." *Perspectives on Politics* 12 (3) 564–81.

Gill, Indermit S., Ana Revenga, and Christian Zeballos. 2016. "Grow, Invest, Insure: A Game Plan to End Extreme Poverty by 2030." Policy Research Working Paper 7892, World Bank, Washington, DC.

Goldin, Claudia. 2014. "A Grand Gender Convergence: Its Last Chapter." *American Economic Review* 104 (4): 1091–119.

Goldin, Claudia, and Cecilia Rouse. 2000. "Orchestrating Impartiality: The Impact of "Blind" Auditions on Female Musicians." *American Economic Review* 90 (4): 715–41.

Granovetter, Mark. 1974. *Getting a Job: A Study of Contacts and Careers.* 1st ed. Cambridge, MA: Harvard University Press.

Granovetter, Mark. 1995. *Getting a Job: A Study of Contacts and Careers.* 2nd ed. Chicago, IL: University of Chicago Press.

Grawe, Nathan D. 2001. *In Search of Intergenerational Credit Constraints among Canadian men: Quantile versus Mean Regression Tests for Binding Credit Constraints.* Analytical Studies Branch, Statistics Canada, Ottawa, Ontario, Canada.

Gregg, Paul, Elizabeth Washbrook, Carol Propper, and Simon Burgess. 2005. "The Effects of a Mother's Return to Work Decision on Child Development in the UK." *Economic Journal* 115 (501): F48-F80.

Groh, Matthew, Nandini Krishnan, David McKenzie, and Tara Vishwanath. 2016. "Do Wage Subsidies Provide a Stepping-Stone to Employment for Recent College Graduates? Evidence from a Randomized Experiment in Jordan." *Review of Economics and Statistics* 98 (3): 488–502.

Gupta, Sanjeev, Michael Keen, Alpa Shah, and Geneviève Verdier. 2017. *Digital Revolutions in Public Finance.* Washington, DC: International Monetary Fund.

Guvenen, Fatih, Serdar Ozkan, and Jae Song. 2014. "The Nature of Countercyclical Income Risk." *Journal of Political Economy* 122 (3): 621–60.

Haushofer, Johannes, and Jeremy Shapiro. 2016. "The Short-Term Impact of Unconditional Cash Transfers to the Poor: Experimental Evidence from Kenya." *Quarterly Journal of Economics* 131(4): 1973–2042.

Hawkins, Summer Sherburne, Lucy Jane Griffiths, Carol Dezateux, Catherine Law, and Millennium Cohort Study Child Health Group. 2007. "The Impact of Maternal Employment on Breast-Feeding Duration in the UK Millennium Cohort Study." *Public Health Nutrition* 10 (9): 891–96.

Hnatkovska, Viktoria, Amartya Lahiri, and Sourabh Paul. 2012. "Castes and Labor Mobility." *American Economic Journal: Applied Economics* 4 (2): 274–307.

Holtz-Eakin, Douglas, David Joulfaian, and Harvey S. Rosen. 1993. "The Carnegie Conjecture: Some Empirical Evidence." *The Quarterly Journal of Economics* 108 (2): 413–35.

Holzer, Harry J. 1998. "Why Do Small Establishments Hire Fewer Blacks than Large Ones?" *Journal of Human Resources* 33 (4): 896–914.

Holzer, Harry, and David Neumark. 2000. "Assessing Affirmative Action." *Journal of Economic Literature* 38 (3): 483–568.

ILO (International Labour Office). 2016. *World Employment and Social Outlook 2016: Trends for Youth*. Geneva: ILO.

IMF (International Monetary Fund). 2013. *Fiscal Monitor: Taxing Times*. Washington, DC: International Monetary Fund.

———. 2014. *Fiscal Monitor: Public Expenditure Reform: Making Difficult Choices*. Washington, DC: International Monetary Fund.

———. 2017. *Fiscal Monitor: IMF Fiscal Monitor: Tackling Inequality*. Washington, DC: International Monetary Fund.

Inchauste, Gabriela, and Nora Lustig. 2017. *The Distributional Impact of Taxes and Transfers: Evidence from Eight Developing Countries*. Directions in Development—Poverty. Washington, DC: World Bank.

Inchauste, Gabriela, João Pedro Azevedo, Boniface Essama-Nssah, Sergio Olivieri, Trang Van Nguyen, Jaime Saavedra-Chanduvi, and Hernan Winkler. 2014. *Understanding Changes in Poverty*. Washington, DC: World Bank.

Ioannides, Yannis M., and Linda D. Loury. 2004. "Job Information Networks, Neighborhood Effects, and Inequality." *Journal of Economic Literature* 42 (4): 1056–93.

Jackson, Matthew O. 2008. *Social and Economic Networks*. Princeton, NJ: Princeton University Press.

Jaumotte, Florence, and Carolina Osorio Buitron. 2015. "Inequality and Labor Market Institutions." Staff Discussion Note 15/14, International Monetary Fund, Washington, DC.

Joshi, Heather, Elizabeth Cooksey, and Georgia Verropoulou. 2009. "Combining Childrearing with Work: Do Maternal Employment Experiences Compromise Child Development?" CLS Working Paper 2009/1, Center for Longitudinal Studies, Institute of Education, University of London, London.

Katz, Lawrence F. 1998. "Wage Subsidies for the Disadvantaged." In *Generating Jobs: How to Create Demand for Low-Skilled Workers*, edited by R. Freeman and P. Gottschalk, 21–53, New York: Russell Sage Foundation.

Keen, Michael, Yitae Kim, and Ricardo Varsano. 2008. "The 'Flat Tax(es)': Principles and Experience." *International Tax and Public Finance* 15 (6): 712–51.

Kline, Patrick, and Enrico Moretti. 2014. "People, Places, and Public Policy: Some Simple Welfare Economics of Local Economic Development Programs." *Annual Review of Economics* 6: 629–62.

Krishnan, Nandini, Gabriel Lara Ibarra, Ambar Narayan, Sailesh Tiwari, and Tara Vishwanath. 2016. *Uneven Odds, Unequal Outcomes: Inequality of Opportunity in the Middle East and North Africa*. Washington, DC: World Bank.

Lang, Kevin, and Jee-Yeon K. Lehmann. 2012. "Racial Discrimination in the Labor Market: Theory and Empirics." *Journal of Economic Literature* 50 (4): 959–1006.

Lefgren, Lars, and Frank McIntyre. 2006. "The Relationship between Women's Education and Marriage Outcomes." *Journal of Labor Economics* 24 (4): 787–830.

Loury, Glenn C. 1981. "Intergenerational Transfers and the Distribution of Earnings." *Econometrica: Journal of the Econometric Society* 49 (4): 843–867.

Lustig, Nora. 2017. "Fiscal Policy, Income Redistribution and Poverty Reduction in Low and Middle-Income Countries." Center for Global Development Working Paper 448, Center for Global Development, London, UK.

Macmillan, Lindsey. 2014. "Intergenerational Worklessness in the UK and the Role of Local Labour Markets." *Oxford Economic Papers* 66 (3): 871–89.

Magruder, Jeremy R. 2010. "Intergenerational Networks, Unemployment, and Persistent Inequality in South Africa." *American Economic Journal: Applied Economics* 2 (1): 62–85.

Mankiw, N. Gregory. 2013. "Defending the One Percent." *Journal of Economic Perspectives* 27 (3): 21–34.

Manoli, Day, and Nick Turner. 2016. "Do Notices Have Permanent Effects on Benefit Take-up." *Tax Law Review* 70: 439.

Mayer, Susan E., and Leonard M. Lopoo. 2008. "Government Spending and Intergenerational Mobility." *Journal of Public Economics* 92 (1–2): 139–58.

Mazumder, Bhashkar. 2005. "Fortunate Sons: New Estimates of Intergenerational Mobility in the United States Using Social Security Earnings Data." *Review of Economics and Statistics* 87 (2): 235–55.

McKenzie, David. 2017. "Identifying and Spurring High-Growth Entrepreneurship: Experimental Evidence from a Business Plan Competition." *American Economic Review* 107 (8): 2278–307.

Mencken, F. Carson, and Idee Winfield. 2000. "Job Search and Sex Segregation: Does Sex of Social Contact Matter?" *Sex Roles* 42 (9–10): 847–64.

Meyer, Bruce D., and Dan T. Rosenbaum. 2001. "Welfare, the Earned Income Tax Credit, and the Labor Supply of Single Mothers." *The Quarterly Journal of Economics* 116 (3): 1063–114.

Mirrlees, James, Stuart Adam, Tim Besley, Richard Blundell, Stephen Bond, Robert Chote, Malcolm Gammie, Paul Johnson, Gareth Myles, and James M. Poterba. 2011. *Tax by Design: The Mirrlees Review*. Vol. 2. London: Oxford University Press.

Molina-Millan, Teresa, Tania Barham, Karen Macours, John A. Maluccio, and Marco Stampini. 2016. "Long-term Impacts of Conditional Cash Transfers in Latin America: Review of the Evidence." IDB Working Paper Series IDB-WP-732. Inter-American Development Bank, Washington, DC.

Mulligan, Casey B. 1997. *Parental Priorities and Economic Inequality.* Chicago, IL: University of Chicago Press.

Neal, Derek A., and William R. Johnson. 1996. "The Role of Premarket Factors in Black–White Wage Differences." *Journal of Political Economy* 104 (5): 869–95.

Norregaard, John. 2015. "Taxing Immovable Property: Revenue Potential and Implementation Challenges," In *Inequality and Fiscal Policy*, edited by Benedict J. Clements, Ruud A. de Mooij, Sanjeev Gupta, and Michael Keen, chapter 11, 191–222. Washington, DC: International Monetary Fund.

O'Higgins, Niall. 2010. "The Impact of the Economic and Financial Crisis on Youth Employment: Measures for Labour Market Recovery in the European Union, Canada and the United States." Employment Working Paper 70, International Labour Organization, Geneva, Switzerland.

O'Neill, June E., and Dave M. O'Neill. 2006. "What Do Wage Differentials Tell about Labor Market Discrimination?" In *The Economics of Immigration and Social Diversity*, edited by Solomon W. Polachek, Carmel Chiswick, and Hillel Rapoport. 293–357. Bingley, UK: Emerald Group.

Page, Benjamin I., Larry M. Bartels, and Jason Seawright. 2013. "Democracy and the Policy Preferences of Wealthy Americans." *Perspectives on Politics* 11 (1): 51–73.

Patnaik, Ankita. 2016. "Reserving Time for Daddy: The Short and Long-Run Consequences of Fathers' Quotas." Working Paper. doi: 10.2139/ssrn.2475970.

Perez-Gonzalez, Francisco. 2006. "Inherited Control and Firm Performance." *American Economic Review* 96 (5): 1559–88.

Peter, Klara Sabirianova, Steve Buttrick, and Denvil Duncan. 2010. "Global Reform of Personal Income Taxation, 1981–2005: Evidence from 189 Countries." *National Tax Journal* 63 (3), 447–78.

Phelps, Edmund S. 1972. *Inflation Policy and Unemployment Theory: The Cost-Benefit Approach to Monetary Planning.* London: Macmillan.

Piketty, Thomas. 2000. "Theories of Persistent Inequality and Intergenerational Mobility." In *Handbook of Income Distribution.* Vol. 1, edited by Anthony B. Atkinson and François Bourguignon, 429–76. New York: Elsevier.

———. 2011. "On the Long-Run Evolution of Inheritance: France 1820–2050." *Quarterly Journal of Economics* 126 (3): 1071–131.

————. 2014. *Capital in the 21st Century.* Cambridge, MA: Harvard University Press.

Piketty, Thomas, Emmanuel Saez, and Stefanie Stantcheva. 2014. "Optimal Taxation of Top Labor Incomes: A Tale of Three Elasticities." *American Economic Journal: Economic Policy* 6 (1): 230–71.

Pissarides, Christopher A. 1992. "Loss of Skill during Unemployment and the Persistence of Employment Shocks." *Quarterly Journal of Economics* 107 (4): 1371–91.

Raaum, Oddbjørn, and Knut Røed. 2006. "Do Business Cycle Conditions at the Time of Labor Market Entry Affect Future Employment Prospects?" *The Review of Economics and Statistics* 88 (2): 193–210.

Rangel, Marcos A. 2006. "Alimony Rights and Intrahousehold Allocation of Resources: Evidence from Brazil." *Economic Journal* 116 (513): 627–58.

Rucci, Graciana. 2004. "The Effects of Macroeconomic Shocks on the Well-being of People in Developing Countries." PhD dissertation, University of California, Los Angeles, CA.

Saez, Emmanuel. 2001. "Using Elasticities to Derive Optimal Income Tax Rates." *The Review of Economic Studies* 68 (1): 205–29.

Siddique, Zahra. 2011. "Evidence on Caste Based Discrimination." *Labour Economics* 18: S146–59.

Sinha, Rishabh. 2018. "Closer, But No Cigar: Intergenerational Mobility across Caste Groups in India." Policy Research Working Paper WPS 8401, World Bank, Washington, DC.

Solon, Gary. 1992. "Intergenerational Income Mobility in the United States." *American Economic Review* 82 (3): 393–408.

Stiglitz, Joseph E. 2012. *The Price of Inequality: How Today's Divided Society Endangers Our Future.* New York: Norton.

Stinson, Martha H., and Peter Gottschalk. 2016. "Is There an Advantage to Working? The Relationship between Maternal Employment and Intergenerational Mobility." In *Inequality: Causes and Consequences (Research in Labor Economics),* Vol. 43, edited by Lorenzo Cappellari, Solomon W. Polachek, and Konstantinos Tatsiramos, 355–405. Bingley, UK: Emerald Group.

Thomas, Duncan, Kathleen Beegle, Elizabeth Frankenberg, Bondan Sikoki, John Strauss, and Graciela Teruel. 2004. "Education in a Crisis." *Journal of Development Economics* 74 (1): 53–85.

Tollefson, Jeff. 2015. "Revolt of the Randomistas." *Nature* 524 (7564): 150.

Van der Weide, Roy, and Branko Milanovic. Forthcoming. "Inequality Is Bad for Growth of the Poor (but Not for That of the Rich)." *World Bank Economic Review.*

Von Wachter, Till, Jae Song, and Joyce Manchester. 2009. *Long-Term Earnings Losses Due to Mass Layoffs during the 1982 Recession: An*

Analysis Using U.S. Administrative Data from 1974 to 2004. Technical Report, Columbia University, New York.

Wang, Shing-Yi. 2013. "Marriage Networks, Nepotism, and Labor Market Outcomes in China." *American Economic Journal: Applied Economics* 5 (3): 91–112.

World Bank. 2006. *World Development Report 2006: Equity and Development.* Washington, DC: World Bank.

———. 2012a. *World Development Report 2013: Jobs.* Washington, DC: World Bank.

———. 2012b. *World Development Report 2012: Gender Equality and Development.* Washington, DC: World Bank.

———. 2015. *Women, Business and the Law 2016.* Washington, DC: World Bank.

———. 2016a. *Poverty and Shared Prosperity 2016: Taking on Inequality.* Washington, DC: World Bank.

———. 2016b. *Global Monitoring Report 2015/16: Development Goals in an Era of Demographic Change.* Washington, DC: World Bank.

———. 2017. *World Development Report 2017: Governance and the Law.* Washington, DC: World Bank.

———. 2018. *Entangled: Localized Effects of Exports on Earnings and Employment in South Asia.* Draft. Washington, DC: World Bank.

Wright, Erik Olin. 2006. "Two Redistributive Proposals–Universal Basic Income and Stakeholder Grants." *Focus* 24 (2): 5–7.

Zhang, Xiaobo, and Guo Li. 2003. "Does Guanxi Matter to Nonfarm Employment?" *Journal of Comparative Economics* 31 (2): 315–31.